Great Conversations
1

SELECTED AND EDITED BY
Daniel Born, *Director of Adult Programs*
Donald H. Whitfield, *Director of Higher Education Programs*

CONTRIBUTORS
Nancy Carr, *Senior Editor*
Anne Gendler, *Editorial Director*
Judith McCue, *Great Books Program Specialist*
Gary Schoepfel, *Vice President for Discussion Groups*
Donald C. Smith, *Senior Trainer*

PRODUCTION EDITORS
A. C. Racette
Jason A. Smith

Great Conversations

1

THE GREAT BOOKS FOUNDATION
A nonprofit educational organization

Published and distributed by

THE GREAT BOOKS FOUNDATION
A nonprofit educational organization

35 East Wacker Drive, Suite 400
Chicago, IL 60601
www.greatbooks.org

Copyright © 2004 by The Great Books Foundation
Chicago, Illinois
ISBN 0-945159-34-X

9 8 7 6 5 4 3 2

Library of Congress Cataloging-in-Publication Data
Great conversations 1 / selected and edited by Daniel Born, Donald H. Whitfield.
        p. cm.
Contents: The epic of Gilgamesh / anonymous—Prometheus bound / Aeschylus—Of
friendship and of solitude / Michel de Montaigne—Pensées / Blaise Pascal—Self-reliance /
Ralph Waldo Emerson—Out of the cradle endlessly rocking / Walt Whitman—Democracy
in America / Alexis de Tocqueville—An enemy of the people / Henrik Ibsen—The value of
science / Henri Poincaré—Thoughts for the times on war and death / Sigmund Freud—The
secret sharer / Joseph Conrad—The theory of the leisure class / Thorstein Veblen—The
stages of life / Carl Jung—Tell me a riddle / Tillie Olsen—Boys and girls / Alice Munro.
        ISBN 0-945159-34-X (paperback)
        1. Literature—Collections. I. Born, Daniel. II. Whitfield, Donald H.

PN6012.G74 2004
808.8—dc22   2004042409

Book cover and interior design:
Judy Sickle, Forward Design
Chicago, Illinois

CONTENTS

Great Conversations 1 is the first in a series of anthologies intended for those who value the lively pleasure of discussing ideas. It is for readers who care as much about the book talk that follows as they do the solitary pleasures of the reading experience. The selections in this book will provide rich material for talking about ideas that are never out of currency, whether the conversation takes place in a book discussion group or a classroom.

Running through all the selections are themes that have been of central importance to many people the world over. These selections, ranging from the ancient Mesopotamian *Epic of Gilgamesh* to Sigmund Freud's thoughts on war, represent writing that is not ephemeral but rather has stood—and, we believe, will stand—the test of time. They speak directly to all serious readers, without requiring any special expertise or background knowledge. At the same time, they are inexhaustibly rereadable, suggesting new questions and interpretations to successive generations of readers as well as to any one reader at different times of life. The selections embody powerful arguments that provoke us to ask fundamental questions about our assumptions and ourselves. As the poet W. H. Auden once put it: "A real book is not one that's read, but one that reads us."

Just as important, such writings speak not only to us, but to each other. Common themes run through works from several centuries—for example, from the portrayal of Gilgamesh and his soulmate, Enkidu, through Michel de Montaigne's reflections on friendship, to Alice Munro's depiction of gender roles. In naming the series *Great Conversations*, we invite readers to become active participants in this dialogue. Each selection, while uniquely powerful in its own right, becomes even more so when considered in light of the others.

A distinguishing characteristic of a true liberal arts education, whether pursued in a college class or through a book discussion group, is the ability to make connections between different modes of understanding the world.

The selections in *Great Conversations* represent thinkers presenting their view of the world through the telling of stories, creating poetry, forming scientific hypotheses, analyzing society and government, probing the workings of the human mind, and engaging in philosophical and religious speculation. That is, they represent the entire range of human intellectual activity across what are often distinguished as separate disciplines. Although the selections in *Great Conversations* are arranged chronologically, there are numerous sequences for organizing these selections to emphasize common themes across disciplines, genres, and historical periods. An appendix to this book, "Connecting Themes," provides some suggestions for thematic clusters of several readings that will help discussion group participants make connections among the selections. These texts do not live in isolation. It is as if they are in continual dialogue with one another—and with us.

One of the most rewarding ways to pursue the questions these selections provoke is through participation in a book discussion group. A successful group becomes a community of active inquirers who engage each other and the authors of the works read in common. Sharing a range of perspectives, insights, and lively questions leads to a deeper understanding of what the authors are saying and how it relates to one's own life.

To assist book group participants and other readers, we have provided brief introductory notes and questions for each selection. The notes provide relevant biographical information about each author and highlight a few of the most prominent themes of the text. The questions are intended to help readers consider each author's ideas critically, and to provide a model for questions to ask in a discussion group. In addition, there are questions for two longer works not reprinted in *Great Conversations 1*: Saul Bellow's *Seize the Day* and Frederick Douglass's *Narrative of the Life of Frederick Douglass, an American Slave*.

The elements of a successful Great Books discussion are simple. To paraphrase one experienced leader: *The discussion begins with a question. All the participants must have the text in their minds and on the table in front of them. Address is polite and responsive. All should participate and support their opinions with thoughtful reasoning rather than simple assertions—when that has been said, all has been said. There is no further method. The rest develops as living conversation.*

The *shared inquiry* method of discussion developed by the Great Books Foundation uses *interpretive questions* and *evaluative questions* to focus the group's discussion. The questions appended to each selection in *Great Conversations* follow this distinction.

Interpretive questions are concerned with the meaning of the text and best pursued by referring to specific portions of the selection being discussed. There is more than one way to answer an interpretive question based on text. These works have been discussed for decades, and sometimes centuries, precisely because they don't invite simple answers. Interpretive questions seek to clarify what the author is saying and can be supported with evidence from the reading. For an expository work, interpretive questions might be directed toward articulating a writer's assumptions and the way the argument of the selection is developed. For works of fiction, drama, and poetry, interpretive questions might ask about the plot, characters, and imagery of the work, and how these elements add up to a coherent view. Of course, a number of strong and often differing interpretations of a work might emerge in the course of a discussion. This is what gives the discussion momentum and liveliness.

The second kind of question, evaluative, invites a broader response and is best taken up after the discussion group has made considerable effort to understand the author's meaning. A group may arrive at one or several interpretations. Evaluative questions tend to invite answers that include participants' life experiences in relation to the author's meaning. They generally ask if what we understand the author to be saying is significant or true.

In the course of a discussion, interpretive and evaluative questions will often merge. Some discussion groups find it helpful to spend the greater portion of their time on questions of interpretation, reserving evaluative considerations for the last half hour or so of the session. Other groups become very adept at blending both approaches throughout the discussion. We strongly recommend focusing on interpretive questions first, then shifting to the more free-ranging mode of evaluation. Our experience as discussion leaders suggests that premature wandering into areas of personal experience, before the text has been thoroughly grappled with through interpretive questions, fails to lead to a satisfying discussion and instead detracts from it. Textual discussion is not quite the same thing as group therapy, although we would be among the first to claim that some of the best discussions of a text can deliver thera-peutic effects.

Robert Maynard Hutchins, in his essay "The Great Conversation," wrote: "Nobody can make so clear and comprehensive and accurate a statement of the basic issues of human life as to close the discussion. Each statement calls for explanation, correction, modification, expansion, or contradiction." We invite you to become active and lifelong participants in this ongoing discussion. And we hope that *Great Conversations* will provide you with one means to do so.

THE EPIC OF GILGAMESH

The oldest written epic of any human civilization, this work of Mesopotamia, published before 2000 BCE, predates Homer by at least 1500 years. It survives on clay tablets, the first of which were excavated by British archaeologists in the mid-nineteenth century in what is modern-day Iraq. Discoveries at sites in Nineveh and Nimrud included thousands of fragments of the inscribed tablets, as well as Assyrian artifacts and sculptures.

The task of deciphering the cuneiform characters began in Baghdad, and continued at the British Museum in London, where many of the tablets had been transported. A couple of decades later, in 1872, the public's imagination was gripped by the Gilgamesh epic when a British scholar announced that the Assyrian collation of the poem, dating from the era of Ashurbanipal (668–627 BCE), the last great Assyrian king, included "an account of the flood." The poem has enjoyed a wide readership ever since, even though the flood portion of the narrative is arguably not the center of the story.

The tragic story line of Gilgamesh is tied to his inheritance: as someone who is one-third god and two-thirds human, he will be forced in his finite time on earth to tether his furious energies to altogether human limitations. Wreaking public havoc in the kingdom at the outset of the poem, young Gilgamesh is provided by the gods with a companion and handler (who has his own rough-hewn image), Enkidu. The two men subsequently go on a journey of daring exploits, followed by some capricious interventions of the gods, who include the ambiguous patriarch Enlil and the vivid siren Ishtar.

Gilgamesh's education, if we can call it that, does not stop at physical exploits. This poem explores the meaning of loss as well as the purely physical well-being of triumphant heroes. It is concerned with the inward and the outward man, and Gilgamesh makes more than one kind of journey before the story ends. His search for the key to immortality, his conversations with Utnapishtim, and his concluding return to Uruk, where he will preside over a city kingdom of architectural distinction and commercial might, all add up to a multidimensional figure of some complexity. While we may think psychological nuance is the province of modern, not primitive, cultural production, it would seem the Mesopotamian Sumerians roughly four millennia ago had developed a few ideas of their own about the human condition—ideas that translate with surprising force and verve for contemporary readers.

There are numerous translations and versions of the Gilgamesh epic. Most are based primarily on the Ashurbanipal version, written in Akkadian, although fragments in Sumerian have also been discovered. Scholarly editions of the poem, based on literal transcriptions and translations from the ancient tablets, generally contain numerous gaps and ellipses due to the missing fragments. This translation by Danny P. Jackson fills in some of those gaps in the interests of a more coherent and readable text.

The Epic of Gilgamesh

MAIN CHARACTERS

GILGAMESH, hero and king of Uruk

ENKIDU, his new friend

NINSUN, wise goddess and mother of Gilgamesh

SHAMHAT, sacred girl who brought the two friends together

ANU, father of the gods and patron of Uruk

HUMBABA, monster god who must be killed

ISHTAR, the king's spurned and vengeful suitor-goddess

ENLIL, god who unleashes the great flood

SIDURI, barmaid with worldly advice

URSHANABI, boatman who gives passage to paradise

UTNAPISHTIM, who holds the secret of eternal life

TABLET I
Column i

Fame haunts the man who visits hell,
who lives to tell my entire tale identically.
So like a sage, a trickster, or saint,
    GILGAMESH
was a hero who knew secrets and saw forbidden places,
who could even speak of the time before the
Flood because he lived long, learned much,
and spoke his life to those who first
cut into clay his birdlike words.

He commanded walls for Uruk and for Eanna,
our holy ground,
walls that you can see still; walls where weep
the weary widows of dead soldiers.
Go to them and touch their immovable presence
with gentle finger to find yourself.
No one else ever built such walls.
Climb Uruk's tower and walk about on a
windy night. Look. Touch. Taste. Sense.
What force creates such mass?
Open up the special box that's hidden in the wall
and read aloud the story of Gilgamesh's life.
Learn what sorrow taught him; learn of those
he overcame by wit or force or fear as he,
a town's best child, acted nobly in the way
one should to lead and acted wisely too
as one who sought no fame.
Child of Lugalbanda's wife and some great force,
Gilgamesh is a fate alive, the
finest babe of Ninsun, she who never
let a man touch her, indeed
so pure and heavenly, so without sin.
He knew the secret paths that reached the eagle's
nest above the mountain, and he knew too how
just to drop a well into the chilly earth.
He sailed the sea to where Shamash comes,
explored the world, sought life, and came at last
to Utnapishtim far away who did bring
back to life the flooded earth.

Is there anywhere a greater king
who can say, as Gilgamesh may,
"I am supreme"?

Column ii

The bigger part of him was made in heaven
and the smaller part somewhere on earth.
She-who-must-be-obeyed fashioned his body's self.
She endowed him.

Gilgamesh watches the flocks of Uruk himself
as if he were a loose bull, nose up in open field.
No one else could come close to fighting like that.
His clan is roused by powdery dreams
And with them all he goes howling through sanctuaries.
But would he ever let his child come
To see him ravish others?
"Is this the shepherd of Uruk's flocks,
our strength, our light, our reason,
who hoards the girls of other men
for his own purpose?"
A prayer of opposition rose from Uruk's other men to heaven;
and the attentive gods asked:
"Who created this awesome beast
with an unmatched strength and a
chant that fosters armies?
This warrior keeps boys from fathers
in the night and in the day.
Is this Gilgamesh,
is this the shepherd of Uruk's flocks,
our strength, our light, our reason,
who hoards the girls of other men
for his own purpose?"

When Anu in the sky heard this,
he said to Aruru, great goddess of creation that she is:
"You created humans; create again in the
image of Gilgamesh and let this imitation be
as quick in heart and as strong in arm
so that these counterforces might first engage,
then disengage, and finally let Uruk's children

live in peace."
Hearing that, Aruru thought of Anu. Then she
wet her creative fingers, fashioned a rock, and tossed it
as far as she could into the woods.
Thus she fathered Enkidu, a forester, and gave birth
in terror and in fright without a single cry of pain,
bringing forth another likeness of Ninurta, god of war.
Hair covered his body and his curls resembled
those of any good girl, growing swiftly like the
fair hair of Nisaba-giver-of-grain.
This Enkidu had neither clan nor race. He went
clothed as one who shepherds well, eating the food
of grass, drinking from the watery holes of herds,
and racing swift as wind or silent water.
Then Enkidu met a hunter at the watery hole
on three consecutive days.
And each time the face of the hunter signaled
recognition of Enkidu.
For the herds were uninvited at
the hunter's oasis, and the hunter was
disturbed by this intrusion. His quiet heart
rushed up in trouble. His eyes darkened.
Fear leaped forth onto a face that looks
as if it expects to doubt for a long, long time.

Column iii

Then with trembling lips the hunter told his father this complaint:
"Sir, one has come to my watery hole from afar and he
is the biggest and best throughout the land. He feels power.
His is a strength like that of Anu's swift star, and
tirelessly does he roam across the land.
He eats the food of beasts and, like the beasts,
he comes at will to drink from my watery hole.
In fear do I see him come to undo
what I have done by wrecking traps, by
bursting mounds, by letting animals slip through my
grasp, beasts that I would bind."

Then with hateful lips, the father told the hunter his reply:
"Boy, your answer lies in Uruk where

there stalks a man of endless strength named Gilgamesh.
He is the biggest and best throughout the land. He feels power.
His is a strength like that of Anu's swift star.
Start out toward Uruk's ancient palace
and tell your tale to Gilgamesh.
In turn he'll say to set a trap, take back with
you a fine lover, some sacred temple girl,
who might let him see what force and charm a girl can have.
Then as Enkidu comes again to the watery hole,
let her strip in nearby isolation to show him all her grace.
If he is drawn toward her, and leaves the herd to mate,
his beasts on high will leave him then behind."

The hunter heard his father well and went that very night
to Uruk where he said this to Gilgamesh:
"There is someone from afar whose
force is great throughout our land.
His is a strength throughout the land. He feels power.
His is a strength like that of Anu's swift star, and
tirelessly does he roam across the land.
He eats the food of beasts and, like the beasts,
he comes at will to drink from my watery hole.
In fear do I see him come to undo
what I have done by wrecking traps, by
bursting mounds, by letting animals slip through my
grasp, beasts that I would bind."

So Gilgamesh replied:
"Go set a trap; take back with
you a fine lover, Shamhat, the sacred temple girl,
who might let him see what charm and force a girl can have.
Then as Enkidu comes again to the watery hole,
let her strip in nearby isolation to show him all her grace.
If he is drawn toward her, and leaves the herd to mate,
his beasts on high will leave him then behind."

The hunter returned, bringing with him the sacred temple girl,
and swift was their journey.
Three days later, at the watery hole, they set their
trap for Enkidu and spoke no word for two
whole days waiting and waiting and waiting.
Then the herd came slowly in to drink.

Column iv

Beasts arose and sleepy limbs began to flutter then.
Enkidu, the boy who walked on mountains,
who eats the food of beasts and, like the beasts,
comes down at will to drink from the watery hole,
with the beasts arose and stretched
his tired limbs to start the day.
She beheld him then, as he was in his beginning,
the one who gave and took life from the far woods.
"Here is he, fine lover; be set to wet him with
your tongue and chest and loins.
Spread forth your happiness. Display your hidden charm.
Jump him fast and kneel upon his shoulders.
Without his wind then, he'll enter near your entrance.
Take off your robe to let him in.
Let him see what force a girl can have.
The friends he has from on wild will exile him
if he presses his person, as he will, into your scented bush."
Shamhat let her garments loose and spread forth
her happiness which Enkidu entered as gusts of wind
enter tunnels bound for hell.
Hot and swollen first, she jumped him fast,
knocking out his rapid breath with
thrust after loving thrust.
She let him see what force a girl can have,
and he stayed within her scented bush for
seven nights, leaping, seeping, weeping, and sleeping there.

After that week of pleasure,
Enkidu returned to the herds
but the beasts fled from him in haste.
They stampeded away from his new self.
He could no longer race as he had once,
legs soft now and ankles stiff. The beasts
left him behind and he grew sad
that he could no longer speed with them.
But he enjoyed the memory that no virgin has
and, returning to his fine lover, he once
more knelt between her legs
as she spoke these words to him:
"Now you are as if a god, my boy,

with no more need of dumb beasts, however fair.
We can now ascend the road to Uruk's palace,
the immaculate domicile, where Anu and Ishtar dwell,
and there we will see Gilgamesh, the powerful,
who rides over the herd like any great king."
These words he heard and he stared at her.
For the first time he wished for just one friend.
Then Enkidu asked the love who was so fine:
"Please come with me and be my love
at the immaculate domicile, where Anu and Ishtar dwell,
and there we will see Gilgamesh, the powerful,
who rides over the herd like any great king.
I wish to call on him; to proclaim all things
aloud and find a friend in him."

Column v

Enkidu continued:
"Uruk will hear me say, 'I am the strongest.
I alone can do all I wish.'
Forester that I am, a mountainous power is mine.
We should march together, face-by-face,
so I can promote your fame."
Then fine lover said these words in invitation:
"Enter Uruk of the herds, Enkidu,
where costumes bright are worn,
where it is always time to party,
where merry music never fades,
where graceful girls do ever play
with toys and boys and men;
for in the night these revelers do
their best to rule the town.
There, with a smile, Enkidu
will see his other self, great Gilgamesh.
Watch him all, please. Note his
face, his fists, his fairest sword,
and all the strength that dwells in him.
Could he be greater than you,
this one who's up and down all day and night?
Fear your own anger, boy; for great Gilgamesh
adores fair Shamash and is adored in turn.

Anu of the blue sky, Enlil from the clouds,
and clever Ea have empowered him.
And before he even sees you,
this great Gilgamesh will have first envisioned you
in Uruk as a rival in a dream."

Gilgamesh awakens to ask his mother, Ninsun,
to leave off the dream.
"Mother," says he, "I saw a star
within my head in sleep just now
that fell at me like Anu's dart
and I could not escape.
Uruk was on high of it,
our people did applaud,
and gathered up to praise his force.
Men clenched fists; women danced.
And I too embraced this rising star,
as a man does the woman he loves best,
then took the new one here to you
so that you could see us both at once."

Gilgamesh's mother, who is wise in all and worries not, replied:
"This bright, new star is your true friend
who fell at you like Anu's dart,
whom you could not escape."

Column vi

Then she who is wise in all and worries not continued:
"So say this friend is one who is almighty,
with strength renowned around the world,
like Anu's dart his force is real
so that he draws you in, as does a wife,
though he is sure to race away, like
that most distant star, with the secrets of your origin.
This dissolves your sleep."

Then again, Gilgamesh said to her in reply:
"Mother, I slept when some with axes then
attacked the herds of Uruk."
So Ninsun reassured the frightened king:
"Enkidu will help.

He will guard his loves
or rescue them from danger;
he is your most faithful friend.
Expect him to shepherd you
and to be sure that all goes well."

Gilgamesh said to his fond source:
I pray for fortune and for fate
to send me such a one
that I may have a friend who's as kind
and patient as a brother."

Then in sleep full of repose
the temple girl enchanted Enkidu
where they lay smiling.

TABLET II
Column i

Then Gilgamesh explained his dream to Ninsun:
"Last night a vision filled my head
with sights of stars and one sent down from heaven.
At first I tried and failed to carry forth
these signs with me. Then all citizens
of Uruk here assisted in my efforts.
So I was able then to bring these omens near to you."

And she said in reply:
"Wisely done, fair son, and rightly so
for one well reared as you were.
All others too will soon acclaim
this god-sent gift to you."

Then Gilgamesh concluded:
"In another dream I saw an ax
and bent toward it with manly interest;
so fair was its appearance
that it seemed wholesome, young, and
ready as a woman."

Column ii

Soon the day came when the fine lover of Enkidu said:
"Now come with me to enter into Uruk
where we shall meet the mighty king,
enormous Gilgamesh.
Now you are as if a god, my boy,
with no more need of dumb beasts, however fair.
We can ascend the road to Uruk's palace,
the immaculate domicile, where Anu and Ishtar dwell,
and there we will see Gilgamesh, the powerful,
who rides over the herd like any great king.
You will see in him a power rare
and fairly learn to love him like yourself."

They journeyed from the forest far and wide
to venture on toward Uruk.
The girl led forth the naked boy
as gently as a mother would,
tearing her garment right in two
to hide their native beauty
and clothed his splendid body then
with her own cloak as they approached.

Column iii

Along the way he learned new human ways
tracking down the gentle sheep
and using weapons for the first time
to fight away the savage beasts
that do attack the herds and
farms of men.

Column iv

Along the way he also learned to eat and drink
as men and women do. The girl did
teach all these things too for Enkidu's first lessons.

And with a man upon the road they spoke
to learn of customs new to one from

16

far-off woods. So Enkidu came then
to know of Gilgamesh who harshly
ruled and was not loved by those men whose girls
he often played with all night long.

And before they entered through the
gates of Uruk's mighty walls, Enkidu
was hailed as one who might
be sent to rival any king who
might treat gentle folk unfairly.

Column v

In the alleys of Uruk
during a display of force
the approach of Enkidu stopped everything.
Uruk rose before him.
The mountain beyond stretched skyward.
All creatures worshiped him.
Youths rallied round.
People adored him as they adore a newborn babe.
For so it is when one comes from nowhere
to do what no one thought could be done.
For Ishara then a wedding bed is set this night
because a guest has come who is as strong as any king.
And Enkidu stood before the gate where new lovers go
and stopped Gilgamesh from coming with nighttime girls.
It is there where they first fight
throughout the night and round about Uruk's walls,
which they chipped and wrecked in places.

Column vi

So the mighty brothers fought at first
pushing and shoving each other
for hours and hours enraged.
Then a calm force gently soothed
their well-matched spirits
to bring a peace and rest their strife.

17

It was Enkidu who sued for rest saying:
"Gilgamesh, enough! I am here to
match some fate with you, not
to destroy or rival any king."

TABLET III
Column i

Then Enkidu and Gilgamesh joined in
sacred friendship and sealed their solemn
bond with noble kiss.

Column ii

Enkidu and Gilgamesh often sat then together,
visited Ninsun's shrine, conversed
of many plans, and fashioned a future together.
Once, informed by fears of
future sorrow, Enkidu began
to weep and warn his friend of
coming horror. He said:
"If we go there beyond here to where
Humbaba the Awful lives,
there will be a gruesome war
in a place no one calls home,
where no one wants to stay for long
or go to rest or rest to gain
the strength to reach the forests."

The Great One rose within
and robed herself appropriately
covering herself,
ringing her curls beneath her crown
to ascend the altar, where she stood
lighting the first signals of charcoal for the incense
and preparing sacred cups that hold the
precious liquids which will be spilled.
Then Ninsun asked Shamash:

"Why?
Why have you called my only son away
and shaped his mind in so disturbed a way?
For now, he says, you invite him to begin a
pilgrimage that ends where Humbaba
directs a never-ending battle,
along a foreign, lonely road
far within the forests dark and damp
where a man like him might just kill
a god like Humbaba or be killed
to dissolve the pain that you, Shamash, oppose."

Column iii

Humbaba stirs within the darkened wood
and in the hearts of men there rises fear.
When Enkidu spoke at last to Gilgamesh
he said these words of warning:
I knew this monster's reputation long ago.
Fire and death mix in his breath,
and I for one do not wish now
to challenge such a demon."
But Gilgamesh retorted: "All glory
will be ours if now we conquer
this unprecedented foe and risk the
woe that frightens others."
And Enkidu said then in swift reply:
"How shall we go toward woods
so fiercely guarded?"

Column iv

Enlil it was who sent Humbaba there
to scare away intruders with fierce
and frightening howls. Great Gilgamesh
remembered that when he spoke words like these
to Enkidu: "Only gods live forever
with Shamash, my friend; for even our
longest days are numbered. Why worry over
being like dust in the wind? Leap up for

this great threat. Fear not. Even if I were
to fail and fall in combat,
all future clans would say I did the job."
Special weapons then were ordered to be made
for their assault upon Humbaba.
Axes, swords, and combat saddles were prepared
and all of Uruk's population flocked round
their great departure.

Column v

The awful monster's reputation
made Uruk's gentle people fear
for their great king. And after
all the plans were made to start
out to fight Humbaba, a group
came forward to see the king.

The elders spoke to Gilgamesh:
"Fear the force that you control, hot-headed boy;
Be sure you watch where you direct
your every, heavy swing in battle.
Vanguards protect.
Friends save friends.
Let Enkidu lead on the way
through forests that he knows.
He knows how to fight in woodlands;
he knows where to pick his fight.
Enkidu will shield his bosom too
as well as that of his companion
so as to protect them both.
He'll traverse any ditch of any width.
Enkidu will guard our king.
Be sure to bring him safely back."
Gilgamesh said to Enkidu:
"Arise, my other self, and speed your way to Egalmah
to where my mother sits, kind Ninsun.
She understands all I need to know.
She'll tell us where we should go and what to do."
Again the men embraced as teammates do.
Gilgamesh and Enkidu set out to Egalmah.

Column vi

Upset by all his thoughts of coming battles
and concerned by his consultations with the gods,
Gilgamesh then sadly set his palace rooms in order.
His weapons were prepared, his helmet shined,
and garments freshly cleaned.
Citizens of Uruk came to say good-bye and
wish their daring king farewell.
"Go careful through this risky, bold adventure,
mighty lord. Be sure of your own safety first of all."
So spoke the elders of his town and then continued:
"Let Enkidu take risks for you and have him
lead the way through woods he knows so well.
Pray that Shamash show him, as your guide,
the nearest path and choicest route to
where you dare to go.
May great Lugalbanda favor you in combat with Humbaba."
Then Enkidu himself spoke finally to his king:
"The time is right for us to now depart.
Follow me, sir, along the savage way
to where a worthy opponent,
the awful beast Humbaba,
waits for your challenge in the
dark woodlands that he guards.
Do not fear this. Rely on me
in every matter and let me act
as careful guide for your most daring venture."

TABLET IV
Columns i, ii

Ten miles into the march, they stopped to eat.
After thirty miles, they rested,
then finished another twenty miles that day.
Within three days they covered
what would take others a month and a half to travel.
They dug for water where
there appeared to be none
in the dry desert on their way
to challenge Humbaba.

Columns iii, iv

Onward ventured Gilgamesh and Enkidu.
And they both knew where danger lurked
at their first destination.
As up they climbed upon the final hill,
they saw a guard put out by Humbaba
as fierce as any watchdog.
Gilgamesh pursued first.

Column v

Gilgamesh heard shouts from
Enkidu who said to his companion:
"Remember promises we made
in the city where we live. Recall
the courage and the force
we vowed to bring upon this mission."
These words dispelled the fear felt
in his heart and Gilgamesh in
return then shouted back:
"Quick. Grab the guard
and don't let go.
Race fearlessly and don't let go.
Our enemy, Humbaba, has set out seven uniforms
but has only dressed in one
so far. So six layers of strength

are yet unused by him."
As one mad brute he is enraged,
bellowing loudly while the foresters warn each other
what he's like.

Column vi

Wounded in combat with the guard they killed,
Enkidu uses words to say:
"I lost my strength in this crushed hand when the gate slammed shut.
What shall I do?"
Then Gilgamesh spoke: "Brother,
as a man in tears would,
you transcend all the rest who've gathered,
for you can cry and kill
with equal force.
Hold my hand in yours,
and we will not fear what hands like ours can do.
Scream in unison, and we will ascend
to death or love, to say in song what we shall do.
Our cry will shoot afar so
this new weakness, awful doubt,
will pass through you.
Stay, brother, let us ascend as one."

TABLET V
Column i

Gilgamesh and Enkidu froze and stared into the woods'
great depth and height. When they spied
Humbaba's path, they found the opening toward
straight passage. Then they were able to find and see
the home of the gods, the paradise of Ishtar's other self,
called Irnini the Most Attractive.
All beauty true is ever there
where gods do dwell, where there is
cool shade and harmony and
sweet-odored food to match their mood.

Column iii

Then Gilgamesh envisioned yet again
another dream
high up in the hills
where boulders crashed.
Again Enkidu said to his brother,
as he unraveled this dreary story for his king:
"Brother, your song is a fine omen.
This dream will make you well.
Brother, that vision you saw is rich
for on that mountain top
we can capture Humbaba and
hurl his earthly form from
towering cliffs through sky to
earth, making his shape
as flat and wide as it is round and high."

"Mountain, mountain in the sky,
Break the god and make him die."

Column iv

Mountain on high then sent the myth into Enkidu's sleep,
and a chill from the high winds forced him to rest,
since he was blown around as grain is on open field.
Curled up in a ball, Gilgamesh rested
in blessed sleep, the best of friends at the worst of times.
But by the moon's halfway course, he rose
and then began to speak:
"Brother, if you made no noise, what sound woke me?
If you didn't jostle me, what shook my body?
There was no god nearby, so why am I so stunned?
Brother, I've had a third vision in sleep
and I am deeply frightened to recall it all.
Sky screamed. And Mother Earth moaned.
Sun went out of light and blackest night
enveloped the heavens.
Then came flashes of lightning, source of fire.
Storm clouds raced nearby and swept all life away
from out of the sky above our heads.
Brightness dissolved, light evaporated;

cinders turned to ash.
When we leave the mountain, this is what we will remember."

When Enkidu learned this myth as told,
he replied to Gilgamesh:
"Shamash, your god, creates a great attraction
for both of us. Shamash now approves
of this attack upon Humbaba. Take the sign
as some divine dream to urge us on."
Shamash himself said such words to Gilgamesh
as if in prayer:
"Do not balk now, favored one.
Brace yourself for battle and proceed."

Heavenly winds blasted down from out of the sky
about and all around Humbaba. From east and
west, with sand and grain, they blew him
back and forth. His giant self became
fatigued. His awesome strength dwindled.
Not even his great right foot could step away in flight.
So in this way, by Shamash's intervention,
Humbaba the awful beast was brought so low.

Column vi

The dying beast called out for mercy once
and part of what he said could still be heard over the howling winds:
"Please, Gilgamesh! Have mercy on me, wounded.
I shall freely give you all the lumber of my mighty realm
and work for you both day and night."
It was Enkidu then who shouted louder
than the beast and with his words he
urged a swift conclusion:
"Kill the beast now, Gilgamesh. Show
no weak or silly mercy toward so sly a foe."

Taking his companion's mean advice, Gilgamesh
swiftly cut the beast, splattering blood upon
his cloak and sandals then. Soiled by this
violent conflict, the friends began their
journey back to Uruk's towering walls
expecting now to be received as heroes who
had fought and won a legendary battle.

TABLET VI
Column i

Gilgamesh bathed himself and cleaned his hair,
as beautiful as it was long.
He cast off bloodied robes and put on his favorite gown,
secured the cincture and stood royal.
Then Gilgamesh put on his crown.

Ishtar looked up at Gilgamesh's handsome pride.
"Come to me," she whispered. "Come to me and be my groom.
Let me taste all parts of you,
treat you as husband, be treated as your wife.
And as a gift I'd give to you
one regal coach of gold and blue
with wheels of yellow and all so new
that I would flatter all your might
with the sight of demons driven off
by my own god, by my own man.
Come to my home, most sweetly scented of all places,
where holy faces wash your feet with tears as
do the priests and priestesses of gods like Anu.
All mighty hands of kings and queens
will open doors for you.
So too will all the countryside donate
in duplicate to your fold.
And the slow will race ahead for you,
so that by association, all that you touch
will turn to gold."
Gilgamesh replied to mighty Ishtar thus:
"But how could I repay you as a wife
and still avoid the bitterness and strife that follow you?
Is it perfume for a dress you want, or me?
My self or something wrapped around a tree?
Do I offer you food, sweet nuts or grapes?
Are those for gods or for the savage apes?
And who will pour a treat to us in bed,
you dressed for life and me as if I'm dead?
Here's a song I made for you
(a little crude, a little rude):

Ishtar's the hearth gone cold,
a broken door, without the gold;

a fort that shuts its soldiers out,
a water well that's filled with doubt;
tar that can't be washed away,
a broken cup, stained and gray;
rock that shatters to dust and sand,
a useless weapon in the hand;
and worse than that or even this,
a god's own sandal filled with piss.
You've had your share of boys, that's true,
but which of them came twice for you?
Let me now list the ones that you just blew away.

Column ii

First was Tammuz, the virgin boy you took
after a three-year-long seductive look.
Then you lusted for a fancy, colored bird
and cut its wing so it could not herd.
Thus in the lovely woods at night
bird sings, 'I'm blind. I have no sight.'
You trapped a lion, too, back then.
Its cock went in your form as hen.
And then you dug him seven holes
in which to fall on sharpened poles.
You let a horse in your back door
by laying on a stable floor;
but then you built the world's first chain
to choke his throat and end his reign.
You let him run with all his might,
as boys will sometimes do at night,
before you harnessed his brute force
with labor fierce, a mean divorce.
So did his mother weep and wail
to see her child's foot set with a nail.
You fondled once a shepherd boy
who baked buns for your tongue's joy
and daily killed his lambs so coy.
So in return for gifts like those
you chose to lupinize his toy.
And when his brothers saw his penis
they knew you'd done something heinous.
Ishullanu trimmed your father's trees
and brought you carrots, dates, and peas.

So mighty you sat down to feasts,
then turned your thoughts to raping beasts.
You saw him naked once and said:
'Come, Ishullanu, into my bed
and force your force into my head.
Place your fingers where men dread
to touch a girl who's dead.'
And he in turn said this to you:
'What is it that you'd have me do?
I know, kind mother, I won't eat
if I can't match your female heat.
But would you have me sing and sin
as my whistle goes both out and in?'
So since he balked to play that role,
you switched his jewel into a mole;
stuck in the muck of a marshy town
his pleasure can't go up or down.
And that is how you'd deal with me
if we got friendly, warm, and free."

When Ishtar heard his words so cruel,
she lost her cool and played the fool
by blasting off for daddy's distant star,
where she said: "Daddy, daddy, daddy, please,
Gilgamesh called me a tease."

Column iii

"Gilgamesh said I sinned and lived
without faith in myself or others," she pouted.

Her father, Anu, said these exact words to Ishtar:
"Now, daughter, did you first insult him,
this Gilgamesh who then began to taunt you
with jibes about your inclinations?"
Ishtar shouted back at him, who is her father:
"You! Now! Make him stop! Loose the
bull who could trample him at once.
Let the bull spill his blood.
And you'd better do this now or I'll
wreak havoc of my own right down to hell.
I'll loose the goddamn devil. I'll rain corpses.

I'll make zombies eat infants and there will be
more dead souls than living ones!"

Her father, Anu, said these exact words to Ishtar:
"But if I do what you seem now to want,
there would be long years of drought
and sorrow. Have you stored enough
reserve to feed the people who
deserve your close protection?"

And she said:
"Yes, I have reserved a plan
for those I love. Now do as I demand
and punish all who insult me."

Then her father, Anu, heard Ishtar's cry
and Ishtar forced her will.

Anu set loose a bull from out of the sky and,
at the bull's proclamation, there cracks the
earth to swallow up nine dozen citizens of Uruk!

Column iv

An earthquake fixed a grave for nine dozen citizens of Uruk.
Two or three or four hundred victims,
maybe more than that, fell into hell.
And when the quake returned for a third time,
it was near to Enkidu,
he who fell upon the abyss so wide and grim.
Enkidu collapsed near the earth-shaking bull.
Then he leaped to grab the bull by his long horns
even with spit upon his face from out the savage mouth,
even with the stench of bowels near his nose.

Then Enkidu said to Gilgamesh:
"Brother, you and I are now hailed as one.
How could we defeat a god?
Brother, I see great challenge here, but can we dare defy such force?
Let's kill it if we can right now.

Be unrelenting and hope that god
gives us the strength.
We must be cold and strong

to cut our enemy's weak neck."
Enkidu surrounds the bull, pursuing heaven's beast
and finally catches him.

So Gilgamesh, like a bull dancer,
svelte and mighty then,
plunged his sword into the throat held fast by Enkidu.
They butchered and bled the bull and then cut out its heart
to offer as sacrifice before Shamash.
Then Gilgamesh and Enkidu retreated
from the altar itself and stood afar
in deep respect as they did pray.
At last the two sat down, bound by war, bound by worship.

Ishtar appeared upon Uruk's walls
looking like a wailing widow.
She shrieked this curse aloud:
"Damn Gilgamesh, who injured me,
by slaughtering a divine bull."
Enkidu reacted to these words of Ishtar quick
by hurling at her head a hunk of meat from the bull's thigh.
And from afar he shouted up to her:
"This bloody mess of a plain bull would
be about what I could make of you
if you came near. I'd tie
your hands with these ropelike intestines."
Ishtar signaled then for her attendants:
coiffured bishops, cantors, and girls
whose charms keep worshipers coming.

Then atop the great wall above the city high
standing by the severed part of its right thigh,
she had them shriek laments for the bull who'd died.
So to complete this ritual and adorn his throne
Gilgamesh summoned artisans of all kinds.
Some measured the diameter of the bull's horns,
each containing thirty pounds of lapis lazuli.
Together those horns could hollow hold
half a dozen quarts of oil.
And that is what Gilgamesh brought as potion
to the altar of Lugalbanda, his special protector.
He carried the horns and enshrined them in a palace
of honor where his clan held rites.

Then Enkidu and Gilgamesh absolved their
bloody hands in the forgiving river,
the deep, eternal Euphrates that does not change.

At last relieved of such a stain, the friends renew
their vows with a brief embrace
before riding through Uruk's crowded streets
amid acclaim. There Gilgamesh stops to
give this speech to gathered girls:

Column v

"What man is most impressive now?
Who is finest, firmest, and most fair?
Isn't Gilgamesh that man above men
and isn't Enkidu the strongest of all?"
Then they party loudly throughout the day
so that, come night, they drop down dead in sleep.
But Enkidu is resurrected quickly
to relieve his soul of fright
and sadly he asks Gilgamesh in tears:
"Oh brother, why would I dream that gods sat round to set my fate?"

TABLET VII
Column i

Enkidu confessed this dream to Gilgamesh:
"The gods all gathered round last night
and Anu told Enlil that one of us should die
because of what we've done against their names.
Though Shamash intervened for us,
saying we had slain Humbaba and the bull
with his consent, the others sought revenge."

Then Enkidu fell ill and soon lost his full strength.
Saying words like these as his friend lay dying,
Gilgamesh intoned:
"Why should you be so condemned and why should
I go right on living?

Will my own sad eyes soon never look on you again?
Shall I descend to depths beneath
this earth to visit worlds reserved
for those who've died?"

Enkidu glanced up, addressing the entryway
on which his hand was morbidly crushed:
"Door of all forests, that confuses wind and rain,
deaf, dumb, and blind portal;
I admired your firm texture
before I first saw the mighty trees
aloft that gave force to you.
There is nothing on earth that could replace
your splendor or your worth.
At two hundred feet in height, at forty feet around are
your mighty posts, your priceless hinge
cut and crafted in Nippur's holy ground.
If I had guessed that you'd become this,
I would have shattered you to pieces
with my ax and have been more careful not
to wound my hand so badly on your frame."

Column iii

Then cursing the hunter whom he first met
and the girl whom he first loved, Enkidu raged:
"Slash him. Cut half his face.
Raise up floods beneath his feet
so that no animal is safe."
And at his sacred, former lover Enkidu did swear:
"Get up, witch, and hear your fortune
guaranteed now and forever.
I damn you off and damn you down.
I'd break your teeth with stones and let
your mouth hang open
until you'd say thanks to your killer
who would favor you by letting you
lie homeless on an open road
in some foul ditch.
May all and any who can hurt you now
often cross the paths you take.

I hope you live in fright, unsure of hope
and starved always for the touch of love."

Shamash responded from on high:
"The fine lover, my Enkidu, is cursed by you
who gave you bread and meat and stew,
the same who offered you some wine,
food and drink almost divine
so that you were taken for a god.
The fine lover, my thoughtless boy, invested you
with robes of gold, robes of blue
and, more important, gave your dear friend
the thought that he should do whatever need
be done and still more too.
Did your brother, Gilgamesh, give you as fine a bed
as any on earth or any there in heaven?
Did he promote the likes of you to fame
unrivaled, so that rulers kneel to kiss
the ground you walk upon?
He will also show the Uruk people how to mourn for you.
An entire people will cry upon your death
and he will go in tears
ignoring the dirt and dust and mud
that stain his hands and hair.
So in despair will his mind be
as off he roams in lonely woods wearing rags."

When Enkidu heard these sad words
he was speechless and in his heart
he knew that Shamash spoke the truth.
His anger fled and Enkidu resolved
to die in peace.

Column iv

With these last words the dying Enkidu did pray
and say to his beloved companion:
"In dreams last night
the heavens and the earth poured out
great groans while I alone
stood facing devastation. Some fierce
and threatening creature flew down at me

33

and pushed me with its talons toward
the horror-filled house of death
wherein Irkalla, queen of shades,
stands in command.
There is darkness which lets no person
again see light of day.
There is a road leading away from
bright and lively life.
There dwell those who eat dry dust
and have no cooling water to quench their awful thirst.

As I stood there I saw all those who've died,
and even kings among those darkened souls
have none of their remote and former glory.
All earthly greatness was forfeit
and I entered then into the house of death.
Others who have been there long
did rise to welcome me."

Hearing this, great Gilgamesh said to his handsome mother:
"My friend, dear Enkidu, has seen his passing now,
and he lies dying here upon a sad and lonely cot.
Each day he weakens more and wonders how much more
life may yet belong to his hands and eyes and tongue."

Then Enkidu resumed his last remarks and said:
"Oh Gilgamesh, some destiny has robbed me
of the honor fixed for those who die in battle.
I lie now in slow disgrace, withering day by day,
deprived as I am of the peace that comes to one
who dies suddenly in a swift clash of arms."

TABLET VIII
Column i

Then once again at break of day
did Gilgamesh conclude the silent night
by being first to raise his hands and voice
and he said:
"Oh Enkidu, whose own mother's grace

was every bit as sweet as any deer's
and whose father
raced just as swift and stood as strong
as any horse that ever ran,
accept all natural customs
within the limitless confines of the wild
where you were raised by those with
tails, by those with hooves, by
those with fur and whiskers.
All the roads in and out of your great forest
now lie silent, but for the sobbing done by your wild friends.
The aged men and women of Uruk mourn today
and raise their withered palms in prayer
as we carry you by, toward Mount Kur.
Grottos weep for you and valleys too
and so do those great trees
upon the shore where you loved to run.
And also crying now are
large bears, little dogs, baby cubs
of lions and of tigers, and even
the hyena now has ceased its laugh.
Wild bull and the rapidest of deer
All, all, all sigh,
All, all, all cry for you.
Ulay's lovely riverbanks are swollen on this day
where you did walk as boys alone can do
upon the banks of rivers that mother
their young thoughts about life and death.
Yes, that great brown god, the river Ulay,
today mourns for you as does the
true Euphrates eternal and silent.
Uruk's rugged men mourn for you
who killed that sacrificial bull.
They all weep tears today
and those in Eridu, who loved your fame,
and say your name aloud,
they too weep tears today
and all in days to come, even those who knew
you not, all may weep tears someday
for your sad lot.
Your favorite aunt, your blessed servant,
your first girlfriend,

your inspiration, your companion, your darling
dear, and she you feared to be alone with,
all women who ever sat and ate with you,
all men you ever helped with food or drink,
every one and all,
lovers fast and strangers slow.
Those you touched or who touched you
and those who never knew just how you felt.
All and every burst into tears
today because they heard that
you were suddenly dead."

Column ii

"I'll cry now, citizens of Uruk, and you
will finally hear what no one else
has ever had the nerve to say in sorrow.
I was family and friend to Enkidu and I shall
fill the woodlands where we stalked with loud, sad sobs today.
I cry now, Enkidu, like some crazed woman. I howl.
I screech for you because you were the ax upon my belt
and the bow in my weak hand; the sword within my sheath,
the shield that covered me in battle; my happiest robe,
the finest clothes I ever wore,
the ones that made me look best in the eyes of the world.
That is what you were; that is what you'll always be.
What devil came to take you off from me?

Brother, you chased down the strongest mule,
the swiftest horse on mountains high,
the quickest panthers in the flatlands.
And they in turn will weep for you.

Birds in the air cry aloud.
Fish in the lake gather together near the shore.
What else heeds this sorrow?
The leaves of the trees and the paths you loved
in the forest grow dark.
Night itself murmurs and so too does the day.
All the eyes of the city that once saw your kind face begin to weep.
Why? Because you were my brother and you died.
When we met and fought and loved,

we went up on mountains high to where we dared to capture
god's own strength in one great beast and then to cut its throat,
thus humbling Humbaba, green god of woodlands steep.
Now there is a sleeplike spell on you, and you
are dark as well as deaf."

Enkidu can move no more.
Enkidu can lift his head no more.

"Now there is a sound throughout the land
that can mean only one thing.
I hear the voice of grief and I know that you have been taken
somewhere by death.
Weep. Let the roads we walked together flood themselves with tears.
Let the beasts we hunted cry out for this:
the lion and the leopard, the tiger and the panther.
Let their strength be put into their tears.
Let the cloudlike mountain where you killed
the guardian of woodland treasures
place grief upon its sky blue top.
Let the river which soothed our feet overflow its banks
as tears do that swell and rush across my dusty cheeks.
Let the clouds and stars race swiftly with you into death.
Let the rain that makes us dream
tell the story of your life tonight.
Who mourns for you now, Brother?
Everyone who knew you does.
The harvesters and the farmers who used to bring you grain
are standing alone in their fields.
The servants who worked in your house
today whispered your name in empty rooms.
The lover who kissed every part of you
touches her chilled lips with scented fingers.
The women of the palace sit
and stare at the queen of the city.
She sobs and sobs and sobs.
The men with whom you played so bold
speak fondly of your name.
Thus they deal with this misfortune.
But what do I do? I only know that a cruel fate robbed me
of my dearest friend too soon.
What state of being holds you now? Are you lost forever?
Do you hear my song?"

"I placed my hand upon your quiet heart."

One brother covered the set face of another
with a bride-white veil.

"I flew above you then as if I were an eagle."

Then, like some great cat whose darling young have sadly died,
Gilgamesh slides back and forth fixed mindlessly on grief.
He commands many men to erect statues of honor, saying:
"Make his chest a noble blue and on his honored body place a jewel
as will allow all viewers then to see how great he was,
how great he'll always be."

Next day, Gilgamesh rose from a restless sleep.

Column iii

Then Gilgamesh continued with his birdlike words:
"On a pedestal I will honor your corpse
by setting you
above all earthly princes who will celebrate you
when people from all distant lands
both rich and poor in spirit
acclaim your memory.
And when you are gone,
never again to wear good clothes or care for food,
I'll still remember how you dressed and how you ate."
When day did break again next morn,
Gilgamesh stripped off the lion's cloak and
rose to say this prayer:
"Your funeral is a precious
gesture I made to hide my own guilt."

Good-bye, dear brother
Ave atque vale, frater [1]
Sal sri akai meri pra [2]
Dehna hune wood wordema [3]
Slan agat, seanchara [4]
Shalom. [5]

1. Latin: Hail and farewell, Brother.
2. Bengali (India): Good-bye, Brother.
3. Amharic (Ethiopia): Farewell, sweet Brother.
4. Gaelic: Go fairly, old Friend.
5. Hebrew: Peace.

Column v

Still grieving reverently
after he arose next day, Gilgamesh imagined the Anunnaki
who decide the fate of
those who go to the underworld.
After learning how to pause his heart,
Gilgamesh created just the same image
in the face of a river.
At break of day,
on the sacred table made of special wood,
the grieving king placed a consecrated bowl of blue
filled with butter and with honey too
and this he offered up in solemn prayer
to Shamash, lord god.

TABLET IX
Column i

Then Gilgamesh wept some more
for his dead friend. He wandered
over barren hills, mumbling to his own spirit:
"Will you too die as Enkidu did?
Will grief become your food? Will we both
fear the lonely hills, so vacant?
I now race from place to place,
dissatisfied with wherever I am and
turn my step toward Utnapishtim,
godchild of Ubaratutu,
who lives a pious life in fair Dilmun
where the morning sun arises as it
does in paradises lost and won.
As if in sleep I come upon the mountain door at midnight
where I face wild-eyed lions and I am afraid.
Then to Sin, the god of mighty light,
I raise my solemn chant to beg:
'Save me, please, my god.'"

Despite respite
he could not sleep or dream that night.

Instead he wandered through the woods
so like a savage beast just then
did he bring death again and again
upon the lions' heads
with an ax he drew
from off his belt.

Column ii

When he finally reached the base of
Mount Mashu, Gilgamesh began to
climb the double cliff
that guides the rising and setting of Shamash.
Now these identical towers touch
the distant, distant sky,
and far below, their breasts descend toward hell.
Those who guard the gate are
poison scorpions
who terrorize all, whose spells bring death.
And then resplendent power
thrives all across the town
where I was born
and rises farther still to
mountain tops.
At dawn and dark they shield Shamash.
And when he sensed them there,
Gilgamesh could not dare to look
upon their threat;
but held his glance away,
suspended fear,
and then approached in dread.
One among the guardians there
said this to his wife:
"The one who comes toward us
is partly divine, my dear."
And then the same one said
to the godlike part of Gilgamesh:
"Eternal heart, why make
this long, long trip

trying to come to us
through travail? Speak now."

Column iii

Gilgamesh said: "I come by here
to visit my elder, my Utnapishtim,
the epitome of both life everlasting and
death that is eternal."

The poison scorpion guardian said:
"No mortal man has ever
come to know what you seek
here. Not one of all your kind
has come so far, the distance
you would fall if you fell
all day and all night into the pit
and through great darkness
where there is no light
without Shamash who raises
and lowers the sun;
to where I let no one go,
to where I forbid anyone to enter."

Column iv

Heartachest pain abounds
with ice or fire all around.
The scorpion one,
I do not know whether a man or a woman,
said then:
"Gilgamesh, I command you
to proceed
to highest peaks
over hills toward heaven.
Godspeed!
With all permissions given here, I approve your venture."
So Gilgamesh set out then over
that sacred, sacred path within the mountains of Mashu,
near that incarnate ray of sunshine

precious to Shamash.
Oh dark, dark, dark, dark.
Oh the night, unholy and blind,
that wrapped him as soon as he stepped
forth upon that path.

Column v

DARKNESS
Beneath a moonless, starless sky,
Gilgamesh was frozen and unseeing
by time before midnight;
by midnight's hollow eye
he was unseen and frozen.
At 1 a.m. he tripped and fell
blinded and frozen.
At 2 a.m. he staggered on
blinded and frozen.
At 3 a.m. he faltered not
blinded and frozen.
By 4 a.m. his second wind warmed him who still was
blinded and frozen.
And at your final dawn,
son of man, you will see only
a heap of broken images in an ascending
light that gives you sight you may not want,
for you will then behold all precious goods
and gardens sweet as home to you, as exile,
boughs of blue, oh unforgotten gem,
as true as any other memory from any other previous life.

Column vi

Then along the path
Gilgamesh traveled fast
and came at length to
shorelines fresh with dew.
And there he met a maiden,
one who knows the secrets of the sea.

TABLET X
Column i

This gentle girl is called Siduri
and she sits by the sea
where she sways from side to side.
She made the water pale; she crafted the first gold bowl
while peeking at the sun
through a slit across her face veil.

King Gilgamesh approached the girl's small cottage by the sea
dressed as a mountain man,
a meat eater,
with an aching heart
and the stare of one setting out upon some
arduous, horrid trek.
The girl who gives her men lifesaving drinks
said to herself, "Beware of the one
coming now. He walks as if he'd kill."
And so Siduri locked the door,
put stones in place, lay on the floor.
When Gilgamesh heard sounds inside
he yelled at her. "Why do you hide?
Shall I have to break through this door?"

The girl whose drinks refresh the soul
then said these words to Gilgamesh:
"Is there a simple reason, sir, why you're so sad
or why your face is drawn and thin?
Has chance worn out your youth or did some
wicked sorrow consume you like food?
You look like one setting out on some arduous, horrid trek,
like one exposed to extremes of hot and cold,
like one who searches everywhere for grace."
He responded then to her who gives her men
lifesaving drinks:
"Girl, there is no simple reason why I'm so sad
or why my face is drawn and thin.
Chance alone did not wear out my youth. Some
wicked sorrow consumes me like food.
But I do look like one setting out on some
arduous, horrid trek, like one exposed
to extreme hot or cold,
like one who searches everywhere

43

for the breath of life
because my brother, my only true friend, met death;
he who raced wild horses there,
who caught orange tigers here.
This was Enkidu, my soul's good half,
who raced wild horses there,
who caught orange tigers here;
who did all things while he conquered mountains
and divine bulls that race
across the sky like clouds;
who gave Humbaba, the woodland god,
reason to weep when he stole through
the wooded path to slaughter lions."

Column ii

Gilgamesh continued:
"I greatly loved my friend who was always there for me.
I loved Enkidu who was always there for me.
What awaits us all caught him first
and I did thirst for one whole week to
see him once again in splendor until his body decomposed.
Then I wept for my future death
and I fled home for mountaintops to breathe
when my friend's death choked off my wind.
On mountaintops I roamed content to breathe
again when my friend's death choked off my wind.
Walking. Walking. Walking over hills.
Could I sit down to rest?
Could I stop crying then
when my best friend had died
as I will someday do?"

Then Gilgamesh said to the fair girl
whose saving drinks gave life to men:
"Tell me, girl, how to get to Utnapishtim.
Where do I look for signs? Show me directions. Help.
Please let me have safe passage over seas.
Give me advice to guide me on my way."
She said to him in swift reply:
"No man has ever gone that way

and lived to say he crossed the sea.
Shamash only ventures there,
only Shamash would dare
to stare into the sun.
Pain joins the voyager soon,
and soon the traveler grows weary
where death surrounds the path
on every side with danger."

Column iii

The girl whose drinks refresh the soul
then said these words to Gilgamesh:
"Remember always, mighty king,
that gods decreed the fates of all
many years ago. They alone are let
to be eternal, while we frail humans die
as you yourself must someday do.
What is best for us to do
is now to sing and dance.
Relish warm food and cool drinks.
Cherish children to whom your love gives life.
Bathe easily in sweet, refreshing waters.
Play joyfully with your chosen wife."

"It is the will of the gods for you to smile
on simple pleasure in the leisure time of your short days."

"And what, after all, my fellow man,
would you do when you got to that
far side where Urshanabi dwells
among the hills of Utnapishtim?
He knows only the dead weight of what is dead
and he is one who plays with deadly snakes.
Would you put your lips near his?
If he befriends you then, go on.
But if he walks away, return to me."
With that in mind
Gilgamesh took up his chore,
unsheathed his sword, slipped toward the shore,
and there joined one who rows the seas of death.
Gilgamesh sliced through the underbrush as an arrow goes through air

while cracking the stones of the sacred columns.
And Urshanabi barely saw the arrow's glint
and too late heard the ax's thud.
And so surprised was he that
there was never any chance to
hide or to deny the daring man
at least a chance at
some safe passage.

Gilgamesh traveled on to where he next
found the ferryman of Utnapishtim. This man,
Urshanabi, said to Gilgamesh:
"Your face seems tense; your eyes do not glance well
and hell itself is part of how you look.
Grief hangs from your shoulders.
You look like one who's been without a home, without a bed
or roof for a long time, wandering the wilds on some random search."
Gilgamesh replied to the ferryman:
"Yes, sir, it's true my face is tense
and that my eyes seem harsh.
My looks are now so hellish,
for I wear my grief as ill as any other.
I'm not this way as some refugee
without a bed or roof for a long time,
and I don't wander the wilds randomly.
I grieve for Enkidu, my fair companion and true friend,
who chased the strongest mule, the swiftest horse
on mountain high, the quickest panther of the flatland.
Together we did all things, climbing sky-high peaks,
stealing divine cattle, humbling the gods, killing Humbaba
and the precious lions, guardians of the sky.
All this I did with my best friend who now is dead.
Mortality reached him first and I am left this week
to weep and wail for his shriveling corpse, which scares me.
I roam aloft and alone now, by death enthralled,
and think of nothing but my dear friend.
I roam the lonely path with death upon my mind
and think of nothing but my dear friend.
Over many seas and across many mountains I roam.
I can't stop pacing. I can't stop crying.
My friend has died and half my heart is torn from me.
Won't I soon be like him, stone cold and dead, for all the days to come?"

Urshanabi replied as he had done before:
"Your face seems tense; your eyes do not glance well
and hell itself is part of how you look.
Grief hangs from your shoulders.
You look like one who's been without a home, without a bed
or roof for a long time, wandering the wilds on some random search."

And Gilgamesh said to him then in swift reply:
"Of course my face seems tense and my eyes seem harsh.
Of course I'm worn out weeping. Why should I not cry?
I've come to ask directions to Utnapishtim, who lives so
free beyond death's deep, deep lake. Where can he be?
Tell me how to venture there where I may learn his secrets."

Finally, Urshanabi uttered these last words to Gilgamesh:
"You yourself have hurt this effort most, sir,
by blasphemy and sacrilege,
by breaking idols and by holding the untouchably sacred stones.
You broke stone images!
So now, Mr. Gilgamesh, raise high your ax."

Thus chastised, Gilgamesh
raised high his ax, unsheathed his sword,
did penance too as he chopped down many trees;
prepared them then, and then brought them
to Urshanabi.
After this, they cast off together,
with push and pull they launched the skiff
upon the waving sea.
They leaped quick, in three short days
covering a span that any other would
traverse only after months of passage
and soon they sailed on to Death's own sea.

Column iv

Still directing the king's new efforts, Urshanabi called:
"Give me another pull, Gilgamesh, upon the mighty oar
and then another. Give ten times twenty
and then give twenty times ten pulls upon the
mighty oars; then ten more twice; then twice
more ten and then confuse the number of

the pulls you put upon the oar
by losing count aloud and starting over."
Halfway through all that pulling,
Gilgamesh had worn the oars to bits
and torn his shirt from off his back
to raise a helping sail upon the mast.
Then Utnapishtim glared down from stars and clouds
and mused aloud, as if to coach the world:
"How could any human dare to break the idols
or steer the craft that gods and goddesses use?
This stranger is not fit to tie the shoes of servants.
I do see, but I am blind.
I do know, but cannot understand
how he behaves like
the beasts of here and there."

Column v

Gilgamesh spoke many words to Utnapishtim
and told of strife in life and
battles rare. He hailed his friend Enkidu,
acclaimed their pride, and grieved the
death that saddened his great heart.
Gilgamesh raised his prayer to the remote Utnapishtim:
"Oh myth-filled god,
I have traveled many roads,
crossed many rivers and mountains.
I never rested. I never slept. Grief consumed me.
My clothing was ragged by the time I met
the girl who would help me.
I killed all manner of animal in order
to eat and clothe myself.
When I was rejected, I stooped to squalor.
Cursed I went,
being unholy."
Utnapishtim replied:
"Why cry over your fate and nature?
Chance fathered you. Your conception was
an accidental combination
of the divine and mortal.
I do not presume to know how to help
the likes of you."

Column vi

Utnapishtim continued:
"No man has ever seen Death.
No one ever heard Death's voice
but Death is real and Death is loud.
How many times must a home be restored
or a contract revised and approved?
How many times must two brothers agree
not to dispute what is theirs?
How many wars and how many floods must there be
with plague and exile in their wake?
Shamash is the one who can say.
But there is no one else who can
see what Shamash only can see within the sun.

Behold the cold, cold corpse from a distance,
and then regard the body of one who sleeps.
There seems no difference. How can we say
which is good and which is bad?
And it is also like that with other things as well.

Somewhere above us, where the goddess Mammetum decides all things,
Mother Chance sits with the Anunnaki
and there she settles all decrees of fable and of fortune.
There they issue lengths of lives;
then they issue times of death.
But the last, last matter
is always veiled from human beings.
The length of lives can only be guessed."
Thus spoke Utnapishtim.

TABLET XI
Column i

To the most distant and removed of semigods, to Utnapishtim,
Gilgamesh said: "When I regard you now, my godlike man,
it's like seeing my own face on calm water
where I dare to study myself.
Like me, you are first of all a fighter
who prefers to war no more.

How could one like you, so human, all too human,
ascend to be at one with other gods?"

Utnapishtim said to him in swift reply:
"Only one as bold as you would dare expect
such knowledge. But I shall tell you what
no person has ever been told.
High up the constant Euphrates
there rests a place you call Shuruppak
where gods and goddesses recline.
Then came the flood, sent by gods' intent.
Mama, Anu, and Enlil were at Shuruppak.
So too was their coachman, Ninurta,
and Ennugi, the beastiarius,
and one who watches over precious infants, the ever vigilant Ea.
And Ea refrained their chant to the high-grown reeds
upon the shore, giving this advice to me:
'Arise! Arise! Oh wall-like reeds.
Arise and hear my words:
Citizen of Shuruppak, child of Ubaratutu,
abandon your home and build a boat.
Reject the corpselike stench of wealth.
Choose to live and choose to love;
choose to rise above and give back
what you yourself were given.
Be moderate as you flee for survival
in a boat that has no place for riches.
Take the seed of all you need aboard
with you and carefully weigh anchor
after securing a roof that will let in no water.'

"Then I said back in reverent prayer:
'I understand, great Ea.
I shall do just as you say to honor god,
but for myself
I'll have to find a reason to give the people.'

"Then Ea voiced a fair reply:
'Tell those who'll need to know
that Enlil hates you.
Say: "I must flee the city now
and go by sea to where Enlil waits to take my life.
I will descend to the brink of hell

to be with Ea, god,
who will send riches to you like the rain:
all manner of birds;
birds . . . bords . . . burds . . .
and the rarest of rare fish.
The land will fill with crops full grown at break of day.
Ea will begin to shower
gifts of life upon you all".' "

Column ii

Then Utnapishtim continued, saying words like these:
"By week's end I engineered designs
for an acre's worth of floor upon the ark we built
so that its walls rose straight toward heaven;
with decks all round did I design its space; 120 cubits measured
   its deck.
With division of six and of seven
I patterned its squares and stairs;
left space for portals too,
secured its beams, and stockpiled
all that ever could be used.
Pitch for the hull I poured into the kiln
and ordered three full volumes of oil
to start with and two times three more yet.
For what is security?
Each day I sacrificed the holy bulls
and chosen sheep for the people
and pushed the laborers to great fatigue
and thirst, allayed alone by wine,
which they drank as if it were water running
from barrels set up for holding cheer
in preparation for a New Year's party they expected.
I set up an ointment box
and cleaned my fingers with its cream.

"After one week, the ark was done,
though launching was more work than fun
since hull boards caught and snapped
until the water burst most of its great ton.
I supplied the craft with all I owned

of silver, gold, and seed.
My clan brought on the food they'd eat
and all the things we thought we'd need.
At last, it was my turn just then
to shepherd beasts and birds and
babies wet and loud.
It was Shamash who ordained the time, saying:
'Prepare the way for your whole boat
and set to sail when the storm
begins to threaten you.'

"The Anunnaki too then cried for them.
The gods themselves, finally suffering, sat up
and let their first tears flow down
cheeks and over lips pressed closed.

Column iii

"For the whole next week
the sky screamed and storms wrecked the earth
and finally broke the war,
which groaned as one in labor's throes.
Even Ishtar then bemoaned the
fates of her sad people.
Ocean silent.
Winds dead.
Flood ended.
Then I see a dawn so still;
all humans beaten to dirt
and earth itself like some vast roof.
I peeked through the portal into a morning sun
then turned, knelt, and cried.
Tears flooded down my face.

"Then I searched high and low for the shoreline,
finally spotting an island near and dear.
Our boat stuck fast beside Mount Nimush.
Mount Nimush held the hull that could not sway for one whole week.

"I released the watch bird, to soar in search of land.
The bird came back within a day
exhausted, unrelieved from lack of rest.

I then released a swallow, to soar in search of land.
The bird came back within a day
exhausted, unrelieved from lack of rest.
I then released a raven, to soar in search of land.
The bird took flight above more shallow seas,
found food and found release and found no
need to fly on back to me.

"These birds I then released to earth's four corners
and offered sacrifice,
a small libation to the heights of many mountains,
from numbered chalices that I arranged.
Under these I spread the scents that gods favored
and when the gods smelled the sweet perfume of sacrifice,
they gathered in flight all above, like apparitions.

Column iv

"From distant heights with heavenly sights,
the female of all female gods descended then;
Aruru who aroused the wry thought
that Anu made for intercourse.
'Great gods from far and wide
keep always in my mind
this thought for intercourse,
tokened by the sacred blue medallion on my neck.
Let me recall with smiles
these days in days to come.
Gods of my shoreline, gods of my sky,
come round this food that I prepared for you;
but do not let Enlil enjoy this too,
since he's the one who drowned my relatives
without telling the gods what he set out to do.'
When Enlil saw the boat, he released
his calm reason and let in the Igigi, monsters of blood.
'What force dares defy my anger!?
How dare a man be still alive!?'
Then with these words Ninurta said to Enlil:
'Can any of us besides Ea, maker of words,
create such things as speech?'
Then with these words Ea himself said to Enlil:

53

'Sly god,
sky darkener,
and tough fighter,
how dare you drown so many little people
without consulting me?
Why not just kill the one who offended you,
drown only the sinner?
Keep hold of his lifecord; harness his destiny.
Rather than killing rains, set cats at people's throats.
Rather than killing rains, set starvation on dry, parched throats.
Rather than killing rains, set sickness on the minds and hearts of people.
I was not the one who revealed our god-awful secrets.
Blame Utnapishtim, Mr. Know-it-all,
who sees everything,
who knows everything.' "

"Reflect on these stories, my Gilgamesh."

"Then Enlil swooped down around my boat;
he gently raised me from the slime,
placed my wife beside my kneeling form
and blessed us both at once with hands upon our bowed heads.
So was it ordained.
So we were ordained."

Earlier than that time, Utnapishtim was not divine.
Then with his wife he was deified
and sent to rule the place where rivers start.
"Gods sent me everywhere to rule the place where rivers start."

"As for you, Gilgamesh, which gods will be called on
to direct your path and future life?
Arise! Be alert! Stay up with stars for
seven long and sleepless nights!"
But even as he tried to stay awake,
foglike sleep rolled over his eyes.
Then Utnapishtim said these words:
"Dear wife, behold the one who tries to pray
while foglike sleep rolls over his eyes."
She said to him who rarely talks:
"Arouse him now and let him
leave unharmed. Permit that one
to go back home at last."

Column v

Then Utnapishtim said these words:
"An upset soul can upset many gods.
Be kind with food and generous to him.
But keep a count of how he
sleeps and what he eats."

She was kind with food and gentle with the man
and she kept count of how he slept.
"One, two, three, alarie,
he slept with death the fairy.
Four, five, six, alarie,
he looked so cold and wary."
Then he returned from death to breath!

So Gilgamesh said to the one who rarely spoke:
"Just as I slipped toward sleep,
you sent my dream."
And to him in reply, Utnapishtim said these words:
"*One, two, three, alarie,*
you slept with death the fairy.
Four, five, six, alarie,
you looked so cold and wary.
Then you arose from death to breath."
So Gilgamesh said to the one who rarely speaks:
"Help me, Utnapishtim. Where is
home for one like me whose self
was robbed of life? My own
bed is where death sleeps and
I crack her spine on every line
where my foot falls."
Utnapishtim calls out to the sailor god:
"Urshanabi, dear, you will never land
again easily or easily sail the seas
to shores where you no more will find safe harbor.
Sandy and disheveled hair does not become
the one you nearly drowned.
Shingles now spoil his hidden beauty.
Better find a place to clean him up.
Better race to pools of saltless water soon
so that by noon he'll shine again for all of us to see.
Tie up his curly hair with ribbon fair.

Place on his shoulders broad the happy robe
so that he may return to his native city easily in triumph.
Allow him to wear the sacred elder's cloak
and see that it is always kept as clean
as it can be."

The sailor god brought Gilgamesh
to where they cleaned his wounds.
By noon he shone again for all to see.
He tied his curly hair with ribbon fair,
and placed upon his shoulder broad the happy robe
so he would return to Uruk easily in triumph
with a cloak unstained and unstainable.
Urshanabi and Gilgamesh launched the boat
over the breakers on the beach and
started to depart across the seas.

Column vi

To her distant husband, Utnapishtim's wife said:
"This Gilgamesh has labored much to come here.
Can you reward him for traveling back?"
At that very moment, Gilgamesh used paddles
to return his craft along the shore.
Then Utnapishtim called out to him:
"Gilgamesh! You labored much to come here.
How can I reward you for traveling back?
May I share a special secret, one
that the gods alone do know?
There is a plant that hides somewhere among the rocks
that thirsts and thrusts itself deep
in the earth, with thistles that sting.
That plant contains eternal life for you."
Immediately, Gilgamesh set out in search.
Weighed down carefully, he dove beneath
the cold, cold waters and saw the plant.
Although it stung him when he grabbed its leaf,
he held it fast as he then slipped off his weights
and soared back to the surface.

Then Gilgamesh said this to Urshanabi, the sailor god:
"Here is the leaf that begins
all life worth having.
I am bound now for Uruk,
town so full of shepherds,
and there I'll dare to give
this plant to aged men as food
and they will call it life giving.
I too intend to eat it
and to be made forever young."
After ten miles they ate.
After fifteen miles they set up camp
where Gilgamesh slipped into a pool;
but in the pool, a cruel snake slithered by
and stole the plant from Gilgamesh
who saw the snake grow young again,
as off it raced with the special, special plant.
Right there and then Gilgamesh began to weep
and, between sobs, said to the sailor god who held his hand:
"Why do I bother working for nothing?
Who even notices what I do?
I don't value what I did
and now only the snake has
won eternal life. In minutes,
swift currents will lose forever
that special sign that god had left for me."

Then they set out again,
this time upon the land.
After ten miles they stopped to eat.
After thirty miles they set up camp.
Next day they came to Uruk, full of shepherds.
Then Gilgamesh said this to the boatman:
"Rise up now, Urshanabi, and examine
Uruk's wall. Study the base, the brick,
the old design. Is it permanent as can be?
Does it look like wisdom designed it?
The house of Ishtar in
Uruk is divided into three parts:
the town itself, the palm grove, and the prairie."

QUESTIONS

1. Why is Enkidu created? (Tablet I, Column ii)

2. What does Enkidu gain and lose through his encounter with the temple girl? (Tablet I, Columns iv, v)

3. Why does Enkidu wrestle with Gilgamesh at Ishara's doorway? (Tablet II, Columns iv, v)

4. Why does Enkidu counsel Gilgamesh to kill rather than show mercy to Humbaba? (Tablet V, Columns iv, vi)

5. What does Gilgamesh's speech in response to Ishtar's offer of herself reveal about him? (Tablet VI, Columns i, ii)

6. In Enkidu's dream following the killing of the divine bull, what does the conversation between Anu, Enlil, and Shamash indicate about the gods' concept of justice? (Tablet VII, Column i)

7. Why does Enkidu die? (Tablet VII) Why does Gilgamesh claim that his own sorrow at the loss of Enkidu is shared by everything and everyone else? (Tablet VIII)

8. Why does Utnapishtim tell the story of the flood when Gilgamesh asks how he came to be immortal like the gods? (Tablet XI, Column i)

9. Who or what causes the flood and controls it? (Tablet XI, Columns i, ii, iii)

10. Why is Gilgamesh denied the gift of eternal life? (Tablet XI, Column vi)

FOR FURTHER REFLECTION

1. What is Gilgamesh's greatest achievement?

2. What does this story say about the connection between love and friendship?

3. In what ways, if any, does Gilgamesh mature in this story?

4. What role or roles in the story do the women characters play?

5. What does Gilgamesh learn from Utnapishtim?

AESCHYLUS

B orn near Athens around 525 BCE, Aeschylus lived through the tumultuous events that marked the defeat of the invading Persians in 490 and 480, the decades of factional striving for political power in Athens, and the emergence of a democratic city-state under the leadership of Pericles in the early 450s. Aeschylus was a member of the older generation of what is often distinguished as classical Greece. He fought at the momentous Battle of Marathon and contributed to the flourishing of Athens as the preeminent intellectual center of the Greek world. In his early years and later when he traveled to Sicily, he had firsthand experience of political regimes that were, in varying degrees, tyrannies. He died in Sicily in 455 BCE.

During his lifetime, Aeschylus was recognized as one of the leading tragic poets. Along with his younger contemporaries Sophocles and Euripides, he developed the many possibilities of dramatic art. Aeschylus is traditionally credited with the innovation of putting more than one character on stage at the same time, making possible a rich interplay of speech and action. He is known to have written more than eighty plays, fifty-two of which won first prize in annual competitions at the Theater of Dionysus. Only seven plays and a few fragments have survived.

Prometheus Bound is generally considered to be one of Aeschylus's final works, the first and only remaining part of a trilogy. Standing alone, it is a powerful depiction of conflicting claims of justice, represented by the benefi-cent actions of Prometheus on behalf of suffering mankind opposed to the violent brutality of Zeus's rule. Having given mankind the gift of reason, Prometheus himself is powerless in using the same faculty to persuade Zeus of the rightness of his appeal. However, far from simply portraying rightful rebellion in the face of tyrannical subjugation, Aeschylus presents us with a subtle and many-sided exploration of what is possible in a world bound by harsh and crushing conditions. Early in the play, Prometheus, the suffering immortal being whose name translates as "Forethought," replies to the questioning chorus that he provided mankind with "blind hopes" in order to cause "mortals to cease foreseeing doom." Here Aeschylus asks us to consider those qualities of the human condition that give stature and meaning to our existence in a world that often seems inimical.

AESCHYLUS
Prometheus Bound

CHARACTERS

MIGHT

VIOLENCE (MUTA PERSONA)

HEPHAESTUS

PROMETHEUS

OCEANOS

IO

HERMES

CHORUS OF DAUGHTERS OF OCEANOS

[*Scene: A bare and desolate crag in the Caucasus. Enter Might and Violence, demons and servants of Zeus, and Hephaestus, the smith.*]

MIGHT
This is the world's limit that we have come to; this is the Scythian country, an untrodden desolation. Hephaestus, it is you that must heed the commands the Father laid upon you to nail this malefactor to the high craggy rocks in fetters unbreakable of adamantine chain. For it was your flower, the brightness of fire that devises all, that he stole and gave to mortal men; this is the sin for which he must pay the gods the penalty—that he may learn to endure and like the sovereignty of Zeus and quit his man-loving disposition.

HEPHAESTUS
Might and Violence, in you the command of Zeus has its perfect fulfillment: in you there is nothing to stand in its way. But, for

myself, I have not the heart to bind violently a god who is my kin here on this wintry cliff. Yet there is constraint upon me to have the heart for just that, for it is a dangerous thing to treat the Father's words lightly.

High-contriving son of Themis of straight counsel: this is not of your will nor of mine; yet I shall nail you in bonds of indissoluble bronze on this crag far from men. Here you shall hear no voice of mortal; here you shall see no form of mortal. You shall be grilled by the sun's bright fire and change the fair bloom of your skin. You shall be glad when Night comes with her mantle of stars and hides the sun's light; but the sun shall scatter the hoarfrost again at dawn. Always the grievous burden of your torture will be there to wear you down; for he that shall cause it to cease has yet to be born.

Such is the reward you reap of your man-loving disposition. For you, a god, feared not the anger of the gods, but gave honors to mortals beyond what was just. Wherefore you shall mount guard on this unlovely rock, upright, sleepless, not bending the knee. Many a groan and many a lamentation you shall utter, but they shall not serve you. For the mind of Zeus is hard to soften with prayer, and every ruler is harsh whose rule is new.

MIGHT

Come, why are you holding back? Why are you pitying in vain? Why is it that you do not hate a god whom the gods hate most of all? Why do you not hate him, since it was your honor that he betrayed to men?

HEPHAESTUS

Our kinship has strange power; that, and our life together.

MIGHT

Yes. But to turn a deaf ear to the Father's words—how can that be? Do you not fear that more?

HEPHAESTUS

You are always pitiless, always full of ruthlessness.

MIGHT

There is no good singing dirges over him. Do not labor uselessly at what helps not at all.

HEPHAESTUS

O handicraft of mine—that I deeply hate!

MIGHT

Why do you hate it? To speak simply, your craft is in no way the author of his present troubles.

HEPHAESTUS

Yet would another had had this craft allotted to him.

MIGHT

There is nothing without discomfort except the overlordship of the gods. For only Zeus is free.

HEPHAESTUS

I know. I have no answer to this.

MIGHT

Hurry now. Throw the chain around him that the Father may not look upon your tarrying.

HEPHAESTUS

There are the fetters, there: you can see them.

MIGHT

Put them on his hands: strong, now with the hammer: strike. Nail him to the rock.

HEPHAESTUS

It is being done now. I am not idling at my work.

MIGHT

Hammer it more; put in the wedge; leave it loose nowhere. He's a cunning fellow at finding a way even out of hopeless difficulties.

HEPHAESTUS

Look now, his arm is fixed immovably!

MIGHT

Nail the other safe, that he may learn, for all his cleverness, that he is duller witted than Zeus.

HEPHAESTUS

No one, save Prometheus, can justly blame me.

MIGHT

Drive the obstinate jaw of the adamantine wedge right through his breast: drive it hard.

HEPHAESTUS

Alas, Prometheus, I groan for your sufferings.

MIGHT

Are you pitying again? Are you groaning for the enemies of Zeus?
Have a care, lest some day you may be pitying yourself.

HEPHAESTUS

You see a sight that hurts the eye.

MIGHT

I see this rascal getting his deserts. Throw the girth around his sides.

HEPHAESTUS

I am forced to do this; do not keep urging me.

MIGHT

Yes, I will urge you, and hound you on as well. Get below now, and
hoop his legs in strongly.

HEPHAESTUS

There now, the task is done. It has not taken long.

MIGHT

Hammer the piercing fetters with all your power, for the Overseer
of our work is severe.

HEPHAESTUS

Your looks and the refrain of your tongue are alike.

MIGHT

You can be softhearted. But do not blame my stubbornness and
harshness of temper.

HEPHAESTUS

Let us go. He has the harness on his limbs.

MIGHT [to *Prometheus*]

Now, play the insolent; now, plunder the gods' privileges and give
them to creatures of a day. What drop of your sufferings can mortals
spare you? The gods named you wrongly when they called you
Forethought; you yourself *need* Forethought to extricate yourself
from this contrivance.

[*Prometheus is left alone on the rock.*]

PROMETHEUS

    Bright light, swift-winged winds, springs of the rivers, numberless
laughter of the sea's waves, earth, mother of all, and the all-seeing
circle of the sun: I call upon you to see what I, a god, suffer
at the hands of gods—
see with what kind of torture
worn down I shall wrestle ten thousand
years of time—
such is the despiteful bond that the Prince
has devised against me, the new Prince
of the Blessed Ones. Oh woe is me!
I groan for the present sorrow,
I groan for the sorrow to come, I groan
questioning when there shall come a time
when he shall ordain a limit to my sufferings.
What am I saying? I have known all before,
all that shall be, and clearly known; to me,
nothing that hurts shall come with a new face.
So must I bear, as lightly as I can,
the destiny that fate has given me;
for I know well against necessity,
against its strength, no one can fight and win.

I cannot speak about my fortune, cannot
hold my tongue either. It was mortal man
to whom I gave great privileges and
for that was yoked in this unyielding harness.
I hunted out the secret spring of fire,
that filled the narthex stem, which when revealed
became the teacher of each craft to men,
a great resource. This is the sin committed
for which I stand accountant, and I pay
nailed in my chains under the open sky.

Ah! Ah!
What sound, what sightless smell approaches me,
god sent, or mortal, or mingled?
Has it come to earth's end
to look on my sufferings,
or what does it wish?
You see me a wretched god in chains,
the enemy of Zeus, hated of all
the gods that enter Zeus's palace hall,
because of my excessive love for man.
What is that? The rustle

of birds' wings near? The air whispers
with the gentle strokes of wings.
Everything that comes toward me is occasion for fear.

[*The Chorus, composed of the daughters of Oceanos, enters, with the members
wearing some formalized representation of wings, so that their general
appearance is birdlike.*]

CHORUS
Fear not: this is a company of friends
that comes to your mountain with swift
rivalry of wings.
Hardly have we persuaded our Father's
mind, and the quick-bearing winds
speeded us hither. The sound
of stroke of bronze rang through our cavern
in its depths, and it shook from us
shamefaced modesty; unsandaled
we have hastened on our chariot of wings.

PROMETHEUS
Alas, children of teeming Tethys and of him
who encircles all the world with stream unsleeping,
Father Ocean,
look, see with what chains
I am nailed on the craggy heights
of this gully to keep a watch
that none would envy me.

CHORUS
I see, Prometheus: and a mist of fear and tears
besets my eyes as I see your form
wasting away on these cliffs
in adamantine bonds of bitter shame.
For new are the steersmen that rule Olympus:
and new are the customs by which Zeus rules,
customs that have no law to them,
but what was great before he brings to nothingness.

PROMETHEUS
Would that he had hurled me
underneath the earth and underneath
the House of Hades, host to the dead—

yes, down to limitless Tartarus,
yes, though he bound me cruelly
in chains unbreakable,
so neither god nor any other being
might have found joy in gloating over me.
Now as I hang, the plaything of the winds,
my enemies can laugh at what I suffer.

CHORUS

Who of the gods is so hard of heart
that he finds joy in this?
Who is that that does not feel
sorrow answering your pain—
save only Zeus? For he malignantly,
always cherishing a mind
that bends not, has subdued the breed
of Uranos, nor shall he cease
until he satisfies his heart,
or someone take the rule from him—that hard-to-capture rule—
by some device of subtlety.

PROMETHEUS

Yes, there shall come a day for me
when he shall need me, me that now am tortured
in bonds and fetters—he shall need me then,
this president of the Blessed—
to show the new plot whereby he may be spoiled
of his throne and his power.
Then not with honeyed tongues
of persuasion shall he enchant me;
he shall not cow me with his threats
to tell him what I know,
until he free me from my cruel chains
and pay me recompense for what I suffer.

CHORUS

You are stout of heart, unyielding
to the bitterness of pain.
You are free of tongue, too free.
It is my mind that piercing fear has fluttered;
your misfortunes frighten me.
Where and when is it fated
to see you reach the term, to see you reach
the harbor free of trouble at the last?

A disposition none can win, a heart
that no persuasions soften—these are his,
the Son of Kronos.

PROMETHEUS

I know that he is savage: and his justice
a thing he keeps by his own standard: still
that will of his shall melt to softness yet
when he is broken in the way I know,
and though his temper now is oaken hard
it shall be softened: hastily he'll come
to meet my haste, to join in amity
and union with me—one day he shall come.

CHORUS

Reveal it all to us: tell us the story of what the charge was on which
Zeus caught you and punished you so cruelly with such dishonor.
Tell us, if the telling will not injure you in any way.

PROMETHEUS

To speak of this is bitterness. To keep silent
bitter no less; and every way is misery.

When first the gods began their angry quarrel,
and god matched god in rising faction, some
eager to drive old Kronos from his throne
that Zeus might rule—the fools!—others again
earnest that Zeus might never be their king—
I then with the best counsel tried to win
the Titans, sons of Uranos and Earth,
but failed. They would have none of crafty schemes
and in their savage arrogance of spirit
thought they would lord it easily by force.
But she that was my mother, Themis, Earth—
she is but one although her names are many—
had prophesied to me how it should be,
even how the Fates decreed it: and she said
that "not by strength nor overmastering force
the Fates allowed the conquerors to conquer
but by guile only": This is what I told them,
but they would not vouchsafe a glance at me.
Then with those things before me it seemed best
to take my mother and join Zeus's side:
he was as willing as we were:

thanks to my plans the dark receptacle
of Tartarus conceals the ancient Kronos,
him and his allies. These were the services
I rendered to this tyrant and these pains
the payment he has given me in requital.
This is a sickness rooted and inherent
in the nature of a tyranny:
that he that holds it does not trust his friends.

But you have asked on what particular
charge he now tortures me: this I will tell you.
As soon as he ascended to the throne
that was his father's, straightway he assigned
to the several gods their several privileges
and portioned out the power, but to the unhappy
breed of mankind he gave no heed, intending
to blot the race out and create a new.
Against these plans none stood save I: I dared.
I rescued men from shattering destruction
that would have carried them to Hades' house;
and therefore I am tortured on this rock,
a bitterness to suffer, and a pain
to pitiful eyes. I gave to mortal man
a precedence over myself in pity: I
can win no pity: pitiless is he
that thus chastises me, a spectacle
bringing dishonor on the name of Zeus.

CHORUS

He would be iron minded and made of stone, indeed, Prometheus,
who did not sympathize with your sufferings. I would not have chosen to see them, and now that I see, my heart is pained.

PROMETHEUS

Yes, to my friends I am pitiable to see.

CHORUS

Did you perhaps go further than you have told us?

PROMETHEUS

I caused mortals to cease foreseeing doom.

CHORUS

What cure did you provide them with against that sickness?

PROMETHEUS
> I placed in them blind hopes.

CHORUS
> That was a great gift you gave to men.

PROMETHEUS
> Besides this, I gave them fire.

CHORUS
> And do creatures of a day now possess bright-faced fire?

PROMETHEUS
> Yes, and from it they shall learn many crafts.

CHORUS
> Then these are the charges on which—

PROMETHEUS
> Zeus tortures me and gives me no respite.

CHORUS
> Is there no limit set for your pain?

PROMETHEUS
> None save when it shall seem good to Zeus.

CHORUS
> How will it ever seem good to him? What hope is there? Do you
> not see how you have erred? It is not pleasure for me to say that
> you have erred, and for you it is a pain to hear. But let us speak
> no more of all this and do you seek some means of deliverance
> from your trials.

PROMETHEUS
> It is an easy thing for one whose foot
> is on the outside of calamity
> to give advice and to rebuke the sufferer.
> I have known all that you have said: I knew,
> I knew when I transgressed nor will deny it.
> In helping man I brought my troubles on me;
> but yet I did not think that with such tortures
> I should be wasted on these airy cliffs,
> this lonely mountaintop, with no one near.
> But do not sorrow for my present suffering;

alight on earth and hear what is to come
that you may know the whole complete: I beg you
alight and join your sorrow with mine: misfortune
wandering the same track lights now upon one
and now upon another.

CHORUS

Willing our ears,
that hear you cry to them, Prometheus,
now with light foot I leave the rushing car
and sky, the holy path of birds, and light
upon this jutting rock: I long
to hear your story to the end.

[*Enter Oceanos, riding on a hippocamp, or sea monster.*]

OCEANOS

I come
on a long journey, speeding past the boundaries,
to visit you, Prometheus: with the mind
alone, no bridle needed, I direct
my swift-winged bird; my heart is sore
for your misfortunes; you know that. I think
that it is kinship makes me feel them so.
Besides, apart from kinship, there is no one
I hold in higher estimation: that
you soon shall know and know beside that in me
there is no mere word-kindness: tell me
how I can help you, and you will never say
that you have any friend more loyal to you
than Oceanos.

PROMETHEUS

What do I see? Have you, too, come to gape
in wonder at this great display, my torture?
How did you have the courage to come here
to this land, Iron Mother, leaving the stream
called after you and the rock-roofed, self-established
caverns? Was it to feast your eyes upon
the spectacle of my suffering and join
in pity for my pain? Now look and see
the sight, this friend of Zeus, that helped set up
his tyranny and see what agonies
twist me, by his instructions!

OCEANOS

Yes, I see,
Prometheus, and I want, indeed I do,
to advise you for the best, for all your cleverness.
Know yourself and reform your ways to new ways,
for new is he that rules among the gods.
But if you throw about such angry words,
words that are whetted swords, soon Zeus will hear you,
even though his seat in glory is far removed,
and then your present multitude of pains
will seem like child's play. My poor friend, give up
this angry mood of yours and look for means
of getting yourself free of trouble. Maybe
what I say seems to you both old and commonplace;
but this is what you pay, Prometheus, for
that tongue of yours, which talked so high and haughty:
you are not yet humble, still you do not yield
to your misfortunes, and you wish, indeed,
to add some more to them; now, if you follow
me as a schoolmaster you will not kick
against the pricks, seeing that he, the king,
that rules alone, is harsh and sends accounts
to no one's audit for the deeds he does.
Now I will go and try if I can free you:
do you be quiet, do not talk so much.
Since your mind is so subtle, don't you know
that a vain tongue is subject to correction?

PROMETHEUS

I envy you, that you stand clear of blame,
yet shared and dared in everything with me!
Now let me be, and have no care for me.
Do what you will, him you will not persuade;
He is not easily won over: look,
take care lest coming here to me should hurt you.

OCEANOS

You are by nature better at advising
others than yourself. I take my cue
from deeds, not words. Do not withhold me now
when I am eager to go to Zeus. I'm sure,
I'm sure that he will grant this favor to me,
to free you from your chains.

PROMETHEUS

    I thank you and will never cease; for loyalty
is not what you are wanting in. Don't trouble,
for you will trouble to no purpose, and no help
to me—if it so be you want to trouble.
No, rest yourself, keep away from this thing;
because I am unlucky I would not,
for that, have everyone unlucky too.
No, for my heart is sore already when
I think about my brothers' fortunes—Atlas,
who stands to westward of the world, supporting
the pillar of earth and heaven on his shoulders,
a load that suits no shoulders; and the earthborn
dweller in caves Cilician, whom I saw
and pitied, hundred-headed, dreadful monster,
fierce Typho, conquered and brought low by force.
Once against all the gods he stood, opposing,
hissing out terror from his grim jaws; his eyes
flashed gorgon glaring lightning as he thought
to sack the sovereign tyranny of Zeus;
but upon him came the unsleeping bolt
of Zeus, the lightning-breathing flame, down rushing,
which cast him from his high aspiring boast.
Struck to the heart, his strength was blasted dead
and burnt to ashes; now a sprawling mass
useless he lies, hard by the narrow seaway
pressed down beneath the roots of Aetna: high
above him on the mountain peak the smith
Hephaestus works at the anvil. Yet one day
there shall burst out rivers of fire, devouring
with savage jaws the fertile, level plains
of Sicily of the fair fruits; such boiling wrath
with weapons of fire-breathing surf, a fiery
unapproachable torrent, shall Typho vomit,
though Zeus's lightning left him but a cinder.

    But all of this you know: you do not need me
to be your schoolmaster: reassure yourself
as you know how: this cup I shall drain myself
till the high mind of Zeus shall cease from anger.

OCEANOS

    Do you not know, Prometheus, that words are healers of the
sick temper?

PROMETHEUS
Yes, if in season due one soothes the heart with them, not tries
violently to reduce the swelling anger.

OCEANOS
Tell me, what danger do you see for me in loyalty to you, and
courage therein?

PROMETHEUS
I see only useless effort and a silly good nature.

OCEANOS
Suffer me then to be sick of this sickness, for it is a profitable thing,
if one is wise, to seem foolish.

PROMETHEUS
This shall seem to be my fault.

OCEANOS
Clearly your words send me home again.

PROMETHEUS
Yes, lest your doings for me bring you enmity.

OCEANOS
His enmity, who newly sits on the all-powerful throne?

PROMETHEUS
His is a heart you should beware of vexing.

OCEANOS
Your own misfortune will be my teacher, Prometheus.

PROMETHEUS
Off with you, then! Begone! Keep your present mind.

OCEANOS
These words fall on very responsive ears. Already my four-legged
bird is pawing the level track of heaven with his wings, and he will
be glad to bend the knee in his own stable.

CHORUS
STROPHE
I cry aloud, Prometheus, and lament your bitter fate,
my tender eyes are trickling tears:

their fountains wet my cheek.
This is a tyrant's deed; this is unlovely,
a thing done by a tyrant's private laws,
and with this thing Zeus shows his haughtiness
of temper toward the gods that were of old.

ANTISTROPHE

Now all the earth has cried aloud, lamenting:
now all that was magnificent of old
laments your fall, laments your brethren's fall
as many as in holy Asia hold
their stablished habitation, all lament
in sympathy for your most grievous woes.

STROPHE

Dwellers in the land of Colchis,
maidens, fearless in the fight,
and the host of Scythia, living
round the lake Maeotis, living
on the edges of the world.

ANTISTROPHE

And Arabia's flower of warriors
and the craggy fortress keepers
near Caucasian mountains, fighters
terrible, crying for battle,
brandishing sharp pointed spears.

STROPHE

One god and one god only I have seen
before this day, in torture and in bonds
unbreakable: he was a Titan,
Alas, whose strength and might
ever exceeded; now he bends his back
and groans beneath the load of earth and heaven.

ANTISTROPHE

The wave cries out as it breaks into surf;
the depth cries out, lamenting you; the dark
Hades, the hollow underneath the world,
sullenly groans below; the springs
of sacred flowing rivers all lament
the pain and pity of your suffering.

PROMETHEUS

Do not think that out of pride or stubbornness I hold my peace; my
heart is eaten away when I am aware of myself, when I see myself
insulted as I am. Who was it but I who in truth dispensed their
honors to these new gods? I will say nothing of this; you know it all;
but hear what troubles there were among men, how I found them
witless and gave them the use of their wits and made them masters
of their minds. I will tell you this, not because I would blame men,
but to explain the goodwill of my gift. For men at first had eyes but
saw to no purpose; they had ears but did not hear. Like the shapes of
dreams they dragged through their long lives and handled all things
in bewilderment and confusion. They did not know of building
houses with bricks to face the sun; they did not know how to work
in wood. They lived like swarming ants in holes in the ground, in
the sunless caves of the earth. For them there was no secure token
by which to tell winter nor the flowering spring nor the summer
with its crops; all their doings were indeed without intelligent
calculation until I showed them the rising of the stars and the set-
tings, hard to observe. And further I discovered to them numbering,
preeminent among subtle devices, and the combining of letters as a
means of remembering all things, the Muses' mother, skilled in
craft. It was I who first yoked beasts for them in the yokes and made
of those beasts the slaves of trace chain and pack saddle that they
might be man's substitute in the hardest tasks; and I harnessed to
the carriage, so that they loved the rein, horses, the crowning pride
of the rich man's luxury. It was I and none other who discovered
ships, the sail-driven wagons that the sea buffets. Such were the
contrivances that I discovered for men—alas for me! For I myself
am without contrivance to rid myself of my present affliction.

CHORUS

What you have suffered is indeed terrible. You are all astray and
bewildered in your mind, and like a bad doctor that has fallen sick
himself, you are cast down and cannot find what sort of drugs would
cure your ailment.

PROMETHEUS

Hear the rest, and you will marvel even more at the crafts and
resources I contrived. Greatest was this: in the former times if a man
fell sick he had no defense against the sickness, neither healing food
nor drink, nor unguent; but through the lack of drugs men wasted
away, until I showed them the blending of mild simples wherewith
they drive out all manner of diseases. It was I who arranged all the
ways of seercraft, and I first adjudged what things come verily true
from dreams; and to men I gave meaning to the ominous cries, hard

to interpret. It was I who set in order the omens of the highway and the flight of crooked-taloned birds, which of them were propitious or lucky by nature, and what manner of life each led, and what were their mutual hates, loves, and companionships; also I taught of the smoothness of the vitals and what color they should have to pleasure the gods and the dappled beauty of the gall and the lobe. It was I who burned thighs wrapped in fat and the long shank bone and set mortals on the road to this murky craft. It was I who made visible to men's eyes the flaming signs of the sky that were before dim. So much for these. Beneath the earth, man's hidden blessing, copper, iron, silver, and gold—will anyone claim to have discovered these before I did? No one, I am very sure, who wants to speak truly and to the purpose. One brief word will tell the whole story: all arts that mortals have come from Prometheus.

CHORUS
Therefore do not help mortals beyond all expediency while neglecting yourself in your troubles. For I am of good hope that once freed of these bonds you will be no less in power than Zeus.

PROMETHEUS
Not yet has fate that brings to fulfillment determined these things to be thus. I must be twisted by ten thousand pangs and agonies, as I now am, to escape my chains at last. Craft is far weaker than necessity.

CHORUS
Who then is the steersman of necessity?

PROMETHEUS
The triple-formed Fates and the remembering Furies.

CHORUS
Is Zeus weaker than these?

PROMETHEUS
Yes, for he, too, cannot escape what is fated.

CHORUS
What is fated for Zeus besides eternal sovereignty?

PROMETHEUS
Inquire of this no further; do not entreat me.

CHORUS
This is some solemn secret, I suppose, that you are hiding.

PROMETHEUS

Think of some other story: this one it is not yet the season to give tongue to, but it must be hidden with all care; for it is only by keeping it that I will escape my despiteful bondage and my agony.

CHORUS

STROPHE

May Zeus never, Zeus that all
the universe controls, oppose
his power against my mind:
may I never dallying
be slow to give my worship at
the sacrificial feasts
when the bulls are killed beside
quenchless Father Ocean:
may I never sin in word:
may these precepts still abide
in my mind nor melt away.

ANTISTROPHE

It is a sweet thing to draw out
a long, long life in cheerful hopes,
and feed the spirit in the bright
benignity of happiness:
but I shiver when I see you
wasted with ten thousand pains,
all because you did not tremble
at the name of Zeus: your mind
was yours, not his, and at its bidding
you regarded mortal men
too high, Prometheus.

STROPHE

Kindness that cannot be requited, tell me,
where is the help in that, my friend? What succor
in creatures of a day? You did not see
the feebleness that draws its breath in gasps,
a dreamlike feebleness by which the race
of man is held in bondage, a blind prisoner.
So the plans of men shall never
pass the ordered law of Zeus.

ANTISTROPHE

This I have learned while I looked on your pains,
deadly pains, Prometheus.
A dirge for you came to my lips, so different
from the other song I sang to crown your marriage
in honor of your couching and your bath,
upon the day you won her with your gifts
to share your bed—of your own race she was,
Hesione—and so you brought her home.

[*Enter Io, a girl wearing horns like an ox.*]

IO

What land is this? What race of men? Who is it
I see here tortured in this rocky bondage?
What is the sin he's paying for? Oh tell me
to what part of the world my wanderings have brought me.
O, O, O,
there it is again, there again—it stings me,
the gadfly, the ghost of earth-born Argos:
keep it away, keep it away, earth!
I'm frightened when I see the shape of Argos,
Argos the herdsman with ten thousand eyes.
He stalks me with his crafty eyes: he died,
but the earth didn't hide him; still he comes
even from the depths of the underworld to hunt me:
he drives me starving by the sands of the sea.

The reed-woven pipe drones on in a hum
and drones and drones its sleep-giving strain:
O, O, O,
Where are you bringing me, my far-wandering wanderings?
Son of Kronos, what fault, what fault
did you find in me that you should yoke me
to a harness of misery like this,
that you should torture me so to madness
driven in fear of the gadfly?
Burn me with fire: hide me in earth: cast me away
to monsters of the deep for food: but do not
grudge me the granting of this prayer, King.
Enough have my much wandering wanderings
exercised me: I cannot find
a way to escape my troubles.
Do you hear the voice of the cow-horned maid?

PROMETHEUS

Surely I hear the voice, the voice of the maiden, gadfly haunted, the daughter of Inachus? She set Zeus's heart on fire with love and now she is violently exercised running on courses overlong, driven by Hera's hate.

IO

How is it you speak my father's name?
Tell me, who are you? Who are you? Oh
who are you that so exactly accosts me by name?
You have spoken of the disease that the gods have sent to me
which wastes me away, pricking with goads,
so that I am moving always
tortured and hungry, wild bounding,
quick sped I come,
a victim of jealous plots.
Some have been wretched
before me, but who of these
suffered as I do?
But declare to me clearly
what I have still to suffer: what would avail
against my sickness, what drug would cure it:
Tell me, if you know:
tell me, declare it to the unlucky, wandering maid.

PROMETHEUS

I shall tell you clearly all that you would know, weaving you no riddles, but in plain words, as it is just to open the lips to friends. You see before you him that gave fire to men, even Prometheus.

IO

O spirit that has appeared as a common blessing to all men, unhappy Prometheus, why are you being punished?

PROMETHEUS

I have just this moment ceased from the lamentable tale of my sorrows.

IO

Will you then grant me this favor?

PROMETHEUS

Say what you are asking for: I will tell you all.

IO

Tell who it was that nailed you to the cliff.

PROMETHEUS

The plan was the plan of Zeus, and the hand the hand of Hephaestus.

IO

And what was the offense of which this is the punishment?

PROMETHEUS

It is enough that I have told you a clear story so far.

IO

In addition, then, indicate to me what date shall be the limit of my wanderings.

PROMETHEUS

Better for you not to know this than know it.

IO

I beg you, do not hide from me what I must endure.

PROMETHEUS

It is not that I grudge you this favor.

IO

Why then delay to tell me all?

PROMETHEUS

It is no grudging, but I hesitate to break your spirit.

IO

Do not have more thought for me than pleases me myself.

PROMETHEUS

Since you are so eager, I must speak; and do you give ear.

CHORUS

Not yet: give me, too, a share of pleasure. First let us question her concerning her sickness, and let her tell us of her desperate fortunes. And then let you be our informant for the sorrows that still await her.

PROMETHEUS

It is your task, Io, to gratify these spirits, for besides other considerations they are your father's sisters. To make wail and lament for one's ill fortune, when one will win a tear from the audience, is well worthwhile.

10

I know not how I should distrust you: clearly
you shall hear all you want to know from me.
Yet even as I speak I groan in bitterness
for that storm sent by god on me, that ruin
of my beauty; I must sorrow when I think
who sent all this upon me. There were always
night visions that kept haunting me and coming
into my maiden chamber and exhorting
with winning words, "O maiden greatly blessed,
why are you still a maiden, you who might
make marriage with the greatest? Zeus is stricken
with lust for you; he is afire to try
the bed of love with you: do not disdain him.
Go, child, to Lerna's meadow, deep in grass,
to where your father's flocks and cattle stand
that Zeus's eye may cease from longing for you."
With such dreams I was cruelly beset
night after night until I took the courage
to tell my father of my nightly terror.
He sent to Pytho many an embassy
and to Dodona seeking to discover
what deed or word of his might please the god,
but those he sent came back with riddling oracles
dark and beyond the power of understanding.
At last the word came clear to Inachus
charging him plainly that he cast me out
of home and country, drive me out footloose
to wander to the limits of the world;
if he should not obey, the oracle said,
the fire-faced thunderbolt would come from Zeus
and blot out his whole race. These were the oracles
of Loxias, and Inachus obeyed them.
He drove me out and shut his doors against me
with tears on both our parts, but Zeus's bit
compelled him to do this against his will.
Immediately my form and mind were changed
and all distorted; horned, as you see,
pricked on by the sharp biting gadfly, leaping
in frenzied jumps I ran beside the river
Kerchneia, good to drink, and Lerna's spring.
The earth-born herdsman Argos followed me
whose anger knew no limits, and he spied
after my tracks with all his hundred eyes.
Then an unlooked-for doom, descending suddenly,

took him from life: I, driven by the gadfly,
that god-sent scourge, was driven always onward
from one land to another: that is my story.
If you can tell me what remains for me,
tell me, and do not out of pity cozen
with kindly ties: there is no sickness worse
for me than words that to be kind must lie.

CHORUS

Hold! Keep away! Alas!
Never did I think that such strange
words would come to my ears:
never did I think such intolerable
sufferings, an offense to the eye,
shameful and frightening, so
would chill my soul with a double-edged point.
Alas, Alas, for your fate!
I shudder when I look on Io's fortune.

PROMETHEUS

You groan too soon: you are full of fear too soon: wait till you hear
besides what is to be.

CHORUS

Speak, tell us to the end. For sufferers it is sweet to know
beforehand clearly the pain that still remains for them.

PROMETHEUS

The first request you made of me you gained
lightly: from her you wished to hear the story
of what she suffered. Now hear what remains,
what sufferings this maid must yet endure
from Hera. Do you listen, child of Inachus,
hear and lay up my words within your heart
that you may know the limits of your journey.
First turn to the sun's rising and walk on
over the fields no plough has broken: then
you will come to the wandering Scythians
who live in wicker houses built above
their well-wheeled wagons; they are an armed people,
armed with the bow that strikes from far away:
do not draw near them; rather let your feet
touch the surf line of the sea where the waves moan,
and cross their country: on your left there live
the Chalybes who work with iron: these

you must beware of; for they are not gentle,
nor people whom a stranger dare approach.
Then you will come to Insolence, a river
that well deserves its name: but cross it not—
it is no stream that you can easily ford—
until you come to Caucasus itself,
the highest mountains, where the river's strength
gushes from its very temples. Cross these peaks,
the neighbors of the stars, and take the road
southward until you reach the Amazons,
the race of women who hate men, who one day
shall live around Thermodon in Themiscyra
where Salmydessos, rocky jaw of the sea,
stands sailor hating, stepmother of ships.
The Amazons will set you on your way
and gladly: you will reach Cimmeria,
the isthmus, at the narrow gates of the lake.
Leave this with a good heart and cross the channel,
the channel of Maeotis: and hereafter
for all time men shall talk about your crossing,
and they shall call the place for you Cow's-ford.*
Leave Europe's mainland then, and go to Asia.

[*To the Chorus.*]

Do you now think this tyrant of the gods
is hard in all things without difference?
He was a god and sought to lie in love
with this girl who was mortal, and on her
he brought this curse of wandering: bitter indeed
you found your marriage with this suitor, maid.
Yet you must think of all that I have told you
as still only in prelude.

IO

    O, O

PROMETHEUS

Again, you are crying and lamenting: what will you do when you
hear of the evils to come?

---

* Cow's-ford: Bosporus.

CHORUS
Is there still something else to her sufferings of which you will speak?

PROMETHEUS
A wintry sea of agony and ruin.

IO
What good is life to me then? Why do I not throw myself at once from some rough crag, to strike the ground and win a quittance of all my troubles? It would be better to die once for all than suffer all one's days.

PROMETHEUS
You would ill bear my trials, then, for whom Fate reserves no death. Death would be a quittance of trouble: but for me there is no limit of suffering set till Zeus fall from power.

IO
Can Zeus ever fall from power?

PROMETHEUS
You would be glad to see that catastrophe, I think.

IO
Surely, since Zeus is my persecutor.

PROMETHEUS
Then know that this shall be.

IO
Who will despoil him of his sovereign scepter?

PROMETHEUS
His own witless plans.

IO
How? Tell me, if there is no harm to telling.

PROMETHEUS
He shall make a marriage that shall hurt him.

IO
With god or mortal? Tell me, if you may say it.

PROMETHEUS
    Why ask what marriage? That is not to be spoken.

IO
    Is it his wife shall cast him from his throne?

PROMETHEUS
    She shall bear him a son mightier than his father.

IO
    Has he no possibility of escaping this downfall?

PROMETHEUS
    None, save through my release from these chains.

IO
    But who will free you, against Zeus's will?

PROMETHEUS
    Fate has determined that it be one of your descendants.

IO
    What, shall a child of mine bring you free?

PROMETHEUS
    Yes, in the thirteenth generation.

IO
    Your prophecy has now passed the limits of understanding.

PROMETHEUS
    Then also do not seek to learn your trials.

IO
    Do not offer me a boon and then withhold it.

PROMETHEUS
    I offer you then one of two stories.

IO
    Which? Tell me and give me the choice.

PROMETHEUS
    I will: choose that I tell you clearly either what remains for you
    or the one that shall deliver me.

CHORUS

> Grant her one and grant me the other and do not deny us the tale.
> Tell her what remains of her wanderings: tell us of the one that shall
> deliver you. That is what I desire.

PROMETHEUS

> Since you have so much eagerness, I will not
> refuse to tell you all that you have asked me.
> First to you, Io, I shall tell the tale
> of your sad wanderings, rich in groans—inscribe
> the story in the tablets of your mind.
> When you shall cross the channel that divides
> Europe from Asia, turn to the rising sun,
> to the burnt plains, sun scorched; cross by the edge
> of the foaming sea till you come to Gorgona
> to the flat stretches of Kisthene's country.
> There live the ancient maids, children of Phorcys:
> these swan-formed hags, with but one common eye,
> single-toothed monsters, such as nowhere else
> the sun's rays look on nor the moon by night.
> Near are their winged sisters, the three Gorgons,
> with snakes to bind their hair up, mortal hating:
> no mortal that but looks on them shall live:
> these are the sentry guards I tell you of.
> Hear, too, of yet another gruesome sight,
> the sharp-toothed hounds of Zeus, that have no bark,
> the vultures—them take heed of—and the host
> of one-eyed Arimaspians, horse riding,
> that live around the spring, which flows with gold,
> the spring of Pluto's river: go not near them.
> A land far off, a nation of black men,
> these you shall come to, men who live hard by
> the fountain of the sun where is the river
> Aethiops—travel by his banks along
> to a waterfall where from the Bibline hills
> Nile pours his holy waters, pure to drink.
> This river shall be your guide to the triangular
> land of the Nile and there, by Fate's decree,
> there, Io, you shall find your distant home,
> a colony for you and your descendants.
> If anything of this is still obscure
> or difficult ask me again and learn
> clearly: I have more leisure than I wish.

CHORUS

If there is still something left for you to tell her of her ruinous
wanderings, tell it; but if you have said everything, grant us the favor
we asked and tell us the story too.

PROMETHEUS

The limit of her wanderings complete
she now has heard: but so that she may know
that she has not been listening to no purpose
I shall recount what she endured before
she came to us here: this I give as pledge,
a witness to the good faith of my words.
The great part of the story I omit
and come to the very boundary of your travels.
When you had come to the Molossian plains
around the sheer back of Dodona where
is the oracular seat of Zeus Thesprotian,
the talking oaks, a wonder past belief,
by them full clearly, in no riddling terms,
you were hailed glorious wife of Zeus that shall be:
does anything of this wake pleasant memories?
Then, goaded by the gadfly, on you hastened
to the great gulf of Rhea by the track
at the side of the sea: but in returning course
you were storm-driven back: in time to come
that inlet of the sea shall bear your name
and shall be called Ionian, a memorial
to all men of your journeying: these are proofs
for you, of how far my mind sees something farther
than what is visible: for what is left,
to you and you this I shall say in common,
taking up again the track of my old tale.
There is a city, furthest in the world,
Canobos, near the mouth and issuing point
of the Nile: there Zeus shall make you sound of mind
touching you with a hand that brings no fear,
and through that touch alone shall come your healing.
You shall bear Epaphos, dark of skin, his name
recalling Zeus's touch and his begetting.
This Epaphos shall reap the fruit of all
the land that is watered by the broad flowing Nile.
From him five generations, and again
to Argos they shall come, against their will,
in number fifty, women, flying from
a marriage with their kinsfolk: but these kinsfolk

their hearts with lust aflutter like the hawks
barely outdistanced by the doves will come
hunting a marriage that the law forbids:
the god shall grudge the men these women's bodies,
and the Pelasgian earth shall welcome them
in death: for death shall claim them in a fight
where women strike in the dark, a murderous vigil.
Each wife shall rob her husband of his life
dipping in blood her two-edged sword: even so
may Love come, too, upon my enemies.
But one among these girls shall love beguile
from killing her bedfellow, blunting her purpose:
and she shall make her choice—to bear the name
of coward and not murder: this girl,
she shall in Argos bear a race of kings.
To tell this clearly needs a longer story,
but from her seed shall spring a man renowned
for archery, and he shall set me free.
Such was the prophecy which ancient Themis
my Titan mother opened up to me;
but how and by what means it shall come true
would take too long to tell, and if you heard
the knowledge would not profit you.

IO

Eleleu, eleleu
It creeps on me again, the twitching spasm,
the mind-destroying madness, burning me up
and the gadfly's sting goads me on—
steel point by no fire tempered—
and my heart in its fear knocks on my breast.
There's a dazing whirl in my eyes as I run
out of my course by the madness driven,
the crazy frenzy; my tongue ungoverned
babbles; the words in a muddy flow strike
on the waves of the mischief I hate, strike wild
without aim or sense.

CHORUS

STROPHE

A wise man indeed he was
that first in judgment weighed this word
and gave it tongue: the best by far
it is to marry in one's rank and station:
let no one working with her hands aspire
to marriage with those lifted high in pride
because of wealth, or of ancestral glory.

ANTISTROPHE

Never, never may you see me,
Fates majestic, drawing nigh
the bed of Zeus, to share it with the kings:
nor ever may I know a heavenly wooer:
I dread such things beholding
Io's sad virginity,
ravaged, ruined; bitter wandering
hers because of Hera's wrath.

EPODE

When a match has equal partners
then I fear not: may the eye
inescapable of the mighty
gods not look on me.
That is a fight that none can fight: a fruitful
source of fruitlessness: I would not
know what I could do: I cannot
see the hope when Zeus is angry
of escaping him.

PROMETHEUS

Yet shall this Zeus, for all his pride of heart
be humble yet: such is the match he plans,
a marriage that shall drive him from his power
and from his throne, out of the sight of all.
So shall at last the final consummation
be brought about of Father Kronos's curse,
which he, driven from his ancient throne, invoked
against the son deposing him: no one
of all the gods save I alone can tell
a way to escape this mischief. I alone
know it and how. So let him confidently
sit on his throne and trust his heavenly thunder
and brandish in his hand his fiery bolt.

Nothing shall all of this avail against
a fall intolerable, a dishonored end.
So strong a wrestler Zeus is now equipping
against himself, a monster hard to fight.
This enemy shall find a plan to best
the thunderbolt, a thunderclap to best
the thunderclap of Zeus: and he shall shiver
Poseidon's trident, curse of sea and land.
So, in his crashing fall shall Zeus discover
how different are rule and slavery.

CHORUS

You voice your wishes for the god's destruction.

PROMETHEUS

They are my wishes, yet shall come to pass.

CHORUS

Must we expect someone to conquer Zeus?

PROMETHEUS

Yes; he shall suffer worse than I do now.

CHORUS

Have you no fear of uttering such words?

PROMETHEUS

Why should I fear, since death is not my fate?

CHORUS

But he might give you pain still worse than this.

PROMETHEUS

Then let him do so; all this I expect.

CHORUS

Wise are the worshipers of Adrasteia.

PROMETHEUS

Worship him, pray; flatter whatever king
is king today; but I care less than nothing
for Zeus. Let him do what he likes,
let him be king for his short time: he shall not
be king for long.

> Look, here is Zeus's footman,
> this fetch-and-carry messenger of him,
> the New King. Certainly he has come here
> with news for us.

HERMES

> You, subtle spirit, you
> bitterly overbitter, you that sinned
> against the immortals, giving honor to
> the creatures of a day, you thief of fire:
> the Father has commanded you to say
> what marriage of his is this you brag about
> that shall drive him from power—and declare it
> in clear terms and no riddles. You, Prometheus,
> do not cause me a double journey; these

[*Pointing to the chains.*]

> will prove to you that Zeus is not softhearted.

PROMETHEUS

> Your speech is pompous sounding, full of pride,
> as fits the lackey of the gods. You are young
> and young your rule, and you think that the tower
> in which you live is free from sorrow: from it
> have I not seen two tyrants thrown? The third,
> who now is king, I shall yet live to see him
> fall, of all three most suddenly, most dishonored.
> Do you think I will crouch before your gods,
> —so new—and tremble? I am far from that.
> Hasten away, back on the road you came.
> You shall learn nothing that you ask of me.

HERMES

> Just such the obstinacy that brought you here,
> to this self-willed calamitous anchorage.

PROMETHEUS

> Be sure of this: when I set my misfortune
> against your slavery, I would not change.

HERMES

> It is better, I suppose, to be a slave
> to this rock, than Zeus's trusted messenger.

PROMETHEUS
Thus must the insolent show their insolence!

HERMES
I think you find your present lot too soft.

PROMETHEUS
Too soft? I would my enemies had it then,
and you are one of those I count as such.

HERMES
Oh, you would blame me too for your calamity?

PROMETHEUS
In a single word, I am the enemy
of all the gods that gave me ill for good.

HERMES
Your words declare you mad, and mad indeed.

PROMETHEUS
Yes, if it's madness to detest my foes.

HERMES
No one could bear you in success.

PROMETHEUS
                    Alas!

HERMES
Alas! Zeus does not know that word.

PROMETHEUS
Time in its aging course teaches all things.

HERMES
But you have not yet learned a wise discretion.

PROMETHEUS
True: or I would not speak so to a servant.

HERMES
It seems you will not grant the Father's wish.

PROMETHEUS
I should be glad, indeed, to requite his kindness!

HERMES
You mock me like a child!

PROMETHEUS
                                                And are you not
a child, and sillier than a child, to think
that I should tell you anything? There is not
a torture or an engine wherewithal
Zeus can induce me to declare these things,
till he has loosed me from these cruel shackles.
So let him hurl his smoky lightning flame,
and throw in turmoil all things in the world
with white-winged snowflakes and deep bellowing
thunder beneath the earth: me he shall not
bend by all this to tell him who is fated
to drive him from his tyranny.

HERMES
Think, here and now, if this seems to your interest.

PROMETHEUS
I have already thought—and laid my plans.

HERMES
Bring your proud heart to know a true discretion—
O foolish spirit—in the face of ruin.

PROMETHEUS
You vex me by these senseless adjurations,
senseless as if you were to advise the waves.
Let it not cross your mind that I will turn
womanish minded from my fixed decision
or that I shall entreat the one I hate
so greatly, with a woman's upturned hands,
to loose me from my chains: I am far from that.

HERMES
I have said too much already—so I think—
and said it to no purpose: you are not softened:
your purpose is not dented by my prayers.
You are a colt new broken, with the bit
clenched in its teeth, fighting against the reins

and bolting. You are far too strong and confident
in your weak cleverness. For obstinacy
standing alone is the weakest of all things
in one whose mind is not possessed by wisdom.
Think what a storm, a triple wave of ruin
will rise against you, if you will not hear me,
and no escape for you. First this rough crag
with thunder and the lightning bolt the Father
shall cleave asunder, and shall hide your body
wrapped in a rocky clasp within its depth;
a tedious length of time you must fulfill
before you see the light again, returning.
Then Zeus's winged hound, the eagle red,
shall tear great shreds of flesh from you, a feaster
coming unbidden, every day: your liver
bloodied to blackness will be his repast.
And of this pain do not expect an end
until some God shall show himself successor
to take your tortures for himself and willing
go down to lightless Hades and the shadows
of Tartarus's depths. Bear this in mind
and so determine. This is no feigned boast
but spoken with too much truth. The mouth of Zeus
does not know how to lie, but every word
brings to fulfillment. Look, you, and reflect
and never think that obstinacy is better
than prudent counsel.

CHORUS

                         Hermes seems to us
to speak not altogether out of season.
He bids you leave your obstinacy and seek
a wise good counsel. Hearken to him. Shame
it were for one so wise to fall in error.

PROMETHEUS

Before he told it me I knew this message:
but there is no disgrace in suffering
at an enemy's hand, when you hate mutually.
So let the curling tendril of the fire
from the lightning bolt be sent against me: let
the air be stirred with thunderclaps, the winds
in savage blasts convulsing all the world.
Let earth to her foundations shake, yes to her root,

before the quivering storm: let it confuse
the paths of heavenly stars and the sea's waves
in a wild surging torrent: this my body
let him raise up on high and dash it down
into black Tartarus with rigorous
compulsive eddies: death he cannot give me.

HERMES

These are a madman's words, a madman's plan:
is there a missing note in this mad harmony?
is there a slack chord in his madness? You,
you, who are so sympathetic with his troubles,
away with you from here, quickly away!
lest you should find your wits stunned by the thunder
and its hard defending roar.

CHORUS

                                    Say something else
different from this: give me some other counsel
that I will listen to: this word of yours
for all its instancy is not for us.
How dare you bid us practice baseness? We
will bear along with him what we must bear.
I have learned to hate all traitors: there is no
disease I spit on more than treachery.

HERMES

Remember then my warning before the act:
when you are trapped by ruin don't blame fortune.
don't say that Zeus has brought you to calamity
that you could not foresee: do not do this:
but blame yourselves: now you know what you're doing:
and with this knowledge neither suddenly
nor secretly your own want of good sense
has tangled you in the net of ruin, past
all hope of rescue.

PROMETHEUS

Now it is words no longer: now in very truth
the earth is staggered: in its depths the thunder
bellows resoundingly, the fiery tendrils
of the lightning flash light up, and whirling clouds
carry the dust along: all the winds' blasts
dance in a fury one against the other

in violent confusion: earth and sea
are one, confused together: such is the storm
that comes against me manifestly from Zeus
to work its terrors. O holy mother mine,
O sky that circling brings the light to all,
you see me, how I suffer, how unjustly.

QUESTIONS

1. Why does Hephaestus say that in Might and Violence "the command of Zeus has its perfect fulfillment"? (63)

2. What is the meaning of the indictment of Prometheus that Hephaestus states: "you . . . gave honors to mortals beyond what was just"? (64)

3. What does it mean to say that "only Zeus is free" when he is also shown to be weaker than the Fates and Furies? (65)

4. Why is Zeus portrayed as a tyrant who rules by "customs that have no law to them"? (68)

5. What does Prometheus mean when he says that he "caused mortals to cease foreseeing doom" and "placed in them blind hopes"? (71, 72)

6. Why does the Chorus emphasize that Zeus "malignantly" subdued the breed of Uranos and showed "haughtiness of temper toward the gods that were of old"? (69, 77)

7. What is Oceanos asking Prometheus to do when he advises him to "reform your ways to new ways"? (74)

8. If not out of pride or stubbornness, why does Prometheus hold his peace?

9. Why is Prometheus, the one who gave "all arts that mortals have," made to suffer punishment? (79)

10. Why does Aeschylus have Io, another victim of Zeus's tyranny, encounter Prometheus?

11. How is Prometheus's attitude toward his punishment affected by knowing that some day he will be freed?

12. Why is it Prometheus, and he alone, who can tell Zeus how to escape falling from power?

FOR FURTHER REFLECTION

1. Why does Zeus punish Prometheus for helping the human race?

2. Why doesn't Prometheus yield to Zeus's power?

3. Why does Prometheus love humanity so much that he will suffer for it?

4. Why does Aeschylus write the play so that Zeus never appears to directly confront Prometheus?

5. When Prometheus claims that he suffers unjustly, does he mean that Zeus is misapplying justice, which is always and everywhere the same? Or does he mean that there is more than one kind of justice in the world?

MICHEL DE MONTAIGNE

M ichel Eyquem de Montaigne was born into a prosperous and civic-minded family near Bordeaux, France, in 1533. During the 1550s and 1560s, Montaigne served for thirteen years in the Bordeaux Parlement, one of the regional courts of justice, where he was dismayed by the inadequacy of the law. We know from his essays that his public service was diffident and dutiful rather than ambitious. During these years, Montaigne formed a strong friendship with Étienne de La Boétie, another counselor, to whom he pays homage in "Of Friendship." After the death of La Boétie in 1563 and that of his father several years later, Montaigne retired to his hereditary estate in 1571, intending to devote his time to reading and writing in "freedom, tranquillity, and leisure." The rationale for this way of life is set out in "Of Solitude."

In 1580, Montaigne published the first two books of the *Essais (Essays)*, consisting of ninety-four chapters. However, during this period and for the remainder of his life, Montaigne was repeatedly drawn back into public life. In France, religious intolerance and civil strife between Catholics and Protestants troubled the second half of the sixteenth century. As a loyal moderate highly respected by leaders of both factions, including Henry III, Montaigne was enlisted to serve two terms as mayor of Bordeaux and later to mediate between the contending parties. He continued to write *Essais*, publishing Book III in 1587 and extensively revising the entire collection during the last years of his life. Montaigne died at home, in bed, in 1592.

In calling his writings "essays," Montaigne was emphasizing that they represent tests, or probes—the meaning of the French word *essais*—of his opinions and outlook. Less concerned with absolute consistency than with communicating the way in which ideas reside in the living, temperamental person, the *Essais* form a kind of autobiography for Montaigne and his readers to reflect on what is permanent and what is transient in themselves.

One of the key questions raised in both "Of Friendship" and "Of Solitude" is about the conditions and relationships in which the most rewarding kinds of communication can occur.

Of Friendship

As I was considering the way a painter I employ went about his work, I had a mind to imitate him. He chooses the best spot, the middle of each wall, to put a picture labored over with all his skill, and the empty space all around it he fills with grotesques, which are fantastic paintings whose only charm lies in their variety and strangeness. And what are these things of mine, in truth, but grotesques and monstrous bodies, pieced together of diverse members, without definite shape, having no order, sequence, or proportion other than accidental?

A lovely woman tapers off into a fish.

HORACE

I do indeed go along with my painter in this second point, but I fall short in the first and better part; for my ability does not go far enough for me to dare to undertake a rich, polished picture, formed according to art. It has occurred to me to borrow one from Étienne de La Boétie, which will do honor to all the rest of this work. It is a discourse to which he gave the name *La Servitude Volontaire*; but those who did not know this have since very fitly rebaptized it *Le Contre Un*.[1] He wrote it by way of essay in his early youth, in honor of liberty against tyrants. It has long been circulating in the hands of men of understanding, not without great and well-merited commendation; for it is a fine thing, and as full as can be. Still, it is far from being the best he could do; and if at the more mature age when I knew him, he had adopted a plan such as mine, of putting his ideas in writing, we should see many rare things that would bring us very close to the glory of antiquity; for particularly in the matter of natural gifts, I know no one who can be compared with him. But nothing of his has remained except this treatise—and that by chance, and I think he never saw it after it left his hands—and some observations on

---

1. [*La Servitude Volontaire*, "Voluntary Servitude." *Le Contre Un*, "Against One Man."—Trans.]

that Edict of January, made famous by our civil wars, which will perhaps yet find their place elsewhere. That was all I could recover of what he left—I, to whom in his will, with such loving recommendation, with death in his throat, he bequeathed his library and his papers—except for the little volume of his works that I have had published.

And yet I am particularly obliged to this work, since it served as the medium of our first acquaintance. For it was shown to me long before I had seen him and gave me my first knowledge of his name, thus starting on its way this friendship, which together we fostered, as long as God willed, so entire and so perfect that certainly you will hardly read of the like, and among men of today you see no trace of it in practice. So many coincidences are needed to build up such a friendship that it is a lot if fortune can do it once in three centuries.

There is nothing to which nature seems to have inclined us more than to society. And Aristotle says that good legislators have had more care for friendship than for justice. Now the ultimate point in the perfection of society is this. For in general, all associations that are forged and nourished by pleasure or profit, by public or private needs, are the less beautiful and noble, and the less friendships, in so far as they mix into friendship another cause and object and reward than friendship itself. Nor do the four ancient types—natural, social, hospitable, erotic—come up to real friendship, either separately or together.

From children toward fathers, it is rather respect. Friendship feeds on communication, which cannot exist between them because of their too great inequality, and might perhaps interfere with the duties of nature. For neither can all the secret thoughts of fathers be communicated to children, lest this beget an unbecoming intimacy, nor could the admonitions and corrections, which are one of the chief duties of friendship, be administered by children to fathers. There have been nations where by custom the children killed their fathers, and others where the fathers killed their children, to avoid the interference that they can sometimes cause each other; and by nature the one depends on the destruction of the other. There have been philosophers who disdained this natural tie, witness Aristippus: when pressed about the affection he owed his children for having come out of him, he began to spit, saying that that had come out of him just as well, and that we also bred lice and worms. And that other, whom Plutarch wanted to reconcile with his brother, said: "I don't think any more of him for having come out of the same hole."

Truly the name of brother is a beautiful name and full of affection, and for that reason he and I made our alliance a brotherhood. But that confusion of ownership, the dividing, and the fact that the richness of one is the poverty of the other, wonderfully softens and loosens the solder of brotherhood. Since brothers have to guide their careers along the same path and at the same rate, it is inevitable that they often jostle, and clash with each other. Furthermore, why should the harmony and kinship that begets these true friendships be found in them? Father and son may be of entirely different dispositions, and brothers also. He is my son, he is my kinsman, but he is an unsociable man, a knave, or a fool. And then, the more they are friendships that law and natural obligation impose on us, the less of our choice and free will there is in them. And our free will has no product more properly its own than affection and friendship. Not that I have not experienced all the friendship that can exist in that situation, having had the best father that ever was, and the most indulgent, even in his extreme old age, and being of a family famous and exemplary, from father to son, in this matter of brotherly concord:

> *Known to others*
> *For fatherly affection toward my brothers.*
>   HORACE

To compare this brotherly affection with affection for women, even though it is the result of our choice—it cannot be done; nor can we put the love of women in the same category. Its ardor, I confess—

> *Of us that goddess is not unaware*
> *Who blends a bitter sweetness with her care*
>   CATULLUS

—is more active, more scorching, and more intense. But it is an impetuous and fickle flame, undulating and variable, a fever flame, subject to fits and lulls, that holds us only by one corner. In friendship it is a general and universal warmth, moderate and even, besides, a constant and settled warmth, all gentleness and smoothness, with nothing bitter and stinging about it. What is more, in love there is nothing but a frantic desire for what flees from us:

> *Just as a huntsman will pursue a hare*
> *O'er hill and dale, in weather cold or fair;*
> *The captured hare is worthless in his sight;*
> *He only hastens after things in flight.*
>   ARIOSTO

As soon as it enters the boundaries of friendship, that is to say harmony of wills, it grows faint and languid. Enjoyment destroys it, as having a fleshly end, subject to satiety. Friendship, on the contrary, is enjoyed according as it is desired; it is bred, nourished, and increased only in enjoyment, since it is spiritual, and the soul grows refined by practice. During the reign of this perfect friendship, those fleeting affections once found a place in me, not to speak of my friend, who confesses only too many of them in these verses. Thus these two passions within me came to be known to each other, but to be compared, never; the first keeping its course in proud and lofty flight, and disdainfully watching the other making its way far, far beneath it.

As for marriage, for one thing it is a bargain to which only the entrance is free—its continuance being constrained and forced, depending otherwise than on our will—and a bargain ordinarily made for other ends. For another, there supervene a thousand foreign tangles to unravel, enough to break the thread and trouble the course of a lively affection; whereas in friendship there are no dealings or business except with itself. Besides, to tell the truth, the ordinary capacity of women is inadequate for that communion and fellowship which is the nurse of this sacred bond; nor does their soul seem firm enough to endure the strain of so tight and durable a knot. And indeed, but for that, if such a relationship, free and voluntary, could be built up, in which not only would the souls have this complete enjoyment, but the bodies would also share in the alliance, so that the entire man would be engaged, it is certain that the resulting friendship would be fuller and more complete. But this sex in no instance has yet succeeded in attaining it, and by the common agreement of the ancient schools is excluded from it.

And that other, licentious Greek love is justly abhorred by our morality. Since it involved, moreover, according to their practice, such a necessary disparity in age and such a difference in the lovers' functions, it did not correspond closely enough with the perfect union and harmony that we require here: *For what is this love of friendship? Why does no one love either an ugly youth, or a handsome old man?* [Cicero]. For even the picture the Academy paints of it will not contradict me, I think, if I say this on the subject: that this first frenzy which the son of Venus inspired in the lover's heart at the sight of the flower of tender youth, in which they allow all the insolent and passionate acts that immoderate ardor can produce, was simply founded on external beauty, the false image of corporeal generation. For it could not be founded on the spirit, the signs of which were still hidden, which was only at its birth and before the age of budding. If this frenzy seized a base heart, the means of his courtship were riches, presents, favor in advancement to dignities, and other such base merchandise, which were generally condemned. If it fell on a nobler heart, the means were also noble: philosophical instruction, precepts to revere religion, obey the laws, die for the good of the country; examples of valor, prudence, justice; the lover studying to make himself acceptable by the grace and beauty of his soul, that of his body being long since faded, and hoping by this mental fellowship to establish a firmer and more lasting pact.

When this courtship attained its effect in due season (for whereas they do not require of the lover that he use leisure and discretion in his enterprise, they strictly require it of the loved one, because be had to judge an inner beauty, difficult to know and hidden from discovery), then there was born in the loved one the desire of spiritual conception through the medium of spiritual beauty. This was the main thing here, and corporeal beauty accidental and secondary; quite the opposite of the lover. For this reason they prefer the loved one, and prove that the gods also prefer him, and strongly rebuke the poet Aeschylus for having, in the love of Achilles and Patroclus, given the lover's part to Achilles, who was in the first beardless bloom of his youth and the handsomest of all the Greeks.

After this general communion was established, the stronger and worthier part of it exercising its functions and predominating, they say that there resulted from it fruits very useful personally and to the public; that it constituted the strength of the countries that accepted the practice, and the principal defense of equity and liberty: witness the salutary loves of Harmodius and Aristogeiton. Therefore they call it sacred and divine. And, by their reckoning, only the violence of tyrants and the cowardice of the common people are hostile to it. In short, all that can be said in favor of the Academy is that this was a love ending in friendship, which corresponds pretty well to the Stoic definition of love: *Love is the attempt to form a friendship inspired by beauty* [Cicero].

I return to my description of a more equitable and more equable kind of friendship. *Only those are to be judged friendships in which the characters have been strengthened and matured by age* [Cicero].

For the rest, what we ordinarily call friends and friendships are nothing but acquaintanceships and familiarities formed by some chance or convenience, by means of which our souls are bound to each other. In the friendship I speak of, our souls mingle and blend with each other so completely that they efface the seam that joined them, and cannot find it again. If you press me to tell why I loved him, I feel that this cannot be expressed, except by answering: Because it was he, because it was I.

Beyond all my understanding, beyond what I can say about this in particular, there was I know not what inexplicable and fateful force that was the mediator of this union. We sought each other before we met because of the reports we heard of each other, which had more effect on our affection than such reports would reasonably have; I think it was by some ordinance from heaven. We embraced each other by our names. And at our first meeting, which by chance came at a great feast and gathering in the city, we found ourselves so taken with each other, so well acquainted, so bound together, that from that time on nothing was so close to us as each other. He wrote an excellent Latin satire, which is published, in which he excuses and explains the precipitancy of our mutual understanding, so promptly grown to its perfection. Having so little time to last, and having begun so late, for we were both grown men, and he a few years older than I, it could not lose time and conform to the pattern of mild and regular friendships, which need so many precautions in the form of long preliminary association. Our friendship has no other model than itself, and can be compared only with itself. It is not one special consideration, nor two, nor three, nor four, nor a thousand: it is I know not what quintessence of all this mixture, which, having seized my whole will, led it to plunge and lose itself in his; which, having seized his whole will, led it to plunge and lose itself in mine, with equal hunger, equal rivalry. I say lose, in truth, for neither of us reserved anything for himself, nor was anything either his or mine.

When Laelius, in the presence of the Roman consuls—who, after condemning Tiberius Gracchus, prosecuted all those who had been in his confidence—came to ask Caius Blossius, who was Gracchus's best friend, how much he would have been willing to do for him, he answered: "Everything." "What, everything?" pursued Laelius. "And what if he had commanded you to set fire to our temples." "He would never have commanded me to do that," replied Blossius. "But what if he had?" Laelius insisted. "I would have obeyed," he replied. If he was such a perfect friend to Gracchus as the histories say, he did not need to offend the consuls by this last bold confession, and he should not have abandoned the assurance be had of Gracchus' will. But nevertheless, those who charge that this answer is seditious do not fully understand this mystery, and fail to assume first what is true, that he had Gracchus' will up his sleeve, both by power over him and by knowledge of him. They were friends more than citizens, friends more than friends or enemies of their country or friends of ambition and disturbance. Having committed themselves absolutely to each other, they held absolutely the reins of each other's inclination; and if you assume that this team was guided by the strength and leadership of reason, as indeed it is quite impossible to harness it without that, Blossius's answer is as it should have been. If their actions went astray, they were by my measure neither friends to each other, nor friends to themselves.

For that matter, this answer has no better ring than would mine if someone questioned me in this fashion: "If your will commanded you to kill your daughter, would you kill her?" and I said yes. For that does not bear witness to any consent to do so, because I have no doubt at all about my will, and just as little about that of such a friend. It is not in the power of all the arguments in the world to dislodge me from the certainty I have of the intentions and judgments of my friend. Not one of his actions could be presented to me, whatever appearance it might have, that I could not immediately find the motive for it. Our souls pulled together in such unison, they regarded each other with such ardent affection, and with a like affection revealed themselves to each other to the very depths of our hearts, that not only did I know his soul as well as mine, but I should certainly have trusted myself to him more readily than to myself.

Let not these other, common friendships be placed in this rank. I have as much knowledge of them as another, and of the most perfect of their type, but I advise you not to confuse the rules of the two; you would make a mistake. You must walk in those other friendships bridle in hand, with prudence and precaution; the knot is not so well tied that there is no cause to mistrust it. "Love him," Chilo used to say, "as if you are to hate him some day; hate him as if you are to love him." This precept, which is so abominable in this sovereign and masterful friendship, is healthy in the practice of ordinary and customary friendships, in regard to which we must use the remark that Aristotle often repeated: "O my friends, there is no friend."

In this noble relationship, services and benefits, on which other friendships feed, do not even deserve to be taken into account; the reason for this is the complete fusion of our wills. For just as the friendship I feel for myself receives no increase from the help I give myself in time of need, whatever the Stoics say, and as I feel no gratitude to myself for the service I do myself; so the union of such friends, being truly perfect, makes them lose the sense of such duties, and hate and banish from between them these words of separation and distinction: benefit, obligation, gratitude, request, thanks, and the like. Everything actually being in common between them—wills, thoughts, judgments, goods, wives, children, honor, and life—and their relationship being that of one soul in two bodies, according to Aristotle's very apt definition, they can neither lend nor give anything to each other. That is why the lawmakers, to honor marriage with some imaginary resemblance to this divine union, forbid gifts between husband and wife, wishing thus to imply that everything should belong to each of them and that they have nothing to divide and split up between them.

If, in the friendship I speak of, one could give to the other, it would be the one who received the benefit who would oblige his friend. For, each of them seeking above all things to benefit the other, the one who provides the matter and the occasion is the liberal one, giving his friend the satisfaction of doing for him what he most wants to do. When the philosopher Diogenes was short of money, he used to say that he asked it back of his friends, not that he asked for it. And to show how this works in practice, I will tell you an ancient example that is singular.

Eudamidas of Corinth had two friends, Charixenus, a Sicyonian, and Aretheus, a Corinthian. When he came to die, he being poor and his two friends rich, he made his will thus: "I leave this to Aretheus, to feed my mother and support her in her old age; this to Charixenus, to see my daughter married and give her the biggest dowry he can; and in case one of them should chance to die, I substitute the survivor in his place." Those who first saw this will laughed at it; but his heirs, having been informed of it, accepted it with singular satisfaction. And when one of them, Charixenus, died five days later, and the place of substitute was opened to Aretheus, he supported the mother with great care, and of five talents he had in his estate, he gave two and a half to his only daughter for her marriage, and two and a half for the marriage of the daughter of Eudamidas, holding their weddings on the same day.

This example is quite complete except for one circumstance, which is the plurality of friends. For this perfect friendship I speak of is indivisible: each one gives himself so wholly to his friend that he has nothing left to distribute elsewhere; on the contrary, he is sorry that he is not double, triple, or quadruple, and that he has not several souls and several wills, to confer them all on this one object. Common friendships can be divided up: one may love in one man his beauty, in another his easygoing ways, in another liberality, in one paternal love, in another brotherly love, and so forth; but this friendship that possesses the soul and rules it with absolute sovereignty cannot possibly be double. If two called for help at the same time, which one would you run to? If they demanded conflicting services of you, how would you arrange it? If one confided to your silence a thing that would be useful for the other to know, how would you extricate yourself? A single dominant friendship dissolves all other obligations. The secret I have sworn to reveal to no other man, I can impart without perjury to the one who is not another man: he is myself. It is a great enough miracle to be doubled, and those who talk of tripling themselves do not realize the loftiness of the thing: nothing is extreme that can be matched. And he who supposes that of two men I love one just as much as the other, and that they love each other and me just as much as I love them, multiplies into a fraternity the most singular and unified of all things, of which even a single one is the rarest thing in the world to find.

The rest of this story fits in very well with what I was saying, for Eudamidas bestows upon his friends the kindness and favor of using them for his need. He leaves them heirs to this liberality of his, which consists of putting into their hands a chance to do him good. And without doubt the strength of friendship is shown much more richly in his action than in that of Aretheus.

In short, these are actions inconceivable to anyone who has not tasted friendship, and which make me honor wonderfully the answer of that young soldier to Cyrus, who asked him for how much he would sell a horse with which he had just won the prize in a race, and whether he would exchange him for a kingdom: "No indeed, Sire, but I would most willingly let him go to gain a friend, if I found a man worthy of such an alliance." That was not badly spoken, "if I found one"; for it is easy to find men fit for a superficial acquaintance. But for this kind, in which we act from the very bottom of our hearts, which holds nothing back, truly it is necessary that all the springs of action be perfectly clean and true.

In the relationships that bind us only by one small part, we need look out only for the imperfections that particularly concern that part. The religion of my doctor or my lawyer cannot matter. That consideration has nothing in common with the functions of the friendship they owe me. And in the domestic relationship between me and those who serve me, I have the same attitude. I scarcely inquire of a lackey whether he is chaste; I try to find out whether he is diligent. And I am not as much afraid of a gambling mule driver as of a weak one, or of a profane cook as of an ignorant one. I do not make it my business to tell the world what it should do—enough others do that—but what I do in it.

That is my practice: do as you see fit.
TERENCE

For the familiarity of the table I look for wit, not prudence; for the bed, beauty before goodness; in conversation, competence, even without uprightness. Likewise in other matters.

Just as the man who was found astride a stick, playing with his children, asked the man who surprised him thus to say nothing about it until he was a father himself, in the belief that the passion which would then be born in his soul would make him an equitable judge of such an act, so I should like to talk to people who have experienced what I tell. But knowing how far from common usage and how rare such a friendship is, I do not expect to find any good judge of it. For the very discourses that antiquity has left us on this subject seem to me weak compared with the feeling I have. And in this particular the facts surpass even the precepts of philosophy:

Nothing shall I, while sane, compare with a dear friend.
HORACE

The ancient Menander declared that man happy who had been able to meet even the shadow of a friend. He was certainly right to say so, especially if be spoke from experience. For in truth, if I compare all the rest of my life—though by the grace of God I have spent it pleasantly, comfortably, and, except for the loss of such a friend, free from any grievous affliction, and full of tranquillity of mind, having accepted my natural and original advantages without seeking other ones—if I compare it all, I say, with the four years which were granted me to enjoy the sweet company and society of that man, it is nothing but smoke, nothing but dark and dreary night. Since the day I lost him,

> *Which I shall ever recall with pain,*
> *Ever with reverence—thus, gods, did you ordain—*
>
> VIRGIL

I only drag on a weary life. And the very pleasures that come my way, instead of consoling me, redouble my grief for his loss. We went halves in everything; it seems to me that I am robbing him of his share,

> *Nor may I rightly taste of pleasures here alone,*
> *—So I resolved—when he who shared my life is gone*
>
> TERENCE

I was already so formed and accustomed to being a second self everywhere that only half of me seems to be alive now.

> *Since an untimely blow has snatched away*
> *Part of my soul, why then do I delay,*
> *I the remaining part, less dear than he,*
> *And not entire surviving? The same day*
> *Brought ruin equally to him and me.*
>
> HORACE

There is no action or thought in which I do not miss him, as indeed he would have missed me. For just as he surpassed me infinitely in every other ability and virtue, so he did in the duty of friendship.

> *Why should I be ashamed or exercise control*
> *Mourning so dear a soul?*
>
> HORACE

> *Brother, your death has left me sad and lone;*
> *Since you departed all our joys have gone,*
> *Which while you lived your sweet affection fed;*
> *My pleasures all lie shattered, with you dead.*
> *Our soul is buried, mine with yours entwined;*
> *And since then I have banished from my mind*
> *My studies, and my spirit's dearest joys.*
> *Shall I ne'er speak to you, or hear your voice?*
> *Or see your face, more dear than life to me?*
> *At least I'll love you to eternity.*
>
> CATULLUS

But let us listen a while to this boy of sixteen.

Because I have found that this work has since been brought to light, and with evil intent, by those who seek to disturb and change the state of our government without worrying whether they will improve it, and because they have mixed his work up with some of their own concoctions, I have changed my mind about putting it in here. And so that the memory of the author may not be damaged in the eyes of those who could not know his opinions and actions at close band, I beg to advise them that this subject was treated by him in his boyhood, only by way of an exercise, as a common theme hashed over in a thousand places in books. I have no doubt that he believed what he wrote, for he was so conscientious as not to lie even in jest. And I know further that if he had had the choice, he would rather have been born in Venice than in Sarlat, and with reason. But he had another maxim sovereignly imprinted in his soul, to obey and submit most religiously to the laws under which he was born. There never was a better citizen, or one more devoted to the tranquillity of his country, or more hostile to the commotions and innovations of his time. He would much rather have used his ability to suppress them than to give them material that would excite them further. His mind was molded in the pattern of other ages than this.

Now, in exchange for this serious work, I shall substitute another, produced in that same season of his life, gayer and more lusty.

Of Solitude

L et us leave aside the usual long comparison between the solitary and the active life; and as for that fine statement under which ambition and avarice take cover—that we are not born for our private selves, but for the public—let us boldly appeal to those who are in the midst of the dance. Let them cudgel their conscience and say whether, on the contrary, the titles, the offices, and the hustle and bustle of the world are not sought out to gain private profit from the public. The evil means men use in our day to push themselves show clearly that the end is not worth much. Let us reply to ambition that it is she herself that gives us a taste for solitude. For what does she shun so much as society? What does she seek so much as elbowroom? There is opportunity everywhere for doing good or evil. However, if Bias' statement is true, that the wicked are in the majority, or what Ecclesiastes says, that not one in a thousand is good—

> *The good are rare: if all their numbers you compile,*
> *They'll scarcely match the gates of Thebes, the mouths of the Nile.*
>
> JUVENAL

—contagion is very dangerous in the crowd. One must either imitate the vicious or hate them. Both these things are dangerous: to imitate them because they are many, and to hate many of them because they are unlike us.

Merchants who go to sea are right to be careful that those who embark on the same ship are not dissolute, blasphemous, or wicked, and to regard such company as unlucky. Wherefore Bias said humorously to those who were undergoing with him the danger of a great tempest and calling on the gods for help: "Be quiet, so they may not realize that you are here with me." And in a more pressing case, Albuquerque, viceroy in the Indies for King Manuel of Portugal, when in great peril of shipwreck at sea, took a young boy upon his shoulders for this purpose alone, that in their common danger the boy's innocence might serve him as a guarantee and a recommendation to divine favor, and bring him to safety.

It is not that the wise man cannot live anywhere content, yes, and alone in a palace crowd; but if he has the choice, says he, he will flee even the sight of a throng. He will endure it, if need be, but if it is up to him, he will choose solitude. He does not feel sufficiently rid of vices if he must still contend with those of other men. Charondas chastised as evil those who were convicted of keeping evil company.

There is nothing so unsociable and so sociable as man; the one by his vice, the other by his nature. And Antisthenes does not seem to me to have given a satisfactory answer to the man who reproached him for associating with wicked men, when he said that doctors lived well enough among the sick; for if they improve the health of the sick, they impair their own by contagion, and by the constant sight and treatment of diseases.

Now the aim of all solitude, I take it, is the same: to live more at leisure and at one's ease. But people do not always look for the right way. Often they think they have left business, and they have only changed it. There is scarcely less trouble in governing a family than in governing an entire state: whatever the mind is wrapped up in, it is all wrapped up in it, and domestic occupations are no less importunate for being less important. Furthermore, by getting rid of the court and the market place we do not get rid of the principal worries of our life:

> *Reason and sense remove anxiety,*
> *Not villas that look out upon the sea.*
> HORACE

Ambition, avarice, irresolution, fear, and lust do not leave us when we change our country.

> *Behind the horseman sits black care.*
> HORACE

They often follow us even into the cloisters and the schools of philosophy. Neither deserts, nor rocky caves, nor hair shirts, nor fastings will free us of them:

> *The fatal shaft sticks in her side.*
> VIRGIL

Someone said to Socrates that a certain man had grown no better by his travels. "I should think not," he said; "he took himself along with him."

> *Why should we move to find*
> *Countries and climates of another kind?*
> *What exile leaves himself behind?*
> HORACE

If a man does not first unburden his soul of the load that weighs upon it, movement will cause it to be crushed still more, as in a ship the cargo is less cumbersome when it is settled. You do a sick man more harm than good by moving him. You imbed the malady by disturbing it, as stakes penetrate deeper and grow firmer when you budge them and shake them. Wherefore it is not enough to have gotten away from the crowd, it is not enough to move; we must get away from the gregarious instincts that are inside us, we must sequester ourselves and repossess ourselves.

> *"At last," you'll say, "I've snapped my chains."*
> *A fleeing dog may well have snapped his, at great pains,*
> *Yet dangling from his neck the greater part remains.*
>
> PERSIUS

We take our chains along with us; our freedom is not complete; we still turn our eyes to what we have left behind, our fancy is full of it.

> *Unless the heart is purged, what must we undergo!*
> *What battles and what perils, to our fruitless woe!*
> *How great the bitter cares of lust that rend apart,*
> *With terrors in their train, an agitated heart!*
> *What ruin, what disasters, follow in the path*
> *Of pride, and lust, and luxury, and sloth, and wrath!*
>
> LUCRETIUS

Our illness grips us by the soul, and the soul cannot escape from itself:

> *The soul's at fault, which ne'er escapes itself.*
>
> HORACE

Therefore we must bring it back and withdraw it into itself: that is the real solitude, which may be enjoyed in the midst of cities and the courts of kings; but it is enjoyed more handily alone.

Now since we are undertaking to live alone and do without company, let us make our contentment depend on ourselves; let us cut loose from all the ties that bind us to others; let us win from ourselves the power to live really alone and to live that way at our ease.

After Stilpo escaped the burning of his city, in which he had lost wife, children, and property, Demetrius Poliorcetes, seeing him unperturbed in expression amid the great ruin of his country, asked him if he had not suffered loss. No, he replied; thanks to God he had lost nothing of his own. The philosopher Antisthenes expressed the same idea humorously: that man should furnish himself with provisions that would float on water and could swim ashore with him from a shipwreck.

Certainly a man of understanding has lost nothing, if he has himself. When the city of Nola was ruined by the barbarians, Paulinus, the bishop of the city, who had lost everything and had been taken prisoner, prayed God thus: "Lord, keep me from feeling this loss; for Thou knowest that they have yet touched nothing of what is mine." The riches that made him rich and the goods that made him good were still entire. That is what it is to choose wisely the treasures that can be secured from harm, and to hide them in a place where no one may go and which can be betrayed only by ourselves.

We should have wife, children, goods, and above all health, if we can; but we must not bind ourselves to them so strongly that our happiness depends on them. We must reserve a back shop all our own, entirely free, in which to establish our real liberty and our principal retreat and solitude. Here our ordinary conversation must be between us and ourselves, and so private that no outside association or communication can find a place; here we must talk and laugh as if without wife, without children, without possessions, without retinue and servants, so that, when the time comes to lose them, it will be nothing new to us to do without them. We have a soul that can be turned upon itself; it can keep itself company; it has the means to attack and the means to defend, the means to receive and the means to give: let us not fear that in this solitude we shall stagnate in tedious idleness:

> *In solitude be to thyself a throng.*
> TIBULLUS

Virtue, says Antisthenes, is content with itself, without rules, without words, without deeds.

Among our customary actions there is not one in a thousand that concerns ourselves. The man you see climbing atop the ruins of that wall, frenzied and beside himself, a mark for so many harquebus shots; and that other, all scarred, pale, and faint with hunger, determined to die rather than open the gates to him—do you think they are there for their own sake? They are there for the sake of a man whom perhaps they never saw, who is not in the least concerned about their doings, and who at that very moment is plunged in idleness and pleasures.

This fellow, all dirty, with running nose and eyes, whom you see coming out of his study after midnight, do you think he is seeking among his books how to make himself a better, happier, and wiser man? No such news. He is going to teach posterity the meter of Plautus's verses and the true spelling of a Latin word, or die in the attempt. Who does not willingly exchange health, rest, and life for reputation and glory, the most useless, worthless, and false coin that is current among us? Our own death does not frighten us enough? Let us burden ourselves also with that of our wives, our children, and our servants. Our own affairs don't give us enough trouble? Let us also torment ourselves and get headaches over those of our neighbors and friends.

> *What! Shall a man establish in his soul, or prize*
> *Anything dearer than himself in his own eyes?*
> TERENCE

Solitude seems to me more appropriate and reasonable for those who have given to the world their most active and flourishing years, following the example of Thales.

We have lived enough for others; let us live at least this remaining bit of life for ourselves. Let us bring back our thoughts and plans to ourselves and our well-being. It is no small matter to arrange our retirement securely; it keeps us busy enough without mixing other undertakings with it. Since God gives us leisure to make arrangements for moving out, let us make them; let us pack our bags; let us take an early leave of the company; let us break free from the violent clutches that engage us elsewhere and draw us away from ourselves. We must untie these bonds that are so powerful, and henceforth love this and that, but be wedded only to ourselves. That is to say, let the other things be ours, but not joined and glued to us so strongly that they cannot be detached without tearing off our skin and some part of our flesh as well. The greatest thing in the world is to know how to belong to oneself.

It is time to untie ourselves from society, since we can contribute nothing to it. And he who cannot lend, let him keep from borrowing. Our powers are failing us; let us withdraw them and concentrate them on ourselves. He who can turn the offices of friendship and fellowship around and fuse them into himself, let him do so. In this decline, which makes him useless, burdensome, and troublesome to others, let him keep from being troublesome to himself, and burdensome, and useless. Let him indulge and care for himself, and especially govern himself, respecting and fearing his reason and his conscience, so that he cannot make a false step in their presence without shame. *For it is rare for anyone to respect himself enough* [Quintilian].

Socrates says that the young should get instruction; that grown men should practice doing good; and that old men should withdraw from all civil and military occupations and live at their own discretion, without being tied down to any fixed office.

There are some temperaments more suited to these precepts for retirement than others. Those whose susceptibility is weak and lax, and whose affection and will are fastidious and slow to enter service or employment—of whom I am one, both by natural disposition and by conviction—will comply with this advice better than will the active and busy souls who embrace everything and engage themselves everywhere, who grow passionate about all things, who offer, present, and give themselves on all occasions. We should use these accidental and external conveniences, so far as they are agreeable to us, but without making them our mainstay; they are not; neither reason nor nature will have it so. Why should we, contrary to their laws, enslave our contentment to the power of others? Moreover, to anticipate the accidents of fortune; to deprive ourselves of the commodities that are in our hands, as many have done through piety and some philosophers through reason; to wait on ourselves; to sleep on the hard ground; to put out our eyes; to throw our riches into the river; to seek pain, some in order to win bliss in another life by torment in this, others to make themselves safe from a new fall by settling on the lowest step—these are the acts of an excessive virtue. Let the sturdier and stronger natures make even their hiding place glorious and exemplary:

> *When riches fail, I praise*
> *The safe and simple life, content with humble ways;*
> *But then, when better, richer fortune smiles on me,*
> *I say that only they live well and sensibly*
> *Whose wealth in country manors glistens brilliantly.*
>
> HORACE

I have enough on my hands without going that far. It is enough for me while under fortune's favor, to prepare for its disfavor, and while I am well-off, to picture the evil that is to come, as far as my imagination can reach; just as we accustom ourselves to jousts and tournaments, and imitate war in the midst of peace.

I do not consider the philosopher Arcesilaus less virtuous because I know that he used gold and silver vessels as much as his fortune allowed him to; and I esteem him more highly for having used them moderately and liberally than if he had given them up.

I see to what limits natural necessity goes; and, thinking about the poor beggar at my door, often merrier and healthier than myself, I put myself in his place, I try to fit my mind to his bias. And running over the other examples in the same way, though I may think that death, poverty, contempt, and disease are at my heels, I easily resolve not to take fright at what a lesser man than I accepts with such patience. I cannot believe that meanness of understanding can do more than vigor, or that the effects of reason cannot match the effects of habit. And knowing how precarious these incidental comforts are, I do not fail, while in full enjoyment of them, to make it my sovereign request of God that he make me content with myself and the good things I bring forth. I see hearty young men who never fail to carry in their baggage a mass of pills to take when afflicted with a cold, which they fear the less because they think they have the remedy at hand. Thus we must do; and further, if we feel ourselves subject to some graver malady, we must provide ourselves with the drugs that benumb and put to sleep the affected part.

The occupation we must choose for such a life must be neither laborious nor annoying; otherwise there would be no point in having come to it in search of rest. This depends on each man's particular taste: mine is not at all adaptable to household management. Those who like it should apply themselves to it with moderation:

Try to bend things to them, not them to things.
HORACE

Besides, the care of an estate is a job for slaves, as Sallust calls it. Some parts of it are more excusable, like the care of gardens, which Xenophon attributes to Cyrus; and a mean may be found between that base and sordid concern, tense and full of anxiety, which is seen in men who plunge themselves deep into it, and that profound and extreme negligence, letting everything go to seed, which we see in others:

> *Democritus's herds devour his season's yield,*
> *While his swift soul without his body roams afield.*
HORACE

But let us hear the counsel that the younger Pliny gives his friend Cornelius Rufus on this matter of solitude: "I advise you, in this full and prosperous retreat of yours, to leave to your servants the sordid and abject care of the household, and to devote yourself to the study of letters, in order to derive from them something that is all your own." He means reputation, being of a like temper with Cicero, who says he wants to use his solitude and rest from public affairs to gain by his writings immortal life:

> *Is knowledge naught to you*
> *Unless another knows that you know all you do?*
PERSIUS

It seems reasonable, when a man talks of retiring from the world, that he should set his gaze outside of it. These men do so only halfway. They indeed arrange their affairs for the time when they will no longer be there; but by a ridiculous contradiction they still aspire to reap the fruit of their plan from the world when they have left it.

The idea of those who seek solitude for religious reasons, filling their hearts with the certainty of divine promises for the other life, is much more sane and consistent. They set before their eyes God, an object infinite both in goodness and in power; in him the soul has the wherewithal to satisfy its desires abundantly in complete freedom. Afflictions, sufferings, come to them as profit, being used for the acquisition of eternal health and rejoicing; death is to be desired, being the passage to so perfect a state. The harshness of their rules is promptly smoothed by habit; and the carnal appetites are frustrated and then put to sleep by denial, for nothing keeps them up but use and exercise. Only this one goal of another life, happily immortal, rightly deserves that we abandon the comforts and pleasures of this life of ours. And he who can really and constantly kindle his soul with the flame of that living faith and hope, builds himself in solitude a life that is voluptuous and delightful beyond any other kind of life.

Therefore I am satisfied with neither the purpose nor the means of Pliny's advice; we still would merely fall out of an ague into a burning fever. This occupation with books is as laborious as any other, and as much an enemy to health, which should be our chief consideration. And we must not let ourselves be lulled to sleep by the pleasure we take in it; it is the same pleasure that ruins the frugal man, the miser, the voluptuous man, and the ambitious man. The sages teach us often enough to beware of the treachery of our appetites, and to distinguish true and entire pleasures from pleasures that are mixed and streaked with a preponderance of pain. For most pleasures, they say, caress and embrace us only to strangle us, like those thieves that the Egyptians called Philistas. If we got our headache before getting drunk, we should take care not to drink too much; but pleasure, to deceive us, walks ahead and hides her sequel from us. Books are pleasant; but if by associating with them we end by losing gaiety and health, the best parts of us, let us leave them. I am one of those who think that their benefits cannot counterbalance this loss.

As men who have long felt weakened by some indisposition at last give themselves up to the mercy of medicine and have certain rules of living prescribed for them by art, rules which are nevermore to be transgressed; so he who retires, annoyed and disgusted with the common way of life, must model his new life on the rules of reason, order it and arrange it by premeditation and reflection. He must have taken leave of every kind of labor, whatever aspect it may bear; he must flee in general the passions that prevent tranquillity of body and soul, and choose the way that suits his humor best:

Let each one know the way that he should go.
PROPERTIUS

In household management, in study, in hunting, and in all other pursuits, we should take part up to the utmost limits of pleasure, but beware of engaging ourselves further, where it begins to be mingled with pain. We must reserve only so much business and occupation as we need to keep us in trim and protect ourselves from the inconveniences that the other extreme, slack and sluggish idleness, brings in its train.

There are sterile and thorny sciences, for the most part created for the busy life; we must leave them to those who are in the service of the world. For myself, I like only pleasant and easy books, which entertain me, or those that console me and counsel me to regulate my life and my death:

To saunter silent through the wholesome wood,
Bent on thoughts worthy of the wise and good.
HORACE

Wiser men, having a strong and vigorous soul, can make for themselves a wholly spiritual repose. But I, who have a commonplace soul, must help support myself by bodily comforts; and since age has lately robbed me of those that were more to my fancy, I train and sharpen my appetite for those that remain and are more suitable to this present season. We must hold on, tooth and nail, to our enjoyment of the pleasures of life, which our years tear, one after the other, from our hands:

> *Let us seize pleasures; life is ours to claim;*
> *Too soon we shall be ashes, ghosts, a name.*
>
> PERSIUS

Now, as for glory, the goal that Pliny and Cicero set up for us, it is very far from my reckoning. The humor most directly opposite to retirement is ambition. Glory and repose are things that cannot lodge in the same dwelling. As far as I can see, these men have only their arms and legs outside the crowd; their souls, their intentions, are more than ever in the thick of it:

> *Old man, do you cull scraps for others' ears?*
>
> PERSIUS

They have only stepped back to make a better jump, to get a stronger impetus wherewith to plunge deeper into the crowd. Do you want to see how they shoot a grain's length too short? Let us put into the scales the advice of two philosophers [Epicurus and Seneca] of two very different sects, one writing to Idomeneus, the other to Lucilius, their friends, to persuade them to give up handling affairs and withdraw from their high positions into solitude.

"You have," they say, "lived until now swimming and floating; come away and die in port. You have given the rest of your life to light; give this part to the shade. It is impossible to abandon occupations if you do not abandon the fruits of them; therefore rid yourself of all care for reputation and glory. There is danger that the gleam of your past actions may give you only too much light and follow you right into your lair. Abandon with the other pleasures that which comes from the approbation of others; and as for your knowledge and ability, don't worry, it will not lose its effect if it makes you yourself a better man. Remember the man who, when asked why he took so much pains in an art which could come to the knowledge of so few people, replied: 'Few are enough for me, one is enough for me, none at all is enough for me.' He spoke truly: you and one companion are an adequate theater for each other, or you for yourself. Let the people be one to you, and let one be a whole people to you. It is a base ambition to want to derive glory from our idleness and our concealment. We must do like the animals that rub out their tracks at the entrance to their lairs.

"Seek no longer that the world should speak of you, but how you should speak to yourself. Retire into yourself, but first prepare to receive yourself there; it would be madness to trust in yourself if you do not know how to govern yourself. There are ways to fail in solitude as well as in company. Until you have made yourself such that you dare not trip up in your own presence, and until you feel both shame and respect for yourself, let true ideals be kept before your mind [Cicero], keep ever in your mind Cato, Phocion, and Aristides, in whose presence even fools would hide their faults; make them controllers of all your intentions; if these intentions get off the track, your reverence for those men will set them right again. They will keep you in a fair way to be content with yourself, to borrow nothing except from yourself, to arrest your mind and fix it on definite and limited thoughts in which it may take pleasure; and, after understanding the true blessings, which we enjoy in so far as we understand them, to rest content with them, without any desire to prolong life and reputation."

That is the counsel of true and natural philosophy, not of an ostentatious and talky philosophy like that of Pliny and Cicero.

QUESTIONS FOR "OF FRIENDSHIP"

1. Why does Montaigne suggest that friendship is no longer practiced in "so entire and so perfect" a way as he and La Boétie practiced it? (106)

2. If Montaigne believes that "our free will has no product more properly its own than affection and friendship," why does he say that friendship "seized his whole will, led it to plunge and lose itself"? (107, 110)

3. For Montaigne, which relationships measure up to the standards of the friendship he describes as ideal? Why don't some relationships measure up to this ideal?

4. Why does Montaigne believe that "a single dominant friendship" dissolves all other obligations? (112)

5. Why does Montaigne say of his friend that "he is myself"? (112)

6. If the discourses on friendship from ancient philosophers and writers seem to Montaigne to be weak in comparison to his own feelings, why does he include them in this essay?

FOR FURTHER REFLECTION

1. Is Montaigne's essay a tribute to his ideal of friendship, or a tribute to his dead friend, La Boétie? Do these different possibilities change the way we interpret Montaigne's language?

2. Who is the "we" Montaigne refers to throughout this essay, and how does that affect our reading of the essay today?

3. Can people develop close friendships only with people like themselves?

4. Following the criteria developed by Montaigne, can men and women be friends?

5. Do we still believe, as Montaigne did, that love and friendship are to be distinguished?

6. What, if anything, does Montaigne's concept of friendship share with the concept of monogamy?

QUESTIONS FOR "OF SOLITUDE"

1. What are the purposes of the leisure and ease that Montaigne assumes are the aims of solitude?

2. What does Montaigne mean when he says, "Certainly a man of understanding has lost nothing, if he has himself"? (119)

3. According to Montaigne, what place do riches and comforts have in the solitude he recommends?

4. Are we meant to believe Montaigne when he says, "For myself, I like only pleasant and easy books, which entertain me, or those that console me and counsel me to regulate my life and my death"? (124)

FOR FURTHER REFLECTION

1. How can we determine when "it is time to untie ourselves from society, since we can contribute nothing to it"? (121)

2. According to Montaigne, how completely should we "cut loose from all the ties that bind us to others"? (119)

CONNECTING QUESTIONS

1. How can Montaigne elevate the "perfect friendship" over all other relationships, but also advocate solitude?

2. Does Montaigne think of solitude as a way to find happiness, or as a way to deal with the death of his friend?

3. When Montaigne asks, "Why should we, contrary to [the] laws [of reason and nature], enslave our contentment to the power of others?" is he questioning the nature of his friendship with La Boétie? (121)

4. At the beginning of "Of Friendship," Montaigne uses images of a painting, a woman, and a fish to begin his meditation on the form of the essay itself. Why does he do this, and is he equally preoccupied with form in "Of Solitude"?

5. Do Montaigne's attitudes toward family life change in these two essays?

6. Are friendship and solitude meant for different stages of one's life, or does Montaigne make a case for holding them in a kind of perpetual, moderating balance?

BLAISE PASCAL

Inventing the first known mechanical calculating machine, discovering the science of hydrostatics, and formulating the mathematical principles of probability theory were among the supremely rational accomplishments of the writer whose most well-known phrase is, "The heart has reasons of which reason knows nothing." Born in France in 1623, Blaise Pascal was raised by a father whose forward-looking educational practices perfectly matched his son's precocious intellectual abilities. Before he was twenty, Pascal had already made original and mature contributions to mathematics and had begun to develop an interest in experimental science. The importance of his work was recognized by some of the most significant thinkers of his time, including Descartes and Fermat. At the same time, Pascal was afflicted almost continuously with painful ailments that would be with him his entire life.

From the mid-1640s onward, Pascal and his family came to embrace an austere and controversial sect of Roman Catholicism called *Jansenism*, which emphasized the need for divine grace as a remedy for mankind's degraded condition. Denying the efficacy of good works to achieve salvation, Jansenism also repudiated free will and advocated denial of worldly involvement and the eradication of self-love. In conflict with the prevailing Jesuitical temperament of the Roman Catholic Church, Jansenism rejected the doctrine that the practice of the sacrament of communion alone, without heartfelt and searching repentance, could atone for a life of continued sin. One of Pascal's sisters entered the Jansenist convent at Port-Royal near Paris, where her brother followed in 1655, after his intense experience of religious conversion the previous November. Following several years of exhausting work searching for the kind of certainty attainable in mathematics and science, Pascal readjusted his life to the rigors of a spiritual community.

At the request of the Port-Royal community, Pascal wrote *The Provincial Letters* (in 1656–57) under a pseudonym. Widely circulated, this work was a brilliantly reasoned defense of Jansenism that has been read not only by those interested in the church's doctrinal controversy, but also by others who appreciated Pascal's wit, clarity of style, and keen observations about human behavior. *The Provincial Letters* above all exemplify Pascal's ability to use his powerful rational abilities to bring readers to an understanding of spiritual doctrines that set severe limits on the use of reason.

Toward the end of his life, Pascal began to compose a full-scale work to be titled *Apology for the Christian Religion.* Not intended as a Jansenist tract, the *Apology* was to be a closely reasoned argument of more universal interest. Its purpose would be to bring people to God through Christ and the Catholic Church, first through a thorough analysis of the human condition, then through an elaborate interpretation of scriptural truths that would show the way to salvation. By the time he died in 1662, Pascal had written his thoughts—or, in French, *pensées*—concerning these matters on hundreds of sheets and scraps of paper as a preliminary to composing the *Apology,* though his failing health had not permitted him to proceed very far with his project. Shortly after his death, these documents were collected and organized, with the order that Pascal had left them providing some guidance. However, there was and remains great uncertainty about how Pascal would have finally used this material had he completed the *Apology.* Subsequent editors have arranged the *Pensées* in many different ways to reflect various thematic concerns. The following selection and ordering were developed for this edition and include the most well-known passages among the hundreds of brief paragraphs that Pascal left.

The doctrinal controversies that preoccupied Pascal have long passed. Of lasting interest are his sharp observations of the ways humans restlessly occupy their time to escape boredom and anxiety; his discussion of the limitations of the scope of scientific investigation; his analysis of how the faculties of sense, reason, and intuition relate; and, above all, his challenge to those who think that studied skepticism is a worthy substitute for a vigorous lifelong pursuit of truth.

BLAISE PASCAL
Pensées (selection)

136 *Diversion.* Sometimes, when I set to thinking about the various activities of men, the dangers and troubles which they face at court or in war, giving rise to so many quarrels and passions, daring and often wicked enterprises and so on, I have often said that the sole cause of man's unhappiness is that he does not know how to stay quietly in his room. A man wealthy enough for life's needs would never leave home to go to sea or besiege some fortress if he knew how to stay at home and enjoy it. Men would never spend so much on a commission in the army if they could bear living in town all their lives, and they only seek after the company and diversion of gambling because they do not enjoy staying at home.

But after closer thought, looking for the particular reasons for all our unhappiness now that I knew its general cause, I found one very cogent reason in the natural unhappiness of our feeble mortal condition, so wretched that nothing can console us when we really think about it.

Imagine any situation you like, add up all the blessings with which you could be endowed, to be king is still the finest thing in the world; yet if you imagine one with all the advantages of his rank, but no means of diversion, left to ponder and reflect on what he is, this limp felicity will not keep him going; he is bound to start thinking of all the threats facing him, of possible revolts, finally of inescapable death and disease, with the result that if he is deprived of so-called diversion he is unhappy, indeed more unhappy than the humblest of his subjects who can enjoy sport and diversion.

The only good thing for men therefore is to be diverted from thinking of what they are, either by some occupation which takes their mind off it, or by some novel and agreeable passion which keeps them busy, like gambling, hunting, some absorbing show, in short by what is called diversion.

That is why gaming and feminine society, war and high office are so popular. It is not that they really bring happiness, nor that anyone imagines that true bliss comes from possessing the money to be won at gaming or the hare that is hunted: no one would take it as a gift. What people want is not the easy peaceful life that allows us to think of our unhappy condition, nor the dangers of war, nor the burdens of office, but the agitation that takes our mind off it and diverts us. That is why we prefer the hunt to the capture.

That is why men are so fond of hustle and bustle; that is why prison is such a fearful punishment; that is why the pleasures of solitude are so incomprehensible. That, in fact, is the main joy of being a king, because people are continually trying to divert him and procure him every kind of pleasure. A king is surrounded by people whose only thought is to divert him and stop him thinking about himself, because, king though he is, he becomes unhappy as soon as he thinks about himself.

That is all that men have been able to devise for attaining happiness; those who philosophize about it, holding that people are quite unreasonable to spend all day chasing a hare that they would not have wanted to buy, have little knowledge of our nature. The hare itself would not save us from thinking about death and the miseries distracting us, but hunting it does so. Thus when Pyrrhus was advised to take the rest toward which he was so strenuously striving, he found it very hard to do so.

Telling a man to rest is the same as telling him to live happily. It means advising him to enjoy a completely happy state which he can contemplate at leisure without cause for distress. It means not understanding nature.

Thus men who are naturally conscious of what they are shun nothing so much as rest; they would do anything to be disturbed.

It is wrong then to blame them; they are not wrong to want excitement—if they only wanted it for the sake of diversion. The trouble is that they want it as though, once they had the things they seek, they could not fail to be truly happy. That is what justifies calling their search a vain one. All this shows that neither the critics nor the criticized understand man's real nature.

When men are reproached for pursuing so eagerly something that could never satisfy them, their proper answer, if they really thought about it, ought to be that they simply want a violent and vigorous occupation to take their minds off themselves, and that is why they choose some attractive object to entice them in ardent pursuit. Their opponents could find no answer to that,

(Vanity, pleasure of showing off. Dancing, you must think where to put your feet.)

but they do not answer like that because they do not know themselves. They do not know that all they want is the hunt and not the capture. The nobleman sincerely believes that hunting is a great sport, the sport of kings, but his huntsman does not feel like that. They imagine that if they secured a certain appointment they would enjoy resting afterward, and they do not realize the insatiable nature of cupidity. They think they genuinely want rest when all they really want is activity.

They have a secret instinct driving them to seek external diversion and occupation, and this is the result of their constant sense of wretchedness. They have another secret instinct, left over from the greatness of our original nature, telling them that the only true happiness lies in rest and not in excitement. These two contrary instincts give rise to a confused plan buried out of sight in the depths of their soul, which leads them to seek rest by way of activity and always to imagine that the satisfaction they miss will come to them once they overcome certain obvious difficulties and can open the door to welcome rest.

All our life passes in this way: we seek rest by struggling against certain obstacles, and once they are overcome, rest proves intolerable because of the boredom it produces. We must get away from it and crave excitement.

We think either of present or of threatened miseries, and even if we felt quite safe on every side, boredom on its own account would not fail to emerge from the depths of our hearts, where it is naturally rooted, and poison our whole mind.

Man is so unhappy that he would be bored even if he had no cause for boredom, by the very nature of his temperament, and he is so vain that, though he has a thousand and one basic reasons for being bored, the slightest thing, like pushing a ball with a billiard cue, will be enough to divert him.

"But," you will say, "what is his object in all this?" Just so that he can boast tomorrow to his friends that he played better than someone else. Likewise others sweat away in their studies to prove to scholars that they have solved some hitherto insoluble problem in algebra. Many others again, just as foolishly in my view, risk the greatest dangers so that they can boast afterward of having captured some stronghold. Then there are others who exhaust themselves observing all these things, not in order to become wiser, but just to show they know them, and these are the biggest fools of the lot, because they know what they are doing, while it is conceivable that the rest would stop being foolish if they knew too.

A given man lives a life free from boredom by gambling a small sum every day. Give him every morning the money he might win that day, but on condition that he does not gamble, and you will make him unhappy. It might be argued that what he wants is the entertainment of gaming and not the winnings. Make him play then for nothing; his interest will not be fired and he will become bored, so it is not just entertainment he wants. A half-hearted entertainment without excitement will bore him. He must have excitement, he must delude himself into imagining that he would be happy to win what he would not want as a gift if it meant giving up gambling. He must create some target for his passions and then arouse his desire, anger, fear, for this object he has created, just like children taking fright at a face they have daubed themselves.

That is why this man, who lost his only son a few months ago and was so troubled and oppressed this morning by lawsuits and quarrels, is not thinking about it any more. Do not be surprised; he is concentrating all his attention on which way the boar will go that his dogs have been so hotly pursuing for the past six hours. That is all he needs. However sad a man may be, if you can persuade him to take up some diversion he will be happy while it lasts, and however happy a man may be, if he lacks diversion and has no absorbing passion or entertainment to keep boredom away, he will soon be depressed and unhappy. Without diversion there is no joy; with diversion there is no sadness. That is what constitutes the happiness of persons of rank, for they have a number of people to divert them and the ability to keep themselves in this state.

Make no mistake about it. What else does it mean to be Superintendent, Chancellor, Chief Justice, but to enjoy a position in which a great number of people come very morning from all parts and do not leave them a single hour of the day to think about themselves? When they are in disgrace and sent off to their country houses, where they lack neither wealth nor servants to meet their needs, they infallibly become miserable and dejected because no one stops them thinking about themselves.

44 *Imagination.* It is the dominant faculty in man, master of error and falsehood, all the more deceptive for not being invariably so; for it would be an infallible criterion of truth if it were infallibly that of lies. Since, however, it is usually false, it gives no indication of its quality, setting the same mark on true and false alike.

I am not speaking of fools, but of the wisest men, amongst whom imagination is best entitled to persuade. Reason may object in vain; it cannot fix the price of things.

This arrogant force, which checks and dominates its enemy, reason, for the pleasure of showing off the power it has in every sphere, has established a second nature in man. Imagination has its happy and unhappy men, its sick and well, its rich and poor; it makes us believe, doubt, deny reason; it deadens the senses, it arouses them; it has its fools and sages, and nothing annoys us more than to see it satisfy its guests more fully and completely than reason ever could. Those who are clever in imagination are far more pleased with themselves than prudent men could reasonably be. They look down on people with a lofty air; they are bold and confident in argument, where others are timid and unsure, and their cheerful demeanor often wins the verdict of their listeners, for those whose wisdom is imaginary enjoy the favor of judges similarly qualified. Imagination cannot make fools wise, but it makes them happy, as against reason, which only makes its friends wretched: one covers them with glory, the other with shame.

Who dispenses reputation? Who makes us respect and revere persons, works, laws, the great? Who but this faculty of imagination? All the riches of the earth are inadequate without its approval. Would you not say that this magistrate, whose venerable age commands universal respect, is ruled by pure, sublime reason, and judges things as they really are, without paying heed to the trivial circumstances which offend only the imagination of weaker men? See him go to hear a sermon in a spirit of pious zeal, the soundness of his judgment strengthened by the ardor of his charity, ready to listen with exemplary respect. If, when the preacher appears, it turns out that nature has given him a hoarse voice and an odd sort of face, that his barber has shaved him badly and he happens not to be too clean either, then, whatever great truths he may announce, I wager that our senator will not be able to keep a straight face.

Put the world's greatest philosopher on a plank that is wider than need be: if there is a precipice below, although his reason may convince him that he is safe, his imagination will prevail. Many could not even stand the thought of it without going pale and breaking into sweat.

I do not intend to list all the effects of imagination. Everyone knows that the sight of cats, or rats, the crunching of a coal, etc., is enough to unhinge reason. The tone of voice influences the wisest of us and alters the force of a speech or a poem.

Love or hate alters the face of justice. An advocate who has been well paid in advance will find the cause he is pleading all the more just. The boldness of his bearing will make it seem all the better to the judges, taken in by appearances. How absurd is reason, the sport of every wind! I should list almost all the actions of men, who hardly stir except when jolted by imagination. For reason has had to yield, and at its wisest adopts those principles which human imagination has rashly introduced at every turn. Anyone who chose to follow reason alone would have proved himself a fool. We must, since reason so pleases, work all day for benefits recognized as imaginary, and, when sleep has refreshed us from the toils of our reason, we must at once jump up to pursue the phantoms and endure the impressions created by this ruler of the world. Here is one of the principles of error, but not the only one.

Man has been quite right to make these two powers into allies, although in this peace imagination enjoys an extensive advantage; for in conflict its advantage is more complete. Reason never wholly overcomes imagination, while the contrary is quite common.

Our magistrates have shown themselves well aware of this mystery. Their red robes, the ermine in which they swaddle themselves like furry cats, the law courts where they sit in judgment, the fleurs-de-lis, all this august panoply was very necessary. If physicians did not have long gowns and mules, if learned doctors did not wear square caps and robes four times too large, they would never have deceived the world, which finds such an authentic display irresistible. If they possessed true justice, and if physicians possessed the true art of healing, they would not need square caps; the majesty of such sciences would command respect in itself. But, as they only possess imaginary science, they have to resort to these vain devices in order to strike the imagination, which is their real concern, and this, in fact, is how they win respect.

Soldiers are the only ones who do not disguise themselves in this way, because their role is really more essential; they establish themselves by force, the others by masquerade.

That is why our kings have not attempted to disguise themselves. They have not dressed up in extraordinary clothes to show what they are, but they have themselves escorted by guards, scarred veterans. These armed troops whose hands and strength are theirs alone, the drums and trumpets that march before them, and these legions which surround them make the most resolute tremble. They do not wear the trappings, they simply have the power. It would take reason at its most refined to see the Grand Turk, surrounded in his superb seraglio by 40,000 janissaries, as a man like any other.

We have only to see a lawyer in cap and gown to form a favorable opinion of his competence.

Imagination decides everything: it creates beauty, justice, and happiness, which is the world's supreme good. I should dearly like to see the Italian book, of which I know only the title, worth many books in itself, *Dell'opinione regina del mondo*. Without knowing the book, I support its views, apart from any evil it may contain.

Such, more or less, are the effects of this deceptive faculty, apparently given to us for the specific purpose of leading us inevitably into error. We have plenty of other principles of error.

Longstanding impressions are not the only ones that can mislead us; the charms of novelty have the same power. Hence all the debate among men, who accuse each other either of following the false impressions of childhood or of rashly pursuing new ones. If anyone has found the golden mean, let him appear and prove it. Any principle, however natural it may be, even implanted in childhood, may be treated as a false impression either of education or of the senses.

"Because," they say, "you have believed since you were a child that a box was empty when you could not see anything in it, you believed that a vacuum could exist. This is just an illusion of your senses, strengthened by habit, and it must be corrected by science." Others say: "When you were taught at school that there is no such thing as a vacuum, your common sense was corrupted; it was quite clear about it before being given the wrong impression, and now it must be corrected by reverting to your original state." Who then is the deceiver, the senses or education?

We have another principle of error in illnesses, which impair our judgment and sense. If serious illnesses do considerable harm, I have no doubt that the less serious ones have a proportionate effect.

Our own interest is another wonderful instrument for blinding us agreeably. The fairest man in the world is not allowed to be judge in his own cause. I know of men who, to avoid the danger of partiality in their own favor, have leaned over to the opposite extreme of injustice. The surest way to lose a perfectly just case was to get close relatives to commend it to them. Justice and truths are two points so fine that our instruments are too blunt to touch them exactly. If they do make contact, they blunt the point and press all round on the false rather than the true.

Man, then, is so happily constituted that he has no exact principle of truth, and several excellent ones of falsehood. Let us now see how many.

But the most absurd cause of his errors is the war between the senses and the reason.

978 *Self-love.* The nature of self-love and of this human self is to love only self and consider only self. But what is it to do? It cannot prevent the object of its love from being full of faults and wretchedness: it wants to be great and sees that it is small; it wants to be happy and sees that it is wretched; it wants to be perfect and sees that it is full of imperfections; it wants to be the object of men's love and esteem and sees that its faults deserve only their dislike and contempt. The predicament in which it thus finds itself arouses in it the most unjust and criminal passion that could possibly be imagined, for it conceives a deadly hatred for the truth which rebukes it and convinces it of its faults. It would like to do away with this truth, and not being able to destroy it as such, it destroys it, as best it can, in the consciousness of itself and others; that is, it takes every care to hide its faults both from itself and others, and cannot bear to have them pointed out or noticed.

It is no doubt an evil to be full of faults, but it is a still greater evil to be full of them and unwilling to recognize them, since this entails the further evil of deliberate self-delusion. We do not want others to deceive us; we do not think it right for them to want us to esteem them more than they deserve; it is therefore not right either that we should deceive them and want them to esteem us more than we deserve.

Thus, when they merely reveal vices and imperfections which we actually possess, it is obvious that they do us no wrong, since they are not responsible for them, but are really doing us good, by helping us to escape from an evil, namely our ignorance of these imperfections. We ought not to be annoyed that they know them and despise us, because it is right that they should know us for what we are and despise us if we are despicable.

These are the feelings which would spring from a heart full of equity and justice. What then should we say of ours, seeing it quite differently disposed? For is it not true that we hate the truth and those who tell it to us, and we like them to be deceived to our advantage, and want to be esteemed by them as other than we actually are?

Here is a proof of it which appalls me. The Catholic religion does not oblige us to reveal our sins indiscriminately to everyone; it allows us to remain hidden from all other men, with one single exception, to whom it bids us reveal our innermost heart and show ourselves for what we are. There is only this one man in the world whom it orders us to disillusion, and it lays on him the obligation of inviolable secrecy, which means that he might as well not possess the knowledge of us that he has. Can anything milder and more charitable be imagined? And yet, such is man's corruption that he finds even this law harsh, and this is one of the main reasons why a large part of Europe has revolted against the church.

How unjust and unreasonable the heart of man is, that he should resent the obligation to behave toward one man as it would be right, in some ways, to behave toward all! For is it right that we should deceive them?

This aversion for the truth exists in differing degrees, but it may be said that it exists in everyone to some degree, because it is inseparable from self-love. It is this false delicacy which makes those who have to correct others choose so many devious ways and qualifications to avoid giving offense. They must minimize our faults, pretend to excuse them, and combine this with praise and marks of affection and esteem. Even then such medicine still tastes bitter to self-love, which takes as little of it as possible, always with disgust and often even with secret resentment against those administering it.

The result is that anyone who has an interest in winning our affection avoids rendering us a service which he knows to be unwelcome; we are treated as we want to be treated; we hate the truth and it is kept from us; we desire to be flattered and we are flattered; we like being deceived and we are deceived.

This is why each rung of fortune's ladder, which brings us up in the world, takes us further from the truth, because people are more wary of offending those whose friendship is most useful and enmity most dangerous. A prince can be the laughingstock of Europe and the only one to know nothing about it. This does not surprise me: telling the truth is useful to the hearer but harmful to those who tell it, because they incur such odium. Now those who live with princes prefer their own interests to that of the prince they serve, and so they have no wish to benefit him by harming themselves.

This misfortune is no doubt greater and more common among those most favored by fortune, but more modest people are not exempt, because we always have some interest in being popular. Thus human life is nothing but a perpetual illusion; there is nothing but mutual deception and flattery. No one talks about us in our presence as he would in our absence. Human relations are only based on this mutual deception; and few friendships would survive if everyone knew what his friend said about him behind his back, even though he spoke sincerely and dispassionately.

Man is therefore nothing but disguise, falsehood, and hypocrisy, both in himself and with regard to others. He does not want to be told the truth. He avoids telling it to others, and all these tendencies, so remote from justice and reason, are naturally rooted in his heart.

512 *Difference between the mathematical and the intuitive mind.* In the one, principles are obvious, but remote from ordinary usage, so that from want of practice we have difficulty turning our heads that way; but once we do turn our heads the principles can be fully seen; and it would take a thoroughly unsound mind to draw false conclusions from principles so patent that they can hardly be missed.

But, with the intuitive mind, the principles are in ordinary usage and there for all to see. There is no need to turn our heads, or strain ourselves: it is only a question of good sight, but it must be good; for the principles are so intricate and numerous that it is almost impossible not to miss some. Now the omission of one principle can lead to error, and so one needs very clear sight to see all the principles as well as an accurate mind to avoid drawing false conclusions from known principles.

All mathematicians would therefore be intuitive if they had good sight, because they do not draw false conclusions from principles that they know. And intuitive minds would be mathematical if they could adapt their sight to the unfamiliar principles of mathematics.

Thus the reason why certain intuitive minds are not mathematical is that they are quite unable to apply themselves to the principles of mathematics, but the reason why mathematicians are not intuitive is that they cannot see what is in front of them: for, being accustomed to the clear-cut, obvious principles of mathematics and to draw no conclusions until they have clearly seen and handled their principles, they become lost in matters requiring intuition, whose principles cannot be handled in this way. These principles can hardly be seen, they are perceived instinctively rather than seen, and it is with endless difficulty that they can be communicated to those who do not perceive them for themselves. These things are so delicate and numerous that it takes a sense of great delicacy and precision to perceive them and judge correctly and accurately from this perception: most often it is not possible to set it out logically as in mathematics, because the necessary principles are not ready to hand, and it would be an endless task to undertake. The thing must be seen all at once, at a glance, and not as a result of progressive reasoning, at least up to a point. Thus it is rare for mathematicians to be intuitive or the intuitive to be mathematicians, because mathematicians try to treat these intuitive matters mathematically, and make themselves ridiculous, by trying to begin with definitions followed by principles, which is not the way to proceed in this kind of reasoning. It is not that the mind does not do this, but it does so tacitly, naturally, and artlessly, for it is beyond any man to express it and given to very few even to apprehend it. Intuitive minds, on the contrary, being thus accustomed to judge at a glance, are taken aback when presented with propositions of which they understand nothing (and of which the necessary preliminaries are definitions and principles so barren that they are not used to looking at them in such detail), and consequently feel repelled and disgusted.

But unsound minds are never either intuitive or mathematical.

Mathematicians who are merely mathematicians therefore reason soundly as long as everything is explained to them by definitions and principles, otherwise they are unsound and intolerable, because they reason soundly only from clearly defined principles.

And intuitive minds which are merely intuitive lack the patience to go right into the first principles of speculative and imaginative matters which they have never seen in practice and are quite outside ordinary experience.

198   When I see the blind and wretched state of man, when I survey the whole universe in its dumbness and man left to himself with no light, as though lost in this corner of the universe, without knowing who put him there, what he has come to do, what will become of him when he dies, incapable of knowing anything, I am moved to terror, like a man transported in his sleep to some terrifying desert island, who wakes up quite lost and with no means of escape. Then I marvel that so wretched a state does not drive people to despair. I see other people around me, made like myself. I ask them if they are

any better informed than I, and they say they are not. Then these lost and wretched creatures look around and find some attractive objects to which they become addicted and attached. For my part I have never been able to form such attachments, and considering how very likely it is that there exists something besides what I can see, I have tried to find out whether God has left any traces of himself.

I see a number of religions in conflict, and therefore all false, except one. Each of them wishes to be believed on its own authority and threatens unbelievers. I do not believe them on that account. Anyone can say that. Anyone can call himself a prophet, but I see Christianity, and find its prophecies, which are not something that anyone can do.

199 *Disproportion of man.* This is where unaided knowledge brings us. If it is not true, there is no truth in man, and if it is true, he has good cause to feel humiliated; in either case he is obliged to humble himself.

And, since he cannot exist without believing this knowledge, before going on to a wider inquiry concerning nature, I want him to consider nature just once, seriously and at leisure, and to look at himself as well, and judge whether there is any proportion between himself and nature by comparing the two.

Let man then contemplate the whole of nature in her full and lofty majesty, let him turn his gaze away from the lowly objects around him; let him behold the dazzling light set like an eternal lamp to light up the universe, let him see the earth as a mere speck compared to the vast orbit described by this star, and let him marvel at finding this vast orbit itself to be no more than the tiniest point compared to that described by the stars revolving in the firmament. But if our eyes stop there, let our imagination proceed further; it will grow weary of conceiving things before nature tires of producing them. The whole visible world is only an imperceptible dot in nature's ample bosom. No idea comes near it; it is no good inflating our conceptions beyond imaginable space, we only bring forth atoms compared to the reality of things. Nature is an infinite sphere whose center is everywhere and circumference nowhere. In short it is the greatest perceptible mark of God's omnipotence that our imagination should lose itself in that thought.

Let man, returning to himself, consider what he is in comparison with what exists; let him regard himself as lost, and from this little dungeon, in which he finds himself lodged, I mean the universe, let him learn to take the earth, its realms, its cities, its houses, and himself at their proper value.

What is a man in the infinite?

But, to offer him another prodigy equally astounding, let him look into the tiniest things he knows. Let a mite show him in its minute body incomparably more minute parts, legs with joints, veins in its legs, blood in the veins, humors in the blood, drops in the humors, vapors in the drops: let him divide these things still further until he has exhausted his powers of imagination, and let the last thing he comes down to now be the subject of our discourse. He will perhaps think that this is the ultimate of minuteness in nature.

I want to show him a new abyss. I want to depict to him not only the visible universe, but all the conceivable immensity of nature enclosed in this miniature atom. Let him see there an infinity of universes, each with its firmament, its planets, its earth, in the same proportions as in the visible world, and on that earth animals, and finally mites, in which he will find again the same results as in the first; and finding the same thing yet again in the others without end or respite, he will be lost in such wonders, as astounding in their minuteness as the others in their amplitude. For who will not marvel that our body, a moment ago imperceptible in a universe, itself imperceptible in the bosom of the whole, should now be a colossus, a world, or rather a whole, compared to the nothingness beyond our reach? Anyone who considers himself in this way will be terrified at himself, and, seeing his mass, as given him by nature, supporting him between these two abysses of infinity and nothingness, will tremble at these marvels. I believe that with his curiosity changing into wonder he will be more disposed to contemplate them in silence than investigate them with presumption.

For, after all, what is man in nature? A nothing compared to the infinite, a whole compared to the nothing, a middle point between all and nothing, infinitely remote from an understanding of the extremes; the end of things and their principles are unattainably hidden from him in impenetrable secrecy; he is equally incapable of seeing the nothingness from which he emerges and the infinity in which he is engulfed.

What else can he do, then, but perceive some semblance of the middle of things, eternally hopeless of knowing either their principles or their end? All things have come out of nothingness and are carried onward to infinity. Who can follow these astonishing processes? The author of these wonders understands them: no one else can.

Because they failed to contemplate these infinities, men have rashly undertaken to probe into nature as if there were some proportion between themselves and her.

Strangely enough they wanted to know the principles of things and go on from there to know everything, inspired by a presumption as infinite as their object. For there can be no doubt that such a plan could not be conceived without infinite presumption or a capacity as infinite as that of nature.

When we know better, we understand that, since nature has engraved her own image and that of her author on all things, they almost all share her double infinity. Thus we see that all the sciences are infinite in the range of their researches, for who can doubt that mathematics, for instance, has an infinity of infinities of propositions to expound? They are infinite also in the multiplicity and subtlety of their principles, for anyone can see that those which are supposed to be ultimate do not stand by themselves, but depend on others, which depend on others again, and thus never allow of any finality.

But we treat as ultimate those which seem so to our reason, as in material things we call a point indivisible when our senses can perceive nothing beyond it, although by its nature it is infinitely divisible.

Of these two infinites of science, that of greatness is much more obvious, and that is why it has occurred to few people to claim that they know everything. "I am going to speak about everything," Democritus used to say.

But the infinitely small is much harder to see. The philosophers have much more readily claimed to have reached it, and that is where they have all tripped up. This is the origin of such familiar titles as *Of the principles of things, Of the principles of philosophy*,[1] and the like, which are really as pretentious, though they do not look it, as this blatant one: *Of all that can be known*.[2]

We naturally believe we are more capable of reaching the center of things than of embracing their circumference, and the visible extent of the world is visibly greater than we. But since we in our turn are greater than small things, we think we are more capable of mastering them, and yet it takes no less capacity to reach nothingness than the whole. In either case it takes an infinite capacity, and it seems to me that anyone who had understood the ultimate principles of things might also succeed in knowing infinity. One depends on the other, and one leads to the other. These extremes touch and join by going in opposite directions, and they meet in God and God alone.

1. [By Descartes (1644).—Trans.]
2. [By Pico della Mirandola (1486).—Trans.]

Let us then realize our limitations. We are something and we are not everything. Such being as we have conceals from us the knowledge of first principles, which arise from nothingness, and the smallness of our being hides infinity from our sight.

Our intelligence occupies the same rank in the order of intellect as our body in the whole range of nature.

Limited in every respect, we find this intermediate state between two extremes reflected in all our faculties. Our senses can perceive nothing extreme; too much noise deafens us, too much light dazzles; when we are too far or too close we cannot see properly; an argument is obscured by being too long or too short; too much truth bewilders us. I know people who cannot understand that 4 from 0 leaves 0. First principles are too obvious for us; too much pleasure causes discomfort; too much harmony in music is displeasing; too much kindness annoys us: we want to be able to pay back the debt with something over. *Kindness is welcome to the extent that it seems the debt can be paid back. When it goes too far gratitude turns into hatred.*[3]

We feel neither extreme heat nor extreme cold. Qualities carried to excess are bad for us and cannot be perceived; we no longer feel them, we suffer them. Excessive youth and excessive age impair thought; so do too much and too little learning.

In a word, extremes are as if they did not exist for us nor we for them; they escape us or we escape them.

Such is our true state. That is what makes us incapable of certain knowledge or absolute ignorance. We are floating in a medium of vast extent, always drifting uncertainly, blown to and fro; whenever we think we have a fixed point to which we can cling and make fast, it shifts and leaves us behind; if we follow it, it eludes our grasp, slips away, and flees eternally before us. Nothing stands still for us. This is our natural state and yet the state most contrary to our inclinations. We burn with desire to find a firm footing, an ultimate, lasting base on which to build a tower rising up to infinity, but our whole foundation cracks and the earth opens up into the depth of the abyss.

Let us then seek neither assurance nor stability; our reason is always deceived by the inconsistency of appearances; nothing can fix the finite between the two infinites which enclose and evade it.

Once that is clearly understood, I think that each of us can stay quietly in the state in which nature has placed him. Since the middle station allotted to us is always far from the extremes, what does it

---

3. [Tacitus, *Annals*, IV. 18.—Trans.]

matter if someone else has a slightly better understanding of things? If he has, and if he takes them a little further, is he not still infinitely remote from the goal? Is not our span of life equally infinitesimal in eternity, even if it is extended by ten years?

In the perspective of these infinites, all finites are equal and I see no reason to settle our imagination on one rather than another. Merely comparing ourselves with the finite is painful.

If man studied himself, he would see how incapable he is of going further. How could a part possibly know the whole? But perhaps he will aspire to know at least the parts to which he bears some proportion. But the parts of the world are all so related and linked together that I think it is impossible to know one without the other and without the whole.

There is, for example, a relationship between man and all he knows. He needs space to contain him, time to exist in, motion to be alive, elements to constitute him, warmth and food for nourishment, air to breathe. He sees light, he feels bodies, everything in short is related to him. To understand man therefore one must know why he needs air to live, and to understand air one must know how it comes to be thus related to the life of man, etc.

Flame cannot exist without air, so, to know one, one must know the other.

Thus, since all things are both caused or causing, assisted and assisting, mediate and immediate, providing mutual support in a chain linking together naturally and imperceptibly the most distant and different things, I consider it as impossible to know the parts without knowing the whole as to know the whole without knowing the individual parts.

The eternity of things in themselves or in God must still amaze our brief span of life.

The fixed and constant immobility of nature, compared to the continual changes going on in us, must produce the same effect.

And what makes our inability to know things absolute is that they are simple in themselves, while we are composed of two opposing natures of different kinds, soul and body. For it is impossible for the part of us which reasons to be anything but spiritual, and even if it were claimed that we are simply corporeal, that would still more preclude us from knowing things, since there is nothing so inconceivable as the idea that matter knows itself. We cannot possibly know how it could know itself.

Thus, if we are simply material, we can know nothing at all, and, if we are composed of mind and matter, we cannot have perfect knowledge of things which are simply spiritual or corporeal.

That is why nearly all philosophers confuse their ideas of things, and speak spiritually of corporeal things and corporeally of spiritual ones, for they boldly assert that bodies tend to fall, that they aspire toward their center, that they flee from destruction, that they fear a void, that they have inclinations, sympathies, antipathies, all things pertaining only to things spiritual. And when they speak of minds, they consider them as being in a place, and attribute to them movement from one place to another, which are things pertaining only to bodies.

Instead of receiving ideas of these things in their purity, we color them with our qualities and stamp our own composite being on all the simple things we contemplate.

Who would not think, to see us compounding everything of mind and matter, that such a mixture is perfectly intelligible to us? Yet this is the thing we understand least; man is to himself the greatest prodigy in nature, for he cannot conceive what body is, and still less what mind is, and least of all how a body can be joined to a mind. This is his supreme difficulty, and yet it is his very being. *The way in which minds are attached to bodies is beyond man's understanding, and yet this is what man is.*[4]

Finally to complete the proof of our weakness, I shall end with these two considerations. . . .

200 Man is only a reed, the weakest in nature, but he is a thinking reed. There is no need for the whole universe to take up arms to crush him: a vapor, a drop of water is enough to kill him. But even if the universe were to crush him, man would still be nobler than his slayer, because he knows that he is dying and the advantage the universe has over him. The universe knows none of this.

Thus all our dignity consists in thought. It is on thought that we must depend for our recovery, not on space and time, which we could never fill. Let us then strive to think well; that is the basic principle of morality.

---

4. [St. Augustine, *City of God*, XXI. 10.—Trans.]

429 This is what I see and what troubles me. I look around in every direction and all I see is darkness. Nature has nothing to offer me that does not give rise to doubt and anxiety. If I saw no sign there of a Divinity I should decide on a negative solution: if I saw signs of a Creator everywhere I should peacefully settle down in the faith. But, seeing too much to deny and not enough to affirm, I am in a pitiful state, where I have wished a hundred times over that, if there is a God supporting nature, she should unequivocally proclaim him, and that, if the signs in nature are deceptive, they should be completely erased; that nature should say all or nothing so that I could see what course I ought to follow. Instead of that, in the state in which I am, not knowing what I am nor what I ought to do, I know neither my condition nor my duty. My whole heart strains to know what the true good is in order to pursue it: no price would be too high to pay for eternity.

I envy those of the faithful whom I see living so unconcernedly, making so little use of a gift which, it seems to me, I should turn to such different account.

430 No other has realized that man is the most excellent of creatures. Some, fully realizing how real his excellence is, have taken for cowardice and ingratitude men's natural feelings of abasement; while others, fully realizing how real this abasement is, have treated with haughty ridicule the feelings of greatness which are just as natural to man.

"Lift up your eyes to God," say some of them, "look at him whom you resemble and who created you to worship him. You can make yourself like him: wisdom will make you his equal, if you want to follow him."—"Hold your heads high, free men," said Epictetus. And others say, "Cast down your eyes toward the ground, puny worm that you are, and look at the beasts whose companion you are."

What then is to become of man? Will he be the equal of God or the beasts? What a terrifying distance! What then shall he be? Who cannot see from all this that man is lost, that he has fallen from his place, that he anxiously seeks it, and cannot find it again? And who then is to direct him there? The greatest men have failed.

678 Man is neither angel nor beast, and it is unfortunately the case that anyone trying to act the angel acts the beast.

12　*Order.* Men despise religion. They hate it and are afraid it may be true. The cure for this is first to show that religion is not contrary to reason, but worthy of reverence and respect.

Next make it attractive, make good men wish it were true, and then show that it is.

Worthy of reverence because it really understands human nature.

Attractive because it promises true good.

427　Let them at least learn what this religion is which they are attacking before attacking it. If this religion boasted that it had a clear sight of God and plain and manifest evidence of his existence, it would be an effective objection to say that there is nothing to be seen in the world which proves him so obviously. But since on the contrary it says that men are in darkness and remote from God, that he has hidden himself from their understanding, that this is the very name which he gives himself in Scripture: *Deus absconditus* [the hidden God];[5] and, in a word, if it strives equally to establish these two facts: that God has appointed visible signs in the church so that he shall be recognized by those who genuinely seek him, and that he has none the less hidden them in such a way that he will only be perceived by those who seek him with all their heart, then what advantage can they derive when, unconcerned to seek the truth as they profess to be, they protest that nothing shows it to them? For the obscurity in which they find themselves, and which they use as an objection against the church, simply establishes one of the things the church maintains without affecting the other, and far from proving her teaching false, confirms it.

In order really to attack the truth they would have to protest that they had made every effort to seek it everywhere, even in what the church offers by way of instruction, but without any satisfaction. If they talked like that they would indeed be attacking one of Christianity's claims. But I hope to show here that no reasonable person could talk like that. I even venture to say that no one has ever done so. We know well enough how people in this frame of mind behave. They think they have made great efforts to learn when they have spent a few hours reading some book of the Bible, and have questioned some ecclesiastic about the truths of the faith. After that they boast that they have sought without success in books and among men. But, in fact, I should say to them what I have often

---

5. [Isaiah 45:15.—Trans.]

said: such negligence is intolerable. It is not a question here of the trifling interest of some stranger prompting such behavior: it is a question of ourselves, and our all.

The immortality of the soul is something of such vital importance to us, affecting us so deeply, that one must have lost all feeling not to care about knowing the facts of the matter. All our actions and thoughts must follow such different paths, according to whether there is hope of eternal blessings or not, that the only possible way of acting with sense and judgment is to decide our course in the light of this point, which ought to be our ultimate objective.

Thus our chief interest and chief duty is to seek enlightenment on this subject, on which all our conduct depends. And that is why, amongst those who are not convinced, I make an absolute distinction between those who strive with all their might to learn and those who live without troubling themselves or thinking about it.

I can feel nothing but compassion for those who sincerely lament their doubt, who regard it as the ultimate misfortune, and who, sparing no effort to escape from it, make their search their principal and most serious business.

But as for those who spend their lives without a thought for this final end of life and who, solely because they do not find within themselves the light of conviction, neglect to look elsewhere, and to examine thoroughly whether this opinion is one of those which people accept out of credulous simplicity or one of those which, though obscure in themselves, none the less have a most solid and unshakeable foundation: as for them, I view them very differently.

This negligence in a matter where they themselves, their eternity, their all are at stake, fills me more with irritation than pity; it astounds and appalls me; it seems quite monstrous to me. I do not say this prompted by the pious zeal of spiritual devotion. I mean on the contrary that we ought to have this feeling from principles of human interest and self-esteem. For that we need only see what the least enlightened see.

One needs no great sublimity of soul to realize that in this life there is no true and solid satisfaction, that all our pleasures are mere vanity, that our afflictions are infinite, and finally that death which threatens us at every moment must in a few years infallibly face us with the inescapable and appalling alternative of being annihilated or wretched throughout eternity.

Nothing could be more real, or more dreadful than that. Let us put on as bold a face as we like: that is the end awaiting the world's most illustrious life. Let us ponder these things, and then say whether it is not beyond doubt that the only good thing in this life is the hope of another life, that we become happy only as we come nearer to it, and that, just as no more unhappiness awaits those who have been quite certain of eternity, so there is no happiness for those who have no inkling of it.

It is therefore quite certainly a great evil to have such doubts, but it is at least an indispensable obligation to seek when one does thus doubt; so the doubter who does not seek is at the same time very unhappy and very wrong. If in addition he feels a calm satisfaction, which he openly professes, and even regards as a reason for joy and vanity, I can find no terms to describe so extravagant a creature.

What can give rise to such feelings? What reason for joy can be found in the expectation of nothing but helpless wretchedness? What reason for vanity in being plunged into impenetrable darkness? And how can such an argument as this occur to a reasonable man?

"I do not know who put me into the world, nor what the world is, nor what I am myself. I am terribly ignorant about everything. I do not know what my body is, or my senses, or my soul, or even that part of me which thinks what I am saying, which reflects about everything and about itself, and does not know itself any better than it knows anything else.

"I see the terrifying spaces of the universe hemming me in, and I find myself attached to one corner of this vast expanse without knowing why I have been put in this place rather than that, or why the brief span of life allotted to me should be assigned to one moment rather than another of all the eternity which went before me and all that which will come after me. I see only infinity on every side, hemming me in like an atom or like the shadow of a fleeting instant. All I know is that I must soon die, but what I know least about is this very death which I cannot evade.

"Just as I do not know whence I come, so I do not know whither I am going. All I know is that when I leave this world I shall fall forever into nothingness or into the hands of a wrathful God, but I do not know which of these two states is to be my eternal lot. Such is my state, full of weakness and uncertainty. And my conclusion from all this is that I must pass my days without a thought of seeking what is to happen to me. Perhaps I might find some enlightenment in my doubts, but I do not want to take the trouble, nor take a step to look for it: and afterward, as I sneer at those who are striving to this end—(whatever certainty they have should arouse despair rather than vanity)—I will go without fear or foresight to face so momentous an event, and allow myself to be carried off limply to my death, uncertain of my future state for all eternity."

Who would wish to have as his friend a man who argued like that? Who would choose him from among others as a confidant in his affairs? Who would resort to him in adversity? To what use in life could he possibly be turned?

It is truly glorious for religion to have such unreasonable men as enemies: their opposition represents so small a danger that it serves on the contrary to establish the truths of religion. For the Christian faith consists almost wholly in establishing these two things: the corruption of nature and the redemption of Christ. Now, I maintain that, if they do not serve to prove the truth of the redemption by the sanctity of their conduct, they do at least admirably serve to prove the corruption of nature by such unnatural sentiments.

Nothing is so important to man as his state: nothing more fearful than eternity. Thus the fact that there exist men who are indifferent to the loss of their being and the peril of an eternity of wretchedness is against nature. With everything else they are quite different; they fear the most trifling things, foresee and feel them; and the same man who spends so many days and nights in fury and despair at losing some office or at some imaginary affront to his honor is the very one who knows that he is going to lose everything through death but feels neither anxiety nor emotion. It is a monstrous thing to see one and the same heart at once so sensitive to minor things and so strangely insensitive to the greatest. It is an incomprehensible spell, a supernatural torpor that points to an omnipotent power as its cause.

Man's nature must have undergone a strange reversal for him to glory in being in a state in which it seems incredible that any single person should be. Yet experience has shown me so many like this that it would be surprising if we did not know that most of those concerned in this are pretending and are not really what they seem. They are people who have heard that it is good form to display such extravagance. This is what they call shaking off the yoke, and what they are trying to imitate. But it would not be difficult to show them how mistaken they are to court esteem in this way. That is not how to acquire it, not even, I would say, among worldly people, who judge things sensibly and who know that the only way to succeed is to appear honest, faithful, judicious, and capable of rendering useful service to one's friends, because by nature men only like what may be of use to them. Now what advantage is it to us to hear someone say he has shaken off the yoke, that he does not believe that there is a God watching over his actions, that he considers himself sole master of his behavior, and that he proposes to account for it to no one but himself? Does he think that by so doing he has henceforth won our full confidence, and made us expect from him consolation, counsel, and assistance in all life's needs? Do they think that they have given us great pleasure by telling us that they hold our soul to be no more than wind or smoke, and saying it moreover in tones of pride and satisfaction? Is this then something to be said gaily? Is it not on the contrary something to be said sadly, as being the saddest thing in the world?

If they thought seriously, they would see that this is so misguided, so contrary to good sense, so opposed to decency, so remote in every way from the good form they seek, that they would be more likely to reform than corrupt those who might feel inclined to follow them. And, indeed, make them describe the feeling and reasons which inspire their doubts about religion: what they say will be so feeble and cheap as to persuade you of the contrary. As someone said to them very aptly one day: "If you go on arguing like that," he said, "you really will convert me." And he was right, for who would not shrink from finding himself sharing the feelings of such contemptible people?

Thus those who only pretend to feel like this would be indeed unhappy if they did violence to their nature in order to become the most impertinent of men. If they are vexed in their inmost heart at not seeing more clearly, they should not try to pretend otherwise: it would be no shame to admit it. There is no shame except in having none. There is no surer sign of extreme weakness of mind than the failure to recognize the unhappy state of a man without God; there is no surer sign of an evil heart than failure to desire that the eternal promises be true; nothing is more cowardly than to brazen it out with God. Let them then leave such impiety to those ill bred enough to be really capable of it; let them at least be decent people if they cannot be Christians; let them, in short, acknowledge that there are only two classes of persons who can be called reasonable: those who serve God with all their heart because they know him and those who seek him with all their heart because they do not know him.

As for those who live without either knowing or seeking him, they consider it so little worth while to take trouble over themselves that they are not worth other people's trouble, and it takes all the charity of that religion they despise not to despise them to the point of abandoning them to their folly. But as this religion obliges us always to regard them, as long as they live, as being capable of receiving grace which may enlighten them, and to believe that in a short time they may be filled with more faith than we are, while we on the contrary may be stricken by the same blindness which is theirs now, we must do for them what we would wish to be done for us in their place, and appeal to them to have pity on themselves, and to take at least a few steps in an attempt to find some light. Let them spend on reading about it a few of the hours they waste on other things: however reluctantly they may approach the task they will perhaps hit upon something, and at least they will not be losing much. But as for those who approach it with absolute sincerity and a real desire to find the truth, I hope that they will be satisfied, and convinced by the proofs of so divine a religion which I have collected here, following more or less this order. . . .

428   Before going into the proofs of the Christian religion, I find it necessary to point out how wrong are those men who live unconcerned to seek the truth about something of such importance to them, and affecting them so closely.

Of all their aberrations it is no doubt this which most convicts them of folly and blindness, and where they can most easily be confounded by the first application of common sense and by natural instincts. For it is indubitable that this life is but an instant of time, that the state of death is eternal, whatever its nature may be, and thus that all our actions and thoughts must follow such different paths according to the state of this eternity, that the only possible way of acting with sense and judgment is to decide our course in the light of this point, which ought to be our ultimate objective.

There is nothing more obvious than this, and it follows, according to rational principles, that men are behaving quite reasonably if they do not choose another path. Let us then judge on that score those who live without a thought for the final end of life, drifting wherever their inclinations and pleasures may take them, without reflection or anxiety, as if they could annihilate eternity by keeping their minds off it, concerned solely with attaining instant happiness.

However, eternity exists, and death, which must begin it and which threatens at every moment, must infallibly face them with the inescapable and appalling alternative of being either eternally annihilated or wretched, without their knowing which of these two forms of eternity stands ready to meet them for ever.

The consequences are undeniably terrible. They risk an eternity of wretchedness; whereupon, as if the matter were not worth their trouble, they omit to consider whether this is one of those opinions which are accepted by the people with too ready credulity or one of those which, though obscure in themselves, have a very solid, though concealed, foundation. Thus they do not know whether the fact is true or false, nor whether the proofs are strong or weak. The proofs lie before their eyes, but they refuse to look, and in this state of ignorance they choose to do everything necessary to fall into this calamity, if it exists, to wait for death before testing the proofs, while yet remaining highly satisfied in that state, professing it openly, and indeed with pride. Can we seriously think how important this matter is without being horrified at such extravagant behaviour?

To settle down in such ignorance is a monstrous thing, and those who spend their lives thus must be made to feel how extravagant and stupid it is by having it pointed out to them so that they are confounded by the sight of their own folly. For this is how men argue when they choose to live without knowing what they are and without seeking enlightenment. "I do not know," they say.

148   Man without faith can know neither true good nor justice.

All men seek happiness. There are no exceptions. However different the means they may employ, they all strive toward this goal. The reason why some go to war and some do not is the same desire in both, but interpreted in two different ways. The will never takes the least step except to that end. This is the motive of every act of every man, including those who go and hang themselves.

Yet for very many years no one without faith has ever reached the goal at which everyone is continually aiming. All men complain: princes, subjects, nobles, commoners, old, young, strong, weak, learned, ignorant, healthy, sick, in every country, at every time, of all ages, and all conditions.

A test which has gone on so long, without pause or change, really ought to convince us that we are incapable of attaining the good by our own efforts. But example teaches us very little. No two examples are so exactly alike that there is not some subtle difference, and that is what makes us expect that our expectations will not be disappointed this time as they were last time. So, while the present never satisfies us, experience deceives us, and leads us on from one misfortune to another until death comes as the ultimate and eternal climax

What else does this craving, and this helplessness, proclaim but that there was once in man a true happiness, of which all that now remains is the empty print and trace? This he tries in vain to fill with everything around him, seeking in things that are not there the help he cannot find in those that are, though none can help, since this infinite abyss can be filled only with an infinite and immutable object; in other words by God himself.

God alone is man's true good, and since man abandoned him it is a strange fact that nothing in nature has been found to take his place: stars, sky, earth, elements, plants, cabbages, leeks, animals, insects, calves, serpents, fever, plague, war, famine, vice, adultery, incest. Since losing his true good, man is capable of seeing it in anything, even his own destruction, although it is so contrary at once to God, to reason, and to nature.

Some seek their good in authority, some in intellectual inquiry and knowledge, some in pleasure.

Others again, who have indeed come closer to it, have found it impossible that this universal good, desired by all men, should lie in any of the particular objects which can only be possessed by one individual and which, once shared, cause their possessors more grief over the part they lack than satisfaction over the part they enjoy as their own. They have realized that the true good must be such that it may be possessed by all men at once without diminution or envy, and that no one should be able to lose it against his will. Their reason is that this desire is natural to man, since all men inevitably feel it, and man cannot be without it, and they therefore conclude. . . .

110   We know the truth not only through our reason but also through our heart. It is through the latter that we know first principles, and reason, which has nothing to do with it, tries in vain to refute them. The skeptics have no other object than that, and they work at it to no purpose. We know that we are not dreaming, but, however unable we may be to prove it rationally, our inability proves nothing but the weakness of our reason, and not the uncertainty of all our knowledge, as they maintain. For knowledge of first principles, like space, time, motion, number, is as solid as any derived through reason, and it is on such knowledge, coming from the heart and instinct, that reason has to depend and base all its argument. The heart feels that there are three spatial dimensions and that there is an infinite series of numbers, and reason goes on to demonstrate that there are no two square numbers of which one is double the other. Principles are felt, propositions proved, and both with certainty though by dif-

ferent means. It is just as pointless and absurd for reason to demand proof of first principles from the heart before agreeing to accept them as it would be absurd for the heart to demand an intuition of all the propositions demonstrated by reason before agreeing to accept them.

Our inability must therefore serve only to humble reason, which would like to be the judge of everything, but not to confute our certainty. As if reason were the only way we could learn! Would to God, on the contrary, that we never needed it and knew everything by instinct and feeling! But nature has refused us this blessing, and has instead given us only very little knowledge of this kind; all other knowledge can be acquired only by reasoning.

That is why those to whom God has given religious faith by moving their hearts are very fortunate, and feel quite legitimately convinced, but to those who do not have it we can only give such faith through reasoning, until God gives it by moving their heart, without which faith is only human and useless for salvation.

423 The heart has its reasons of which reason knows nothing: we know this in countless ways.

I say that it is natural for the heart to love the universal being or itself, according to its allegiance, and it hardens itself against either as it chooses. You have rejected one and kept the other. Is it reason that makes you love yourself?

424 It is the heart which perceives God and not the reason. That is what faith is: God perceived by the heart, not by the reason.

418 *Infinity—nothing.* Our soul is cast into the body where it finds number, time, dimensions; it reasons about these things and calls them natural, or necessary, and can believe nothing else.

Unity added to infinity does not increase it at all, any more than a foot added to an infinite measurement: the finite is annihilated in the presence of the infinite and becomes pure nothingness. So it is with our mind before God, with our justice before divine justice. There is not so great a disproportion between our justice and God's as between unity and infinity.

God's justice must be as vast as his mercy. Now his justice toward the damned is less vast and ought to be less startling to us than his mercy toward the elect.

We know that the infinite exists without knowing its nature, just as we know that it is untrue that numbers are finite. Thus it is true that there is an infinite number, but we do not know what it is. It is untrue that it is even, untrue that it is odd, for by adding a unit it does not change its nature. Yet it is a number, and every number is even or odd. (It is true that this applies to every finite number.)

Therefore we may well know that God exists without knowing what he is.

Is there no substantial truth, seeing that there are so many true things which are not truth itself?

Thus we know the existence and nature of the finite because we too are finite and extended in space.

We know the existence of the infinite without knowing its nature, because it too has extension but unlike us no limits.

But we do not know either the existence or the nature of God, because he has neither extension nor limits.

But by faith we know his existence, through glory we shall know his nature.

Now I have already proved that it is quite possible to know that something exists without knowing its nature.

Let us now speak according to our natural lights.

If there is a God, he is infinitely beyond our comprehension, since, being indivisible and without limits, he bears no relation to us. We are therefore incapable of knowing either what he is or whether he is. That being so, who would dare to attempt an answer to the question? Certainly not we, who bear no relation to him.

Who then will condemn Christians for being unable to give rational grounds for their belief, professing as they do a religion for which they cannot give rational grounds? They declare that it is a folly, *stultitiam*, in expounding it to the world, and then you complain that they do not prove it. If they did prove it they would not be keeping their word. It is by being without proof that they show they are not without sense. "Yes, but although that excuses those who offer their religion as such, and absolves them from the criticism of producing it without rational grounds, it does not absolve those who accept it." Let us then examine this point, and let us say: "Either God is or he is not." But to which view shall we be inclined? Reason cannot decide this question. Infinite chaos separates us. At the far end of this infinite distance a coin is being spun which will come down heads or tails. How will you wager? Reason cannot make you choose either, reason cannot prove either wrong.

Do not then condemn as wrong those who have made a choice, for you know nothing about it. "No, but I will condemn them not for having made this particular choice, but any choice, for, although the one who calls heads and the other one are equally at fault, the fact is that they are both at fault: the right thing is not to wager at all."

Yes, but you must wager. There is no choice, you are already committed. Which will you choose then? Let us see: since a choice must be made, let us see which offers you the least interest. You have two things to lose: the true and the good; and two things to stake: your reason and your will, your knowledge and your happiness; and your nature has two things to avoid: error and wretchedness. Since you must necessarily choose, your reason is no more affronted by choosing one rather than the other. That is one point cleared up. But your happiness? Let us weigh up the gain and the loss involved in calling heads that God exists. Let us assess the two cases: if you win you win everything, if you lose you lose nothing. Do not hesitate then; wager that he does exist. "That is wonderful. Yes, I must wager, but perhaps I am wagering too much." Let us see: since there is an equal chance of gain and loss, if you stood to win only two lives for one you could still wager, but supposing you stood to win three?

You would have to play (since you must necessarily play) and it would be unwise of you, once you are obliged to play, not to risk your life in order to win three lives at a game in which there is an equal chance of losing and winning. But there is an eternity of life and happiness. That being so, even though there were an infinite number of chances, of which only one was in your favor, you would still be right to wager one in order to win two; and you would be acting wrongly, being obliged to play, in refusing to stake one life against three in a game, where out of an infinite number of chances there is one in your favor, if there were an infinity of infinitely happy life to be won. But here there is an infinity of infinitely happy life to be won, one chance of winning against a finite number of chances of losing, and what you are staking is finite. That leaves no choice; wherever there is infinity, and where there are not infinite chances of losing against that of winning, there is no room for hesitation, you must give everything. And thus, since you are obliged to play, you must be renouncing reason if you hoard your life rather than risk it for an infinite gain, just as likely to occur as a loss amounting to nothing.

For it is no good saying that it is uncertain whether you will win, that it is certain that you are taking a risk, and that the infinite distance between the certainty of what you are risking and the uncertainty of what you may gain makes the finite good you are certainly risking equal to the infinite good that you are not certain to gain. This is not the case. Every gambler takes a certain risk for an uncertain gain, and yet he is taking a certain finite risk for an uncertain finite gain without sinning against reason. Here there is no infinite distance between the certain risk and the uncertain gain: that is not true. There is, indeed, an infinite distance between the certainty of winning and the certainty of losing, but the proportion between the uncertainty of winning and the certainty of what is being risked is in proportion to the chances of winning or losing. And hence if there are as many chances on one side as on the other you are playing for even odds. And in that case the certainty of what you are risking is equal to the uncertainty of what you may win; it is by no means infinitely distant from it. Thus our argument carries infinite weight, when the stakes are finite in a game where there are even chances of winning and losing and an infinite prize to be won.

This is conclusive and if men are capable of any truth this is it.

"I confess, I admit it, but is there really no way of seeing what the cards are?"—"Yes. Scripture and the rest, etc."—"Yes, but my hands are tied and my lips are sealed; I am being forced to wager and I am not free; I am being held fast and I am so made that I cannot believe. What do you want me to do then?"—"That is true, but at least get it into your head that, if you are unable to believe, it is because of your passions, since reason impels you to believe and yet you cannot do so. Concentrate then not on convincing yourself by multiplying proofs of God's existence but by diminishing your passions. You want to find faith and you do not know the road. You want to be cured of unbelief and you ask for the remedy: learn from those who were once bound like you and who now wager all they have. These are people who know the road you wish to follow, who have been cured of the affliction of which you wish to be cured: follow the way by which they began. They behaved just as if they did believe, taking holy water, having masses said, and so on. That will make you believe quite naturally, and will make you more docile."—"But that is what I am afraid of."—"But why? What have you to lose? But to show you that this is the way, the fact is that this diminishes the passions which are your great obstacles. . . ."

End of this address. "Now what harm will come to you from choosing this course? You will be faithful, honest, humble, grateful, full of good works, a sincere, true friend. . . . It is true you will not enjoy noxious pleasures, glory, and good living, but will you not have others?

"I tell you that you will gain even in this life, and that at every step you take along this road you will see that your gain is so certain and your risk so negligible that in the end you will realize that you have wagered on something certain and infinite for which you have paid nothing."

"How these words fill me with rapture and delight!—"

"If my words please you and seem cogent, you must know that they come from a man who went down upon his knees before and after to pray this infinite and indivisible being, to whom he submits his own, that he might bring your being also to submit to him for your own good and for his glory: and that strength might thus be reconciled with lowliness."

QUESTIONS

Note: Section numbers, not page numbers, are given for this selection from *Pensées*.

1. What is the unhappy condition that according to Pascal drives people to seek diversion? (136)

2. According to Pascal, what is it about man's nature that makes "two contrary instincts give rise to a confused plan buried out of sight in the depths of their soul"? (136)

3. Does Pascal think people are aware of the real reason they seek diversion? (136)

4. What does Pascal mean when he says that imagination "has established a second nature in man"? (44)

5. Why does Pascal claim that "reason never wholly overcomes imagination"? (44)

6. When Pascal says that imagination "creates beauty, justice, and happiness, which is the world's supreme good," is he claiming that the products of imagination are not always deceptive and full of error? (44)

7. Why does Pascal claim that self-love inevitably leads to a hatred of the truth? (978)

8. Does Pascal think that the mathematical and intuitive minds are fundamentally opposed? Does he think that one has more insight than the other? (512)

9. Does Pascal think that man's disproportion to the infinite extent of the universe precludes any certain knowledge? (199)

10. Would Pascal allow that natural science has any value? (199)

11. Why does Pascal claim that "all of our dignity consists in thought" and that "it is on thought that we must depend for our recovery"? (200)

12. If man is "neither angel nor beast," where is his proper place, according to Pascal? What does Pascal mean in saying that "anyone trying to act the angel acts the beast"? (678)

13. Is Pascal correct in saying that even "those who go and hang themselves" are seeking happiness? (148)

14. What is the nature of man's true good that Pascal says will satisfy his natural desires? If, as he says, "we are incapable of attaining the good by our own efforts," what remedy does he propose? (148)

15. According to Pascal, why does reason depend on the "knowledge of first principles" that comes "from the heart and instinct"? (110)

16. When Pascal says that "the heart has its reasons of which reason knows nothing," is he claiming that people cannot have knowledge of why the heart chooses one thing or another? (423)

17. Why does Pascal dismiss the objection of the person who says that "the right thing is not to wager at all" by responding ". . . you must wager. There is no choice, you are already committed"? (418)

18. According to Pascal, does it matter if the one wagering that God exists will have no immediate confirmation of the bet's result? (418)

19. What does Pascal mean when he says that his argument about why one should wager that God exists "carries infinite weight"? (418)

FOR FURTHER REFLECTION

1. Is the scientific understanding of the world necessarily diminished by belief in God?

2. Is it possible for people to be happy living with well-reasoned skepticism about the existence of God and the fate of their souls?

3. Is it important to show that religion is not contrary to reason?

RALPH WALDO EMERSON

R alph Waldo Emerson (1803–1882) is considered by many scholars to be the most influential American writer and philosopher of the nineteenth century. His ideas register heavily in the work of Walt Whitman and Henry David Thoreau, among others. Influenced by British Romantic writers as well as by wide reading in Eastern philosophy and religion, Emerson stressed the primacy of individual human experience and the importance of cultivating a sense of one's own self.

Emerson was the son of a Unitarian minister, and following studies at Harvard College and Harvard Divinity School, he was appointed junior pastor at the Second Church in Boston when he was only twenty-three years old. He would leave the Unitarians in 1831 following the death of his nineteen-year-old wife, the poet Ellen Tucker, and his increasing skepticism about the validity of the sacrament of communion. That same year he traveled to Europe where he met Samuel Taylor Coleridge and Thomas Carlyle, who both exercised a formative influence on his thinking.

In 1836, Emerson published anonymously the book that would establish his reputation. *Nature* was a bold and freewheeling disquisition on the relationship of the individual to the universe and to Emerson's radically reinterpreted notion of God. Emerson's manifesto called for an understanding of the essential unity of all things. Even more important, it declared that new and original thinking was called for in order to discern the outline of that unity: "Our age is introspective. It builds the sepulchres of the fathers. . . . The foregoing generations beheld God and nature face to face; we, through their eyes. Why should not we also enjoy an original relation to the universe? Why should not we have a poetry and philosophy of insight and not of tradition . . . ?"

Also during this time, Emerson helped to form a salon discussion group in Concord, Massachusetts. The group called itself the Symposium, but became popularly known as the Transcendental Club. Its members included the abolitionist Theodore Parker and the utopian reformer George Ripley, who founded Brook Farm in 1841. Transcendentalism is significant in that it breaks not only with the Calvinist doctrine of the New England Puritans, but also with the rationalist theology of the Unitarian church.

Throughout the rest of his career, Emerson's writings and lectures—his very fame, one can argue—would depend on his articulation of a spiritual vision married to a deeply secular creed in which the subject must continually define what he is leaving behind even as he attempts to discern exactly what it is he is trying to embrace. Though he left the formal ministry, Emerson would continue to write and speak prolifically, often employing a style that exhorted his listeners to listen carefully not only to voices outside themselves, but also to the voice within. "Self-Reliance" is one of Emerson's most famous essays, and it shows Emerson at his full power, developing the theme of nonconformity as essential to any genuine notion of selfhood.

RALPH WALDO EMERSON

Self-Reliance

I read the other day some verses written by an eminent painter which were original and not conventional. The soul always hears an admonition in such lines, let the subject be what it may. The sentiment they instill is of more value than any thought they may contain. To believe your own thought, to believe that what is true for you in your private heart is true for all men—that is genius. Speak your latent conviction, and it shall be the universal sense; for the inmost in due time becomes the outmost, and our first thought is rendered back to us by the trumpets of the Last Judgment. Familiar as the voice of the mind is to each, the highest merit we ascribe to Moses, Plato, and Milton is that they set at naught books and traditions, and spoke not what men, but what *they* thought. A man should learn to detect and watch that gleam of light which flashes across his mind from within more than the luster of the firmament of bards and sages. Yet he dismisses without notice his thought, because it is his. In every work of genius we recognize our own rejected thoughts; they come back to us with a certain alienated majesty. Great works of art have no more affecting lesson for us than this. They teach us to abide by our spontaneous impression with good-humored inflexibility the most when the whole cry of voices is on the other side. Else tomorrow a stranger will say with masterly good sense precisely what we have thought and felt all the time, and we shall be forced to take with shame our own opinion from another.

There is a time in every man's education when he arrives at the conviction that envy is ignorance; that imitation is suicide; that he must take himself for better for worse as his portion; that though the wide universe is full of good, no kernel of nourishing corn can come to him but through his toil bestowed on that plot of ground which is given to him to till. The power which resides in him is new in nature, and none but he knows what that is which he can do, nor does he know until he has tried. Not for nothing one face, one character, one fact, makes much impression on him, and another none. This sculpture in the memory is not without preestablished harmony. The eye was placed where one ray should fall, that it might testify of that particular ray. We but half express ourselves, and are ashamed of that divine idea which each of us represents. It may be safely trusted as proportionate and of good issues, so it be faithfully imparted, but God will not have his work made manifest by cowards. A man is relieved and gay when he has put his heart into his work and done his best; but what he has said or done otherwise shall give him no peace. It is a deliverance which does not deliver. In the attempt his genius deserts him; no muse befriends; no invention, no hope.

Trust thyself: every heart vibrates to that iron string. Accept the place the divine providence has found for you, the society of your contemporaries, the connection of events. Great men have always done so, and confided themselves childlike to the genius of their age, betraying their perception that the absolutely trustworthy was seated at their heart, working through their hands, predominating in all their being. And we are now men, and must accept in the highest mind the same transcendent destiny; and not minors and invalids in a protected corner, not cowards fleeing before a revolution, but guides, redeemers and benefactors, obeying the Almighty effort and advancing on Chaos and the Dark.

What pretty oracles nature yields us on this text in the face and behavior of children, babes, and even brutes! That divided and rebel mind, that distrust of a sentiment because our arithmetic has computed the strength and means opposed to our purpose, these have not. Their mind being whole, their eye is as yet unconquered, and when we look in their faces we are disconcerted. Infancy conforms to nobody; all conform to it; so that one babe commonly makes four or five out of the adults who prattle and play to it. So God has armed youth and puberty and manhood no less with its own piquancy and charm, and made it enviable and gracious and its claims not to be put by, if it will stand by itself. Do not think the youth has no force, because he cannot speak to you and me. Hark! In the next room his voice is sufficiently clear and emphatic. It seems he knows how to speak to his contemporaries. Bashful or bold then, he will know how to make us seniors very unnecessary.

The nonchalance of boys who are sure of a dinner, and would disdain as much as a lord to do or say aught to conciliate one, is the healthy attitude of human nature. A boy is in the parlor what the pit is in the playhouse; independent, irresponsible, looking out from his corner on such people and facts as pass by, he tries and sentences them on their merits, in the swift, summary way of boys, as good, bad, interesting, silly, eloquent, troublesome. He cumbers himself never about consequences, about interests; he gives an independent, genuine verdict. You must court him;

he does not court you. But the man is as it were clapped into jail by his consciousness. As soon as he has once acted or spoken with *éclat* he is a committed person, watched by the sympathy or the hatred of hundreds, whose affections must now enter into his account. There is no Lethe for this. Ah, that he could pass again into his neutrality! Who can thus avoid all pledges and, have observed, observe again from the same unaffected, unbiased, unbribable, unaffrighted innocence—must always be formidable. He would utter opinions on all passing affairs, which being seen to be not private but necessary, would sink like darts into the ear of men and put them in fear.

These are the voices which we hear in solitude, but they grow faint and inaudible as we enter into the world. Society everywhere is in conspiracy against the manhood of every one of its members. Society is a joint-stock company, in which the members agree, for the better securing of his bread to each shareholder, to surrender the liberty and culture of the eater. The virtue in most request is conformity. Self-reliance is its aversion. It loves not realities and creators, but names and customs.

Whoso would be a man, must be a nonconformist. He who would gather immortal palms must not be hindered by the name of goodness, but must explore if it be goodness. Nothing is at last sacred but the integrity of your own mind. Absolve you to yourself, and you shall have the suffrage of the world. I remember an answer which when quite young I was prompted to make to a valued adviser who was wont to importune me with the dear old doctrines of the church. On my saying, "What have I to do with the sacredness of traditions, if I live wholly from within?" my friend suggested—"But these impulses may be from below, not from above." I replied, "They do not seem to me to be such; but if I am the Devil's child, I will live then from the Devil." No law can be sacred to me but that of my nature. Good and bad are but names very readily transferable to that or this; the only right is what is after my constitution; the only wrong what is against it. A man is to carry himself in the presence of all opposition as if everything were titular and ephemeral but he. I am ashamed to think how easily we capitulate to badges and names, to large societies and dead institutions. Every decent and well-spoken individual affects and sways me more than is right. I ought to go upright and vital, and speak the rude truth in all ways. If malice and vanity wear the coat of philanthropy, shall that pass? If an angry bigot assumes this bountiful cause of abolition, and comes to me with his last news from Barbados, why should I not say to him, "Go love thy infant; love thy woodchopper; be good natured and modest; have that grace; and never varnish your hard, uncharitable ambition with this incredible tenderness for black folk a thousand miles off. Thy love afar is spite at home." Rough and graceless would be such greeting, but truth is handsomer than the affectation of love. Your goodness must have some edge to it—else it is none. The doctrine of hatred must be preached, as the counteraction of the doctrine of love, when that pules and whines. I shun father and mother and wife and brother when my genius calls me. I would write on the lintels of the doorpost, *Whim*. I hope it is somewhat better than whim at last, but we cannot spend the day in explanation. Expect me not to show cause why I seek or why I exclude company. Then again, do not tell me, as a good man did today, of my obligation to put all poor men in good situations. Are they *my* poor? I tell thee, thou foolish philanthropist, that I grudge the dollar, the dime, the cent I give to such men as do not belong to me and to whom I do not belong. There is a class of persons to whom by all spiritual affinity I am bought and sold; for them I will go to prison if need be; but your miscellaneous popular charities; the education at college of fools; the building of meetinghouses to the vain end to which many now stand; alms to sots, and the thousandfold relief societies—though I confess with shame I sometimes succumb and give the dollar, it is a wicked dollar, which by and by I shall have the manhood to withhold.

Virtues are, in the popular estimate, rather the exception than the rule. There is the man *and* his virtues. Men do what is called a good action, as some piece of courage or charity, much as they would pay a fine in expiation of daily nonappearance on parade. Their works are done as an apology or extenuation of their living in the world—as invalids and the insane pay a high board. Their virtues are penances. I do not wish to expiate, but to live. My life is for itself and not for a spectacle. I much prefer that it should be of a lower strain, so it be genuine and equal, than that it should be glittering and unsteady. I wish it to be sound and sweet, and not to need diet and bleeding. I ask primary evidence that you are a man, and refuse this appeal from the man to his actions. I know that for myself it makes no difference whether I do or forbear those actions which are reckoned excellent. I cannot consent to pay for a privilege where I have intrinsic right. Few and mean as my gifts may be, I actually am, and do not need for my own assurance or the assurance of my fellows any secondary testimony.

What I must do is all that concerns me, not what the people think. This rule, equally arduous in actual and in intellectual life, may serve for the whole distinction between greatness and meanness. It is the harder because you will always find those who think they know what is your duty better than you know it. It is easy in the world to live after the world's opinion; it is easy in solitude to live after our own; but the great man is he who in the midst of the crowd keeps with perfect sweetness the independence of solitude.

The objection to conforming to usages that have become dead to you is that it scatters your force. It loses your time and blurs the impression of your character. If you maintain a dead church, contribute to a dead Bible society, vote with a great party either for the government or against it, spread your table like base housekeepers—under all these screens I have difficulty to detect the precise man you are: and of course so much force is withdrawn from your proper life. But do your work, and I shall know you. Do your work, and you shall reinforce yourself. A man must consider what a blindman's buff is this game of conformity. If I know your sect I anticipate your argument. I hear a preacher announce for his text and topic the expediency of one of the institutions of his church. Do I not know beforehand that not possibly can he say a new and spontaneous word? Do I not know that with all this ostentation of examining the grounds of the institution he will do no such thing? Do I not know that he is pledged to himself not to look but at one side, the permitted side, not as a man, but as a parish minister? He is a retained attorney, and these airs of the bench are the emptiest affectation. Well, most men have bound their eyes with one or another handkerchief, and attached themselves to some one of these communities of opinion. This conformity makes them not false in a few particulars, authors of a few lies, but false in all particulars. Their every truth is not quite true. Their two is not the real two, their four not the real four; so that every word they say chagrins us and we know not where to begin to set them right. Meantime nature is not slow to equip us in the prison uniform of the party to which we adhere. We come to wear one cut of face and figure, and acquire by degrees the gentlest asinine expression. There is a mortifying experience in particular, which does not fail to wreak itself also in the general history; I mean "the foolish face of praise," the forced smile which we put on in company where we do not feel at ease, in answer to conversation which does not interest us. The muscles, not spontaneously moved but moved by a low usurping willfulness, grow tight about the outline of the face, with the most disagreeable sensation.

For nonconformity the world whips you with its displeasure. And therefore a man must know how to estimate a sour face. The bystanders look askance on him in the public street or in the friend's parlor. If this aversion had its origin in contempt and resistance like his own he might well go home with a sad countenance; but the sour faces of the multitude, like their sweet faces, have no deep cause, but are put on and off as the wind blows and a newspaper directs. Yet is the discontent of the multitude more formidable than that of the senate and the college. It is easy enough for a firm man who knows the world to brook the rage of the cultivated classes. Their rage is decorous and prudent, for they are timid, as being very vulnerable themselves. But when to their feminine rage the indignation of the people is added, when the ignorant and the poor are aroused, when the unintelligent brute force that lies at the bottom of society is made to growl and mow, it needs the habit of magnanimity and religion to treat it godlike as a trifle of no concernment.

The other terror that scares us from self-trust is our consistency; a reverence for our past act or word because the eyes of others have no other data for computing our orbit than our past acts, and we are loth to disappoint them.

But why should you keep your head over your shoulder? Why drag about this corpse of your memory, lest you contradict some what you have stated in this or that public place? Suppose you should contradict yourself; what then? It seems to be a rule of wisdom never to rely on your memory, but to bring the past for judgment into the thousand-eyed present, and live ever in a new day. In your metaphysics you have denied personality to the Deity, yet when the devout motions of the soul come, yield to them heart and life, though they should clothe God with shape and color. Leave your theory, as Joseph his coat in the hand of the harlot, and flee.

A foolish consistency is the hobgoblin of little minds, adored by little statesmen and philosophers and divines. With consistency a great soul has simply nothing to do. He may as well concern himself with his shadow on the wall. Speak what you think now in hard words and tomorrow speak what tomorrow thinks in hard words again, though it contradict everything you said today.—"Ah, so you shall be sure to be misunderstood."—Is it so bad then to be misunderstood? Pythagoras was misunderstood, and Socrates, and Jesus, and Luther, and Copernicus, and Galileo, and Newton, and every pure and wise spirit that ever took flesh. To be great is to be misunderstood.

I suppose no man can violate his nature. All the sallies of his will are rounded in by the law of his being, as the inequalities of Andes and Himmaleh are insignificant in the curve of the sphere. Nor does it matter how you gauge and try him. A character is like an acrostic or Alexandrian stanza—read it forward, backward, or across, it still spells the same thing. In this pleasing contrite wood life which God allows me, let me record day by day my honest thought without prospect or retrospect, and, I cannot doubt, it will be found symmetrical, though I mean it not and see it not. My book should smell of pines and resound with the hum of insects. The swallow over my window should interweave that thread or straw he carries in his bill into my web also. We pass for what we are. Character teaches above our wills. Men imagine that they communicate their virtue or vice only by overt actions, and do not see that virtue or vice emit a breath every moment.

There will be an agreement in whatever variety of actions, so they be each honest and natural in their hour. For of one will, the actions will be harmonious, however unlike they seem. These varieties are lost sight of at a little distance, at a little height of thought. One tendency unites them all. The voyage of the best ship is a zigzag line of a hundred tacks. See the line from a sufficient distance, and it straightens itself to the average tendency. Your genuine action will explain itself and will explain your other genuine actions. Your conformity explains nothing. Act singly, and what you have already done singly will justify you now. Greatness appeals to the future. If I can be firm enough today to do right and scorn eyes, I must have done so much right before as to defend me now. Be it how it will, do right now. Always scorn appearances and you always may. The force of character is cumulative. All the foregone days of virtue work their health into this. What makes the majesty of the heroes of the senate and the field, which so fills the imagination? The consciousness of a train of great days and victories behind. They shed a united light on the advancing actor. He is attended as by a visible escort of angels. That is it which throws thunder into Chatham's voice, and dignity into Washington's port, and America into Adams's eye. Honor is venerable to us because it is no ephemera. It is always ancient virtue. We worship it today because it is not of today. We love it and pay it homage because it is not a trap for our love and homage, but is self-dependent, self-derived, and therefore of an old immaculate pedigree, even if shown in a young person.

I hope in these days we have heard the last of conformity and consistency. Let the words be gazetted and ridiculous henceforward. Instead of the gong for dinner, let us hear a whistle from the Spartan fife. Let us never bow and apologize more. A great man is coming to eat at my house. I do not wish to please him; I wish that he should wish to please me. I will stand here for humanity, and though I would make it kind, I would make it true. Let us affront and reprimand the smooth mediocrity and squalid contentment of the times, and hurl in the face of custom and trade and office, the fact which is the upshot of all history, that there is a great responsible Thinker and Actor working wherever a man works; that a true man belongs to no other time or place, but is the center of things. Where he is, there is nature. He measures you and all men and all events. Ordinarily, everybody in society reminds us of somewhat else, or of some other person. Character, reality, reminds you of nothing else; it takes place of the whole creation. The man must be so much that he must make all circumstances indifferent. Every true man is a cause, a country, and an age; requires infinite spaces and numbers and time fully to accomplish his design—and posterity seems to follow his steps as a train of clients. A man Caesar is born, and for ages after we have a Roman Empire. Christ is born, and millions of minds so grow and cleave to his genius that he is confounded with virtue and the possible of man. An institution is the lengthened shadow of one man; as, monachism, of the Hermit Antony; the Reformation, of Luther; Quakerism, of Fox; Methodism, of Wesley; abolition, of Clarkson. Scipio, Milton called "the height of Rome"; and all history resolves itself very easily into the biography of a few stout and earnest persons.

Let a man then know his worth, and keep things under his feet. Let him not peep or steal, or skulk up and down with the air of a charity boy, a bastard, or an interloper in the world which exists for him. But the man in the street, finding no worth in himself which corresponds to the force which built a tower or sculptured a marble god, feels poor when he looks on these. To him a palace, a statue, or a costly book have an alien and forbidding air, much like a gay equipage, and seem to say like that, "Who are you, sir?" Yet they all are his, suitors for his notice, petitioners to his faculties that they will come out and take possession. The picture waits for my verdict; it is not to command me, but I am to settle its claims to praise. That popular fable of the sot who was picked up dead drunk in the street, carried to the duke's house, washed and dressed and laid in the duke's bed, and, on his waking, treated with all obsequious ceremony like the duke, and assured that he had been insane, owes its popularity to the fact that it symbolizes so well the state of man, who is in the world a sort of sot, but now and then wakes up, exercises his reason, and finds himself a true prince.

Our reading is mendicant and sycophantic. In history our imagination plays us false. Kingdom and lordship, power and estate, are a gaudier vocabulary than private John and Edward in a small house and common day's work; but the things of life are the same to both; the sum total of both is the same. Why all this deference to Alfred and Scanderbeg and Gustavus? Suppose they were virtuous; did they wear out virtue? As great a stake depends on your private act today as followed their public and renowned steps. When private men shall act with original views, the luster will be transferred from the actions of kings to those of gentlemen.

The world has been instructed by its kings, who have so magnetized the eyes of nations. It has been taught by this colossal symbol the mutual reverence that is due from man to man. The joyful loyalty with which men have everywhere suffered the king, the noble, or the great proprietor to walk among them by a law of his own, make his own scale of men and things and reverse theirs, pay for benefits not with money but with honor, and represent the law in his person, was the hieroglyphic by which they obscurely signified their consciousness of their own right and come-liness, the right of every man.

The magnetism which all original action exerts is explained when we inquire the reason of self-trust. Who is the Trustee? What is the aboriginal Self, on which a universal reliance may be grounded? What is the nature and power of that science-baffling star, without parallax, without calculable elements, which shoots a ray of beauty even into trivial and impure actions, if the least mark of independence appear? The inquiry leads us to that source, at once the essence of genius, of virtue, and of life, which we call Spontaneity or Instinct. We denote this primary wisdom as Intuition, while all later teachings are tuitions. In that deep force, the last fact behind which analysis cannot go, all things find their common origin. For the sense of being which in calm hours rises, we know not how, in the soul, is not diverse from things, from space, from light, from time, from man, but one with them and proceeds obviously from the same source whence their life and being also proceed. We first share the life by which things exist and afterward see them as appearances in nature and forget that we have shared their cause. Here is the fountain of action and of thought. Here are the lungs of that inspiration which giveth man wisdom and which cannot be denied without impiety and atheism. We lie in the lap of immense intelligence, which makes us receivers of its truth and organs of its activity. When we discern justice, when we discern truth, we do nothing of ourselves, but allow a passage to its beams. If we ask whence this comes, if we seek to pry into the soul that causes, all philosophy is at fault. Its presence or its absence is all we can affirm. Every man discriminates between the voluntary acts of his mind and his involuntary perceptions, and knows that to his involuntary perceptions a perfect faith is due. He may err in the expression of them, but he knows that these things are so, like day and night, not to be disputed. My willful actions and acquisitions are but roving—the idlest reverie, the faintest native emotion, command my curiosity and respect. Thoughtless people contradict as readily the statement of perceptions as of opinions, or rather much more readily; for they do not distinguish between perception and notion. They fancy that I choose to see this or that thing. But perception is not whimsical, but fatal. If I see a trait, my children will see it after me, and in course of time all mankind—although it may chance that no one has seen it before me. For my perception of it is as much a fact as the sun.

The relations of the soul to the divine spirit are so pure that it is profane to seek to interpose helps. It must be that when God speaketh he should communicate, not one thing, but all things; should fill the world with his voice; should scatter forth light, nature, time, souls, from the center of the present thought; and new date and new create the whole. Whenever a mind is simple and receives a divine wisdom, old things pass away—means, teachers, texts, temples fall; it lives now, and absorbs past and future into the present hour. All things are made sacred by relation to it—one as much as another. All things are dissolved to their center by their cause, and in the universal miracle petty and particular miracles disappear. If therefore a man claims to know and speak of God and carries you backward to the phraseology of some old moldered nation in another country, in another world, believe him not. Is the acorn better than the oak which is its fullness and completion? Is the parent better than the child into whom he has cast his ripened being? Whence then this worship of the past? The centuries are conspirators against the sanity and authority of the soul. Time and space are but physiological colors which the eye makes, but the soul is light: where it is, is day; where it was, is night; and history is an impertinence and an injury if it be anything more than a cheerful apologue or parable of my being and becoming.

Man is timid and apologetic; he is no longer upright; he dares not to say "I think," "I am," but quotes some saint or sage. He is ashamed before the blade of grass or the blowing rose. These roses under my window make no reference to former roses or to better ones; they are for what they are; they exist with God today. There is no time to them. There is simply the rose; it is perfect in every moment of its existence. Before a leaf bud has burst, its whole life acts; in the full-blown flower there is no more; in the leafless root there is no less. Its nature is satisfied and it satisfies nature in all moments alike. But man postpones or remembers; he does not live in the present, but with reverted eye laments the past, or, heedless of the riches that surround him, stands on tiptoe to foresee the future. He cannot be happy and strong until he too lives with nature in the present, above time.

This should be plain enough. Yet see what strong intellects dare not yet hear God himself unless he speak the phraseology of I know not what David, or Jeremiah, or Paul. We shall not always set so great a price on a few texts, on a few lives. We are like children who repeat by rote the sentences of grandames and tutors, and, as they grow older, of the men of talents and character they chance to see—painfully recollecting the exact words they spoke; afterward, when they come into the point of view which those had who uttered these sayings, they understand them and are willing to let the words go; for at any time they can use words as good when occasion comes. If we live truly, we shall see truly. It is as easy for the strong man to be strong as it is for the weak to be weak. When we have new perception, we shall gladly disburden the memory of its hoarded treasures as old rubbish. When a man lives with God, his voice shall be as sweet as the murmur of the brook and the rustle of the corn.

And now at last the highest truth on this subject remains unsaid; probably cannot be said; for all that we say is the far-off remembering of the intuition. That thought by what I can now nearest approach to say it, is this. When good is near you, when you have life in yourself, it is not by any known or accustomed way; you shall not discern the footprints of any other; you shall not see the face of man; you shall not hear any name—the way, the thought, the good, shall be wholly strange and new. It shall exclude example and experience. You take the way from man, not to man. All persons that ever existed are its forgotten ministers. Fear and hope are alike beneath it. There is somewhat low even in hope. In the hour of vision there is nothing that can be called gratitude, nor properly joy. The soul raised over passion beholds identity and eternal causation, perceives the self-existence of Truth and Right, and calms itself with knowing that all things go well. Vast spaces of nature, the Atlantic Ocean, the South Sea; long intervals of time, years, centuries, are of no account. This which I think and feel underlay every former state of life and circumstances, as it does underlie my present, and what is called life and what is called death.

Life only avails, not the having lived. Power ceases in the instant of repose; it resides in the moment of transition from a past to a new state, in the shooting of the gulf, in the darting to an aim. This one fact the world hates; that the soul *becomes*; for that forever degrades the past, turns all riches to poverty, all reputation to a shame, confounds the saint with the rogue, shoves Jesus and Judas equally aside. Why then do we prate of self-reliance? Inasmuch as the soul is present there will be power not confident but agent. To talk of reliance is a poor external way of speaking. Speak rather of that which relies because it works and is. Who has more obedience than I masters me, though he should not raise his finger. Round him I must revolve by the gravitation of spirits. We fancy it rhetoric when we speak of eminent virtue. We do not yet see that virtue is Height, and that a man or a company of men, plastic and permeable to principles, by the law of nature must overpower and ride all cities, nations, kings, rich men, poets, who are not.

This is the ultimate fact which we so quickly reach on this, as on every topic, the resolution of all into the ever-blessed ONE. Self-existence is the attribute of the Supreme Cause, and it constitutes the measure of good by the degree in which it enters into all lower forms. All things real are so by so much virtue as they contain. Commerce, husbandry, hunting, whaling, war, eloquence, personal weight, are somewhat, and engage my respect as examples of its presence and impure action. I see the same law working in nature for conservation and growth. Power is, in nature, the essential measure of right. Nature suffers nothing to

remain in her kingdoms which cannot help itself. The genesis and matu-
ration of a planet, its poise and orbit, the bended tree recovering itself
from the strong wind, the vital resources of every animal and vegetable,
are demonstrations of the self-sufficing and therefore self-relying soul.

Thus all concentrates: let us not rove; let us sit at home with the
cause. Let us stun and astonish the intruding rabble of men and books
and institutions by a simple declaration of the divine fact. Bid the
invaders take the shoes from off their feet, for God is here within. Let our
simplicity judge them, and our docility to our own law demonstrate the
poverty of nature and fortune beside our native riches.

But now we are a mob. Man does not stand in awe of man, nor is his
genius admonished to stay at home, to put itself in communication with
the internal ocean, but it goes abroad to beg a cup of water of the urns of
other men. We must go alone. I like the silent church before the service
begins better than any preaching. How far off, how cool, how chaste the
persons look, begirt each one with a precinct or sanctuary! So let us
always sit. Why should we assume the faults of our friend, or wife, or
father, or child, because they sit around our heart, or are said to have the
same blood? All men have my blood and I all men's. Not for that will I
adopt their petulance or folly, even to the extent of being ashamed of it.
But your isolation must not be mechanical, but spiritual, that is, must be
elevation. At times the whole world seems to be in conspiracy to importune you with emphatic trifles. Friend, client, child, sickness, fear, want,
charity, all knock at once at thy closet door and say—"Come out unto
us." But keep thy state; come not into their confusion. The power men
possess to annoy me I give them by a weak curiosity. No man can come
near me but through my act. "What we love that we have, but by desire
we bereave ourselves of the love."

If we cannot at once rise to the sanctities of obedience and faith, let
us at least resist our temptations; let us enter into the state of war and
wake Thor and Woden, courage and constancy, in our Saxon breasts.
This is to be done in our smooth times by speaking the truth. Check this
lying hospitality and lying affection. Live no longer to the expectation of
these deceived and deceiving people with whom we converse. Say to
them, "O father, O mother, O wife, O brother, O friend, I have lived with
you after appearances hitherto. Henceforward I am the truth's. Be it
known unto you that henceforward I obey no law less than the eternal
law. I will have no covenants but proximities. I shall endeavor to nourish
my parents, to support my family, to be the chaste husband of one wife—
but these relations I must fill after a new and unprecedented way. I appeal
from your customs. I must be myself. I cannot break myself any longer
for you, or you. If you can love me for what I am, we shall be the happier.

If you cannot, I will still seek to deserve that you should. I will not hide my tastes or aversions. I will so trust that what is deep is holy, that I will do strongly before the sun and moon whatever inly rejoices me and the heart appoints. If you are noble, I will love you; if you are not, I will not hurt you and myself by hypocritical attentions. If you are true, but not in the same truth with me, cleave to your companions; I will seek my own. I do this not selfishly but humbly and truly. It is alike your interest, and mine, and all men's, however long we have dwelt in lies, to live in truth. Does this sound harsh today? You will soon love what is dictated by your nature as well as mine, and if we follow the truth it will bring us out safe at last." But so may you give these friends pain. Yes, but I cannot sell my liberty and my power, to save their sensibility. Besides, all persons have their moments of reason, when they look out into the region of absolute truth; then will they justify me and do the same thing.

The populace think that your rejection of popular standards is a rejection of all standard, and mere antinomianism; and the bold sensualist will use the name of philosophy to gild his crimes. But the law of consciousness abides. There are two confessionals, in one or the other of which we must be shriven. You may fulfill your round of duties by clearing yourself in the *direct*, or in the *reflex* way. Consider whether you have satisfied your relations to father, mother, cousin, neighbor, town, cat, and dog—whether any of these can upbraid you. But I may also neglect this reflex standard and absolve me to myself. I have my own stern claims and perfect circle. It denies the name of duty to many offices that are called duties. But if I can discharge its debts it enables me to dispense with the popular code. If anyone imagines that this law is lax, let him keep its commandments one day.

And truly it demands something godlike in him who has cast off the common motives of humanity and has ventured to trust himself for a taskmaster. High be his heart, faithful his will, clear his sight, that he may in good earnest be doctrine, society, law, to himself, that a simple purpose may be to him as strong as iron necessity is to others!

If any man consider the present aspects of what is called by distinction *society*, he will see the need of these ethics. The sinew and heart of man seem to be drawn out, and we are become timorous, desponding whimperers. We are afraid of truth, afraid of fortune, afraid of death, and afraid of each other. Our age yields no great and perfect persons. We want men and women who shall renovate life and our social state, but we see that most natures are insolvent, cannot satisfy their own wants, have an ambition out of all proportion to their practical force and do lean and beg day and night continually. Our housekeeping is mendicant, our arts, our occupations, our marriages, our religion we have not chosen, but society has chosen for us. We are parlor soldiers. We shun the rugged battle of fate, where strength is born.

If our young men miscarry in their first enterprises they lose all heart. If the young merchant fails, men say he is *ruined*. If the finest genius studies at one of our colleges and is not installed in an office within one year afterward in the cities or suburbs of Boston or New York, it seems to his friends and to himself that he is right in being disheartened and in complaining the rest of his life. A sturdy farm lad from New Hampshire or Vermont, who in turn tries all the professions, who *teams it, farms it, peddles*, keeps a school, preaches, edits a newspaper, goes to Congress, buys a township, and so forth, in successive years, and always like a cat falls on his feet, is worth a hundred of these city dolls. He walks abreast with his days and feels no shame in not "studying a profession," for he does not postpone his life, but lives already. He has not one chance, but a hundred chances. Let a Stoic open the resources of man and tell men they are not leaning willows, but can and must detach themselves; that with the exercise of self-trust, new powers shall appear; that a man is the word made flesh, born to shed healing to the nations; that he should be ashamed of our compassion, and that the moment be acts from himself, tossing the laws, the books, idolatries, and customs out of the window, we pity him no more but thank and revere him—and that teacher shall restore the life of man to splendor and make his name dear to all history.

It is easy to see that a greater self-reliance must work a revolution in all the offices and relations of men; in their religion; in their education; in their pursuits; their modes of living; their association; in their property; in their speculative views.

1. In what prayers do men allow themselves! That which they call a holy office is not so much as brave and manly. Prayer looks abroad and asks for some foreign addition to come through some foreign virtue, and loses itself in endless mazes of natural and supernatural, and mediatorial and miraculous. Prayer that craves a particular commodity, anything less than all good, is vicious. Prayer is the contemplation of the facts of life from the highest point of view. It is the soliloquy of a beholding and jubilant soul. It is the spirit of God pronouncing his works good. But prayer as a means to effect a private end is meanness and theft. It supposes dualism and not unity in nature and consciousness. As soon as the man is at one with God, he will not beg. He will then see prayer in all action. The prayer of the farmer kneeling in his field to weed it, the prayer of the rower kneeling with the stroke of his oar, are true prayers heard throughout nature, though for cheap ends. Caratach, in Fletcher's "Bonduca," when admonished to inquire the mind of the god Audate, replies,

> *His hidden meaning lies in our endeavors;*
> *Our valors are our best gods.*

Another sort of false prayers are our regrets. Discontent is the want of self-reliance; it is infirmity of will. Regret calamities if you can thereby help the sufferer; if not, attend your own work and already the evil begins to be repaired. Our sympathy is just as base. We come to them who weep foolishly and sit down and cry for company, instead of imparting to them truth and health in rough electric shocks, putting them once more in communication with their own reason. The secret of fortune is joy in our hands. Welcome evermore to gods and men is the self-helping man. For him all doors are flung wide; him all tongues greet, all honors crown, all eyes follow with desire. Our love goes out to him and embraces him because he did not need it. We solicitously and apologetically caress and celebrate him because he held on his way and scorned our disapprobation. The gods love him because men hated him. "To the persevering mortal," said Zoroaster, "the blessed Immortals are swift."

As men's prayers are a disease of the will, so are their creeds a disease of the intellect. They say with those foolish Israelites, "Let not God speak to us, lest we die. Speak thou, speak any man with us, and we will obey." Everywhere I am hindered of meeting God in my brother, because he has shut his own temple doors and recites fables merely of his brother's, or his brother's brother's God. Every new mind is a new classification. If it prove a mind of uncommon activity and power, a Locke, a Lavoisier, a Hutton, a Bentham, a Fourier, it imposes its classification on other men, and lo! a new system. In proportion to the depth of the thought, and so to the number of the objects it touches and brings within reach of the pupil, is his complacency. But chiefly is this apparent in creeds and churches, which are also classifications of some powerful mind acting on the elemental thought of duty and man's relation to the Highest. Such is Calvinism, Quakerism, Swedenborgism. The pupil takes the same delight in subordinating everything to the new terminology as a girl who has just learned botany in seeing a new earth and new seasons thereby. It will happen for a time that the pupil will find his intellectual power has grown by the study of his master's mind. But in all unbalanced minds the classification is idolized, passes for the end and not for a speedily exhaustible means, so that the walls of the system blend to their eye in the remote horizon with the walls of the universe; the luminaries of heaven seem to them hung on the arch their master built. They cannot imagine how you aliens have any right to see—how you can see; "It must be somehow that you stole the light from us." They do not yet perceive that light, unsystematic, indomitable, will break into any cabin, even into theirs. Let them chirp awhile and call it their own. If they are honest and do well, presently their neat new pinfold will be too strait and low, will crack, will lean, will rot, and vanish, and the immortal light, all young and joyful, million-orbed, million-colored, will beam over the universe as on the first morning.

2. It is for want of self-culture that the superstition of Traveling, whose idols are Italy, England, Egypt, retains its fascination for all educated Americans. They who made England, Italy, or Greece venerable in the imagination, did so by sticking fast where they were, like an axis of the earth. In manly hours we feel that duty is our place. The soul is no traveler; the wise man stays at home, and when his necessities, his duties, on any occasion call him from his house, or into foreign lands, he is at home still and shall make men sensible by the expression of his countenance that he goes, the missionary of wisdom and virtue, and visits cities and men like a sovereign and not like an interloper or a valet.

I have no churlish objection to the circumnavigation of the globe for the purpose of art, of study, and benevolence, so that the man is first domesticated, or does not go abroad with the hope of finding somewhat greater than he knows. He who travels to be amused, or to get somewhat which he does not carry, travels away from himself, and grows old even in youth among old things. In Thebes, in Palmyra, his will and mind have become old and dilapidated as they. He carries ruins to ruins.

Traveling is a fool's paradise. Our first journeys discover to us the indifference of places. At home I dream that at Naples, at Rome, I can be intoxicated with beauty and lose my sadness. I pack my trunk, embrace my friends, embark on the sea, and at last wake up in Naples, and there beside me is the stern fact, the sad self, unrelenting, identical, that I fled from. I seek the Vatican and the palaces. I affect to be intoxicated with sights and suggestions, but I am not intoxicated. My giant goes with me wherever I go.

3. But the rage of traveling is a symptom of a deeper unsoundness affecting the whole intellectual action. The intellect is vagabond, and our system of education fosters restlessness. Our minds travel when our bodies are forced to stay at home. We imitate; and what is imitation but the traveling of the mind? Our houses are built with foreign taste; our shelves are garnished with foreign ornaments; our opinions, our tastes, our faculties, lean, and follow the Past and the Distant. The soul created the arts wherever they have flourished. It was in his own mind that the artist sought his model. It was an application of his own thought to the thing to be done and the conditions to be observed. And why need we copy the Doric or the Gothic model? Beauty, convenience, grandeur of thought and quaint expression are as near to us as to any, and if the

American artist will study with hope and love the precise thing to be done by him, considering the climate, the soil, the length of the day, the wants of the people, the habit and form of the government, he will create a house in which all these will find themselves fitted, and taste and sentiment will be satisfied also.

Insist on yourself; never imitate. Your own gift you can present every moment with the cumulative force of a whole life's cultivation; but of the adopted talent of another you have only an extemporaneous half possession. That which each can do best none but his Maker can teach him. No man yet knows what it is, nor can, till that person has exhibited it. Where is the master who could have taught Shakespeare? Where is the master who could have instructed Franklin, or Washington, or Bacon, or Newton? Every great man is a unique. The Scipionism of Scipio is precisely that part he could not borrow. Shakespeare will never be made by the study of Shakespeare. Do that which is assigned you, and you cannot hope too much or dare too much. There is at this moment for you an utterance brave and grand as that of the colossal chisel of Phidias, or trowel of the Egyptians, or the pen of Moses or Dante, but different from all these. Not possibly will the soul, all rich, all eloquent, with thousand-cloven tongue, deign to repeat itself; but if you can hear what these patriarchs say, surely you can reply to them in the same pitch of voice; for the ear and the tongue are two organs of one nature. Abide in the simple and noble regions of thy life, obey thy heart, and thou shalt reproduce the Foreworld again.

4. As our religion, our education, our art look abroad, so does our spirit of society. All men plume themselves on the improvement of society, and no man improves.

Society never advances. It recedes as fast on one side as it gains on the other. It undergoes continual changes; it is barbarous, it is civilized, it is Christianized, it is rich, it is scientific; but this change is not amelioration. For everything that is given something is taken. Society acquires new arts and loses old instincts. What a contrast between the well-clad, reading, writing, thinking American, with a watch, a pencil, and a bill of exchange in his pocket, and the naked New Zealander, whose property is a club, a spear, a mat, and an undivided twentieth of a shed to sleep under! But compare the health of the two men and you shall see that the white man has lost his aboriginal strength. If the traveler tell us truly, strike the savage with a broadax and in a day or two the flesh shall unite and heal as if you struck the blow into soft pitch, and the same blow shall send the white to his grave.

The civilized man has built a coach, but has lost the use of his feet. He is supported on crutches, but lacks so much support of muscle. He has a fine Geneva watch, but he fails of the skill to tell the hour by the sun. A

Greenwich nautical almanac he has, and so being sure of the information when he wants it, the man in the street does not know a star in the sky. The solstice he does not observe; the equinox he knows as little; and the whole bright calendar of the year is without a dial in his mind. His note-books impair his memory; his libraries overload his wit; the insurance office increases the number of accidents; and it may be a question whether machinery does not encumber; whether we have not lost by refinement some energy, by a Christianity, entrenched in establishments and forms, some vigor of wild virtue. For every Stoic was a Stoic; but in Christendom where is the Christian?

There is no more deviation in the moral standard than in the standard of height or bulk. No greater men are now than ever were. A singular equality may be observed between the great men of the first and of the last ages; nor can all the science, art, religion, and philosophy of the nineteenth century avail to educate greater men than Plutarch's heroes, three or four and twenty centuries ago. Not in time is the race progressive. Phocion, Socrates, Anaxagoras, Diogenes, are great men, but they leave no class. He who is really of their class will not be called by their name, but will be his own man, and in his turn the founder of a sect. The arts and inventions of each period are only its costume and do not invigorate men. The harm of the improved machinery may compensate its good. Hudson and Behring accomplished so much in their fishing boats as to astonish Parry and Franklin, whose equipment exhausted the resources of science and art. Galileo, with an opera glass, discovered a more splendid series of celestial phenomena than any one since. Columbus found the New World in an undecked boat. It is curious to see the periodical disuse and perishing of means and machinery which were introduced with loud laudation a few years or centuries before. The great genius returns to essential man. We reckoned the improvements of the art of war among the triumphs of science, and yet Napoleon conquered Europe by the bivouac, which consisted of falling back on naked valor and disencumbering it of all aids. The emperor held it impossible to make a perfect army, says Las Casas, "without abolishing our arms, magazines, commissaries and carriages, until, in imitation of the Roman custom, the soldier should receive his supply of corn, grind it in his hand mill, and bake his bread himself."

Society is a wave. The wave moves onward, but the water of which it is composed does not. The same particle does not rise from the valley to the ridge. Its unity is only phenomenal. The persons who make up a nation today, next year die, and their experience dies with them.

And so the reliance on property, including the reliance on govern-ments which protect it, is the want of self-reliance. Men have looked away from themselves and at things so long that they have come to esteem the religious, learned, and civil institutions as guards of property, and they deprecate assaults on these, because they feel them to be assaults on property. They measure their esteem of each other by what each has, and not by what each is. But a cultivated man becomes ashamed of his property, out of new respect for his nature. Especially he hates what he has if he sees that it is accidental—came to him by inheritance, or gift, or crime; then he feels that it is not having; it does not belong to him, has no root in him, and merely lies there because no revolution or no robber takes it away. But that which a man is, does always by necessity acquire; and what the man acquires is living property, which does not wait the beck of rulers, or mobs, or revolutions, or fire, or storm, or bankruptcies, but perpetually renews itself wherever the man breathes. "Thy lot or portion of life," said the Caliph Ali, "is seeking after thee; therefore be at rest from seeking after it." Our dependence on these foreign goods leads us to our slavish respect for numbers. The political parties meet in numerous conventions; the greater the concourse and with each new uproar of an announcement, The Delegation from Essex! The Democrats from New Hampshire! The Whigs of Maine! the young patriot feels himself stronger than before by a new thousand of eyes and arms. In like manner the reformers summon conventions and vote and resolve in multitude. Not so, O friends! will the God deign to enter and inhabit you, but by a method precisely the reverse. It is only as a man puts off all foreign support and stands alone that I see him to be strong and to prevail. He is weaker by every recruit to his banner. Is not a man better than a town? Ask nothing of men, and, in the endless mutation, thy only firm column must presently appear the upholder of all that surrounds thee. He who knows that power is inborn, that he is weak because he has looked for good out of him and elsewhere, and, so perceiving, throws himself unhesitatingly on his thought, instantly rights himself, stands in the erect position, commands his limbs, works miracles; just as a man who stands on his feet is stronger than a man who stands on his head.

So use all that is called Fortune. Most men gamble with her, and gain all, and lose all, as her wheel rolls. But do thou leave as unlawful these winnings, and deal with Cause and Effect, the chancellors of God. In the Will work and acquire, and thou hast chained the wheel of Chance, and shall sit hereafter out of fear from her rotations. A political victory, a rise of rents, the recovery of your sick or the return of your absent friend, or some other favorable event, raises your spirits, and you think good days are preparing for you. Do not believe it. Nothing can bring you peace but yourself. Nothing can bring you peace but the triumph of principles.

QUESTIONS

1. Why does Emerson think it is genius to believe that what is true for you in your private heart is true for all others?

2. What does Emerson mean when he says that each of us represents a divine idea? What does this reveal about Emerson's view of human nature?

3. How, according to Emerson, does one come to understand and accept the place that "divine providence" has for each person? What is the relationship between "divine providence" and "the genius of their age"? (170)

4. What, according to Emerson, is the primary reason that individuals are inclined not to be self-reliant?

5. Why does Emerson believe that "Whoso would be a man, must be a nonconformist"? (171)

6. Why does Emerson think that "your goodness must have some edge to it—else it is none"? (172)

7. Why does Emerson argue against giving to charities?

8. What, according to Emerson, is the force of a "proper life"? (173)

9. What "work" does Emerson think is proper work? (173)

10. Why is the great soul going to be misunderstood?

11. What is the "law of [one's] being"? (174)

12. If "no man can violate his nature," why does Emerson feel compelled to exhort individuals to be nonconformists? (174)

13. How would Emerson answer his own question: "What is the aboriginal Self, on which a universal reliance may be grounded"? (177)

14. Why does Emerson think that man "cannot be happy and strong until he too lives with nature in the present, above time"? According to Emerson, how does one live "above time"? (178)

15. Why does Emerson think that nothing can bring you peace but yourself?

FOR FURTHER REFLECTION

1. Describe someone you think fits Emerson's notion of the self-reliant person.

2. How do Emerson's definitions of "good" and "bad" follow from or depart from traditional religious teachings about "good" and "bad"?

3. Do you believe as Emerson does that "our age yields no great and perfect persons"? (181)

4. Do you agree with Emerson that the principle of "self-reliance" should govern all that we do?

5. What, if ever, should you compromise about your beliefs to please others?

6. If the poor are not Emerson's poor, then whose poor are they?

7. In what ways does Emerson appeal to ancient religious traditions? In what ways does he shake them off?

WALT WHITMAN

In his essay of 1844, "The Poet," Ralph Waldo Emerson expressed his hope that the United States would soon produce a poet who could give voice to the vast and noble experiment of America itself: "The poet is . . . the man without impediment, who sees and handles that which others dream of, traverses the whole scale of experience, and is representative of man, in virtue of being the largest power to receive and to impart." That man would be Walt Whitman (1803-1892), and his self-published volume of poetry, *Leaves of Grass* (1855), seemed to answer directly Emerson's call.

Indeed, Whitman sent Emerson an inscribed copy of the volume, bearing the now-famous portrait of the young, casually-posed bard with shirt open at the neck, self-confidently looking out at his audience. Emerson promptly wrote back to congratulate him "at the beginning of a great career." *Leaves of Grass* was revised and enlarged through eight subsequent editions. Its final version included the familiar "Song of Myself" and "Crossing Brooklyn Ferry," but also the more controversial poems—with their overt sexual content—in the "Calamus" cycle, as well as poems about the Civil War (*Drum-Taps*). The latter poems were inspired by Whitman's experience as a medical volunteer who witnessed the carnage of battle and the sometimes equally horrific surgical procedures and amputations carried out afterward in crude field hospitals.

Whitman was born on Long Island to parents with radical and nonconformist ideas. His father had been a friend of Tom Paine's, and his parents were influenced both by feminist and Quaker thinkers. Whitman read widely and independently, but he ceased his formal education at the age of twelve to become a printer's apprentice. He was editing the weekly *Long Islander* newspaper before he turned twenty. During his life, he worked as a rural schoolteacher, as a newspaper editor in New Orleans and Brooklyn, and as a federal government employee in the office of the attorney general in Washington, D.C. While in D.C., he wrote his most important prose work,

"Democratic Vistas" (1871), an essay that still captures Whitman's early Emersonian hopefulness, but also roundly excoriates the young nation for failing to live up to its bold promise and ideals. By the time of his death in 1882 in Camden, New Jersey, Whitman was a literary celebrity in America and abroad.

"Out of the Cradle Endlessly Rocking" originally appeared in the third edition of *Leaves of Grass* (1860), under the title "A Word Out of the Sea." It suggests that the poet sees his poetic vocation as a calling based on deep personal and spiritual experience, and that experience must be necessarily understood as the mature reflection by an adult on a childhood incident—in this case, trauma. Whitman's poem perfectly embodies Wordsworth's theory of poetry as "powerful feelings . . . recollected in tranquillity." The poem also prefigures Joyce's theory of the "epiphany," a profound breakthrough in understanding and insight that disrupts the pattern of ordinary everyday experience or that heightens that experience in some jarring way.

Out of the Cradle Endlessly Rocking

Out of the cradle endlessly rocking,
Out of the mocking-bird's throat, the musical shuttle,
Out of the Ninth-month midnight,
Over the sterile sands and the fields beyond, where the child leaving his
    bed wander'd alone, bareheaded, barefoot,
Down from the shower'd halo,
Up from the mystic play of shadows twining and twisting as if they
    were alive,
Out from the patches of briers and blackberries,
From the memories of the bird that chanted to me,
From your memories sad brother, from the fitful risings and fallings
    I heard,
From under that yellow half-moon late-risen and swollen as if with tears,
From those beginning notes of yearning and love there in the mist,
From the thousand responses of my heart never to cease,
From the myriad thence-arous'd words,
From the word stronger and more delicious than any,
From such as now they start the scene revisiting,
As a flock, twittering, rising, or overhead passing,
Borne hither, ere all eludes me, hurriedly,
A man, yet by these tears a little boy again,
Throwing myself on the sand, confronting the waves,
I, chanter of pains and joys, uniter of here and hereafter,
Taking all hints to use them, but swiftly leaping beyond them,
A reminiscence sing.

Once Paumanok,
When the lilac-scent was in the air and Fifth-month grass was growing,
Up this seashore in some briers,
Two feather'd guests from Alabama, two together,

And their nest, and four light-green eggs spotted with brown,
And every day the he-bird to and fro near at hand,
And every day the she-bird crouch'd on her nest, silent, with bright eyes,
And every day I, a curious boy, never too close, never disturbing them,
Cautiously peering, absorbing, translating.

Shine! shine! shine!
Pour down your warmth, great sun!
While we bask, we two together.

Two together!
Winds blow south, or winds blow north,
Day come white, or night come black,
Home, or rivers and mountains from home,
Singing all time, minding no time,
While we two keep together.

Till of a sudden,
May-be kill'd, unknown to her mate,
One forenoon the she-bird crouch'd not on the nest,
Nor return'd that afternoon, nor the next,
Nor ever appear'd again.

And thenceforward all summer in the sound of the sea,
And at night under the full of the moon in calmer weather,
Over the hoarse surging of the sea,
Or flitting from brier to brier by day,
I saw, I heard at intervals the remaining one, the he-bird,
The solitary guest from Alabama.

Blow! blow! blow!
Blow up sea-winds along Paumanok's shore;
I wait and I wait till you blow my mate to me.

Yes, when the stars glisten'd,
All night long on the prong of a moss-scallop'd stake,
Down almost amid the slapping waves,
Sat the lone singer wonderful causing tears.

He call'd on his mate,
He pour'd forth the meanings which I of all men know.

Yes my brother I know,
The rest might not, but I have treasur'd every note,
For more than once dimly down to the beach gliding,
Silent, avoiding the moonbeams, blending myself with the shadows,
Recalling now the obscure shapes, the echoes, the sounds and sights
    after their sorts,
The white arms out in the breakers tirelessly tossing,
I, with bare feet, a child, the wind wafting my hair,
Listen'd long and long.

Listen'd to keep, to sing, now translating the notes,
Following you my brother.

Soothe! soothe! soothe!
Close on its wave soothes the wave behind,
And again another behind embracing and lapping, every one close,
But my love soothes not me, not me.

Low hangs the moon, it rose late,
It is lagging—O I think it is heavy with love, with love.

O madly the sea pushes upon the land,
With love, with love.

O night! do I not see my love fluttering out among the breakers?
What is that little black thing I see there in the white?

Loud! loud! loud!
Loud I call to you, my love!

High and clear I shoot my voice over the waves,
Surely you must know who is here, is here,
You must know who I am, my love.

Low-hanging moon!
What is that dusky spot in your brown yellow?
O it is the shape, the shape of my mate!
O moon do not keep her from me any longer.

Land! land! O land!
Whichever way I turn, O I think you could give me my mate back
    again if you only would,
For I am almost sure I see her dimly whichever way I look.

O rising stars!
Perhaps the one I want so much will rise, will rise with some of you.

O throat! O trembling throat!
Sound clearer through the atmosphere!
Pierce the woods, the earth,
Somewhere listening to catch you must be the one I want.

Shake out carols!
Solitary here, the night's carols!
Carols of lonesome love! death's carols!
Carols under that lagging, yellow, waning moon!
O under that moon where she droops almost down into the sea!
O reckless despairing carols.

But soft! sink low!
Soft! let me just murmur,
And do you wait a moment you husky-nois'd sea,
For somewhere I believe I heard my mate responding to me,
So faint, I must be still, be still to listen,
But not altogether still, for then she might not come immediately to me.

Hither my love!
Here I am! here!
With this just-sustain'd note I announce myself to you,
This gentle call is for you my love, for you.

Do not be decoy'd elsewhere,
That is the whistle of the wind, it is not my voice,
That is the fluttering, the fluttering of the spray,
Those are the shadows of leaves.

O darkness! O in vain!
O I am very sick and sorrowful.

O brown halo in the sky near the moon, drooping upon the sea!
O troubled reflection in the sea!
O throat! O throbbing heart!
And I singing uselessly, uselessly all the night.

O past! O happy life! O songs of joy!
In the air, in the woods, over fields,
Loved! loved! loved! loved! loved!
But my mate no more, no more with me!
We two together no more.

The aria sinking,
All else continuing, the stars shining,
The winds blowing, the notes of the bird continuous echoing,
With angry moans the fierce old mother incessantly moaning,
On the sands of Paumanok's shore gray and rustling,
The yellow half-moon enlarged, sagging down, drooping, the face
    of the sea almost touching,
The boy ecstatic, with his bare feet the waves, with his hair the
    atmosphere dallying,
The love in the heart long pent, now loose, now at last tumultuously
    bursting,
The aria's meaning, the ears, the soul, swiftly depositing,
The strange tears down the cheeks coursing,
The colloquy there, the trio, each uttering,
The undertone, the savage old mother incessantly crying,
To the boy's soul's questions sullenly timing, some drown'd secret hissing,
To the outsetting bard.

Demon or bird! (said the boy's soul,)
Is it indeed toward your mate you sing? or is it really to me?
For I, that was a child, my tongue's use sleeping, now I have heard you,
Now in a moment I know what I am for, I awake,
And already a thousand singers, a thousand songs, clearer, louder,
    and more sorrowful than yours,
A thousand warbling echoes have started to life within me, never to die.

O you singer solitary, singing by yourself, projecting me,
O solitary me listening, never more shall I cease perpetuating you,
Never more shall I escape, never more the reverberations,
Never more the cries of unsatisfied love be absent from me,
Never again leave me to be the peaceful child I was before what there
    in the night,
By the sea under the yellow and sagging moon,
The messenger there arous'd, the fire, the sweet hell within,
The unknown want, the destiny of me.

O give me the clew! (it lurks in the night here somewhere,)
O if I am to have so much, let me have more!

A word then, (for I will conquer it,)
The word final, superior to all,
Subtle, sent up—what is it?—I listen;
Are you whispering it, and have been all the time, you seawaves?
Is that it from your liquid rims and wet sands?

Whereto answering, the sea,
Delaying not, hurrying not,
Whisper'd me through the night, and very plainly before daybreak,
Lisp'd to me the low and delicious word death,
And again death, death, death, death,
Hissing melodious, neither like the bird nor like my arous'd
    child's heart,
But edging near as privately for me rustling at my feet,
Creeping thence steadily up to my ears and laving me softly all over,
Death, death, death, death, death.

Which I do not forget,
But fuse the song of my dusky demon and brother,
That he sang to me in the moonlight on Paumanok's gray beach,
With the thousand responsive songs at random,
My own songs awaked from that hour,
And with them the key, the word up from the waves,
The word of the sweetest song and all songs,
That strong and delicious word which, creeping to my feet,
(Or like some old crone rocking the cradle, swathed in sweet garments,
    bending aside,)
The sea whisper'd me.

QUESTIONS

1. Why does the poet sing this reminiscence?

2. Why does the poet think that he "of all men" knows the he-bird's meanings? (194)

3. Why does his experience on the sands of Paumanok let loose the poet's long pent-up love?

4. Why does the poet personify the sea in this particular way?

5. What is the "colloquy"? The "trio"? (197) What are they doing to the poet?

6. Why does hearing the he-bird's song awaken the child to what he is for?

7. Why is the boy's soul uncertain whether the singer is demon or bird?

8. In what sense is the bird "projecting" the poet? (197)

9. Why does the poet tell the solitary singer, "Never again leave me to be the peaceful child I was before what there in the night, / . . . The messenger there arous'd, the fire, the sweet hell within"? (197)

10. To whom does the poet address the query, "O give me the clew!"? (197)

11. Why does the poet insist that he will "conquer" the "word"? (197)

12. Why is the word *death* "delicious" to the poet? In what sense is it "the key"? (198)

13. Why is the sea "hissing melodious, neither like the bird nor like my arous'd child's heart"? (198)

14. How are we meant to feel about the "old crone rocking the cradle"? (198) What does she represent?

FOR FURTHER REFLECTION

1. Why is death represented in this poem as a woman?

2. What does the poet learn from the mocking-bird's insistence on "singing uselessly, uselessly all the night"? (196) In what way is the poet like the bird?

3. What experience or epiphany in childhood or adolescence produced your sense of vocation? Can a sense of vocation come about in any other way?

ALEXIS DE TOCQUEVILLE

The author of one of the most significant studies of American democratic society and government was a liberal French aristocrat whose father had survived the excesses of the Reign of Terror during the French Revolution. Alexis de Tocqueville, born in 1805, was thus keenly aware of both the advantages and shortcomings of the Old Regime, as well as the potential dangers in the transition to democratic rule based on principles of social and political equality.

Though he is now known primarily for his writings, including *Democracy in America* and *The Old Regime and the Revolution*, throughout his life Tocqueville's ambition was to be a career politician. As the first step toward this goal, he moved easily and early into government service through his father's close ties to the court of Charles X at Versailles. Following the July revolution of 1830 that deposed the Bourbon king, Tocqueville became more convinced than ever that France was headed toward the kind of egalitarian society that was already flourishing in America.

In 1831 and 1832, Tocqueville traveled to the United States to conduct a study of the prison system for the purpose of providing France with a model for its own reforms. Although he did in fact publish his findings on this topic, the more important result of his trip was *Democracy in America.* A highly efficient itinerary during his nine-month stay allowed Tocqueville to experience the entire range of regions and living conditions that comprised America, from the Eastern cities to the Western frontier. In addition, he met Americans of all classes, including such prominent figures as John Quincy Adams, Andrew Jackson, Daniel Webster, and Sam Houston. Published in two parts in 1835 and 1840, *Democracy in America* was immediately recognized as the work of a significant political scientist and brought Tocqueville to the center of the most important intellectual circles in France and England. As a result, he corresponded frequently with the English philosopher John Stuart Mill.

After 1839, Tocqueville realized his political ambitions through his election to the Chamber of Deputies and later the Constituent Assembly, where he served on the committee that wrote the constitution for the Second Republic. His experience of the revolution of 1848 led Tocqueville to view the dependence on state welfare advocated by the revolution leaders as incompatible with individual economic independence, which he valued as a key component of democracy.

Written during his last years, *The Old Regime and the Revolution* expressed Tocqueville's deep concern at what he perceived as a dangerous tendency of democratic societies, especially that of his contemporary France, to become susceptible to stagnation and new forms of despotism. Tocqueville died in 1859 while returning from one of his many visits to England, a country that, along with America, he valued as a useful example for his own.

The first part of *Democracy in America* deals incisively with the ways that the structure and form of government in the United States are conducive to the maintenance and evolution of democratic society. However, the far longer second part, from which the following selection is taken, is a searching study of how equality influences all aspects of that society.

In this selection, Tocqueville asks us to consider the characteristics of American democracy through the ways in which society, government, and the self-interest of individuals are inextricably bound with each other. When he asks his readers, "What do you expect from society and its government?" he is challenging us to reflect, as he does, on both the advantages and disadvantages that arise from a society in which equality of condition results in constant agitation and restlessness at all levels.

Democracy in America (selection)

What the Real Advantages Are Which American Society Derives from the Government of the Democracy

B efore I enter upon the subject of the present chapter, I am induced to remind the reader of what I have more than once adverted to in the course of this book. The political institutions of the United States appear to me to be one of the forms of government that a democracy may adopt; but I do not regard the American Constitution as the best, or as the only one, that a democratic people may establish. In showing the advantages which the Americans derive from the government of democracy, I am therefore very far from meaning, or from believing, that similar advantages can only be obtained from the same laws.

General Tendency of the Laws Under the Rule of the American Democracy and Habits of Those Who Apply Them

Defects of a democratic government easy to be discovered. Its advantages only to be discerned by long observation. Democracy in America often inexpert, but the general tendency of the laws advantageous. In the American democracy public officers have no permanent interests distinct from those of the majority. Result of this state of things.

The defects and the weaknesses of a democratic government may very readily be discovered; they are demonstrated by the most flagrant instances, while its beneficial influence is less perceptibly exercised. A single glance suffices to detect its evil consequences, but its good qualities can only be discerned by long observation. The laws of the American democracy are frequently defective or incomplete; they sometimes attack vested rights or give a sanction to others that are dangerous to the com-

This selection is taken from Chapter 14, "What the Real Advantages Are Which American Society Derives from the Government of the Democracy."

munity; but even if they were good, the frequent changes which they undergo would be an evil. How comes it, then, that the American republics prosper and maintain their position?

In the consideration of laws, a distinction must be carefully observed between the end at which they aim and the means by which they are directed to that end, and between their absolute and their relative excellence. If it be the intention of the legislator to favor the interests of the minority at the expense of the majority, and if the measures he takes are so combined as to accomplish the object he has in view with the least possible expense of time and exertion, the law may be well drawn up, although its purpose be bad; the more efficacious it is, the greater is the mischief that it causes.

Democratic laws generally tend to promote the welfare of the greatest possible number; for they emanate from the majority of the citizens, who are subject to error, but who cannot have an interest opposed to their own advantage. The laws of an aristocracy tend, on the contrary, to concentrate wealth and power in the hands of the minority because an aristocracy, by its very nature, constitutes a minority. It may therefore be asserted, as a general proposition, that the purpose of a democracy in the conduct of its legislation, is useful to a greater number of citizens than that of an aristocracy. This is, however, the sum total of its advantages.

Aristocracies are infinitely more expert in the science of legislation than democracies ever can be. They are possessed of a self-control that protects them from the errors of temporary excitement; and they form lasting designs, which they mature with the assistance of favorable opportunities. Aristocratic government proceeds with the dexterity of art; it understands how to make the collective force of all its laws converge at the same time to a given point. Such is not the case with democracies, whose laws are almost always ineffective or inopportune. The means of democracy are therefore more imperfect than those of aristocracy, and the measures which it unwittingly adopts are frequently opposed to its own cause; but the object it has in view is more useful.

Let us now imagine a community so organized by nature, or by its constitution, that it can support the transitory action of bad laws, and that it can await, without destruction, the general tendency of the legislation: we shall then be able to conceive that a democratic government, notwit standing its defects, will be most fitted to conduce to the prosperity of this community. This is precisely what has occurred in the United States; and I repeat, what I have before remarked, that the great advantage of the Americans consists in their being able to commit faults that they may afterward repair.

An analogous observation may be made respecting public officers. It is easy to perceive that the American democracy frequently errs in the choice of the individuals to whom it entrusts the power of the administration; but it is more difficult to say why the state prospers under their rule. In the first place it is to be remarked, that if in a democratic state the governors have less honesty and less capacity than elsewhere, the governed on the other hand are more enlightened and more attentive to their interests. As the people in democracies is more incessantly vigilant in its affairs and more jealous of its rights, it prevents its representatives from abandoning that general line of conduct which its own interest prescribes. In the second place it must be remembered that if the democratic magistrate is more apt to misuse his power, he possesses it for a shorter period of time. But there is yet another reason which is still more general and conclusive. It is no doubt of importance to the welfare of nations that they should be governed by men of talents and virtue; but it is perhaps still more important that the interests of those men should not differ from the interests of the community at large; for if such were the case, virtues of a high order might become useless, and talents might be turned to a bad account. I say that it is important that the interests of the persons in authority should not conflict with or oppose the interests of the community at large. But I do not insist upon their having the same interests as the *whole* population, because I am not aware that such a state of things ever existed in any country.

No political form has hitherto been discovered, which is equally favorable to the prosperity and the development of all the classes into which society is divided. These classes continue to form, as it were, a certain number of distinct nations in the same nation; and experience has shown that it is no less dangerous to place the fate of these classes exclusively in the hands of any one of them, than it is to make one people the arbiter of the destiny of another. When the rich alone govern, the interest of the poor is always endangered; and when the poor make the laws, that of the rich incurs very serious risks. The advantage of democracy does not consist, therefore, as has sometimes been asserted, in favoring the prosperity of all, but simply in contributing to the well-being of the greatest possible number.

The men who are entrusted with the direction of public affairs in the United States are frequently inferior, both in point of capacity and of morality, to those whom aristocratic institutions would raise to power. But their interest is identified and confounded with that of the majority of their fellow citizens. They may frequently be faithless and frequently mistaken, but they will never systematically adopt a line of conduct opposed to the will of the majority. It is impossible that they should give a dangerous or an exclusive tendency to the government.

The maladministration of a democratic magistrate is a mere isolated fact, which only occurs during the short period for which he is elected. Corruption and incapacity do not act as common interests, which may connect men permanently with one another. A corrupt or an incapable magistrate will not concert his measures with another magistrate, simply because that individual is as corrupt and as incapable as himself; and these two men will never unite their endeavors to promote the corruption and inaptitude of their remote posterity. The ambition and the maneuvers of the one will serve, on the contrary, to unmask the other. The vices of a magistrate, in democratic states, are usually peculiar to his own person.

But under aristocratic governments public men are swayed by the interest of their order, which, if it is sometimes confounded with the interests of the majority, is very frequently distinct from them. This interest is the common and lasting bond that unites them together; it induces them to coalesce and to combine their efforts in order to attain an end that does not always ensure the greatest happiness of the greatest number. It serves not only to connect the persons in authority, but to unite them to a considerable portion of the community, since a numerous body of citizens belongs to the aristocracy, without being invested with official functions. The aristocratic magistrate is therefore constantly supported by a portion of the community, as well as by the government of which he is a member.

The common purpose that connects the interest of the magistrates in aristocracies, with that of a portion of their contemporaries, identifies it with that of future generations. Their influence belongs to the future as much as to the present. The aristocratic magistrate is urged at the same time, toward the same point, by the passions of the community, by his own, and I may almost add by those of his posterity. Is it, then, wonderful that he does not resist such repeated impulses? And indeed aristocracies are often carried away by the spirit of their order without being corrupted by it. They unconsciously fashion society to their own ends and prepare it for their own descendants.

The English aristocracy is perhaps the most liberal that ever existed, and no body of men has ever, uninterruptedly, furnished so many honorable and enlightened individuals to the government of a country. It cannot, however, escape observation, that in the legislation of England the good of the poor has been sacrificed to the advantage of the rich, and the rights of the majority to the privileges of the few. The consequence is, that England, at the present day, combines the extremes of fortune in the bosom of her society; and her perils and calamities are almost equal to her power and her renown.

In the United States, where the public officers have no interests to promote connected with their caste, the general and constant influence of the government is beneficial, although the individuals who conduct it are frequently unskillful and sometimes contemptible. There is indeed a secret tendency in democratic institutions to render the exertions of the citizens subservient to the prosperity of the community, notwithstanding their private vices and mistakes; while in aristocratic institutions there is a propensity, which, notwithstanding the talents and the virtues of those who conduct the government, leads them to contribute to the evils which oppress their fellow creatures. In aristocratic governments public men may frequently do injuries which they do not intend and in democratic states they produce advantages which they never thought of.

Public Spirit in the United States

Patriotism of instinct. Patriotism of reflection. Their different characteristics. Nations ought to strive to acquire the second when the first has disappeared. Efforts of the Americans to acquire it. Interest of the individual intimately connected with that of the country.

There is one sort of patriotic attachment which principally arises from that instinctive, disinterested, and undefinable feeling that connects the affections of man with his birthplace. This natural fondness is united to a taste for ancient customs and to a reverence for ancestral traditions of the past; those who cherish it love their country as they love the mansion of their fathers. They enjoy the tranquillity that it affords them; they cling to the peaceful habits that they have contracted within its bosom; they are attached to the reminiscences that it awakens, and they are even pleased by the state of obedience in which they are placed. This patriotism is sometimes stimulated by religious enthusiasm, and then it is capable of making the most prodigious efforts. It is in itself a kind of religion: it does not reason, but it acts from the impulse of faith and of sentiment. By some nations the monarch has been regarded as a personification of the country; and the fervor of patriotism being converted into the fervor of loyalty, they took a sympathetic pride in his conquests, and gloried in his power. At one time, under the ancient monarchy, the French felt a sort of satisfaction in the sense of their dependence upon the arbitrary pleasure of their king, and they were wont to say with pride, "We are the subjects of the most powerful king in the world."

But, like all instinctive passions, this kind of patriotism is more apt to prompt transient exertion than to supply the motives of continuous endeavor. It may save the state in critical circumstances, but it will not unfrequently allow the nation to decline in the midst of peace. While the manners of a people are simple, and its faith unshaken; while society is steadily based upon traditional institutions, whose legitimacy has never been contested, this instinctive patriotism is wont to endure.

But there is another species of attachment to a country which is more rational than the one we have been describing. It is perhaps less generous and less ardent, but it is more fruitful and more lasting; it is coeval with the spread of knowledge, it is nurtured by the laws, it grows by the exercise of civil rights, and, in the end, it is confounded with the personal interest of the citizen. A man comprehends the influence that the prosperity of his country has upon his own welfare; he is aware that the laws authorize him to contribute his assistance to that prosperity, and he labors to promote it as a portion of his interest in the first place and as a portion of his right in the second.

But epochs sometimes occur in the course of the existence of a nation, at which the ancient customs of a people are changed, public morality destroyed, religious belief disturbed, and the spell of tradition broken, while the diffusion of knowledge yet imperfect, and the civil rights of the community are ill secured or confined within very narrow limits. The country their assumes a dim and dubious shape in the eyes of the citizens; they no longer behold it in the soil that they inhabit, for that soil is to them a dull inanimate clod; nor in the usages of their forefathers, which they have been taught to took upon as a debasing yoke; nor in religion, for of that they doubt; nor in the laws, which do not originate in their own authority; nor in the legislator, whom they fear and despise. The country is lost to their senses, they can neither discover it under its own nor under borrowed features, and they entrench themselves within the dull precincts of a narrow egotism. They are emancipated from prejudice without having acknowledged the empire of reason; they are neither animated by the instinctive patriotism of monarchical subjects, nor by the thinking patriotism of republican citizens; but they have stopped halfway between the two, in the midst of confusion and of distress.

In this predicament, to retreat is impossible; for a people cannot restore the vivacity of its earlier times, any more than a man can return to the innocence and the bloom of childhood: such things may be regretted, but they cannot be renewed. The only thing, then, that remains to be done is to proceed and to accelerate the union of private with public interests, since the period of disinterested patriotism is gone by forever.

I am certainly very far from averring that, in order to obtain this result, the exercise of political rights should be immediately granted to all the members of the community. But I maintain that the most powerful, and perhaps the only means of interesting men in the welfare of their country, which we still possess, is to make them partakers in the government. At the present time civic zeal seems to me to be inseparable from the exercise of political rights; and I hold that the number of citizens will be found to augment or to decrease in Europe in proportion as those rights are extended.

In the United States, the inhabitants were thrown but as yesterday upon the soil that they now occupy, and they brought neither customs nor traditions with them there; they meet each other for the first time with no previous acquaintance; in short, the instinctive love of their country can scarcely exist in their minds. But every one takes as zealous an interest in the affairs of his township, his county, and of the whole state, as if they were his own, because everyone, in his sphere, takes an active part in the government of society.

The lower orders in the United States are alive to the perception of the influence exercised by the general prosperity upon their own welfare; and simple as this observation is, it is one that is but too rarely made by the people. But in America the people regards this prosperity as the result of its own exertions; the citizen looks upon the fortune of the public as his private interest, and he cooperates in its success, not so much from a sense of pride or of duty, as from, what I shall venture to term, cupidity.

It is unnecessary to study the institutions and the history of the Americans in order to discover the truth of this remark, for their manners render it sufficiently evident. As the American participates in all that is done in his country, he thinks himself obliged to defend whatever may be censured; for it is not only his country that is attacked upon these occasions, but it is himself. The consequence is that his national pride resorts to a thousand artifices and to all the petty tricks of individual vanity.

Nothing is more embarrassing in the ordinary intercourse of life than this irritable patriotism of the Americans. A stranger may be very well inclined to praise many of the institutions of their country, but he begs permission to blame some of the peculiarities that he observes—a permission that is however inexorably refused. America is therefore a free country, in which, lest anybody should be hurt by your remarks, you are not allowed to speak freely of private individuals or of the state, of the citizens or of the authorities, of public or of private undertakings, or, in short, of anything at all, except it be of the climate and the soil. Even then Americans will be found ready to defend either the one or the other as if they had been contrived by the inhabitants of the country.

In our times, option must be made between the patriotism of all and the government of a few; for the force and activity that the first confers are irreconcilable with the guarantees of tranquillity that the second furnishes.

Notion of Rights in the United States

No great people without a notion of rights. How the notion of rights can be given to people. Respect of rights in the United States. Whence it arises.

After the idea of virtue, I know no higher principle than that of right; or to speak more accurately, these two ideas are commingled in one. The idea of right is simply that of virtue introduced into the political world. It is the idea of right that enabled men to define anarchy and tyranny and that taught them to remain independent without arrogance, as well as to obey without servility. The man who submits to violence is debased by his compliance; but when he obeys the mandate of one who possesses that right of authority which he acknowledges in a fellow creature, he rises in some measure above the person who delivers the command. There are no great men without virtue, and there are no great nations—it may almost be added that there would be no society—without the notion of rights; for what is the condition of a mass of rational and intelligent beings who are only united together by the bond of force?

I am persuaded that the only means that we possess at the present time of inculcating the notion of rights and of rendering it, as it were, palpable to the senses, is to invest all the members of the community with the peaceful exercise of certain rights: this is very clearly seen in children, who are men without the strength and the experience of manhood. When a child begins to move in the midst of the objects that surround him, he is instinctively led to turn everything that he can lay his hands upon to his own purposes; he has no notion of the property of others; but as he gradually learns the value of things and begins to perceive that he may in his turn be deprived of his possessions, he becomes more circumspect, and he observes those rights in others which he wishes to have respected in himself. The principle that the child derives from the possession of his toys is taught to the man by the objects that he may call his own. In America those complaints against property in general, which are so frequent in Europe, are never heard, because in America there are no paupers. As everyone has property of his own to defend, everyone recognizes the principle upon which he holds it.

The same thing occurs in the political world. In America the lowest classes have conceived a very high notion of political rights, because they exercise those rights. They refrain from attacking those of other people, in order to ensure their own from attack. While in Europe the same classes sometimes recalcitrate even against the supreme power, the American submits without a murmur to the authority of the pettiest magistrate.

This truth is exemplified by the most trivial details of national peculiarities. In France very few pleasures are exclusively reserved for the higher classes. The poor are admitted wherever the rich are received, and they consequently behave with propriety and respect whatever contributes to the enjoyments in which they themselves participate. In England, where wealth has a monopoly of amusement as well as of power, complaints are made that whenever the poor happen to steal into the enclosures that are reserved for the pleasures of the rich, they commit acts of wanton mischief. Can this be wondered at, since care has been taken that they should have nothing to lose?

The government of the democracy brings the notion of political rights to the level of the humblest citizens, just as the dissemination of wealth brings the notion of property within the reach of all the members of the community. I confess that, to my mind, this is one of its greatest advantages. I do not assert that it is easy to teach men to exercise political rights; but I maintain that when it is possible, the effects that result from it are highly important. I add that if there ever was a time at which such an attempt ought to be made, that time is our own. It is clear that the influence of religious belief is shaken and that the notion of divine rights is declining. It is evident that public morality is vitiated, and the notion of moral rights is also disappearing. These are general symptoms of the substitution of argument for faith, and of calculation for the impulses of sentiment. If, in the midst of this general disruption, you do not succeed in connecting the notion of rights with that of personal interest, which is the only immutable point in the human heart, what means will you have of governing the world except by fear? When I am told that since the laws are weak and the populace is wild, since passions are excited and the authority of virtue is paralyzed, no measures must be taken to increase the rights of the democracy, I reply that it is for these very reasons that some measures of the kind must be taken. I am persuaded that governments are still more interested in taking them than society at large, because governments are liable to be destroyed, and society cannot perish.

I am not, however, inclined to exaggerate the example that America furnishes. In those states the people are invested with political rights at a time when they could scarcely be abused, for the citizens were few in number and simple in their manners. As they have increased, the Americans have not augmented the power of the democracy, but they have, if I may use the expression, extended its dominions.

It cannot be doubted that the moment at which political rights are granted to a people that had before been without them, is a very critical, though it be a necessary, one. A child may kill before he is aware of the value of life; he may deprive another person of his property before he is aware that his own may be taken away from him. The lower orders, when first they are invested with political rights, stand, in relation to those rights, in the same position as the child does to the whole of nature, and the celebrated adage may then be applied to them: *homo puer robustus*. This truth may even be perceived in America. The states in which the citizens have enjoyed their rights longest are those in which they make the best use of them.

It cannot be repeated too often that nothing is more fertile in prodigies than the art of being free, but there is nothing more arduous than the apprenticeship of liberty. Such is not the case with despotic institutions. Despotism often promises to make amends for a thousand previous ills. It supports the right, it protects the oppressed, and it maintains public order. The nation is lulled by the temporary prosperity that accrues to it, until it is roused to a sense of its own misery. Liberty, on the contrary, is generally established in the midst of agitation, it is perfected by civil discord, and its benefits cannot be appreciated until it is already old.

Respect for the Law in the United States

Respect of the Americans for the law. Parental affection that they entertain for it. Personal interest of everyone to increase the authority of the law.

It is not always feasible to consult the whole people, either directly or indirectly, in the formation of the law. But it cannot be denied that when such a measure is possible, the authority of the law is very much augmented. This popular origin, which impairs the excellence and the wisdom of legislation, contributes prodigiously to increase its power. There is an amazing strength in the expression of the determination of a whole people; and when it declares itself, the imagination of those who are most inclined to contest it is overawed by its authority. The truth of this fact is very well known by parties. They consequently strive to make out a majority whenever they can. If they have not the greater numbers of voters on their side, they assert that the true majority abstained from voting. If they are foiled even there, they have recourse to the body of those persons who had no votes to give.

In the United States, except slaves, servants, and paupers in the receipt of relief from the townships, there is no class of persons who do not exercise the elective franchise and who do not indirectly contribute to make the laws. Those who design to attack the laws must consequently either modify the opinion of the nation or trample upon its decision.

A second reason, which is still more weighty, may be further adduced. In the United States every one is personally interested in enforcing the obedience of the whole community to the law; for as the minority may shortly rally the majority to its principles, it is interested in professing that respect for the decrees of the legislator, which it may soon have occasion to claim for its own. However irksome an enactment may be, the citizen of the United States complies with it, not only because it is the work of the majority, but because it originates in his own authority; and he regards it as a contract to which he is himself a party.

In the United States, then, that numerous and turbulent multitude does not exist, which always looks upon the law as its natural enemy and accordingly surveys it with fear and with distrust. It is impossible, on the other hand, not to perceive that all classes display the utmost reliance upon the legislation of their country, and that they are attached to it by a kind of parental affection.

I am wrong, however, in saying all classes; for as in America the European scale of authority is inverted. The wealthy are there placed in a position analogous to that of the poor in the Old World, and it is the opulent classes that frequently look upon the law with suspicion. I have already observed that the advantage of democracy is not, as has been sometimes asserted, that it protects the interests of the whole community, but simply that it protects those of the majority. In the United States, where the poor rule, the rich have always some reason to dread the abuses of their power. This natural anxiety of the rich may produce a sullen dissatisfaction, but society is not disturbed by it; for the same reason that induces the rich to withhold their confidence in the legislative authority makes them obey its mandates. Their wealth, which prevents them from making the law, prevents them from withstanding it. Among civilized nations revolts are rarely excited except by such persons as have nothing to lose by them. If the laws of a democracy are not always worthy of respect, at least they always obtain it: for those who usually infringe the laws have no excuse for not complying with the enactments they have themselves made, and by which they are themselves benefited, while the citizens whose interests might be promoted by the infraction of them, are induced, by their character and their station, to submit to the decisions of the legislature, whatever they may be. Besides which, the people in America obey the law not only because it emanates from the popular authority, but because that authority may modify it in any points that may prove vexatory. A law is observed because it is a self-imposed evil in the first place and an evil of transient duration in the second.

Activity Which Pervades All The Branches Of The Body Politic In The United States; Influence Which It Exercises Upon Society

> More difficult to conceive the political activity that pervades the United States than the freedom and equality that reign there. The great activity that perpetually agitates the legislative bodies is only an episode to the general activity. Difficult for an American to confine himself to his own business. Political agitation extends to all social intercourse. Commercial activity of the Americans partly attributable to this cause. Indirect advantages that society derives from a democratic government.

On passing from a country in which free institutions are established to one where they do not exist, the traveler is struck by the change. In the former all is bustle and activity; in the latter everything is calm and motionless. In the one, amelioration and progress are the general topics of inquiry; in the other, it seems as if the community only aspired to repose in the enjoyment of the advantages that it has acquired. Nevertheless, the country that exerts itself so strenuously to promote its welfare is generally more wealthy and more prosperous than the country that appears to be so contented with its lot. And when we compare them together, we can scarcely conceive how so many new wants are daily felt in the former, while so few seem to occur in the latter.

If this remark is applicable to those free countries in which monarchical and aristocratic institutions subsist, it is still more striking with regard to democratic republics. In these states it is not only a portion of the people that is busied with the amelioration of its social condition, but the whole community is engaged in the task. It is not the exigencies and the convenience of a single class for which a provision is to be made, but the exigencies and the convenience of all ranks of life.

It is not impossible to conceive the surpassing liberty that the Americans enjoy. Some idea may likewise be formed of the extreme equality that subsists among them, but the political activity that pervades the United States must be seen in order to be understood. No sooner do you set foot upon the American soil than you are stunned by a kind of tumult. A confused clamor is heard on every side, and a thousand simultaneous voices demand the immediate satisfaction of their social wants. Everything is in motion around you. Here, the people of one quarter of a town are met to decide upon the building of a church. There, the election of a representative is going on. A little further, the delegates of a district are posting to the town in order to consult upon some local improvements. Or in another place the laborers of a village quit their plows to deliberate upon the project of a road or a public school. Meetings are called for the sole purpose of declaring their disapprobation of the line of conduct pursued by the government, while in other assemblies the citizens salute the authorities of the day as the fathers of their country. Societies are formed that regard drunkenness as the principal cause of the evils under which the state labors, and which solemnly bind themselves to give a constant example of temperance.[1]

The great political agitation of the American legislative bodies, which is the only kind of excitement that attracts the attention of foreign countries, is a mere episode or a sort of continuation of the universal movement that originates in the lowest classes of the people and extends

---

1. At the time of my stay in the United States, the temperance societies already consisted of more than 270,000 members. Their effect had been to diminish the consumption of fermented liquors by 500,000 gallons per annum in the state of Pennsylvania alone.

successively to all the ranks of society. It is impossible to spend more efforts in the pursuit of enjoyment.

The cares of political life engross a most prominent place in the occupation of a citizen in the United States. And almost the only pleasure of which an American has any idea, is to take a part in the government and to discuss the part he has taken. This feeling pervades the most trifling habits of life. Even the women frequently attend public meetings and listen to political harangues as a recreation after their household labors. Debating clubs are to a certain extent a substitute for theatrical entertainments: an American cannot converse, but he can discuss; and when he attempts to talk he falls into a dissertation. He speaks to you as if he was addressing a meeting. If he should chance to warm in the course of the discussion, he will infallibly say "Gentlemen," to the person with whom he is conversing.

In some countries the inhabitants display a certain repugnance to avail themselves of the political privileges with which the law invests them. It would seem that they set too high a value upon their time to spend it on the interests of the community. They prefer to withdraw within the exact limits of a wholesome egotism, marked out by four sunk fences and a quickset hedge. But if an American were condemned to confine his activity to his own affairs, he would be robbed of one half of his existence. He would feel an immense void in the life which he is accustomed to lead, and his wretchedness would be unbearable.[2] I am persuaded that if ever a despotic government is established in America, it will find it more difficult to surmount the habits which free institutions have engendered, than to conquer the attachment of the citizens to freedom.

This ceaseless agitation, which democratic government has introduced into the political world, influences all social intercourse. I am not sure that upon the whole this is not the greatest advantage of democracy. I am much less inclined to applaud it for what it does, than for what it causes to be done.

It is incontestable that people frequently conduct public business very ill. But it is impossible that the lower orders should take a part in public business without extending the circle of their ideas and without quitting the ordinary routine of their mental acquirements. The humblest individual who is called upon to cooperate in the government of society acquires a certain degree of self-respect. As he possesses authority, he can command the services of minds much more enlightened than

---

2. The same remark was made at Rome under the first Caesars. Montesquieu somewhere alludes to the excessive despondency of certain Roman citizens who, after the excitement of political life, were all at once flung back into the stagnation of private life.

his own. He is canvassed by a multitude of applicants, who seek to deceive him in a thousand different ways, but who instruct him by their deceit. He takes a part in political undertakings that did not originate in his own conception, but that give him a taste for undertakings of the kind. New ameliorations are daily pointed out in the property that he holds in common with others, and this gives him the desire of improving that property which is more peculiarly his own. He is perhaps neither happier nor better than those who came before him, but be is better informed and more active. I have no doubt that the democratic institutions of the United States, joined to the physical constitution of the country, are the cause (not the direct, as is so often asserted, but the indirect cause) of the prodigious commercial activity of the inhabitants. It is not engendered by the laws, but the people learn how to promote it by the experience derived from legislation.

When the opponents of democracy assert that a single individual performs the duties which he undertakes, much better than the government of the community, it appears to me that they are perfectly right. The government of an individual, supposing an equality of instruction on either side, is more consistent, more persevering, and more accurate than that of a multitude, and it is much better qualified judiciously to discriminate the characters of the men it employs. If any deny what I advance, they have certainly never seen a democratic government or have formed their opinion upon very partial evidence. It is true that even when local circumstances and the disposition of the people allow democratic institutions to subsist, they never display a regular and methodical system of government. Democratic liberty is far from accomplishing all the projects it undertakes, with the skill of an adroit despotism. It frequently abandons them before they have borne their fruits or risks them when the consequences may prove dangerous. In the end it produces more than any absolute government, and if it does fewer things well, it does a greater number of things. Under its sway, the transactions of the public administration are not nearly so important as what is done by private exertion. Democracy does not confer the most skillful kind of government upon the people, but it produces that which the most skillful governments are frequently unable to awaken, namely, an all-pervading and restless activity, a superabundant force, and an energy that is inseparable from it, and which may under favorable circumstances, beget the most amazing benefits. These are the true advantages of democracy.

In the present age, when the destinies of Christendom seem to be in suspense, some hasten to assail democracy as its foe while it is yet in its early growth; and others are ready with their vows of adoration for this new deity which is springing forth from chaos. But both parties are very imperfectly acquainted with the object of their hatred or of their desires. They strike in the dark and distribute their blows by mere chance.

We must first understand what the purport of society and the aim of government is held to be. If it be your intention to confer a certain elevation upon the human mind and to teach it to regard the things of this world with generous feelings, to inspire men with a scorn of mere temporal advantage, to give birth to living convictions, and to keep alive the spirit of honorable devotedness; if you hold it to be a good thing to refine the habits, to embellish the manners, to cultivate the arts of a nation, and to promote the love of poetry, of beauty, and of renown; if you would constitute a people not unfitted to act with power upon all other nations, nor unprepared for those high enterprises which, whatever be the result of its efforts, will leave a name for ever famous in time—if you believe such to be the principal object of society, you must avoid the government of democracy, which would be a very uncertain guide to the end you have in view.

But if you hold it to be expedient to divert the moral and intellectual activity of man to the production of comfort, and to the acquirement of the necessaries of life; if a clear understanding be more profitable to man than genius; if your object be not to stimulate the virtues of heroism, but to create habits of peace; if you had rather witness vices than crimes, and are content to meet with fewer noble deeds, provided offences be diminished in the same proportion; if, instead of living in the midst of a brilliant state of society, you are contented to have prosperity around you; if, in short, you are of opinion that the principal object of a government is not to confer the greatest possible share of power and of glory upon the body of the nation, but to ensure the greatest degree of enjoyment, and the least degree of misery to each of the individuals who compose it—if such be your desires, you can have no surer means of satisfying them, than by equalizing the conditions of men and establishing democratic institutions.

But if the time be past at which such a choice was possible, and if some superhuman power impel us toward one or the other of these two governments without consulting our wishes, let us at least endeavor to make the best of that which is allotted to us; and let us so inquire into its good and its evil propensities as to be able to foster the former, and repress the latter to the utmost.

QUESTIONS

1. Why does Tocqueville say of American laws that "even if they were good, the frequent changes which they undergo would be an evil"? (204)

2. Why does Tocqueville believe that "the great advantage of the Americans consists in their being able to commit faults that they may afterward repair"? (204)

3. Why does Tocqueville argue that democracy is more likely than aristocracy to help individuals do good in spite of their incompetence or evil?

4. Does Tocqueville regard American patriotism as a weakness or a strength?

5. What does Tocqueville mean by "irritable patriotism"? (209)

6. What place does Tocqueville think that property rights have in the general affirmation of democratic principles in America?

7. Why does Tocqueville refer to the granting of political rights to people formerly deprived of them as "critical"? (211)

8. What does Tocqueville mean when he says that "there is nothing more arduous than the apprenticeship of liberty"? (211–212)

9. Why does Tocqueville claim that "in the United States, where the poor rule, the rich have always some reason to dread the abuses of their power"? (213)

10. What does Tocqueville mean when he says that "an American cannot converse, but he can discuss"? (215)

11. Why does Tocqueville say, "Democracy does not confer the most skillful kind of government upon the people"? (216)

12. Why does Tocqueville deny that the choice of democracy will lead to the kind of eminence that characterizes "poetry," "beauty," and "reknown" and many of the other qualities that people hold in high regard? (217)

FOR FURTHER REFLECTION

1. How can Tocqueville claim that in a democracy, though its leaders "are frequently unskillful and sometimes contemptible," nonetheless the course of government is generally benign? (206)

2. Do you agree with Tocqueville that "the idea of right is simply that of virtue introduced into the political world"? (210)

3. Would Tocqueville still affirm today that American democracy is relatively incorruptible even though individuals and laws may be corrupt? Explain.

4. Which, if any, of Tocqueville's ideas about democracy in America hold true today?

HENRIK IBSEN

When *An Enemy of the People* was published in the fall of 1882, playwright Henrik Ibsen (1828–1906) was in the prime of his career and a figure of international renown. He had already spent more than eighteen years outside his native Norway, and it was as an expatriate—living nearly three decades of his life in the great cities of Europe, including Rome and Munich—that Ibsen wrote most of his major works. By century's end, he would come to exercise major literary influence on such writers as George Bernard Shaw and James Joyce.

Vicious attacks by the critics only contributed to Ibsen's notoriety. In the year preceding production of *Enemy,* the *London Daily Telegraph* had described his play *Ghosts*—which concerns a family's struggle with its secret of syphilis—as "an open drain; a loathsome sore unbandaged; a dirty act done publicly; a lazar-house with all its doors and windows open . . . absolutely loathsome and fetid." The public didn't seem to care. They were transfixed by the powerful realism of Ibsen's characters and daring range of subject matter, which included or would come to include war and profiteering (*Pillars of Society,* 1877), a woman's decision to walk away from her husband and children (*A Doll's House,* 1879), and suicide (*Hedda Gabler,* 1890). With *An Enemy of the People,* Ibsen was sufficiently well established to demand that the Christiania (now Oslo) Theater more than double what he had asked in fees for production rights to his previous plays.

Ibsen's success was hard earned. He was familiar with the sting of rejection; as a boy he had experienced the pain of his family's downward economic mobility when his father's lumber business went bankrupt, and he was painfully conscious of being denied access to the best schools. He was apprenticed to a pharmacist at the age of sixteen, though during this time he also started to write plays and articles. His hopes for a career in medicine ended when he failed his university entrance examination. After landing a job as "stage poet" at a small theater in Bergen in 1851, he began writing for the stage in earnest. Several of his plays over the next decade received tepid reviews, prompting his decision to go abroad in 1864.

An Enemy of the People has as its central character a physician, Dr. Thomas Stockmann, a man who possesses difficult truths about his small town and the spa baths upon which its economy is based. As in any number of Ibsen's plays, the conflict encompasses decisions on whether to face squarely or avoid ugly facts, and the ways that one individual's handling of this knowledge can permanently alter relationships—to siblings, to spouse, to children. The play also opens interesting vistas on Ibsen's personal political beliefs, many of which were shaped in the cauldron of Europe's revolutionary year of 1848. Ibsen's beliefs are rather difficult to pinpoint, even though in his time he was variously labeled as an "anarchist" and a "liberal." Maybe more pertinent is the way the play addresses the uncomfortable friction between maintaining integrity in one's personal relations and making politically responsible decisions.

HENRIK IBSEN

An Enemy of the People

CHARACTERS

DOCTOR THOMAS STOCKMANN, medical officer of the baths

MRS. STOCKMANN, his wife

PETRA, their daughter, a teacher

EILIF, MORTEN, their sons, thirteen and ten years old respectively

MAYOR PETER STOCKMANN, the doctor's elder brother, mayor and chief
    of police, chairman of the Baths Committee

MORTEN KIIL, master tanner, Mrs. Stockmann's adoptive father

HOVSTAD, editor of the *People's Messenger*

BILLING, on the staff of the paper

HORSTER, a ship's captain

ASLAKSEN, a printer

Participants in a meeting of citizens: all sorts and conditions of men,
some women, and a band of schoolboys.

The action passes in a town on the south coast of Norway.

ACT I

[*Evening. Dr. Stockmann's sitting room; simply but neatly decorated and furnished. In the wall to the right are two doors, the further one leading to the hall, the nearer one to the doctor's study. In the opposite wall, facing the hall door, a door leading to the other rooms of the house. Against the middle of this wall stands the stove; further forward a sofa with a mirror above it, and in front of it an oval table with a cover. On the table a lighted lamp, with a shade. In the back wall an open door leading to the dining room, in which is seen a supper table, with a lamp on it.*]

Billing is seated at the supper table, with a napkin under his chin. Mrs. Stockmann is standing by the table and placing before him a dish with a large joint of roast beef. The other seats round the table are empty; the table is in disorder, as after a meal.]

MRS. STOCKMANN   If you come an hour late, Mr. Billing, you must put up with a cold supper.

BILLING   [*Eating.*] It is excellent—really first rate.

MRS. STOCKMANN   You know how Stockmann insists on regular meal hours—

BILLING   Oh, I don't mind at all. I almost think I enjoy my supper more when I can sit down to it like this, alone and undisturbed.

MRS. STOCKMANN   Oh, well, if you enjoy it— [*Listening in the direction of the hall.*] I believe this is Mr. Hovstad coming too.

BILLING   Very likely.

[*Mayor Stockmann enters, wearing an overcoat and an official gold-laced cap, and carrying a stick.*]

MAYOR STOCKMANN   Good evening, sister-in-law.

MRS. STOCKMANN   [*Coming forward into the sitting room.*] Oh, good evening; is it you? It is good of you to look in.

MAYOR STOCKMANN   I was just passing, and so— [*Looks toward the drawing room.*] Ah, I see you have company.

MRS. STOCKMANN   [*Rather embarrassed.*] Oh no, not at all; it's the merest chance. [*Hurriedly.*] Won't you sit down and have a little supper?

MAYOR STOCKMANN   I? No, thank you. Good gracious! Hot meat in the evening? That wouldn't suit my digestion.

MRS. STOCKMANN   Oh, for once in a way—

MAYOR STOCKMANN   No, no—much obliged to you. I stick to tea and bread and butter. It's more wholesome in the long run—and rather more economical, too.

MRS. STOCKMANN   [*Smiling.*] You mustn't think Thomas and I are mere spendthrifts, either.

MAYOR STOCKMANN   You are not, sister-in-law; far be it from me to say that. [*Pointing to the doctor's study.*] Is he not at home?

MRS. STOCKMANN   No, he has gone for a little turn after supper—with the boys.

MAYOR STOCKMANN   I wonder if that is a good thing to do? [*Listening.*] There he is, no doubt.

MRS. STOCKMANN   No, that is not he. [*A knock.*] Come in!

[*Hovstad enters from the hall.*]

MRS. STOCKMANN   Ah, it's Mr. Hovstad—

HOVSTAD   You must excuse me; I was detained at the printer's. Good evening, Mayor.

MAYOR STOCKMANN   [*Bowing rather stiffly.*] Mr. Hovstad? You come on business, I presume?

HOVSTAD   Partly. About an article for the paper.

MAYOR STOCKMANN   So I supposed. I hear my brother is an extremely prolific contributor to the *People's Messenger*.

HOVSTAD   Yes, when he wants to unburden his mind on one thing or another, he gives the *Messenger* the benefit.

MRS. STOCKMANN   [*To Hovstad.*] But will you not—? [*Points to the dining room.*]

MAYOR STOCKMANN Well, well, I am far from blaming him for writing for the class of readers he finds most in sympathy with him. And, personally, I have no reason to bear your paper any ill will, Mr. Hovstad.

HOVSTAD No, I should think not.

MAYOR STOCKMANN One may say, on the whole, that a fine spirit of mutual tolerance prevails in our town—an excellent public spirit. And that is because we have a great common interest to hold us together—an interest in which all right-minded citizens are equally concerned—

HOVSTAD Yes—the baths.

MAYOR STOCKMANN Just so. We have our magnificent new baths. Mark my words! The whole life of the town will center around the baths, Mr. Hovstad. There can be no doubt of it!

MRS. STOCKMANN That is just what Thomas says.

MAYOR STOCKMANN How marvelously the place has developed, even in this couple of years! Money has come into circulation, and brought life and movement with it. Houses and ground rents rise in value every day.

HOVSTAD And there are fewer people out of work.

MAYOR STOCKMANN That is true. There is a gratifying diminution in the burden imposed on the well-to-do classes by the poor rates; and they will be still further lightened if only we have a really good summer this year—a rush of visitors—plenty of invalids, to give the baths a reputation.

HOVSTAD I hear there is every prospect of that.

MAYOR STOCKMANN Things look most promising. Inquiries about apartments and so forth keep on pouring in.

HOVSTAD Then the doctor's paper will come in very opportunely.

MAYOR STOCKMANN Has he been writing again?

HOVSTAD This is a thing he wrote in the winter, enlarging on the virtues of the baths, and on the excellent sanitary conditions of the town. But at that time I held it over.

MAYOR STOCKMANN Ah—I suppose there was something not quite judicious about it?

HOVSTAD Not at all. But I thought it better to keep it till the spring, when people are beginning to look about them, and think of their summer quarters—

MAYOR STOCKMANN You were right, quite right, Mr. Hovstad.

MRS. STOCKMANN Yes, Thomas is really indefatigable where the baths are concerned.

MAYOR STOCKMANN It is his duty as one of the staff.

HOVSTAD And of course he was really their creator.

MAYOR STOCKMANN Was he? Indeed! I gather that certain persons are of that opinion. But I should have thought that I, too, had a modest share in that undertaking.

MRS. STOCKMANN Yes, that is what Thomas is always saying.

HOVSTAD No one dreams of denying it, Mr. Mayor. You set the thing going and put it on a practical basis; everybody knows that. I only meant that the original idea was the doctor's.

MAYOR STOCKMANN Yes, my brother has certainly had ideas enough in his time—worse luck! But when it comes to realizing them, Mr. Hovstad, we want men of another stamp. I should have thought that in this house at any rate—

MRS. STOCKMANN Why, my dear brother-in-law—

HOVSTAD Mr. Mayor, how can you—?

MRS. STOCKMANN Do go in and have some supper, Mr. Hovstad; my husband is sure to be home directly.

HOVSTAD Thanks; just a mouthful, perhaps.

[*He goes into the dining room.*]

MAYOR STOCKMANN [*Speaking in a low voice.*] It is extraordinary how people who spring direct from the peasant class never can get over their want of tact.

MRS. STOCKMANN But why should you care? Surely you and Thomas can share the honor, like brothers.

MAYOR STOCKMANN Yes, one would suppose so; but it seems a share of the honor is not enough for some persons.

MRS. STOCKMANN What nonsense! You and Thomas always get on so well together. [*Listening.*] There, I think I hear him.

[*Goes and opens the door to the hall.*]

DR. STOCKMANN [*Laughing and talking loudly, without.*] Here's another visitor for you, Katrina. Isn't it capital, eh? Come in, Captain Horster. Hang your coat on that peg. What! You don't wear an overcoat? Fancy, Katrina, I caught him in the street, and I could hardly get him to come in.

[*Captain Horster enters and bows to Mrs. Stockmann.*]

DR. STOCKMANN [*In the doorway.*] In with you, boys. They're famishing again! Come along, Captain Horster; you must try our roast beef—

[*He forces Horster into the dining room. Eilif and Morten follow them.*]

MRS. STOCKMANN But, Thomas, don't you see—

DR. STOCKMANN [*Turning round in the doorway.*] Oh, is that you, Peter! [*Goes up to him and holds out his hand.*] Now this is really capital.

MAYOR STOCKMANN Unfortunately, I have only a moment to spare—

DR. STOCKMANN Nonsense! We shall have some toddy in a minute. You're not forgetting the toddy, Katrina?

MRS. STOCKMANN Of course not; the water's boiling.

[*She goes into the dining room.*]

MAYOR STOCKMANN Toddy too—!

DR. STOCKMANN Yes. Sit down, and let's make ourselves comfortable.

MAYOR STOCKMANN Thanks. I never join in drinking parties.

DR. STOCKMANN But this isn't a party.

MAYOR STOCKMANN I don't know what else— [*Looks toward the dining room.*] It's extraordinary how they can get through all that food.

DR. STOCKMANN [*Rubbing his hands.*] Yes, doesn't it do one good to see young people eat? Always hungry! That's as it should be. They need good, solid meat to put stamina into them! It is they that have got to whip up the ferment of the future, Peter.

MAYOR STOCKMANN May I ask what there is to be "whipped up," as you call it?

DR. STOCKMANN You'll have to ask the young people that—when the time comes. We won't see it, of course. Two old fogies like you and me—

MAYOR STOCKMANN Come, come! Surely that is a very extraordinary expression to use—

DR. STOCKMANN Oh, you mustn't mind my nonsense, Peter. I'm in such glorious spirits, you see. I feel so unspeakably happy in the midst of all this growing, germinating life. Isn't it a marvelous time we live in! It seems as though a whole new world were springing up around us.

MAYOR STOCKMANN Do you really think so?

DR. STOCKMANN Of course, you can't see it as clearly as I do. You have passed your life in the midst of it all, and that deadens the impression. But I who had to vegetate all those years in that little hole in the north, hardly ever seeing a soul that could speak a stimulating word to me—all this affects me as if I had suddenly dropped into the heart of some teeming metropolis.

MAYOR STOCKMANN Well, metropolis—

DR. STOCKMANN Oh, I know well enough that things are on a small scale here, compared with many other places. But there's life here— there's promise—there's an infinity of things to work and strive for, and that is the main point. [*Calling.*] Katrina, haven't there been any letters?

MRS. STOCKMANN [*In the dining room.*] No, none at all.

DR. STOCKMANN And then a good income, Peter! That's a thing one learns to appreciate when one has lived on starvation wages—

MAYOR STOCKMANN Good heavens—!

DR. STOCKMANN Oh yes, I can tell you we often had hard times of it up there. And now we can live like princes! Today, for example, we had roast beef for dinner; and we've had some of it for supper too. Won't you have some? Come along—just look at it, at any rate—

MAYOR STOCKMANN No, no, certainly not—

DR. STOCKMANN Well then, look here—do you see we've bought a tablecover?

MAYOR STOCKMANN Yes, so I observed.

DR. STOCKMANN And a lampshade, too. Do you see? Katrina has been saving up for them. They make the room look comfortable, don't they? Come over here. No, no, no, not there. So—yes! Now you see how it concentrates the light—. I really think it has quite an artistic effect. Eh?

MAYOR STOCKMANN Yes, when one can afford such luxuries—

DR. STOCKMANN Oh, I can afford it now. Katrina says I make almost as much as we spend.

MAYOR STOCKMANN Ah—almost!

DR. STOCKMANN Besides, a man of science must live in some style. Why, I believe a mere sheriff spends much more a year than I do.

MAYOR STOCKMANN Yes, I should think so! A member of the superior magistracy—

DR. STOCKMANN Well then, even a common shipowner! A man of that sort will get through many times as much—

MAYOR STOCKMANN That is natural, in your relative positions.

DR. STOCKMANN And after all, Peter, I really don't squander any money. But I can't deny myself the delight of having people about me. I must have them. After living so long out of the world, I find it a necessity of life to have bright, cheerful, freedom-loving, hard-working young fellows around me—and that's what they are, all of them, that are sitting there eating so heartily. I wish you knew more of Hovstad—

MAYOR STOCKMANN   Ah, that reminds me—Hovstad was telling me that he is going to publish another article of yours.

DR. STOCKMANN   An article of mine?

MAYOR STOCKMANN   Yes, about the baths. An article you wrote last winter.

DR. STOCKMANN   Oh, that one! But I don't want that to appear for the present.

MAYOR STOCKMANN   Why not? It seems to me this is the very time for it.

DR. STOCKMANN   Very likely—under ordinary circumstances—

[*Crosses the room.*]

MAYOR STOCKMANN   [*Following him with his eyes.*] And what is unusual in the circumstances now?

DR. STOCKMANN   [*Standing still.*] The fact is, Peter, I really cannot tell you just now, not this evening, at all events. There may prove to be a great deal that is unusual in the circumstances. On the other hand, there may be nothing at all. Very likely it's only my fancy.

MAYOR STOCKMANN   Upon my word, you are very enigmatical. Is there anything in the wind? Anything I am to be kept in the dark about? I should think, as chairman of the Bath Committee—

DR. STOCKMANN   And I should think that I—Well, well, don't let us get our backs up, Peter.

MAYOR STOCKMANN   God forbid! I am not in the habit of "getting my back up," as you express it. But I must absolutely insist that all arrangements shall be made and carried out in a businesslike manner, and through the properly constituted authorities. I cannot be a party to crooked or underhand courses.

DR. STOCKMANN   Have *I* ever been given to crooked or underhand courses?

MAYOR STOCKMANN   At any rate you have an ingrained propensity to taking your own course. And that, in a well-ordered community, is almost as inadmissible. The individual must subordinate himself to society or, more precisely, to the authorities whose business it is to watch over the welfare of society.

DR. STOCKMANN   Maybe. But what the devil has that to do with me?

MAYOR STOCKMANN   Why this is the very thing, my dear Thomas, that it seems you will never learn. But take care; you will have to pay for it—sooner or later. Now I have warned you. Good-bye.

DR. STOCKMANN   Are you stark mad? You're on a totally wrong track—

MAYOR STOCKMANN   I am not often on the wrong track. Moreover, I must protest against— [*Bowing toward the dining room.*] Good-bye, sister-in-law; good day to you, gentlemen.

[*He goes.*]

MRS. STOCKMANN   [*Entering the sitting room.*] Has he gone?

DR. STOCKMANN   Yes, and in a fine temper, too.

MRS. STOCKMANN   Why, my dear Thomas, what have you been doing to him now?

DR. STOCKMANN   Nothing at all. He can't possibly expect me to account to him for everything—before the time comes.

MRS. STOCKMANN   What have you to account to him for?

DR. STOCKMANN   H'm—never mind about that, Katrina—It's very odd the postman doesn't come.

[*Hovstad, Billing, and Horster have risen from table and come forward into the sitting room. Eilif and Morten presently follow.*]

BILLING   [*Stretching himself.*] Ah! Strike me dead if one doesn't feel a new man after such a meal.

HOVSTAD   The mayor didn't seem in the best of tempers this evening.

DR. STOCKMANN   That's his stomach. He has a very poor digestion.

HOVSTAD   I fancy it's the staff of the *Messenger* he finds it hardest to stomach.

MRS. STOCKMANN   I thought you got on well enough with him.

HOVSTAD   Oh, yes, but it's only a sort of armistice between us.

BILLING That's it! That word sums up the situation.

DR. STOCKMANN We must remember that Peter is a lonely bachelor, poor devil! He has no home to be happy in, only business, business. And then all that cursed weak tea he goes and pours down his throat! Now then, chairs round the table, boys! Katrina, shouldn't we have the toddy now?

MRS. STOCKMANN [*Going toward the dining room.*] I am just getting it.

DR. STOCKMANN And you, Captain Horster, sit beside me on the sofa. So rare a guest as you—Sit down, gentlemen, sit down.

[*The men sit round the table; Mrs. Stockmann brings in a tray with kettle, glasses, decanters, etc.*]

MRS. STOCKMANN Here you have it: here's arrak, and this is rum, and this cognac. Now, help yourselves.

DR. STOCKMANN [*Taking a glass.*] So we will. [*While the toddy is being mixed.*] And now out with the cigars. Eilif, I think you know where the box is. And Morten, you may fetch my pipe. [*The boys go into the room on the right.*] I have a suspicion that Eilif sneaks a cigar now and then, but I pretend not to notice. [*Calls.*] And my smoking cap, Morten! Katrina, can't you tell him where I left it. Ah, he's got it. [*The boys bring in the things.*] Now, friends, help yourselves. I stick to my pipe, you know—this one has been on many a stormy journey with me, up there in the north. [*They clink glasses.*] Your health! Ah, I can tell you it's better fun to sit cosily here, safe from wind and weather.

MRS. STOCKMANN [*Who sits knitting.*] Do you sail soon, Captain Horster?

HORSTER I hope to be ready for a start by next week.

MRS. STOCKMANN And you're going to America?

HORSTER Yes, that's the intention.

BILLING But then you'll miss the election of the new town council.

HORSTER Is there to be an election again?

BILLING Didn't you know?

HORSTER No, I don't trouble myself about those things.

BILLING But I suppose you take an interest in public affairs?

HORSTER No, I don't understand anything about them.

BILLING All the same, one ought at least to vote.

HORSTER Even those who don't understand anything about it?

BILLING Understand? Why, what do you mean by that? Society is like a ship: every man must put his hand to the helm.

HORSTER That may be all right on shore, but at sea it wouldn't do at all.

HOVSTAD It's remarkable how little sailors care about public affairs as a rule.

BILLING Most extraordinary.

DR. STOCKMANN Sailors are like birds of passage: they are at home both in the south and in the north. So it behooves the rest of us to be all the more energetic, Mr. Hovstad. Will there be anything of public interest in the *People's Messenger* tomorrow?

HOVSTAD Nothing of local interest. But the day after tomorrow I think of printing your article—

DR. STOCKMANN Oh confound it, that article! No, you'll have to hold it over.

HOVSTAD Really? We happen to have plenty of space, and I should say this was the very time for it—

DR. STOCKMANN Yes, yes, you may be right, but you must hold it over all the same. I shall explain to you by and by.

[*Petra, wearing a hat and cloak, and with a number of exercise books under her arm, enters from the hall.*]

PETRA Good evening.

DR. STOCKMANN Good evening, Petra. Is that you?

[*General greetings. Petra puts her cloak, hat, and books on a chair by the door.*]

PETRA   Here you all are, enjoying yourselves, while I've been out slaving.

DR. STOCKMANN   Well then, you come and enjoy yourself too.

BILLING   May I mix you a little—?

PETRA   [*Coming toward the table.*] Thank you, I'd rather help myself—you always make it too strong. By the way, father, I have a letter for you.

[*Goes to the chair where her things are lying.*]

DR. STOCKMANN   A letter! From whom?

PETRA   [*Searching in the pocket of her cloak.*] I got it from the postman just as I was going out—

DR. STOCKMANN   [*Rising and going toward her.*] And you only bring it me now?

PETRA   I really hadn't time to run up again. Here it is.

DR. STOCKMANN   [*Seizing the letter.*] Let me see, let me see, child. [*Reads the address.*] Yes; this is it—!

MRS. STOCKMANN   Is it the one you have been so anxious about, Thomas?

DR. STOCKMANN   Yes it is. I must go at once. Where shall I find a light, Katrina? Is there no lamp in my study again!

MRS. STOCKMANN   Yes—the lamp is lighted. It's on the writing table.

DR. STOCKMANN   Good, good. Excuse me one moment—

[*He goes into the room on the right.*]

PETRA   What can it be, mother?

MRS. STOCKMANN   I don't know. For the last few days he has been continually on the lookout for the postman.

BILLING   Probably a country patient—

PETRA   Poor father! He'll soon have far too much to do. [*Mixes her toddy.*] Ah, this will taste good!

HOVSTAD   Have you been teaching in the night school as well today?

PETRA [*Sipping from her glass.*] Two hours.

BILLING And four hours in the morning at the institute—

PETRA [*Sitting down by the table.*] Five hours.

MRS. STOCKMANN And I see you have exercises to correct this evening.

PETRA Yes, a heap of them.

HORSTER It seems to me you have plenty to do, too.

PETRA Yes, but I like it. You feel so delightfully tired after it.

BILLING Do you like that?

PETRA Yes, for then you sleep so well.

MORTEN I say, Petra, you must be a great sinner.

PETRA A sinner?

MORTEN Yes, if you work so hard. Mr. Rörlund says work is a punishment for our sins.

EILIF [*Contemptuously.*] Bosh! What a silly you are, to believe such stuff as that.

MRS. STOCKMANN Come come, Eilif.

BILLING [*Laughing.*] Capital, capital!

HOVSTAD Should you not like to work so hard, Morten?

MORTEN No, I shouldn't.

HOVSTAD Then what will you do with yourself in the world?

MORTEN I should like to be a Viking.

EILIF But then you'd have to be a heathen.

MORTEN Well, so I would.

BILLING There I agree with you, Morten! I say just the same thing.

MRS. STOCKMANN [*Making a sign to him.*] No, no, Mr. Billing, I'm sure you don't.

BILLING Strike me dead but I do, though. I am a heathen, and I'm proud of it. You'll see we shall all be heathens soon.

MORTEN And shall we be able to do anything we like then?

BILLING Well, you see, Morten—

MRS. STOCKMANN Now run away, boys; I'm sure you have lessons to prepare for tomorrow.

EILIF You might let me stay just a little longer—

MRS. STOCKMANN No, you must go too. Be off, both of you.

[*The boys say good night and go into the room on the left.*]

HOVSTAD Do you really think it can hurt the boys to hear these things?

MRS. STOCKMANN Well, I don't know; I don't like it.

PETRA Really, mother, I think you are quite wrong there.

MRS. STOCKMANN Perhaps. But I don't like it—not here, at home.

PETRA There's no end of hypocrisy both at home and at school. At home you must hold your tongue, and at school you have to stand up and tell lies to the children.

HORSTER Have you to tell lies?

PETRA Yes; do you think we don't have to tell them many and many a thing we don't believe ourselves?

BILLING Ah, that's too true.

PETRA If only I could afford it, I should start a school myself, and things should be very different there.

BILLING Oh, afford it—!

HORSTER If you really think of doing that, Miss Stockmann, I shall be delighted to let you have a room at my place. You know my father's old house is nearly empty; there's a great big dining room on the ground floor—

PETRA [*Laughing.*] Oh, thank you very much—but I'm afraid it won't come to anything.

HOVSTAD No, I fancy Miss Petra is more likely to go over to journalism. By the way, have you had time to look into the English novel you promised to translate for us?

PETRA Not yet. But you shall have it in good time.

[*Dr. Stockmann enters from his room, with the letter open in his hand.*]

DR. STOCKMANN [*Flourishing the letter.*] Here's news, I can tell you, that will wake up the town!

BILLING News?

MRS. STOCKMANN What news?

DR. STOCKMANN A great discovery, Katrina!

HOVSTAD Indeed?

MRS. STOCKMANN Made by you?

DR. STOCKMANN Precisely—by me! [*Walks up and down.*] Now let them go on accusing me of fads and crack-brained notions. But they won't dare to! Ha-ha! I tell you they won't dare!

PETRA Do tell us what it is, father.

DR. STOCKMANN Well, well, give me time, and you shall hear all about it. If only I had Peter here now! This just shows how we men can go about forming judgments like the blindest moles—

HOVSTAD What do you mean, Doctor?

DR. STOCKMANN [*Stopping beside the table.*] Isn't it the general opinion that our town is a healthy place?

HOVSTAD Of course.

DR. STOCKMANN A quite exceptionally healthy place, indeed—a place to be warmly recommended, both to invalids and people in health—

MRS. STOCKMANN My dear Thomas—

DR. STOCKMANN And assuredly we haven't failed to recommend and belaud it. I've sung its praises again and again, both in the *Messenger* and in pamphlets—

HOVSTAD Well, what then?

DR. STOCKMANN These baths, that we have called the pulse of the town, its vital nerve, and—and the devil knows what else—

BILLING "Our city's palpitating heart," I once ventured to call them in a convivial moment—

DR. STOCKMANN Yes, I daresay. Well—do you know what they really are, these mighty, magnificent, belauded baths, that have cost so much money—do you know what they are?

HOVSTAD No, what are they?

MRS. STOCKMANN Do tell us.

DR. STOCKMANN Simply a pestiferous hole.

PETRA The baths, father?

MRS. STOCKMANN [*At the same time.*] Our baths!

HOVSTAD [*Also at the same time.*] But, Doctor—!

BILLING Oh, it's incredible!

DR. STOCKMANN I tell you the whole place is a poisonous whited-sepulcher; noxious in the highest degree! All that filth up there in the Mill Dale—the stuff that smells so horribly—taints the water in the feed pipes of the pump room; and the same accursed poisonous refuse oozes out by the beach—

HOVSTAD Where the sea baths are?

DR. STOCKMANN Exactly.

HOVSTAD But how are you so sure of all this, Doctor?

DR. STOCKMANN I've investigated the whole thing as conscientiously as possible. I've long had my suspicions about it. Last year we had some extraordinary cases of illness among the patients—both typhoid and gastric attacks—

MRS. STOCKMANN Yes, I remember.

DR. STOCKMANN We thought at the time that the visitors had brought the infection with them; but afterward—last winter—I began to question that. So I set about testing the water as well as I could.

MRS. STOCKMANN It was that you were working so hard at!

DR. STOCKMANN Yes, you may well say I've worked, Katrina. But here, you know, I hadn't the necessary scientific appliances; so I sent samples both of our drinking water and of our sea water to the university, for exact analysis by a chemist.

HOVSTAD And you have received his report?

DR. STOCKMANN [*Showing letter.*] Here it is! And it proves beyond dispute the presence of putrefying organic matter in the water— millions of infusoria. It's absolutely pernicious to health, whether used internally or externally.

MRS. STOCKMANN What a blessing you found it out in time.

DR. STOCKMANN Yes, you may well say that.

HOVSTAD And what do you intend to do now, Doctor?

DR. STOCKMANN Why, to set things right, of course.

HOVSTAD You think it can be done, then?

DR. STOCKMANN It must be done. Else the whole baths are useless, ruined. But there's no fear. I am quite clear as to what is required.

MRS. STOCKMANN But, my dear Thomas, why should you have made such a secret of all this?

DR. STOCKMANN Would you have had me rush all over the town and chatter about it, before I was quite certain? No, thank you; I'm not so mad as that.

PETRA   But to us at home—

DR. STOCKMANN   I couldn't say a word to a living soul. But tomorrow you may look in at the Badger's—

MRS. STOCKMANN   Oh, Thomas!

DR. STOCKMANN   Well well, at your grandfather's. The old fellow will be astonished! He thinks I'm not quite right in my head—yes, and plenty of others think the same, I've noticed. But now these good people shall see—yes, they shall see now! [*Walks up and down rubbing his hands.*] What a stir there will be in the town, Katrina! Just think of it! All the water pipes will have to be relaid.

HOVSTAD   [*Rising.*] All the water pipes—?

DR. STOCKMANN   Why, of course. The intake is too low down; it must be moved much higher up.

PETRA   So you were right, after all.

DR. STOCKMANN   Yes, do you remember, Petra? I wrote against it when they were beginning the works. But no one would listen to me then. Now, you may be sure, I shall give them my full broadside— for of course I've prepared a statement for the directors; it has been lying ready a whole week; I've only been waiting for this report. [*Points to letter.*] But now they shall have it at once. [*Goes into his room and returns with a manuscript in his hand.*] See! Four closely written sheets! And I'll enclose the report. A newspaper, Katrina! Get me something to wrap them up in. There—that's it. Give it to—to [*Stamps.*]—what the devil's her name? Give it to the girl, I mean, and tell her to take it at once to the mayor.

[*Mrs. Stockmann goes out with the packet through the dining room.*]

PETRA   What do you think Uncle Peter will say, Father?

DR. STOCKMANN   What should he say? He can't possibly be otherwise than pleased that so important a fact has been brought to light.

HOVSTAD   I suppose you will let me put a short announcement of your discovery in the *Messenger*.

DR. STOCKMANN   Yes, I shall be much obliged if you will.

HOVSTAD It is highly desirable that the public should know about it as soon as possible.

DR. STOCKMANN Yes, certainly.

MRS. STOCKMANN [*Returning.*] She's gone with it.

BILLING Strike me dead if you won't be the first man in the town, Doctor!

DR. STOCKMANN [*Walks up and down in high glee.*] Oh, nonsense! After all, I have done no more than my duty. I've been a lucky treasure hunter, that's all. But all the same—

BILLING Hovstad, don't you think the town ought to get up a torchlight procession in honor of Dr. Stockmann?

HOVSTAD I shall certainly propose it.

BILLING And I'll talk it over with Aslaksen.

DR. STOCKMANN No, my dear friends; let all such claptrap alone. I won't hear of anything of the sort. And if the directors should want to raise my salary, I won't accept it. I tell you, Katrina, I will not accept it.

MRS. STOCKMANN You are quite right, Thomas.

PETRA [*Raising her glass.*] Your health, Father!

HOVSTAD AND BILLING Your health, your health, Doctor!

HORSTER [*Clinking glasses with the doctor.*] I hope you may have nothing but joy of your discovery.

DR. STOCKMANN Thanks, thanks, my dear friends! I can't tell you how happy I am—! Oh, what a blessing it is to feel that you have deserved well of your native town and your fellow citizens. Hurrah, Katrina!

[*He puts both his arms round her neck and whirls her round with him. Mrs. Stockmann screams and struggles. A burst of laughter, applause, and cheers for the doctor. The boys thrust their heads in at the door.*]

ACT II

[*The doctor's sitting room. The dining room door is closed. Morning.*]

MRS. STOCKMANN   [*Enters from the dining room with a sealed letter in her hand, goes to the foremost door on the right and peeps in.*] Are you there, Thomas?

DR. STOCKMANN   [*Within.*] Yes, I have just come in. [*Enters.*] What is it?

MRS. STOCKMANN   A letter from your brother.

[*Hands it to him.*]

DR. STOCKMANN   Aha, let us see. [*Opens the envelope and reads.*] "The manuscript sent me is returned herewith—" [*Reads on, mumbling to himself.*] H'm—

MRS. STOCKMANN   Well, what does he say?

DR. STOCKMANN   [*Putting the paper in his pocket.*] Nothing; only that he'll come up himself about midday.

MRS. STOCKMANN   Then be sure you remember to stay at home.

DR. STOCKMANN   Oh, I can easily manage that; I've finished my morning's visits.

MRS. STOCKMANN   I am very curious to know how he takes it.

DR. STOCKMANN   You'll see he won't be overpleased that it is I that have made the discovery, and not he himself.

MRS. STOCKMANN   Ah, that's just what I'm afraid of.

DR. STOCKMANN   Of course at bottom he'll be glad. But still—Peter is damnably unwilling that any one but himself should do anything for the good of the town.

MRS. STOCKMANN   Do you know, Thomas, I think you might stretch a point, and share the honor with him. Couldn't it appear that it was he that put you on the track—?

DR. STOCKMANN   By all means, for aught I care. If only I can get things put straight—

[*Old Morten Kiil puts his head in at the hall door, and asks slyly:*]

MORTEN KIIL Is it—is it true?

MRS. STOCKMANN [*Going toward him.*] Father—is that you?

DR. STOCKMANN Hallo, father-in-law! Good morning, good morning.

MRS. STOCKMANN Do come in.

MORTEN KIIL Yes, if it's true; if not, I'm off again.

DR. STOCKMANN If what is true?

MORTEN KIIL This crazy business about the waterworks. Now is it true?

DR. STOCKMANN Why, of course it is. But how came you to hear of it?

MORTEN KIIL [*Coming in.*] Petra looked in on her way to the school—

DR. STOCKMANN Oh, did she?

MORTEN KIIL Ay, ay—and she told me—I thought she was only making game of me, but that's not like Petra either.

DR. STOCKMANN No, indeed; how could you think so?

MORTEN KIIL Oh, you can never be sure of anybody. You may be made a fool of before you know where you are. So it is true, after all?

DR. STOCKMANN Most certainly it is. Do sit down, father-in-law. [*Forces him down on the sofa.*] Now isn't it a real blessing for the town—?

MORTEN KIIL [*Suppressing his laughter.*] A blessing for the town?

DR. STOCKMANN Yes, that I made this discovery in time—

MORTEN KIIL [*As before.*] Ay, ay, ay!—Well, I could never have believed that you would play monkey tricks with your very own brother.

DR. STOCKMANN Monkey tricks!

MRS. STOCKMANN Why, father dear—

MORTEN KIIL   [*Resting his hands and chin on the top of his stick and blinking slyly at the doctor.*] What was it again? Wasn't it that some animals had got into the water pipes?

DR. STOCKMANN   Yes, infusorial animals.

MORTEN KIIL   And any number of these animals had got in, Petra said— whole swarms of them.

DR. STOCKMANN   Certainly, hundreds of thousands.

MORTEN KIIL   But no one can see them—isn't that it?

DR. STOCKMANN   Quite right. No one can see them.

MORTEN KIIL   [*With a quiet, chuckling laugh.*] I'll be damned if that isn't the best thing I've heard of you yet.

DR. STOCKMANN   What do you mean?

MORTEN KIIL   But you'll never in this world make the mayor take in anything of the sort.

DR. STOCKMANN   Well, that we shall see.

MORTEN KIIL   Do you really think he'll be so crazy?

DR. STOCKMANN   I hope the whole town will be so crazy.

MORTEN KIIL   The whole town! Well, I don't say but it may. But it serves them right; it'll teach them a lesson. They wanted to be so much cleverer than we old fellows. They hounded me out of the town council. Yes, I tell you they hounded me out like a dog, that they did. But now it's their turn. Just you keep up the game with them, Stockmann.

DR. STOCKMANN   Yes, but, father-in-law—

MORTEN KIIL   Keep it up, I say. [*Rising.*] If you can make the mayor and his gang eat humble pie, I'll give a hundred crowns straight away to the poor.

DR. STOCKMANN   Come, that's good of you.

MORTEN KIIL   Of course, I've little enough to throw away; but if you can manage that, I shall certainly remember the poor at Christmastime, to the tune of fifty crowns.

[*Hovstad enters from hall.*]

HOVSTAD Good morning! [*Pausing.*] Oh! I beg your pardon—

DR. STOCKMANN Not at all. Come in, come in.

MORTEN KIIL [*Chuckling again.*] He! Is he in it too?

HOVSTAD What do you mean?

DR. STOCKMANN Yes, of course he is.

MORTEN KIIL I might have known it! It's to go into the papers. Ah, you're the one, Stockmann! Do you two lay your heads together; I'm off.

DR. STOCKMANN Oh no, don't go yet, father-in-law.

MORTEN KIIL No, I'm off now. Play them all the monkey tricks you can think of. Devil take me but you won't lose by it. [*He goes, Mrs. Stockmann accompanying him.*]

DR. STOCKMANN [*Laughing.*] What do you think—? The old fellow doesn't believe a word of all this about the waterworks.

HOVSTAD Was that what he—?

DR. STOCKMANN Yes, that was what we were talking about. And I daresay you have come on the same business?

HOVSTAD Yes. Have you a moment to spare, Doctor?

DR. STOCKMANN As many as you like, my dear fellow.

HOVSTAD Have you heard anything from the mayor?

DR. STOCKMANN Not yet. He'll be here presently.

HOVSTAD I have been thinking the matter over since last evening.

DR. STOCKMANN Well?

HOVSTAD To you, as a doctor and a man of science, this business of the waterworks appears an isolated affair. I daresay it hasn't occurred to you that a good many other things are bound up with it?

DR. STOCKMANN   Indeed! In what way? Let us sit down, my dear fellow—No, there, on the sofa.

[*Hovstad sits on sofa; the doctor in an easy chair on the other side of the table.*]

DR. STOCKMANN   Well, so you think—?

HOVSTAD   You said yesterday that the water is polluted by impurities in the soil.

DR. STOCKMANN   Yes, undoubtedly; the mischief comes from that poisonous swamp up in the Mill Dale.

HOVSTAD   Excuse me, Doctor, but I think it comes from a very different swamp.

DR. STOCKMANN   What swamp may that be?

HOVSTAD   The swamp in which our whole municipal life is rotting.

DR. STOCKMANN   The devil, Mr. Hovstad! What notion is this you've got hold of?

HOVSTAD   All the affairs of the town have gradually drifted into the hands of a pack of bureaucrats—

DR. STOCKMANN   Come now, they're not all bureaucrats.

HOVSTAD   No; but those who are not are the friends and adherents of those who are. We are entirely under the thumb of a ring of wealthy men, men of old family and position in the town.

DR. STOCKMANN   Yes, but they are also men of ability and insight.

HOVSTAD   Did they show ability and insight when they laid the water pipes where they are?

DR. STOCKMANN   No. That, of course, was a piece of stupidity. But that will be set right now.

HOVSTAD   Do you think it will go so smoothly?

DR. STOCKMANN   Well, smoothly or not, it will have to be done.

HOVSTAD   Yes, if the press exerts its influence.

DR. STOCKMANN Not at all necessary, my dear fellow; I am sure my brother—

HOVSTAD Excuse me, Doctor, but I must tell you that I think of taking the matter up.

DR. STOCKMANN In the paper?

HOVSTAD Yes. When I took over the *People's Messenger*, I was determined to break up the ring of obstinate old blockheads who held everything in their hands.

DR. STOCKMANN But you told me yourself what came of it. You nearly ruined the paper.

HOVSTAD Yes, at that time we had to draw in our horns; that's true enough. The whole bath scheme might have fallen through if these men had been sent about their business. But now the baths are an accomplished fact, and we can get on without these august personages.

DR. STOCKMANN Get on without them, yes, but still we owe them a great deal.

HOVSTAD The debt shall be duly acknowledged. But a journalist of my democratic tendencies cannot let such an opportunity slip through his fingers. We must explode the tradition of official infallibility. That rubbish must be got rid of, like every other superstition.

DR. STOCKMANN There I am with you with all my heart, Mr. Hovstad. If it's a superstition, away with it!

HOVSTAD I should be sorry to attack the mayor, as he is your brother. But I know you think with me—the truth before all other considerations.

DR. STOCKMANN Why, of course. [*Vehemently.*] But still—! But still—!

HOVSTAD You mustn't think ill of me. I am neither more self-interested nor more ambitious than other men.

DR. STOCKMANN Why, my dear fellow—who says you are?

HOVSTAD I come of humble folk, as you know; and I have had ample opportunities of seeing what the lower classes really require. And that is to have a share in the direction of public affairs, Doctor. That is what develops ability and knowledge and self-respect—

DR. STOCKMANN   I understand that perfectly.

HOVSTAD   Yes, and I think a journalist incurs a heavy responsibility if
he lets slip a chance of helping to emancipate the downtrodden
masses. I know well enough that our oligarchy will denounce me as
an agitator, and so forth; but what do I care? If only my conscience
is clear, I—

DR. STOCKMANN   Just so, just so, my dear Mr. Hovstad. But still—devil
take it—! [*A knock at the door.*] Come in!

[*Aslaksen, the printer, appears at the door leading to the hall. He is humbly but
respectably dressed in black, wears a white necktie, slightly crumpled, and has a
silk hat and gloves in his hand.*]

ASLAKSEN   [*Bowing.*] I beg pardon, Doctor, for making so bold—

DR. STOCKMANN   [*Rising.*] Hallo! If it isn't Mr. Aslaksen!

ASLAKSEN   Yes, it's me, Doctor.

HOVSTAD   [*Rising.*] Is it me you want, Aslaksen?

ASLAKSEN   No, not at all. I didn't know you were here. No, it's the
doctor himself—

DR. STOCKMANN   Well, what can I do for you?

ASLAKSEN   Is it true, what Mr. Billing tells me, that you're going to
get us a better set of waterworks?

DR. STOCKMANN   Yes, for the baths.

ASLAKSEN   Of course, of course. Then I just looked in to say that I'll
back up the movement with all my might.

HOVSTAD   [*To the doctor.*] You see!

DR. STOCKMANN   I'm sure I thank you heartily; but—

ASLAKSEN   You may find it no such bad thing to have us small
middle-class men at your back. We form what you may call a solid
majority in the town—when we really make up our minds, that's
to say. And it's always well to have the majority with you, Doctor.

DR. STOCKMANN No doubt, no doubt; but I can't conceive that any special measures will be necessary in this case. I should think in so clear and straightforward a matter—

ASLAKSEN Yes, but all the same, it can do no harm. I know the local authorities very well—the powers that be are not over ready to adopt suggestions from outsiders. So I think it wouldn't be amiss if we made some sort of a demonstration.

HOVSTAD Precisely my opinion.

DR. STOCKMANN A demonstration, you say? But in what way would you demonstrate?

ASLAKSEN Of course with great moderation, Doctor. I always insist upon moderation; for moderation is a citizen's first virtue—at least that's my way of thinking.

DR. STOCKMANN We all know that, Mr. Aslaksen.

ASLAKSEN Yes, I think my moderation is generally recognized. And this affair of the waterworks is very important for us small middle-class men. The baths bid fair to become, as you might say, a little gold mine for the town. We shall all have to live by the baths, especially we homeowners. So we want to support the baths all we can; and as I am chairman of the Homeowners' Association—

DR. STOCKMANN Well—?

ASLAKSEN And as I'm an active worker for the Temperance Society— of course you know, Doctor, that I'm a temperance man?

DR. STOCKMANN To be sure, to be sure.

ASLAKSEN Well, you'll understand that I come in contact with a great many people. And as I'm known to be a prudent and law-abiding citizen, as you yourself remarked, Doctor, I have certain influence in the town, and hold some power in my hands—if I do say so myself.

DR. STOCKMANN I know that very well, Mr. Aslaksen.

ASLAKSEN Well then, you see—it would be easy for me to get up an address, if it came to a pinch.

DR. STOCKMANN An address?

ASLAKSEN   Yes, a kind of vote of thanks to you, from the citizens of the town, for your action in a matter of such general concern. Of course it will have to be drawn up with all fitting moderation, so as to give no offence to the authorities and parties in power. But so long as we're careful about that, no one can take it ill, I should think.

HOVSTAD   Well, even if they didn't particularly like it—

ASLAKSEN   No, no, no; no offence to the powers that be, Mr. Hovstad. No opposition to people that can take it out of us again so easily. I've had enough of that in my time; no good ever comes of it. But no one can object to the free but temperate expression of a citizen's opinion.

DR. STOCKMANN   [*Shaking his hand.*] I can't tell you, my dear Mr. Aslaksen, how heartily it delights me to find so much support among my fellow townsmen. I'm so happy—so happy! Come, you'll have a glass of sherry? Eh?

ASLAKSEN   No, thank you. I never touch spirituous liquors.

DR. STOCKMANN   Well, then, a glass of beer—what do you say to that?

ASLAKSEN   Thanks, not that either, Doctor. I never take anything so early in the day. And now I'll be off round the town, and talk to some of the homeowners, and prepare public opinion.

DR. STOCKMANN   It's extremely kind of you, Mr. Aslaksen, but I really cannot get it into my head that all these preparations are necessary. The affair seems to me so simple and self-evident.

ASLAKSEN   The authorities always move slowly, Doctor—God forbid I should blame them for it—

HOVSTAD   We'll stir them up in the paper tomorrow, Aslaksen.

ASLAKSEN   No violence, Mr. Hovstad. Proceed with moderation, or you'll do nothing with them. Take my advice; I've picked up experience in the school of life. And now I'll say good morning, Doctor. You know now that at least you have us small middle-class men behind you, solid as a wall. You have the majority on your side, Doctor.

DR. STOCKMANN   Many thanks, my dear Mr. Aslaksen. [*Holds out his hand.*] Good-bye, good-bye.

ASLAKSEN Are you coming to the office, Mr. Hovstad?

HOVSTAD I shall come on presently. I have still one or two things to arrange.

ASLAKSEN Very well.

[*Bows and goes. Dr. Stockmann accompanies him into the hall.*]

HOVSTAD [*As the doctor reenters.*] Well, what do you say to that, Doctor? Don't you think it is high time we should give all this weak-kneed, half-hearted cowardice a good shaking up?

DR. STOCKMANN Are you speaking of Aslaksen?

HOVSTAD Yes, I am. He's a decent enough fellow, but he's one of those who are sunk in the swamp. And most people here are just like him: they are forever wavering and wobbling from side to side; what with scruples and misgivings, they never dare advance a step.

DR. STOCKMANN Yes, but Aslaksen seems to me thoroughly well-intentioned.

HOVSTAD There is one thing I value more than good intentions, and that is an attitude of manly self-reliance.

DR. STOCKMANN There I am quite with you.

HOVSTAD So I am going to seize this opportunity, and try whether I can't for once put a little grit into their good intentions. The worship of authority must be rooted up in this town. This gross, inexcusable blunder of the waterworks must be brought home clearly to every voter.

DR. STOCKMANN Very well. If you think it's for the good of the community, so be it; but not till I have spoken to my brother.

HOVSTAD At all events, I shall be writing my leader in the meantime. And if the mayor won't take the matter up—

DR. STOCKMANN But how can you conceive his refusing?

HOVSTAD Oh, it's not inconceivable. And then—

DR. STOCKMANN Well then, I promise you—look here, in that case you may print my paper; put it in just as it is.

HOVSTAD   May I? Is that a promise?

DR. STOCKMANN   [*Handing him the manuscript.*] There it is; take it
with you. You may as well read it in any case; you can return it to
me afterward.

HOVSTAD   Very good; I shall do so. And now, good-bye, Doctor.

DR. STOCKMANN   Good-bye, good-bye. You'll see it will all go smoothly,
Mr. Hovstad—as smoothly as possible.

HOVSTAD   H'm—we shall see.

[*Bows and goes out through the hall.*]

DR. STOCKMANN   [*Going to the dining room door and looking in.*] Katrina!
Hallo! Are you back, Petra?

PETRA   [*Entering.*] Yes, I've just got back from school.

MRS. STOCKMANN   [*Entering.*] Hasn't he been here yet?

DR. STOCKMANN   Peter? No. But I have been having a long talk with
Hovstad. He's quite enthusiastic about my discovery. It turns out
to be of much wider import than I thought at first. So he has placed
his paper at my disposal, if I should require it.

MRS. STOCKMANN   Do you think you will?

DR. STOCKMANN   Not I! But at the same time, one cannot but be proud
to know that the enlightened, independent press is on one's side.
And what do you think? I have had a visit from the chairman of
the Homeowners' Association too.

MRS. STOCKMANN   Really? What did he want?

DR. STOCKMANN   To assure me of his support. They will all stand by
me at a pinch. Katrina, do you know what I have behind me?

MRS. STOCKMANN   Behind you? No. What have you behind you?

DR. STOCKMANN   The solid majority!

MRS. STOCKMANN   Oh! Is that good for you, Thomas?

DR. STOCKMANN Yes, indeed; I should think it was good. [*Rubbing his hands as he walks up and down.*] Great God! What a delight it is to feel oneself in such brotherly unison with one's fellow townsmen!

PETRA And to do so much that's good and useful, Father!

DR. STOCKMANN And all for one's native town, too!

MRS. STOCKMANN There's the bell.

DR. STOCKMANN That must be he. [*Knock at the door.*] Come in!

[*Enter Mayor Stockmann from the hall.*]

MAYOR STOCKMANN Good morning.

DR. STOCKMANN I'm glad to see you, Peter.

MRS. STOCKMANN Good morning, brother-in-law. How are you?

MAYOR STOCKMANN Oh, thanks, so-so. [*To the doctor.*] Yesterday evening, after office hours, I received from you a dissertation upon the state of the water at the baths.

DR. STOCKMANN Yes. Have you read it?

MAYOR STOCKMANN I have.

DR. STOCKMANN And what do you think of the affair?

MAYOR STOCKMANN H'm—

[*With a sidelong glance.*]

MRS. STOCKMAN Come, Petra.

[*She and Petra go into the room on the left.*]

MAYOR STOCKMANN [*After a pause.*] Was it necessary to make all these investigations behind my back?

DR. STOCKMANN Yes, till I was absolutely certain, I—

MAYOR STOCKMANN And are you absolutely certain now?

DR. STOCKMANN My paper must surely have convinced you of that.

MAYOR STOCKMANN Is it your intention to submit this statement to the board of directors, as a sort of official document?

DR. STOCKMANN Of course. Something must be done in the matter, and that promptly.

MAYOR STOCKMANN As usual, you use very strong expressions in your statement. Among other things, you say that what we offer our visitors is a slow poison.

DR. STOCKMANN Why, Peter, what else can it be called? Only think— poisoned water both internally and externally! And that to poor invalids who come to us in all confidence, and pay us handsomely to cure them!

MAYOR STOCKMANN And then you announce as your conclusion that we must build a sewer to carry off the alleged impurities from the Mill Dale, and must re-lay all the water pipes.

DR. STOCKMANN Yes. Can you suggest any other plan?—I know of none.

MAYOR STOCKMANN I found a pretext for looking in at the town engineer's this morning, and—in a half-jesting way—I mentioned these alterations as things we might possibly have to consider at some future time.

DR. STOCKMANN At some future time!

MAYOR STOCKMANN Of course, he smiled at what he thought my extravagance. Have you taken the trouble to think what your proposed alterations would cost? From what the engineer said, I gathered that the expenses would probably amount to up to several hundred thousand crowns.

DR. STOCKMANN So much as that?

MAYOR STOCKMANN Yes. But that is not the worst. The work would take at least two years.

DR. STOCKMANN Two years! Do you mean to say two whole years?

MAYOR STOCKMANN At least. And what are we to do with the baths in the meanwhile? Are we to close them? We should have no alternative. Do you think anyone would come here, if it got abroad that the water was pestilential?

DR. STOCKMANN But, Peter, that's precisely what it is.

MAYOR STOCKMANN And all this now, just now, when the baths are doing so well! Neighboring towns, too, are not without their claims to rank as health resorts. Do you think they would not at once set to work to divert the full stream of visitors to themselves? Undoubtedly they would, and we should be left stranded. We should probably have to give up the whole costly undertaking, and so you would have ruined your native town.

DR. STOCKMANN I—ruined—!

MAYOR STOCKMANN It is only through the baths that the town has any future worth speaking of. You surely know that as well as I do.

DR. STOCKMANN Then what do you think should be done?

MAYOR STOCKMANN I have not succeeded in convincing myself that the condition of the water at the baths is as serious as your statement represents.

DR. STOCKMANN I tell you it's if anything worse—or will be in the summer, when the hot weather sets in.

MAYOR STOCKMANN I repeat that I believe you exaggerate greatly. A competent physician should know what measures to take—he should be able to obviate deleterious influences, and to counteract them in case they should make themselves unmistakably felt.

DR. STOCKMANN Indeed—? And then—?

MAYOR STOCKMANN The existing waterworks are, once for all, a fact, and must naturally be treated as such. But when the time comes, the directors will probably not be indisposed to consider whether it may not be possible, without unreasonable pecuniary sacrifices, to introduce certain improvements.

DR. STOCKMANN And do you imagine I could ever be a party to such dishonesty?

MAYOR STOCKMANN Dishonesty?

DR. STOCKMANN Yes, it would be dishonesty—a fraud, a lie, an absolute crime against the public, against society as a whole!

MAYOR STOCKMANN I have not, as I before remarked, been able to convince myself that there is really any such imminent danger.

DR. STOCKMANN You have! You must have! I know that my demonstration is absolutely clear and convincing. And you understand it perfectly, Peter, only you won't admit it. It was you who insisted that both the bath buildings and the waterworks should be placed where they now are; and it's that—it's that damned blunder that you won't confess. Pshaw! Do you think I don't see through you?

MAYOR STOCKMANN And even if it were so? If I do watch over my reputation with a certain anxiety, I do it for the good of the town. Without moral authority I cannot guide and direct affairs in the way I consider most conducive to the general welfare. Therefore— and on various other grounds—it is of great moment to me that your statement should not be submitted to the board of directors. It must be kept back, for the good of the community. Later on I will bring up the matter for discussion, and we will do the best we can, quietly; but not a word, not a whisper, of this unfortunate business must come to the public ears.

DR. STOCKMANN But it can't be prevented now, my dear Peter.

MAYOR STOCKMANN It must and shall be prevented.

DR. STOCKMANN It can't be, I tell you; far too many people know about it already.

MAYOR STOCKMANN Know about it! Who? Surely not those fellows on the *People's Messenger*—?

DR. STOCKMANN Oh yes, they know. The liberal, independent press will take good care that you do your duty.

MAYOR STOCKMANN [*After a short pause.*] You are an amazingly reckless man, Thomas. Have not you reflected what the consequences of this may be to yourself?

DR. STOCKMANN Consequences?—Consequences to me?

MAYOR STOCKMANN Yes—to you and yours.

DR. STOCKMANN What the devil do you mean?

MAYOR STOCKMANN I believe I have always shown myself ready and willing to lend you a helping hand.

DR. STOCKMANN Yes, you have, and I thank you for it.

MAYOR STOCKMANN I ask for no thanks. Indeed, I was in some measure forced to act as I did—for my own sake. I always hoped I should be able to keep you a little in check, if I helped to improve your pecuniary position.

DR. STOCKMANN What! So it was only for your own sake—!

MAYOR STOCKMANN In a measure, I say. It is painful for a man in an official position, when his nearest relative goes and compromises himself time after time.

DR. STOCKMANN And you think I do that?

MAYOR STOCKMANN Yes, unfortunately, you do, without knowing it. Yours is a turbulent, unruly, rebellious spirit. And then you have an unhappy propensity for rushing into print upon every possible and impossible occasion. You no sooner hit upon an idea than you must write a newspaper article or a whole pamphlet about it.

DR. STOCKMANN Isn't it a citizen's duty, when he has conceived a new idea, to communicate it to the public!

MAYOR STOCKMANN Oh, the public has no need for new ideas. The public gets on best with the good old recognized ideas it has already.

DR. STOCKMANN You say that right out!

MAYOR STOCKMANN Yes, I must speak frankly to you for once. Hitherto I have tried to avoid it, for I know how irritable you are; but now I must tell you the truth, Thomas. You have no conception how much you injure yourself by your officiousness. You complain of the authorities, ay, of the government itself—you cry them down and maintain that you have been slighted, persecuted. But what else can you expect, with your impossible disposition?

DR. STOCKMANN Oh, indeed! So I am impossible, am I?

MAYOR STOCKMANN Yes, Thomas, you are an impossible man to work with. I know that from experience. You have no consideration for anyone or anything; you seem quite to forget that you have me to thank for your position as medical officer of the baths—

DR. STOCKMANN It was mine by right! Mine and no one else's! I was the first to discover the town's capabilities as a watering place; I saw them, and, at that time, I alone. For years I fought single-handed for this idea of mine; I wrote and wrote—

MAYOR STOCKMANN No doubt, but then the right time had not come. Of course, in that out-of-the-way corner, you could not judge of that. As soon as the propitious moment arrived, I—and others— took the matter in hand—

DR. STOCKMANN Yes, and you went and bungled the whole of my glorious plan. Oh, we see now what wise men you were!

MAYOR STOCKMANN All *I* can see is that you are again seeking an outlet for your pugnacity. You want to make an onslaught on your superiors— that is an old habit of yours. You cannot endure any authority over you; you look askance at anyone who holds a higher post than your own; you regard him as a personal enemy—and then you care nothing what kind of weapon you use against him. But now I have shown you how much is at stake for the town, and consequently for me too. And therefore I warn you, Thomas, that I am inexorable in the demand I am about to make of you!

DR. STOCKMANN What demand?

MAYOR STOCKMANN As you have not had the sense to refrain from chattering to outsiders about this delicate business, which should have been kept an official secret, of course it cannot now be hushed up. All sorts of rumors will get abroad, and evil-disposed persons will invent all sorts of additions to them. It will therefore be necessary for you publicly to contradict these rumors.

DR. STOCKMANN I! How? I don't understand you.

MAYOR STOCKMANN We expect that, after further investigation, you will come to the conclusion that the affair is not nearly so serious or pressing as you had at first imagined.

DR. STOCKMANN Aha! So you expect that?

MAYOR STOCKMANN Furthermore, we expect you to express your confidence that the board of directors will thoroughly and conscientiously carry out all measures for the remedying of any possible defects.

DR. STOCKMANN Yes, but that you'll never be able to do, so long as you go on tinkering and patching. I tell you that, Peter; and it's my deepest, sincerest conviction—

MAYOR STOCKMANN As an official, you have no right to hold any individual conviction.

DR. STOCKMANN [*Starting.*] No right to—?

MAYOR STOCKMANN As an official, I say. In your private capacity, of course, it is another matter. But as a subordinate official of the baths, you have no right to express any conviction at issue with that of your superiors.

DR. STOCKMANN This is too much! I, a doctor, a man of science, have no right to—

MAYOR STOCKMANN The matter in question is not a purely scientific one; it is a complex affair. It has both a technical and an economic side.

DR. STOCKMANN What the devil do I care what it is! I will be free to speak my mind upon any subject under the sun!

MAYOR STOCKMANN As you please—so long as it does not concern the baths. With them we forbid you to meddle.

DR. STOCKMANN [*Shouts.*] You forbid—! You! A set of—

MAYOR STOCKMANN *I* forbid it—*I*, your chief; and when I issue an order, you have simply to obey.

DR. STOCKMANN [*Controlling himself.*] Upon my word, Peter, if you weren't my brother—

PETRA [*Tears open the door.*] Father, you cannot submit to this!

MRS. STOCKMANN [*Following her.*] Petra, Petra!

MAYOR STOCKMANN Ah! So we have been listening!

MRS. STOCKMANN The partition is so thin, we couldn't help—

PETRA I stood and listened on purpose.

MAYOR STOCKMANN Well, on the whole, I am not sorry—

DR. STOCKMANN [*Coming nearer to him.*] You spoke to me of forbidding and obeying—

MAYOR STOCKMANN You have forced me to adopt that tone.

DR. STOCKMANN And am I to give myself the lie, in a public declaration?

MAYOR STOCKMAN We consider it absolutely necessary that you should issue a statement in the terms indicated.

DR. STOCKMANN And if I do not obey?

MAYOR STOCKMANN Then we shall ourselves put forth a statement to reassure the public.

DR. STOCKMANN Well and good; then I shall write against you. I shall stick to my point and prove that *I* am right, and you wrong. And what will you do then?

MAYOR STOCKMANN Then I shall be unable to prevent your dismissal.

DR. STOCKMANN What—!

PETRA Father! Dismissal!

MRS. STOCKMANN Dismissal!

MAYOR STOCKMANN Your dismissal from the baths. I shall be compelled to move that notice be given you at once, and that you have henceforth no connection whatever with the baths.

DR. STOCKMANN You would dare to do that!

MAYOR STOCKMANN It is you who are playing the daring game.

PETRA Uncle, this is a shameful way to treat a man like father!

MRS. STOCKMANN Do be quiet, Petra!

MAYOR STOCKMANN [*Looking at Petra.*] Aha! We have opinions of our own already, eh? To be sure, to be sure! [*To Mrs. Stockmann.*] Sister-in-law, you are presumably the most rational member of this household. Use all your influence with your husband; try to make him realize what all this will involve both for his family—

DR. STOCKMANN My family concerns myself alone!

MAYOR STOCKMANN —both for his family, I say, and for the town he lives in.

DR. STOCKMANN It is I that have the real good of the town at heart! I want to lay bare the evils that, sooner or later, must come to light. Ah! You shall see whether I love my native town.

MAYOR STOCKMANN You, who, in your blind obstinacy, want to cut off the town's chief source of prosperity!

DR. STOCKMANN That source is poisoned, man! Are you mad? We live by trafficking in filth and corruption! The whole of our flourishing social life is rooted in a lie!

MAYOR STOCKMANN Idle fancies—or worse. The man who broadcasts such offensive insinuations against his native place must be an enemy of society.

DR. STOCKMANN [*Going toward him.*] You dare to—!

MRS. STOCKMANN [*Throwing herself between them.*] Thomas!

PETRA [*Seizing her father's arm.*] Keep calm, father!

MAYOR STOCKMANN I will not expose myself to violence. You have had your warning now. Reflect upon what is due to yourself and to your family. Good-bye.

[*He goes.*]

DR. STOCKMANN [*Walking up and down.*] And I must put up with such treatment! In my own house, Katrina! What do you say to that!

MRS. STOCKMANN Indeed, it's a shame and a disgrace, Thomas—

PETRA Oh, if I could only get hold of uncle—!

DR. STOCKMANN It's my own fault. I ought to have stood up against them long ago—to have shown my teeth—and used them too!— And to be called an enemy of society! Me! I won't bear it; by Heaven, I won't!

MRS. STOCKMANN But my dear Thomas, after all, your brother has the power—

DR. STOCKMANN   Yes, but I have the right.

MRS. STOCKMANN   Ah yes, right, right! What good does it do to have the right, if you haven't any might?

PETRA   Oh, mother—how can you talk so?

DR. STOCKMANN   What! No good, in a free community, to have right on your side? What an absurd idea, Katrina! And besides—haven't I the free and independent press before me—and the majority at my back? That is might enough, I should think!

MRS. STOCKMANN   Why, good heavens, Thomas! You're surely not thinking of—

DR. STOCKMANN   What am I not thinking of?

MRS. STOCKMANN   —of setting yourself up against your brother, I mean.

DR. STOCKMANN   What the devil would you have me do, if not stick to what is right and true?

PETRA   Yes, that's what I should like to know.

MRS. STOCKMANN   But it will be of no earthly use. If they won't, they won't.

DR. STOCKMANN   Ho-ho, Katrina! Just wait a while, and you shall see whether I can fight my battles to the end.

MRS. STOCKMANN   Yes, to the end of getting your dismissal; that is what will happen.

DR. STOCKMANN   Well then, I shall at any rate have done my duty toward the public, toward society—I who am called an enemy of society!

MRS. STOCKMANN   But toward your family, Thomas? Toward us at home? Do you think that is doing your duty toward those who are dependent on you?

PETRA   Oh, mother, don't always think first of us.

MRS. STOCKMANN   Yes, it's easy for you to talk; you can stand alone if need be. But remember the boys, Thomas, and think a little of yourself too, and of me—

DR. STOCKMANN You're surely out of your senses, Katrina! If I were to be such a pitiful coward as to knuckle under to this Peter and his confounded crew—should I ever have another happy hour in all my life?

MRS. STOCKMANN I don't know about that, but God preserve us from the happiness we shall all of us have if you persist in defying them. There you will be again, with nothing to live on, with no regular income. I should have thought we had had enough of that in the old days. Remember them, Thomas; think of what it all means.

DR. STOCKMANN [*Struggling with himself and clenching his hands.*] And this is what these jacks-in-office can bring upon a free and honest man! Isn't it revolting, Katrina?

MRS. STOCKMANN Yes, no doubt they are treating you shamefully. But God knows there's plenty of injustice one must just submit to in this world. Here are the boys, Thomas. Look at them! What is to become of them? Oh no, no! You can never have the heart—

[*Eilif and Morten, with schoolbooks, have meanwhile entered.*]

DR. STOCKMANN The boys—! [*With a sudden access of firmness and decision.*] Never, though the whole earth should crumble, will I bow my neck beneath the yoke.

[*Goes toward his room.*]

MRS. STOCKMANN [*Following him.*] Thomas—what are you going to do?

DR. STOCKMANN [*At the door.*] I must have the right to look my boys in the face when they have grown into free men.

[*Goes into his room.*]

MRS. STOCKMANN [*Bursts into tears.*] Ah, God help us all!

PETRA Father is true to the core. He will never give in!

[*The boys ask wonderingly what it all means; Petra signs to them to be quiet.*]

ACT III

[*The Editor's Room of the* People's Messenger. *In the background, to the left, an entrance door; to the right another door, with glass panes, through which can be seen the composing room. A door in the right-hand wall. In the middle of the room a large table covered with papers, newspapers, and books. In front, on the left, a window, and by it a desk with a high stool. A couple of armchairs beside the table; some other chairs along the walls. The room is dingy and cheerless, the furniture shabby, the armchairs dirty and torn. In the composing room are seen a few compositors at work; further back, a hand press in operation.*

Hovstad is seated at the desk, writing. Presently Billing enters from the right, with the doctor's manuscript in his hand.]

BILLING   Well, I must say—

HOVSTAD   [*Writing.*] Have you read it through?

BILLING   [*Laying the manuscript on the desk.*] Yes, I should think I had.

HOVSTAD   Don't you think the doctor comes out strong?

BILLING   Strong! Why, strike me dead if he isn't crushing! Every word falls like a—well, like a sledgehammer.

HOVSTAD   Yes, but these fellows won't collapse at the first blow.

BILLING   True enough; but we'll keep on hammering away, blow after blow, till the whole officialdom comes crashing down. As I sat in there reading that article, I seemed to hear the revolution thundering afar.

HOVSTAD   [*Turning round.*] Hush! Don't let Aslaksen hear that.

BILLING   [*In a lower voice.*] Aslaksen's a white-livered, cowardly fellow, without a spark of manhood in him. But this time you'll surely carry your point? Eh? You'll print the doctor's paper?

HOVSTAD   Yes, if only the mayor doesn't give in—

BILLING   That would be damned annoying.

HOVSTAD Well, whatever happens, fortunately we can turn the situation to account. If the mayor won't agree to the doctor's proposal, he'll have all the small middle-class down upon him—all the Homeowners' Association, and the rest of them. And if he does agree to it, he'll fall out with the whole crew of big shareholders in the baths, who have hitherto been his main support—

BILLING Yes, of course; for no doubt they'll have to fork out a lot of money—

HOVSTAD You may take your oath of that. And then, don't you see, when the ring is broken up, we'll din it into the public day by day that the mayor is incompetent in every respect, and that all responsible positions in the town, the whole municipal government in short, must be entrusted to men of liberal ideas.

BILLING Strike me dead if that isn't the square truth! I see it—I see it: we are on the eve of a revolution!

[*A knock at the door.*]

HOVSTAD Hush! [*Calls.*] Come in!

[*Dr. Stockmann enters from the back, left.*]

HOVSTAD [*Going toward him.*] Ah, here is the doctor. Well?

DR. STOCKMANN Print away, Mr. Hovstad!

HOVSTAD So it has come to that?

BILLING Hurrah!

DR. STOCKMANN Print away, I tell you. To be sure it has come to that. Since they will have it so, they must. War is declared, Mr. Billing!

BILLING War to the knife, say I! War to the death, Doctor!

DR. STOCKMANN This article is only the beginning. I have four or five others sketched out in my head already. But where do you keep Aslaksen?

BILLING [*Calling into the printing room.*] Aslaksen! Just come here a moment.

HOVSTAD Four or five more articles, eh? On the same subject?

DR. STOCKMANN   Oh no—not at all, my dear fellow. No; they will deal with quite different matters. But they're all of a piece with the waterworks and sewer question. One thing leads to another. It's just like beginning to pick at an old house, don't you know?

BILLING   Strike me dead, but that's true! You feel you can't leave off till you've pulled the whole lumber heap to pieces.

ASLAKSEN   [*Enters from the printing room.*] Pulled to pieces! Surely the doctor isn't thinking of pulling the baths to pieces?

HOVSTAD   Not at all. Don't be alarmed.

DR. STOCKMANN   No, we were talking of something quite different. Well, what do you think of my article, Mr. Hovstad?

HOVSTAD   I think it's simply a masterpiece—

DR. STOCKMANN   Yes, isn't it? I'm glad you think so—very glad.

HOVSTAD   It's so clear and to the point. One doesn't in the least need to be a specialist to understand the gist of it. I am certain every intelligent man will be on your side.

ASLAKSEN   And all the prudent ones too, I hope?

BILLING   Both the prudent and imprudent—in fact, almost the whole town.

ASLAKSEN   Then I suppose we may venture to print it.

DR. STOCKMANN   I should think so!

HOVSTAD   It shall go in tomorrow.

DR. STOCKMANN   Yes, plague take it, not a day must be lost. Look here, Mr. Aslaksen, this is what I wanted to ask you: won't you take personal charge of the article?

ASLAKSEN   Certainly I will.

DR. STOCKMANN   Be as careful as if it were gold. No printers' errors; every word is important. I shall look in again presently; perhaps you'll be able to let me see a proof—Ah! I can't tell you how I long to have the thing in print—to see it launched—

BILLING Yes, like a thunderbolt!

DR. STOCKMANN —and submitted to the judgment of every intelligent citizen. Oh, you have no idea what I have had to put up with today. I've been threatened with all sorts of things. I was to be robbed of my clearest rights as a human being—

BILLING What! Your rights as a human being!

DR. STOCKMANN —I was to humble myself and eat the dust; I was to set my personal interests above my deepest, holiest convictions—

BILLING Strike me dead, but that's too outrageous!

HOVSTAD Oh, what can you expect from that quarter?

DR. STOCKMANN But they shall find they were mistaken in me; they shall learn that in black and white, I promise them! I shall throw myself into the breach every day in the *Messenger*, bombard them with one explosive article after another—

ASLAKSEN Yes, but look here—

BILLING Hurrah! It's war! War!

DR. STOCKMANN I shall smite them to the earth, I shall crush them, I shall level their entrenchments to the ground in the eyes of all right-thinking men! That's what I shall do!

ASLAKSEN But above all things be temperate, Doctor; bombard with moderation—

BILLING Not at all, not at all! Don't spare the dynamite!

DR. STOCKMANN [*Going on imperturbably.*] For now it's no mere question of waterworks and sewers, you see. No, the whole community must be purged, disinfected—

BILLING There sounds the word of salvation!

DR. STOCKMANN All the old bunglers must be sent packing, you understand. And that in every possible department! Such endless vistas have opened out before me today. I am not quite clear about everything yet, but I shall see my way presently. It's young and vigorous standard-bearers we must look for, my friends; we must have new captains at all the outposts.

BILLING Hear, hear!

DR. STOCKMANN And if only we hold together, it will go so smoothly, so smoothly! The whole revolution will glide off the stocks just like a ship. Don't you think so?

HOVSTAD For my part, I believe we have now every prospect of placing our municipal affairs in the right hands.

ASLAKSEN And if only we proceed with moderation, I really don't think there can be any danger.

DR. STOCKMANN Who the hell cares whether there's danger or not! What I do, I do in the name of truth and for conscience' sake.

HOVSTAD You are a man to be backed up, Doctor.

ASLAKSEN Yes, there's no doubt the doctor is a true friend to the town; he's what I call a friend of society.

BILLING Strike me dead if Dr. Stockmann isn't a friend of the people, Aslaksen!

ASLAKSEN I have no doubt the Homeowners' Association will soon adopt that expression.

DR. STOCKMANN [*Shaking their hands, deeply moved.*] Thanks, thanks, my dear, faithful friends; it does me good to hear you. My respected brother called me something very different. Never mind! Trust me to pay him back with interest! But I must be off now to see a poor devil of a patient. I shall look in again, though. Be sure you look after the article, Mr. Aslaksen; and, whatever you do, don't leave out any of my notes of exclamation! Rather put in a few more! Well, good-bye for the present, good-bye, good-bye.

[*Mutual salutations while they accompany him to the door. He goes out.*]

HOVSTAD He will be invaluable to us.

ASLAKSEN Yes, so long as he confines himself to this matter of the baths. But if he goes further, it will scarcely be advisable to follow him.

HOVSTAD H'm—that entirely depends on—

BILLING You're always so confoundedly timid, Aslaksen.

ASLAKSEN Timid? Yes, when it's a question of attacking local authorities, I am timid, Mr. Billing; I have learned caution in the school of experience, let me tell you. But start me on the higher politics, confront me with the government itself, and then see if I'm timid.

BILLING No, you're not, but that's just where your inconsistency comes in.

ASLAKSEN The fact is, I am keenly alive to my responsibilities. If you attack the government, you at least do society no harm; for the men attacked don't care a straw, you see—they stay where they are all the same. But local authorities can be turned out; and then we might get some incompetent set into power, to the irreparable injury both of homeowners and other people.

HOVSTAD But the education of citizens by self-government—do you never think of that?

ASLAKSEN When a man has solid interests to protect, he can't think of everything, Mr. Hovstad.

HOVSTAD Then I hope I may never have solid interests to protect.

BILLING Hear, hear!

ASLAKSEN [*Smiling.*] H'm! [*Points to the desk.*] Governor Stensgård sat in that editorial chair before you.

BILLING [*Spitting.*] Pooh! A turncoat like that!

HOVSTAD I am no weathercock—and never will be.

ASLAKSEN A politician should never be too sure of anything on earth, Mr. Hovstad. And as for you, Mr. Billing, you ought to take in a reef or two, I should say, now that you are applying for the secretaryship to the town council.

BILLING I—!

HOVSTAD Is that so, Billing?

BILLING Well, yes—but, devil take it, you understand, I'm only doing it to spite their high-and-mightinesses.

ASLAKSEN Well, that has nothing to do with me. But if I am to be accused of cowardice and inconsistency, I should just like to point out this: my political record is open to every one. I have not changed at all, except in becoming more moderate. My heart still belongs to the people; but I don't deny that my reason inclines somewhat toward the authorities—the local ones, I mean.

[*Goes into the printing room.*]

BILLING   Don't you think we should try to get rid of him, Hovstad?

HOVSTAD   Do you know of anyone else that will pay for our paper and printing?

BILLING   What a confounded nuisance it is to have no capital!

HOVSTAD   [*Sitting down by the desk.*] Yes, if we only had that—

BILLING   Suppose you applied to Dr. Stockmann?

HOVSTAD   [*Turning over his papers.*] What would be the good? He hasn't a rap.

BILLING   No, but he has a good man behind him—old Morten Kiil— "The Badger," as they call him.

HOVSTAD   [*Writing.*] Are you so sure he has money?

BILLING   Yes, strike me dead if he hasn't! And part of it must certainly go to Stockmann's family. He's bound to provide for—for the children at any rate.

HOVSTAD   [*Half turning.*] Are you counting on that?

BILLING   Counting? How should I be counting on it?

HOVSTAD   Best not! And that secretaryship you shouldn't count on either, for I can assure you you won't get it.

BILLING   Do you think I don't know that? A refusal is the very thing I want. Such a rebuff fires the spirit of opposition in you, gives you a fresh supply of gall, as it were; and that's just what you need in a godforsaken hole like this, where anything really stimulating so seldom happens.

HOVSTAD   [*Writing.*] Yes, yes.

BILLING   Well—they shall soon hear from me!—Now I'll go and write the appeal to the Homeowners' Association.

[*Goes into the room on the right.*]

HOVSTAD [*Sits at his desk, biting his penholder, and says slowly:*] H'm—
so that's the way of it.— [*A knock at the door.*] Come in.

[*Petra enters from the back, left.*]

HOVSTAD [*Rising.*] What! Is it you? Here?

PETRA Yes; please excuse me—

HOVSTAD [*Offering her an armchair.*] Won't you sit down?

PETRA No, thanks; I must go again directly.

HOVSTAD Perhaps you bring a message from your father—?

PETRA No, I have come on my own account. [*Takes a book from the pocket
of her cloak.*] Here is that English story.

HOVSTAD Why have you brought it back?

PETRA Because I won't translate it.

HOVSTAD But you promised—

PETRA Yes; but then I hadn't read it. I suppose you have not read it either?

HOVSTAD No. You know I can't read English, but—

PETRA Exactly, and that's why I wanted to tell you that you must find
something else. [*Putting the book on the table.*] This will never do for
the *Messenger*.

HOVSTAD Why not?

PETRA Because it flies in the face of all your convictions.

HOVSTAD Well, for that matter—

PETRA You don't understand me. It makes out that a supernatural
power looks after the so-called good people in this world, and turns
everything to their advantage at last, while all the so-called bad
people are punished.

HOVSTAD Yes, but that's all right. That's the very thing the public like.

PETRA   And would you supply the public with such stuff? You don't believe a word of it yourself. You know well enough that things do not really happen like that.

HOVSTAD   Of course not, but an editor can't always do as he likes. He has often to humor people's fancies in minor matters. After all, politics is the chief thing in life—at any rate for a newspaper; and if I want the people to follow me along the path of emancipation and progress, I mustn't scare them away. If they find a moral story like this down in the cellar, they are all the more ready to take in what we tell them above—they feel themselves safer.

PETRA   For shame! You're not such a hypocrite as to set traps like that for your readers. You're not a spider.

HOVSTAD   [*Smiling.*] Thanks for your good opinion. It's true that the idea is Billing's, not mine.

PETRA   Mr. Billing's!

HOVSTAD   Yes, at least he was talking in that strain the other day. It was Billing that was so anxious to get the story into the paper; I don't even know the book.

PETRA   But how can Mr. Billing, with his advanced views—

HOVSTAD   Well, Billing is many sided. He's applying for the secretaryship to the town council, I hear.

PETRA   I don't believe that, Mr. Hovstad. How could he descend to such a thing?

HOVSTAD   That you must ask him.

PETRA   I could never have thought it of Billing!

HOVSTAD   [*Looking more closely at her.*] No? Is it such a surprise to you?

PETRA   Yes. And yet—perhaps not. Oh, I don't know—

HOVSTAD   We journalists are not worth much, Miss Petra.

PETRA   Do you really say that?

HOVSTAD   I think so, now and then.

PETRA Yes, in the little everyday squabbles—that I can understand.
  But now that you have taken up a great cause—

HOVSTAD You mean this affair of your father's?

PETRA Of course. I should think you must feel yourself worth more
  than the general run of people now.

HOVSTAD Yes, today I do feel something of the sort.

PETRA Yes, surely you must. Oh, it's a glorious career you have chosen!
  To be the pioneer of unrecognized truths and new and daring
  ways of thought—even, if that were all, to stand forth fearlessly in
  support of an injured man—

HOVSTAD Especially when the injured man is—I hardly know how
  to put it—

PETRA You mean when he is so upright and true?

HOVSTAD [*In a low voice.*] I mean—especially when he is your father.

PETRA [*Suddenly taken aback.*] That?

HOVSTAD Yes, Petra—Miss Petra.

PETRA So that is your chief thought, is it? Not the cause itself? Not
  the truth? Not father's great, warm heart?

HOVSTAD Oh, that too, of course.

PETRA No, thank you; you said too much that time, Mr. Hovstad.
  Now I shall never trust you again, in anything.

HOVSTAD Can you be so hard on me because it's mainly for your sake—?

PETRA What I blame you for is that you have not acted straight-
  forwardly toward father. You have talked to him as if you cared
  only for the truth and the good of the community. You have trifled
  with both father and me. You are not the man you pretended to
  be. And that I will never forgive you—never.

HOVSTAD You shouldn't say that so bitterly, Miss Petra—least of all now.

PETRA Why not now?

HOVSTAD   Because your father cannot do without my help.

PETRA   [*Measuring him from head to foot.*] So you are capable of that, too? Oh, shame!

HOVSTAD   No, no. I spoke without thinking. You mustn't believe that of me.

PETRA   I know what to believe. Good-bye.

[*Aslaksen enters from printing room, hurriedly and mysteriously.*]

ASLAKSEN   What do you think, Mr. Hovstad— [*Seeing Petra.*] Ow, that's awkward—

PETRA   Well, there is the book. You must give it to someone else.

[*Going toward the main door.*]

HOVSTAD   [*Following her.*] But, Miss Petra—

PETRA   Good-bye.

[*She goes.*]

ASLAKSEN   I say, Mr. Hovstad!

HOVSTAD   Well, well; what is it?

ASLAKSEN   The mayor's out there, in the printing office.

HOVSTAD   The mayor?

ASLAKSEN   Yes. He wants to speak to you; he came in by the back way— he didn't want to be seen, you understand.

HOVSTAD   What can be the meaning of this? Stop, I'll go myself—

[*Goes toward the printing room, opens the door, bows, and invites the mayor to enter.*]

HOVSTAD   Keep a lookout, Aslaksen, that no one—

ASLAKSEN   I understand.

[*Goes into the printing room.*]

MAYOR STOCKMANN   You didn't expect to see me here, Mr. Hovstad.

HOVSTAD   No, I cannot say that I did.

MAYOR STOCKMANN   [*Looking about him.*] You are very comfortably installed here—capital quarters.

HOVSTAD   Oh—

MAYOR STOCKMANN   And here have I come, without with your leave or by your leave, to take up your time—

HOVSTAD   You are very welcome, Mr. Mayor; I am at your service. Let me take your cap and stick. [*He does so, and puts them on a chair.*] And won't you be seated?

MAYOR STOCKMANN   [*Sitting down by the table.*] Thanks. [*Hovsta also sits by the table.*] I have been much—very much worried today, Mr. Hovstad.

HOVSTAD   Really? Well, I suppose with all your various duties, Mr. Mayor—

MAYOR STOCKMANN   It is the doctor that has been causing me annoyance today.

HOVSTAD   Indeed! The doctor?

MAYOR STOCKMANN   He has written a sort of memorandum to the directors about some alleged shortcomings in the baths.

HOVSTAD   Has he really?

MAYOR STOCKMANN   Yes; hasn't he told you? I thought he said—

HOVSTAD   Oh yes, by the bye, he did mention something—

ASLAKSEN   [*From the printing office.*] I've just come for the manuscript—

HOVSTAD   [*In a tone of vexation.*] Oh—there it is on the desk.

ASLAKSEN   [*Finding it.*] All right.

MAYOR STOCKMANN   Why, that is the very thing—

ASLAKSEN   Yes, this is the doctor's article, Mr. Mayor.

HOVSTAD   Oh, is that what you were speaking of?

MAYOR STOCKMANN   Precisely. What do you think of it?

HOVSTAD   I have no technical knowledge of the matter, and I've only glanced through it.

MAYOR STOCKMANN   And yet you are going to print it!

HOVSTAD   I can't very well refuse a signed communication—

ASLAKSEN   I have nothing to do with the editing of the paper, Mr. Mayor—

MAYOR STOCKMANN   Of course not.

ASLAKSEN   I merely print what is placed in my hands.

MAYOR STOCKMANN   Quite right, quite right.

ASLAKSEN   So I must—

[*Goes toward the printing room.*]

MAYOR STOCKMANN   No, stop a moment, Mr. Aslaksen. With your permission, Mr. Hovstad—

HOVSTAD   By all means, Mr. Mayor.

MAYOR STOCKMANN   You are a discreet and thoughtful man, Mr. Aslaksen.

ASLAKSEN   I am glad you think so, Mr. Mayor.

MAYOR STOCKMANN   And a man of very wide influence.

ASLAKSEN   Well—chiefly among the lower middle class.

MAYOR STOCKMANN   The small taxpayers form the majority—here as everywhere.

ASLAKSEN   That's very true.

MAYOR STOCKMANN   And I have no doubt that you know the general feeling among them. Am I right?

ASLAKSEN   Yes, I think I may say that I do, Mr. Mayor.

MAYOR STOCKMANN   Well—since our townsfolk of the poorer class appear to be so heroically eager to make sacrifices—

ASLAKSEN How so?

HOVSTAD Sacrifices?

MAYOR STOCKMANN It is a pleasing evidence of public spirit—a most
pleasing evidence. I admit it is more than I should quite have
expected. But, of course, you know public feeling better than I do.

ASLAKSEN Yes, but, Mr. Mayor—

MAYOR STOCKMANN And assuredly it is no small sacrifice the town will
have to make.

HOVSTAD The town?

ASLAKSEN But I don't understand—It's the baths—

MAYOR STOCKMANN At a rough provisional estimate, the alterations
the doctor thinks desirable will come to two or three hundred
thousand crowns.

ASLAKSEN That's a lot of money, but—

MAYOR STOCKMANN Of course we shall be obliged to raise a
municipal loan.

HOVSTAD [*Rising.*] You surely can't mean that the town—?

ASLAKSEN Would you come upon the rates? Upon the scanty savings
of the lower middle class?

MAYOR STOCKMANN Why, my dear Mr. Aslaksen, where else are the
funds to come from?

ASLAKSEN The proprietors of the baths must see to that.

MAYOR STOCKMANN The proprietors are not in a position to go to
any further expense.

ASLAKSEN Are you quite sure of that, Mr. Mayor?

MAYOR STOCKMANN I have positive information. So if these extensive
alterations are called for, the town itself will have to bear the cost.

ASLAKSEN Oh, plague take it all—I beg your pardon!—but this is
quite another matter, Mr. Hovstad.

HOVSTAD   Yes, it certainly is.

MAYOR STOCKMANN   The worst of it is that we shall be obliged to close the establishment for a couple of years.

HOVSTAD   To close it? Completely?

ASLAKSEN   For two years!

MAYOR STOCKMANN   Yes, the work will require that time—at least.

ASLAKSEN   But, damn it all! We can't stand that, Mr. Mayor. What are we homeowners to live on in the meantime?

MAYOR STOCKMANN   It's extremely difficult to say, Mr. Aslaksen. But what would you have us do? Do you think a single visitor will come here if we go about making them fancy that the water is poisoned, that the place is pestilential, that the whole town—

ASLAKSEN   And it's all nothing but fancy?

MAYOR STOCKMANN   With the best will in the world, I have failed to convince myself that it is anything else.

ASLAKSEN   In that case it's simply inexcusable of Dr. Stockmann—I beg your pardon, Mr. Mayor, but—

MAYOR STOCKMANN   I'm sorry to say you are only speaking the truth, Mr. Aslaksen. Unfortunately, my brother has always been noted for his rashness.

ASLAKSEN   And yet you want to back him up in this, Mr. Hovstad!

HOVSTAD   But who could possibly imagine that—?

MAYOR STOCKMANN   I have drawn up a short statement of the facts, as they appear from a sober-minded standpoint; and I have intimated that any drawbacks that may possibly exist can no doubt be remedied by measures compatible with the finances of the baths.

HOVSTAD   Have you the article with you, Mr. Mayor?

MAYOR STOCKMANN   [*Feeling in his pockets.*] Yes, I brought it with me, in case you—

ASLAKSEN   [*Quickly.*] Plague take it, there he is!

MAYOR STOCKMANN Who? My brother?

HOVSTAD Where? Where?

ASLAKSEN He's coming through the composing room.

MAYOR STOCKMANN Most unfortunate! I don't want to meet him here, and yet there are several things I want to talk to you about.

HOVSTAD [*Pointing to the door on the right.*] Go in there for a moment.

MAYOR STOCKMANN But—?

HOVSTAD You'll find nobody but Billing there.

ASLAKSEN Quick, quick, Mr. Mayor; he's just coming.

MAYOR STOCKMANN Very well, then. But try to get rid of him quickly.

[*He goes out by the door on the right, which Aslaksen opens and closes behind him.*]

HOVSTAD Pretend to be busy, Aslaksen.

[*He sits down and writes. Aslaksen turns over a heap of newspapers on a chair, right.*]

DR. STOCKMANN [*Entering from the composing room.*] Here I am, back again.

[*Puts down his hat and stick.*]

HOVSTAD [*Writing.*] Already, Doctor? Make haste with what we were speaking of, Aslaksen. We've no time to lose today.

DR. STOCKMANN [*To Aslaksen.*] No proof yet, I hear.

ASLAKSEN [*Without turning round.*] No, how could you expect it?

DR. STOCKMANN Of course not, but you understand my impatience. I can have no rest or peace until I see the thing in print.

HOVSTAD H'm. It will take a good while yet. Don't you think so, Aslaksen?

ASLAKSEN I'm afraid it will.

DR. STOCKMANN   All right, all right, my good friend, then I shall look in again. I'll look in twice if necessary. With so much at stake—the welfare of the whole town—one mustn't grudge a little trouble. [*Is on the point of going but stops and comes back.*] Oh, by the way—there's one other thing I must speak to you about.

HOVSTAD   Excuse me; wouldn't some other time—?

DR. STOCKMANN   I can tell you in two words. You see it's this: when people read my article in the paper tomorrow, and find I have spent the whole winter working quietly for the good of the town—

HOVSTAD   Yes, but, Doctor—

DR. STOCKMANN   I know what you're going to say. You don't think it was a bit more than my duty—my simple duty as a citizen. Of course, I know that as well as you do. But you see, my fellow townsmen—good Lord!—the poor souls think so much of me—

ASLAKSEN   Yes, the townspeople have hitherto thought very highly of you, Doctor.

DR. STOCKMANN   That's exactly why I'm afraid that—what I wanted to say was this: when all this comes to them—especially to the poorer classes—as a summons to take the affairs of the town into their own hands for the future—

HOVSTAD   [*Rising.*] H'm, Doctor, I won't conceal from you—

DR. STOCKMANN   Aha! I thought there was something brewing! But I won't hear of it. If they are getting up anything of that sort—

HOVSTAD   Of what sort?

DR. STOCKMANN   Well, anything of any sort—a procession with banners, or a banquet, or a subscription for a testimonial, or whatever it may be—you must give me your solemn promise to put a stop to it. And you too, Mr. Aslaksen; do you hear?

HOVSTAD   Excuse me, Doctor; we may as well tell you the whole truth first as last—

[*Mrs. Stockmann enters from the back, left.*]

MRS. STOCKMANN   [*Seeing the doctor.*] Ah! just as I thought!

HOVSTAD [*Going toward her.*] Mrs. Stockmann, too?

DR. STOCKMANN What the devil do you want here, Katrina?

MRS. STOCKMANN You know very well what I want.

HOVSTAD Won't you sit down? Or perhaps—

MRS. STOCKMANN Thanks, please don't trouble. And you must forgive my following my husband here; remember, I am the mother of three children.

DR. STOCKMANN Stuff and nonsense! We all know that well enough.

MRS. STOCKMANN Well, it doesn't look as if you thought very much about your wife and children today, or you wouldn't be so ready to plunge us all into ruin.

DR. STOCKMANN Are you quite mad, Katrina? Has a man with a wife and children no right to proclaim the truth? Has he no right to be an active and useful citizen? Has he no right to do his duty by the town he lives in?

MRS. STOCKMANN Everything in moderation, Thomas!

ASLAKSEN That's just what I say. Moderation in everything.

MRS. STOCKMANN You are doing us a great wrong, Mr. Hovstad, in enticing my husband away from house and home, and befooling him in this way.

HOVSTAD I am not befooling anyone—

DR. STOCKMANN Befooling! Do you think I should let myself be befooled?

MRS. STOCKMANN Yes, that's just what you do. I know very well that you are the cleverest man in the town, but you're very easily made a fool of, Thomas. [*To Hovstad.*] Remember that he loses his post at the baths if you print what he has written—

ASLAKSEN What!

HOVSTAD Well now, really, Doctor—

DR. STOCKMANN   [*Laughing.*] Ha ha! just let them try—! No no, my dear, they'll think twice about that. I have the solid majority behind me, you see!

MRS. STOCKMANN   That's just the misfortune, that you should have such a horrid thing behind you.

DR. STOCKMANN   Nonsense, Katrina—you go home and look after your house and let me take care of society. How can you be in such a fright when you see me so confident and happy? [*Rubbing his hands and walking up and down.*] Truth and the People must win the day; you may be perfectly sure of that. Oh! I can see all our free-souled citizens standing shoulder to shoulder like a conquering army—! [*Stopping by a chair.*] Why, what the devil is that?

ASLAKSEN   [*Looking at it.*] Oh Lord!

HOVSTAD   [*The same.*] H'm—

DR. STOCKMANN   Why, here's the topknot of authority!

[*He takes the mayor's official cap carefully between the tips of his fingers and holds it up.*]

MRS. STOCKMANN   The mayor's cap!

DR. STOCKMANN   And here's the staff of office, too! But how in the devil's name did they—?

HOVSTAD   Well then—

DR. STOCKMANN   Ah, I understand! He has been here to talk you over. Ha, ha! He reckoned without his host that time! And when he caught sight of me in the printing room— [*Bursts out laughing.*] He took to his heels, eh, Mr. Aslaksen?

ASLAKSEN   [*Hurriedly.*] Exactly, he took to his heels, Doctor.

DR. STOCKMANN   Made off without his stick and—no, that won't do! Peter never left anything behind him. But where the devil have you stowed him? Ah—in here, of course. Now you shall see, Katrina!

MRS. STOCKMANN   Thomas—I implore you—!

ASLAKSEN   Take care, Doctor!

[*Dr. Stockmann has put on the mayor's cap and grasped his stick; he now goes up to the door, throws it open, and makes a military salute. The mayor enters, red with anger. Behind him comes Billing.*]

MAYOR STOCKMANN What is the meaning of these antics?

DR. STOCKMANN Respect, my good Peter! Now, it's I that am in power in this town.

[*He struts up and down.*]

MRS. STOCKMANN [*Almost in tears.*] Oh, Thomas!

MAYOR STOCKMANN [*Following him.*] Give me my cap and stick!

DR. STOCKMANN [*As before.*] You may be chief of police, but I am mayor. I am master of the whole town I tell you!

MAYOR STOCKMANN Put down my cap, I say. Remember it is an official cap, as prescribed by law!

DR. STOCKMANN Pshaw! Do you think the awakening lion of the democracy will let itself be scared by a gold-laced cap? There's to be a revolution in the town tomorrow, let me tell you. You threatened me with dismissal; but now *I* dismiss you—dismiss you from all your offices of trust. You think I can't do it? Oh, yes, I can! I have the irresistible forces of society on my side. Hovstad and Billing will thunder in the *People's Messenger*, and Aslaksen will take the field at the head of the Homeowners' Association—

ASLAKSEN No, Doctor, I shall not.

DR. STOCKMANN Why, of course you will—

MAYOR STOCKMANN Aha! Perhaps Mr. Hovstad would like to join the agitation after all?

HOVSTAD No, Mr. Mayor.

ASLAKSEN No, Mr. Hovstad isn't such a fool as to ruin both himself and the paper for the sake of a delusion.

DR. STOCKMANN [*Looking about him.*] What does all this mean?

HOVSTAD You have presented your case in a false light, Doctor; therefore I am unable to give you my support.

BILLING   And after what the mayor has been so kind as to explain to me, I—

DR. STOCKMANN   In a false light! Well, I am responsible for that. Just you print my article, and I promise you I shall prove it up to the hilt.

HOVSTAD   I shall not print it. I cannot, and will not, and dare not print it.

DR. STOCKMANN   You dare not? What nonsense is this? You are editor, and I suppose it's the editor that controls a paper.

ASLAKSEN   No, it's the subscribers, Doctor.

MAYOR STOCKMANN   Fortunately.

ASLAKSEN   It's public opinion, the enlightened majority, the homeowners and all the rest. It's they who control a paper.

DR. STOCKMANN   [*Calmly.*] And all these powers I have against me?

ASLAKSEN   Yes, you have. It would mean absolute ruin for the town if your article were inserted.

DR. STOCKMANN   So that is the way of it!

MAYOR STOCKMANN   My hat and stick!

[*Dr. Stockmann takes off the cap and lays it on the table along with the stick.*]

MAYOR STOCKMANN   [*Taking them both.*] Your term of office has come to an untimely end.

DR. STOCKMANN   The end is not yet. [*To Hovstad.*] So you are quite determined not to print my article in the *Messenger*?

HOVSTAD   Quite; for the sake of your family, if for no other reason.

MRS. STOCKMANN   Oh, be kind enough to leave his family out of the question, Mr. Hovstad.

MAYOR STOCKMANN   [*Takes a manuscript from his pocket.*] When this appears, the public will be in possession of all necessary information; it is an authentic statement. I place it in your hands.

HOVSTAD   [*Taking the manuscript.*] Good. It shall appear in due course.

DR. STOCKMANN And not mine! You imagine you can kill me and the
truth by a conspiracy of silence! But it won't be so easy as you
think. Mr. Aslaksen, will you be good enough to print my article at
once, as a pamphlet? I'll pay for it myself and be my own publisher.
I'll have four hundred copies—no, five—six hundred.

ASLAKSEN No. If you offered me its weight in gold, I dare not lend my
press to such a purpose, Doctor. I dare not fly in the face of public
opinion. You won't get it printed anywhere in the whole town.

DR. STOCKMANN Then give it back to me.

HOVSTAD [*Handing him the manuscript.*] By all means.

DR. STOCKMANN [*Taking up his hat and cane.*] It shall be made public
all the same. I shall read it at a great mass meeting; all my fellow
citizens shall hear the voice of truth!

MAYOR STOCKMANN Not a single society in the town would let you
their hall for such a purpose.

ASLAKSEN Not one, I'm quite certain.

BILLING No, strike me dead if they would!

MRS. STOCKMANN That would be too disgraceful! Why do they turn
against you like this, every one of them?

DR. STOCKMANN [*Irritated.*] I'll tell you why. It's because in this town
all the men are old women—like you. They all think of nothing
but their families, not of the general good.

MRS. STOCKMANN [*Taking his arm.*] Then I'll show them that an—an old
woman can be a man for once in a way. For now I'll stand by you,
Thomas.

DR. STOCKMANN Bravely said, Katrina! I swear by my soul and
conscience the truth shall out! If they won't let me a hall, I'll hire
a drum and march through the town with it, and I'll read my paper
at every street corner.

MAYOR STOCKMANN You can scarcely be such a raving lunatic as that?

DR. STOCKMANN I am.

ASLAKSEN   You would not get a single man in the whole town to go with you.

BILLING   No, strike me dead if you would!

MRS. STOCKMANN   Don't give in, Thomas. I'll ask the boys to go with you.

DR. STOCKMANN   That's a splendid idea!

MRS. STOCKMANN   Morten will be delighted, and Eilif will go too, I daresay.

DR. STOCKMANN   Yes, and so will Petra! And you yourself, Katrina!

MRS. STOCKMANN   No no, not I. But I'll stand at the window and watch you—that I will.

DR. STOCKMANN   [*Throwing his arms about her and kissing her.*] Thank you for that! Now, my good sirs, we're ready for the fight! Now we shall see whether your despicable tactics can stop the mouth of the patriot who wants to purge society!

[*He and his wife go out together by the door in the back, left.*]

MAYOR STOCKMANN   [*Shaking his head dubiously.*] Now he has turned her head too!

ACT IV

[*A large old-fashioned room in Captain Horster's house. An open folding door in the background leads to an anteroom. In the wall on the left are three windows. About the middle of the opposite wall is a platform, and on it a small table, two candles, a water bottle and glass, and a bell. For the rest, the room is lighted by sconces placed between the windows. In front, on the left, is a table with a candle on it, and by it a chair. In front, to the right, a door, and near it a few chairs.*

Large assemblage of all classes of townsfolk. In the crowd are a few women and schoolboys. More and more people gradually stream in from the back until the room is quite full.]

FIRST CITIZEN   [*To another standing near him.*] So you're here too, Lamstad?

SECOND CITIZEN   I never miss a public meeting.

A BYSTANDER I suppose you've brought your whistle?

SECOND CITIZEN Of course I have; haven't you?

THIRD CITIZEN I should think so. And Skipper Evensen said he'd bring a thumping big horn.

SECOND CITIZEN He's a good 'un, is Evensen! [*Laughter in the group.*]

A FOURTH CITIZEN [*Joining them.*] I say, what's it all about? What's going on here tonight?

SECOND CITIZEN Why, it's Dr. Stockmann that's going to lecture against the mayor.

FOURTH CITIZEN But the mayor's his brother.

FIRST CITIZEN That makes no difference. Dr. Stockmann's not afraid of him.

THIRD CITIZEN But he's all wrong; the *People's Messenger* says so.

SECOND CITIZEN Yes, he must be wrong this time; for neither the Homeowners' Association nor the Citizens' Club would let him have a hall.

FIRST CITIZEN They wouldn't even lend him the hall at the baths.

SECOND CITIZEN No, you may be sure they wouldn't.

A MAN [*In another group.*] Now, who's the one to follow in this business, eh?

ANOTHER MAN [*In the same group.*] Just keep your eye on Aslaksen, and do as he does.

BILLING [*With a portfolio under his arm, makes his way through the crowd.*] Excuse me, gentlemen. Will you allow me to pass? I'm here to report for the *People's Messenger*. Many thanks.

[*Sits by the table on the left.*]

A WORKINGMAN Who's he?

ANOTHER WORKINGMAN Don't you know him? It's that fellow Billing, that writes for Aslaksen's paper.

[*Captain Horster enters by the door in front on the right, escorting Mrs. Stockmann and Petra. Eilif and Morten follow them.*]

HORSTER This is where I thought you might sit; you can so easily slip out if anything should happen.

MRS. STOCKMANN Do you think there will be any disturbance?

HORSTER One can never tell—with such a crowd. But there's no occasion for anxiety.

MRS. STOCKMANN [*Sitting down.*] How kind it was of you to offer Stockmann this room.

HORSTER Since no one else would, I—

PETRA [*Who has also seated herself.*] And it was brave too, Captain Horster.

HORSTER Oh, I don't see where the bravery comes in.

[*Hovstad and Aslaksen enter at the same moment, but make their way through the crowd separately.*]

ASLAKSEN [*Going up to Horster.*] Hasn't the doctor come yet?

HORSTER He's waiting in there.

[*A movement at the door in the background.*]

HOVSTAD [*To Billing.*] There's the mayor! Look!

BILLING Yes, strike me dead if he hasn't put in an appearance after all!

[*Mayor Stockmann makes his way blandly through the meeting, bowing politely to both sides, and takes his stand by the wall on the left. Soon afterward, Dr. Stockmann enters by the door on the right. He wears a black frockcoat and white necktie. Faint applause, met by a subdued hissing. Then silence.*]

DR. STOCKMANN [*In a low tone.*] How do you feel, Katrina?

MRS. STOCKMANN Quite comfortable, thank you. [*In a low voice.*] Now do keep your temper, Thomas.

DR. STOCKMANN Oh, I shall keep myself well in hand. [*Looks at his watch, ascends the platform, and bows.*] It's a quarter past the hour, so I shall begin—

[*Takes out his manuscript.*]

ASLAKSEN But surely a chairman must be elected first.

DR. STOCKMANN No, that's not at all necessary.

SEVERAL GENTLEMEN [*Shouting.*] Yes, yes.

MAYOR STOCKMANN I should certainly say that a chairman ought to be elected.

DR. STOCKMANN But I've called this meeting to give a lecture, Peter!

MAYOR STOCKMANN Dr. Stockmann's lecture may possibly lead to differences of opinion.

SEVERAL VOICES IN THE CROWD A chairman! A chairman!

HOVSTAD The general voice of the meeting seems to be for a chairman!

DR. STOCKMANN [*Controlling himself.*] Very well then; let the meeting have its way.

ASLAKSEN Will not the mayor take the chair?

THREE GENTLEMEN [*Clapping.*] Bravo! Bravo!

MAYOR STOCKMANN For reasons you will easily understand, I must decline. But, fortunately, we have among us one whom I think we can all accept. I allude to the president of the Homeowners' Association, Mr. Aslaksen.

MANY VOICES Yes, yes! Bravo, Aslaksen! Hurrah for Aslaksen!

[*Dr. Stockmann takes his manuscript and descends from the platform.*]

ASLAKSEN Since my fellow citizens repose this trust in me, I cannot refuse—

[*Applause and cheers. Aslaksen ascends the platform.*]

BILLING [*Writing.*] So—"Mr. Aslaksen was elected by acclamation—"

ASLAKSEN   And now, as I have been called to the chair, I take the liberty of saying a few brief words. I am a quiet, peace-loving man; I am in favor of discreet moderation, and of—and of moderate discretion. Everyone who knows me, knows that.

MANY VOICES   Yes, yes, Aslaksen!

ASLAKSEN   I have learned in the school of life and of experience that moderation is the virtue in which the individual citizen finds his best advantage—

MAYOR STOCKMANN   Hear, hear!

ASLAKSEN   —and it is discretion and moderation, too, that best serve the community. I could therefore suggest to our respected fellow citizen, who has called this meeting, that he should endeavor to keep within the bounds of moderation.

A MAN   [*By the door.*] Three cheers for the Temperance Society!

A VOICE   Go to the devil!

VOICES   Hush! hush!

ASLAKSEN   No interruptions, gentlemen!—Does anyone wish to offer any observations?

MAYOR STOCKMANN   Mr. Chairman.

ASLAKSEN   Mayor Stockmann will address the meeting.

MAYOR STOCKMANN   On account of my close relationship—of which you are probably aware—to the present medical officer of the baths, I should have preferred not to speak here this evening. But my position as chairman of the baths, and my care for the vital interests of this town, force me to move a resolution. I may doubtless assume that not a single citizen here present thinks it desirable that untrustworthy and exaggerated statements should get abroad as to the sanitary condition of the baths and of our town.

MANY VOICES   No, no, no! Certainly not! We protest!

MAYOR STOCKMANN   I therefore beg to move, "That this meeting declines to hear the proposed lecture or speech on the subject by the medical officer of the baths."

DR. STOCKMANN [*Flaring up.*] Declines to hear—! What do you mean?

MRS. STOCKMANN [*Coughing.*] H'm! h'm!

DR. STOCKMANN [*Controlling himself.*] So I am not to be heard?

MAYOR STOCKMANN In my statement in the *People's Messenger* I have made the public acquainted with the essential facts, so that all well-disposed citizens can easily form their own judgment. From that statement it will be seen that the medical officer's proposal—besides amounting to a vote of censure upon the leading men of the town—at bottom only means saddling the ratepayers with an unnecessary outlay of at least a hundred thousand crowns.

[*Sounds of protest and some hissing.*]

ASLAKSEN [*Ringing the bell.*] Order, gentlemen! I must beg leave to support the mayor's resolution. I quite agree with him that there is something beneath the surface of the doctor's agitation. In all his talk about the baths, it is really a revolution he is aiming at; he wants to effect a redistribution of power. No one doubts the excellence of Dr. Stockmann's intentions—of course, there cannot be two opinions as to that. I, too, am in favor of self-government by the people, if only it doesn't cost the ratepayers too much. But in this case it would do so; and therefore I'll be hanged if—excuse me—in short, I cannot go with Dr. Stockmann upon this occasion. You can buy even gold too dear; that's my opinion.

[*Loud applause on all sides.*]

HOVSTAD I, too feel bound to explain my attitude. Dr. Stockmann's agitation seemed at first to find favor in several quarters, and I supported it as impartially as I could. But it presently appeared that we had been misled by a false representation of the facts—

DR. STOCKMANN False—!

HOVSTAD Well then, an untrustworthy representation. This the mayor's report has proved. I trust no one here present doubts my liberal principles; the attitude of the *Messenger* on all great political questions is well known to you all. But I have learned from men of judgment and experience that in purely local matters a paper must observe a certain amount of caution.

ASLAKSEN I entirely agree with the speaker.

HOVSTAD And in the matter under discussion it is quite evident that Dr. Stockmann has public opinion against him. But, gentlemen, what is an editor's clearest and most imperative duty? Is it not to work in harmony with his readers? Has he not in some sort received a tacit mandate to further assiduously and unweariedly the interests of his constituents? Or am I mistaken in this?

MANY VOICES No, no, no! Hovstad is right!

HOVSTAD It has cost me a bitter struggle to break with a man in whose house I have of late been a frequent guest—with a man who, up to this day, has enjoyed the unqualified goodwill of his fellow citizens— with a man whose only, or, at any rate, whose chief fault is that he consults his heart rather than his head.

A FEW SCATTERED VOICES That's true! Hurrah for Dr. Stockmann!

HOVSTAD But my duty toward the community has constrained me to break with him. Then, too, there is another consideration that impels me to oppose him, and, if possible, to block the ill-omened path upon which he is entering: consideration for his family—

DR. STOCKMANN Keep to the waterworks and sewers!

HOVSTAD —consideration for his wife and his unprotected children.

MORTEN Is that us, mother?

MRS. STOCKMANN Hush!

ASLAKSEN I will now put the mayor's resolution to the vote.

DR. STOCKMANN You need not. I have no intention of saying anything this evening of all the filth at the baths. No! You shall hear something quite different.

MAYOR STOCKMANN [*Half aloud.*] What next, I wonder?

A DRUNKEN MAN [*At the main entrance.*] I'm a ratepayer, so I've a right to my opinion! And it's my full, firm, incomprehensible opinion that—

SEVERAL VOICES Silence up there!

OTHERS He's drunk! Turn him out!

[*The drunken man is turned out.*]

DR. STOCKMANN Can I speak?

ASLAKSEN [*Ringing the bell.*] Dr. Stockmann will address the meeting.

DR. STOCKMANN A few days ago, I should have liked to see anyone
venture upon such an attempt to gag me as has been made here
tonight! I would have fought like a lion for my sacred rights! But
now I care little enough, for now I have more important things to
speak of.

[*The people crowd closer round him. Morten Kiil comes in sight among
the bystanders.*]

DR. STOCKMANN [*Continuing.*] I have been pondering a great many
things during these last days—thinking such a multitude of
thoughts, that at last my head was positively in a whirl—

MAYOR STOCKMANN [*Coughing.*] H'm—!

DR. STOCKMANN But presently things seemed to straighten themselves
out, and I saw them clearly in all their bearings. That is why I stand
here this evening. I am about to make great revelations, my fellow
citizens! I am going to announce to you a far-reaching discovery,
beside which the trifling fact that our waterworks are poisoned,
and that our health resort is built on pestilential ground, sinks into
insignificance.

MANY VOICES [*Shouting.*] Don't speak about the baths! We won't listen
to that! No more of that!

DR. STOCKMANN I have said I would speak of the great discovery I have
made within the last few days—the discovery that all our sources of
spiritual life are poisoned, and that our whole society rests upon a
pestilential basis of falsehood.

SEVERAL VOICES [*In astonishment and half aloud.*] What's he saying?

MAYOR STOCKMANN Such an insinuation—!

ASLAKSEN [*With his hand on the bell.*] I must call upon the speaker to
moderate his expressions.

DR. STOCKMANN I have loved my native town as dearly as any man
can love the home of his childhood. I was young when I left our
town, and distance, homesickness, and memory threw, as it were,
a glamour over the place and its people.

[*Some applause and cries of approval.*]

DR. STOCKMANN   Then for years I was imprisoned in a horrible hole, far away in the north. As I went about among the people scattered here and there over the stony wilderness, it seemed to me, many a time, that it would have been better for these poor famishing creatures to have had a cattle doctor to attend them, instead of a man like me.

[*Murmurs in the room.*]

BILLING   [*Laying down his pen.*] Strike me dead if I've ever heard—!

HOVSTAD   What an insult to an estimable peasantry!

DR. STOCKMANN   Wait a moment—I don't think anyone can reproach me with forgetting my native town up there. I sat brooding like an eider duck, and what I hatched was—the plan of the baths.

[*Applause and expressions of dissent.*]

DR. STOCKMANN   And when, at last, fate ordered things so happily that I could come home again—then, fellow citizens, it seemed to me that I hadn't another desire in the world. Yes, one desire I had: an eager, constant, burning desire to be of service to my birthplace and to its people.

MAYOR STOCKMANN   [*Gazing into vacancy.*] A strange method to select—!

DR. STOCKMANN   So I went about reveling in my happy illusions. But yesterday morning—no, it was really two nights ago—my mind's eyes were opened wide, and the first thing I saw was the colossal stupidity of the authorities—

[*Noise, cries, and laughter. Mrs. Stockmann coughs repeatedly.*]

MAYOR STOCKMANN   Mr. Chairman!

ASLAKSEN   [*Ringing his bell.*] In virtue of my position—!

DR. STOCKMANN   It's petty to catch me up on a word, Mr. Aslaksen! I only mean that I became alive to the extraordinary muddle our leading men had been guilty of, down at the baths. I cannot for the life of me abide leading men —I've seen enough of them in my time. They are like goats in a young plantation: they do harm at every point; they block the path of a free man wherever he turns—and I should be glad if we could exterminate them like other noxious animals—

[*Uproar in the room.*]

MAYOR STOCKMANN   Mr. Chairman, are such expressions permissible?

ASLAKSEN   [*With his hand on the bell.*] Dr. Stockmann—

DR. STOCKMANN   I can't conceive how it is that I have only now seen through these gentry; for haven't I had a magnificent example before my eyes here every day—my brother Peter—slow of understanding, tenacious in prejudice—

[*Laughter, noise, and whistling. Mrs. Stockmann coughs. Aslaksen rings violently.*]

THE DRUNKEN MAN   [*Who has come in again.*] Is it me you're alluding to? Sure enough, my name's Petersen, but devil take me if—

ANGRY VOICES   Out with that drunken man! Turn him out!

[*The man is again turned out.*]

MAYOR STOCKMANN   Who is that person?

A BYSTANDER   I don't know him, mayor.

ANOTHER   He doesn't belong to the town.

A THIRD   I believe he's a timber dealer from—

[*The rest is inaudible.*]

ASLAKSEN   The man was evidently intoxicated. Continue, Dr. Stockmann, but pray endeavor to be moderate.

DR. STOCKMANN   Well, fellow citizens, I shall say no more about our leading men. If anyone imagines, from what I have just said, that it's these gentlemen I want to make short work of tonight, he is mistaken—altogether mistaken. For I cherish the comfortable conviction that these laggards, these relics of a decaying order of thought, are diligently cutting their own throats. They need no doctor to hasten their end. And it is not people of that sort that constitute the real danger to society; it is not they who are most active in poisoning the sources of our spiritual life and making a plague-spot of the ground beneath our feet; it is not they who are the most dangerous enemies of truth and freedom in our society.

CRIES FROM ALL SIDES   Who, then? Who is it? Name, name!

DR. STOCKMANN   Yes, you may be sure I shall name them! For this is the great discovery I made yesterday: [*In a louder tone.*] The most dangerous foe to truth and freedom in our midst is the majority. Yes, it's the confounded, solid, liberal majority—that, and nothing else! There, I've told you.

[*Immense disturbance in the room. Most of the audience are shouting, stamping, and whistling. Several elderly gentlemen exchange furtive glances and seem to be enjoying the scene. Mrs. Stockmann rises in alarm. Eilif and Morten advance threateningly toward the schoolboys, who are making noises. Aslaksen rings the bell and calls for order. Hovstad and Billing both speak, but nothing can be heard. At last quiet is restored.*]

ASLAKSEN   I must request the speaker to withdraw his ill-considered expressions.

DR. STOCKMANN   Never, Mr. Aslaksen! For it's this very majority that robs me of my freedom, and wants to forbid me to speak the truth.

HOVSTAD   The majority always has right on its side.

BILLING   Yes, and truth too, strike me dead!

DR. STOCKMANN   The majority never has right on its side. Never I say! That is one of the social lies that a free, thinking man is bound to rebel against. Who makes up the majority in any given country? Is it the wise men or the fools? I think we must agree that the fools are in a terrible, overwhelming majority, all the wide world over. But how in the devil's name can it ever be right for the fools to rule over the wise men?

[*Uproar and yells.*]

DR. STOCKMANN   Yes, yes, you can shout me down, but you cannot gainsay me. The majority has might —unhappily—but right it has not. It is I, and the few, the individuals, that are in the right. The minority is always right.

[*Renewed uproar.*]

HOVSTAD   Ha ha! Dr. Stockmann has turned aristocrat since the day before yesterday!

DR. STOCKMANN   I have said that I have no words to waste on the little, narrow-chested, short-winded crew that lie in our wake. Pulsating life has nothing more to do with them. I am speaking of the few, the individuals among us, who have made all the new, germinating truths their own. These men stand, as it were, at the outposts, so far in the van that the majority has not yet reached them—and there they fight for truths that are too lately born into the world's consciousness to have won over the majority.

HOVSTAD   So the doctor's a revolutionist now!

DR. STOCKMANN   Yes, by heaven, I am, Mr. Hovstad! I am going to revolt against the lie that truth belongs exclusively to the majority. What sort of truths do the majority rally round? Truths so stricken in years that they are sinking into decrepitude. When a truth is so old as that, gentlemen, it's in a fair way to become a lie.

[*Laughter and jeers.*]

DR. STOCKMANN   Yes, yes. You may believe me or not, as you please, but truths are by no means the wiry Methusalehs some people think them. A normally constituted truth lives—let us say—as a rule, seventeen or eighteen years, at the outside twenty, very seldom more. And truths so patriarchal as that are always shockingly emaciated; yet it's not till then that the majority takes them up and recommends them to society as wholesome food. I can assure you there's not much nutriment in that sort of fare; you may take my word as a doctor for that. All these majority truths are like last year's salt pork; they're like rancid, moldy ham, producing all the moral scurvy that devastates society.

ASLAKSEN   It seems to me that the honorable speaker is wandering rather far from the subject.

MAYOR STOCKMANN   I beg to endorse the chairman's remark.

DR. STOCKMANN   Why you're surely mad, Peter! I'm keeping as closely to my text as I possibly can; for my text is precisely this: that the masses, the majority, this devil's own majority, it's that, I say, that's poisoning the sources of our spiritual life and making a plague-spot of the ground beneath our feet.

HOVSTAD   And you make this charge against the great, independent majority, just because they have the sense to accept only certain and acknowledged truths?

DR. STOCKMANN   Ah, my dear Mr. Hovstad, don't talk about certain truths! The truths acknowledged by the masses, the multitude, were certain truths to the vanguard in our grandfathers' days. We, the vanguard of today, don't acknowledge them any longer; and I don't believe there exists any other certain truth but this: that no society can live a healthy life upon truths so old and marrowless.

HOVSTAD   But instead of all this vague talk, suppose you were to give us some specimens of these old marrowless truths that we are living upon.

[*Approval from several quarters.*]

DR. STOCKMANN   Oh, I could give you no end of samples from the rubbish heap. But, for the present, I shall keep to one acknowledged truth, which is a hideous lie at bottom, but which Mr. Hovstad, and the *Messenger*, and all adherents of the *Messenger*, live on all the same.

HOVSTAD   And that is—

DR. STOCKMANN   That is the doctrine you have inherited from your forefathers, and go on thoughtlessly proclaiming far and wide—the doctrine that the multitude, the vulgar herd, the masses, are the heart of the people—that they are the people—that the common man, the ignorant, undeveloped member of society, has the same right to sanction and to condemn, to counsel and to govern, as the intellectually distinguished few.

BILLING   Well, now, strike me dead—!

HOVSTAD   [*Shouting at the same time.*] Citizens, please note this!

ANGRY VOICES   Ho-ho! Aren't we the people? Is it only the grand folks that are to govern?

A WORKINGMAN   Out with the fellow that talks like that!

OTHERS   Turn him out!

A CITIZEN   [*Shouting.*] Blow your horn, Evensen.

[*The deep notes of a horn are heard; whistling and terrific noise in the room.*]

DR. STOCKMANN [*When the noise has somewhat subsided.*] Now do be
reasonable! Can't you bear even for once in a way to hear the voice
of truth? I don't ask you all to agree with me on the instant. But I
certainly should have expected Mr. Hovstad to back me up, as
soon as he had collected himself a bit. Mr. Hovstad sets up to be
a freethinker—

SEVERAL VOICES [*Subdued and wondering.*] Freethinker, did he say? What?
Mr. Hovstad a freethinker?

HOVSTAD [*Shouting.*] Prove it, Dr. Stockmann. When have I said so
in print?

DR. STOCKMANN [*Reflecting.*] No, upon my soul, you're right there;
you've never had the frankness to do that. Well, well, I won't put
you on the rack, Mr. Hovstad. Let me be the freethinker then. And
now I'll make it clear to you all, and on scientific grounds too, that
the *Messenger* is leading you shamefully by the nose when it tells
you that you, the masses, the crowd, are the true heart of the people.
I tell you that's only a newspaper lie. The masses are nothing but
the raw material that must be fashioned into a People.

[*Murmurs, laughter, and disturbance in the room.*]

DR. STOCKMANN Is it not so with all other living creatures? What a
difference between a cultivated and an uncultivated breed of animals!
Just look at a common barn-door hen. What meat do you get from
such a skinny carcass? Not much, I can tell you! And what sort of
eggs does she lay? A decent crow or raven can lay nearly as good.
Then take a cultivated Spanish or Japanese hen, or take a fine
pheasant or turkey—ah!—then you'll see the difference! And now
look at the dog, our near relation. Think first of an ordinary vulgar
cur—I mean one of those wretched, ragged, plebeian mongrels that
haunt the gutters, and soil the sidewalks. Then place such a mongrel
by the side of a poodle, descended through many generations from
an aristocratic stock, who have lived on delicate food and heard
harmonious voices and music. Do you think the brain of the poodle
isn't very differently developed from that of the mongrel? Yes, you
may be sure it is! It's well-bred poodle pups like this that jugglers
train to perform the most marvelous tricks. A common mongrel
could never learn anything of the sort—not if he tried till doomsday.

[*Noise and laughter are heard all round.*]

A CITIZEN [*Shouting.*] Do you want to make dogs of us now?

ANOTHER MAN   We're not animals, Doctor!

DR. STOCKMANN   Yes, on my soul, but we are animals, my good sir! We're one and all of us animals, whether we like it or not. But truly there are few enough aristocratic animals among us. Oh, there's a terrible difference between poodle-men and mongrel-men! And the ridiculous part of it is that Mr. Hovstad quite agrees with me so long as it's four-legged animals we're talking of—

HOVSTAD   Oh, beasts are only beasts.

DR. STOCKMANN   Well and good—but no sooner do I apply the law to two-legged animals than Mr. Hovstad stops short. Then he dare not hold his own opinions or think out his own thoughts; then he turns the whole principle upside down, and proclaims in the *People's Messenger* that the barn-door hen and the gutter mongrel are precisely the finest specimens in the menagerie. But that's always the way, so long as the commonness still lingers in your system, and you haven't worked your way up to spiritual distinction.

HOVSTAD   I make no pretence to any sort of distinction. I come of simple peasant folk, and I am proud that my root should lie deep down among the common people, who are here being insulted.

WORKMEN   Hurrah for Hovstad. Hurrah! hurrah!

DR. STOCKMANN   The sort of common people I am speaking of are not found among the lower classes alone; they crawl and swarm all around us—up to the very summits of society. Just look at your own smug, respectable mayor! Why, my brother Peter belongs as clearly to the common people as any man that walks on two legs—

[*Laughter and hisses.*]

MAYOR STOCKMANN   I protest against such personalities.

DR. STOCKMANN   [*Imperturbably.*] —and that not because, like myself, he's descended from a good-for-nothing old pirate from Pomerania, or thereabouts—for that's our ancestry—

MAYOR STOCKMANN   An absurd tradition! Utterly groundless.

DR. STOCKMANN —but he is so because he thinks the thoughts and holds the opinions of his official superiors. Men who do that belong, intellectually speaking, to the common people; and that is why my distinguished brother Peter is at bottom so undistinguished—and consequently so illiberal.

MAYOR STOCKMANN Mr. Chairman—

HOVSTAD So that the distinguished people in this country are the liberals? That's quite a new light on the subject.

[*Laughter.*]

DR. STOCKMANN Yes, that is part of my new discovery. And this, too, follows: that liberality of thought is almost precisely the same thing as morality. Therefore I say it's absolutely unpardonable of the *Messenger* to proclaim, day in, day out, the false doctrine that it's the masses, the multitude, the solid majority, that monopolize liberality and morality—and that vice and corruption and all sorts of spiritual uncleanness ooze out of culture, as all that filth oozes down to the baths from the Mill Dale tan-works!

[*Noise and interruptions.*]

DR. STOCKMANN [*Goes on imperturbably, smiling in his eagerness.*] And yet this same *Messenger* can preach about elevating the masses and the multitude to a higher level of well-being! Why, devil take it, if the *Messenger*'s own doctrine holds good, the elevation of the masses would simply mean hurling them straight to perdition! But, happily, the notion that culture demoralizes is nothing but an old traditional lie. No it's stupidity, poverty, the ugliness of life, that do the devil's work! In a house that isn't aired and swept every day—my wife maintains that the floors ought to be scrubbed too, but perhaps that is going too far—well—in such a house, I say, within two or three years, people lose the power of thinking or acting morally. Lack of oxygen enervates the conscience. And there seems to be precious little oxygen in many and many a house in this town, since the whole solid majority is unscrupulous enough to want to found its future upon a quagmire of lies and fraud.

ASLAKSEN I cannot allow so gross an insult to be leveled against a whole community.

A GENTLEMAN I move that the chairman order the speaker to sit down.

EAGER VOICES   Yes, yes! That's right! Sit down! Sit down!

DR. STOCKMANN   [*Flaring up.*] Then I shall proclaim the truth at every street corner! I shall write to newspapers in other towns! The whole country shall know how matters stand here!

HOVSTAD   It almost seems as if the doctor's object were to ruin the town.

DR. STOCKMANN   Yes, so well do I love my native town that I would rather ruin it than see it flourishing upon a lie.

ASLAKSEN   That's plain speaking.

[*Noise and whistling. Mrs. Stockmann coughs in vain; the doctor no longer heeds her.*]

HOVSTAD   [*Shouting amid the tumult.*] The man who would ruin a whole community must be an enemy to his fellow citizens!

DR. STOCKMANN   [*With growing excitement.*] What does it matter if a lying community is ruined! Let it be leveled to the ground, say I! All men who live upon a lie ought to be exterminated like vermin! You'll end by poisoning the whole country; you'll bring it to such a pass that the whole country will deserve to perish. And if ever it comes to that, I shall say, from the bottom of my heart: perish the country! Perish all its people!

A MAN   [*In the crowd.*] Why, he talks like a regular enemy of the people!

BILLING   Strike me dead but there spoke the people's voice!

THE WHOLE ASSEMBLY   [*Shouting.*] Yes! yes! yes! He's an enemy of the people! He hates his country! He hates the whole people!

ASLAKSEN   Both as a citizen of this town and as a human being, I am deeply shocked at what it has been my lot to hear tonight. Dr. Stockmann has unmasked himself in a manner I should never have dreamed of. I must reluctantly subscribe to the opinion just expressed by some estimable citizens, and I think we ought to formulate this opinion in a resolution. I therefore beg to move, "That this meeting declares the medical officer of the baths, Dr. Thomas Stockmann, to be an enemy of the people."

[*Thunders of applause and cheers. Many form a circle round the doctor and hoot at him. Mrs. Stockmann and Petra have risen. Morten and Eilif fight the other schoolboys, who have also been hooting. Some grown-up persons separate them.*]

DR. STOCKMANN [*To the people hooting.*] Ah, fools that you are! I tell you that—

ASLAKSEN [*Ringing.*] The doctor is out of order in speaking. A formal vote must be taken, but out of consideration for personal feelings, it will be taken in writing and without names. Have you any blank paper, Mr. Billing?

BILLING Here's both blue and white paper—

ASLAKSEN Capital; that will save time. Cut it up into slips. That's it. [*To the meeting.*] Blue means no, white means aye. I myself will go round and collect the votes.

[*The mayor leaves the room. Aslaksen and a few others go round with pieces of paper in hats.*]

A GENTLEMAN [*To Hovstad.*] What can be the matter with the doctor? What does it all mean?

HOVSTAD Why, you know what a hare-brained creature he is.

ANOTHER GENTLEMAN [*To Billing.*] I say, you're often at his house. Have you ever noticed if the fellow drinks?

BILLING Strike me dead if I know what to say. The toddy's always on the table when anyone looks in.

A THIRD GENTLEMAN No, I should rather say he went off his head at times.

FIRST GENTLEMAN I wonder if there's madness in the family?

BILLING I shouldn't be surprised.

A FOURTH GENTLEMAN No, it's pure malice. He wants to be revenged for something or other.

BILLING He was certainly talking about a rise in his salary the other day, but he didn't get it.

ALL THE GENTLEMAN [*Together.*] Aha! That explains everything.

THE DRUNKEN MAN [*In the crowd.*] I want a blue one, I do! And I'll have a white one, too.

SEVERAL PEOPLE There's the tipsy man again! Turn him out.

MORTEN KIIL   [*Approaching the doctor.*] Well, Stockmann, you see now what such monkey tricks lead to?

DR. STOCKMANN   I have done my duty.

MORTEN KIIL   What was that you said about the Mill Dale tanneries?

DR. STOCKMANN   You heard what I said—that all the filth comes from them.

MORTEN KIIL   From my tannery as well?

DR. STOCKMANN   I'm sorry to say yours is the worst of all.

MORTEN KIIL   Are you going to put that in the papers, too?

DR. STOCKMANN   I can't gloss anything over.

MORTEN KIIL   This may cost you dear, Stockmann!

[*He goes out.*]

A FAT GENTLEMAN   [*Goes up to Horster, without bowing to the ladies.*] Well, Captain, so you lend your house to enemies of the people.

HORSTER   I suppose I can do as I please with my own property, Sir.

THE GENTLEMAN   Then of course you can have no objection if I follow your example?

HORSTER   What do you mean, Sir?

THE GENTLEMAN   You shall hear from me tomorrow.

[*Turns away and goes out.*]

PETRA   Wasn't that the owner of your ship, Captain Horster?

HORSTER   Yes, that was Mr. Vik.

ASLAKSEN   [*With the voting papers in his hands, ascends the platform and rings.*] Gentlemen! I have now to announce the result of the vote. All the voters, with one exception—

A YOUNG GENTLEMAN   That's the tipsy man!

ASLAKSEN With the exception of one intoxicated person, this meeting of citizens unanimously declares the medical officer of the baths, Dr. Thomas Stockmann, to be an enemy of the people. [*Cheers and applause.*] Three cheers for our fine old municipality! [*Cheers.*] Three cheers for our able and energetic mayor, who has so loyally set family prejudice aside! [*Cheers.*] The meeting is dissolved.

[*He descends.*]

BILLING Three cheers for the chairman!

ALL Hurrah for Aslaksen!

DR. STOCKMANN My hat and coat, Petra. Captain, have you room for passengers to the new world?

HORSTER For you and yours, Doctor, we'll make room.

DR. STOCKMANN [*While Petra helps him to put on his coat.*] Good. Come Katrina, come boys!

[*He gives his wife his arm.*]

MRS. STOCKMANN [*In a low voice.*] Thomas, dear, let us go out by the back way.

DR. STOCKMANN No back ways, Katrina! [*In a loud voice.*] You shall hear from the enemy of the people, before he shakes the dust from his feet! I am not so forbearing as a certain person. I don't say: I forgive you, for you know not what you do.

ASLAKSEN [*Shouts.*] That is a blasphemous comparison, Dr. Stockmann!

BILLING Strike me—! This is more than a serious man can stand!

A COARSE VOICE And he threatens us into the bargain!

ANGRY CRIES Let's smash his windows! Duck him in the fiord!

A MAN [*In the crowd.*] Blow your horn, Evensen! Blow, man, blow!

[*Horn blowing, whistling, and wild shouting. The doctor, with his family, goes toward the door. Horster clears the way for them.*]

ALL [*Yelling after them as they go out.*] Enemy of the people! Enemy of the people! Enemy of the people!

BILLING   Strike me dead if I'd care to drink toddy at Stockmann's
tonight!

[*The people throng toward the door; the shouting is taken up by others outside;
from the street are heard cries of "Enemy of the people! Enemy of the people!"*]

ACT V

[*Dr. Stockmann's study. Bookshelves and glass cases with various collections along
the walls. In the back, a door leading to the hall; in front, on the left, a door to
the sitting room. In the wall to the right are two windows, all the panes of which
are smashed. In the middle of the room is the doctor's writing table,
covered with books and papers. The room is in disorder. It is forenoon.*

*Dr. Stockmann, in dressing gown, slippers, and skull cap, is bending down and
raking with an umbrella under one of the cabinets; at last he rakes out a stone.*]

DR. STOCKMANN   [*Speaking through the sitting-room doorway.*] Katrina, I've
found another!

MRS. STOCKMANN   [*In the sitting room.*] Oh, I'm sure you'll find plenty more.

DR. STOCKMANN   [*Placing the stone on a pile of others on the table.*] I shall
keep these stones as sacred relics. Eilif and Morten shall see them
every day, and when I die they shall be heirlooms. [*Raking under the
bookcase.*] Hasn't—what the devil is her name?—the girl—hasn't she
been for the glazier yet?

MRS. STOCKMANN   [*Coming in.*] Yes, but he said he didn't know whether
he would be able to come today.

DR. STOCKMANN   I believe, if the truth were told, he dare not come.

MRS. STOCKMANN   Well, Randina, too, had an idea he was afraid to
come, because of the neighbors. [*Speaks through the sitting-room
doorway.*] What is it, Randina?—Very well. [*Goes out, and returns
immediately.*] Here is a letter for you, Thomas.

DR. STOCKMANN   Let me see. [*Opens the letter and reads.*] Aha!

MRS. STOCKMANN   Who is it from?

DR. STOCKMANN   From the landlord. He gives us notice.

MRS. STOCKMANN Is it possible? He is such a nice man—

DR. STOCKMANN [*Looking at the letter.*] He dare not do otherwise, he says. He is very unwilling to do it; but he dare not do otherwise—on account of his fellow citizens, out of respect for public opinion, is in a dependent position, doesn't dare to offend certain influential men—

MRS. STOCKMANN There, you see, Thomas.

DR. STOCKMANN Yes, yes, I see well enough; they are all cowards, every one of them in this town; no one dares do anything for fear of all the rest. [*Throws the letter on the table.*] But it's all the same to us, Katrina. We will shape our course for the new world, and then—

MRS. STOCKMANN But are you sure this idea of going abroad is altogether wise, Thomas?

DR. STOCKMANN Would you have me stay here, where they have pilloried me as an enemy of the people, branded me, smashed my windows! And look here, Katrina, they've torn a hole in my black trousers, too.

MRS. STOCKMANN Oh dear, and these are the best you have!

DR. STOCKMANN A man should never put on his best trousers when he goes out to battle for freedom and truth. Well, I don't care so much about the trousers; them you can always patch up for me. But that the mob, the rabble, should dare to attack me as if they were my equals—that is what I can't, for the life of me, stomach!

MRS. STOCKMANN Yes, they have behaved abominably to you here, Thomas, but is that any reason for leaving the country altogether?

DR. STOCKMANN Do you think the plebeians aren't just as insolent in other towns? Oh yes, they are, my dear; it's six of one and half a dozen of the other. Well, never mind; let the curs yelp; that's not the worst; the worst is that everyone, all over the country, is the slave of his party. Not that I suppose—very likely it's no better in the free West either; the solid majority, and enlightened public opinion, and all the other devil's trash is rampant there too. But you see the conditions are larger there than here; they may kill you, but they don't slow torture you; they don't screw up a free soul in a vice, as they do at home here. And then, if need be, you can keep out of it all. [*Walks up and down.*] If I only knew of any primeval forest, or a little South Sea island to be sold cheap—

MRS. STOCKMANN   Yes, but the boys, Thomas.

DR. STOCKMANN   [*Comes to a standstill.*] What an extraordinary woman you are, Katrina! Would you rather have the boys grow up in such a society as ours? Why, you could see for yourself yesterday evening that one half of the population is stark mad, and if the other half hasn't lost its wits, that's only because they are brute beasts who haven't any wits to lose.

MRS. STOCKMANN   But really, my dear Thomas, you do say such imprudent things.

DR. STOCKMANN   What! Isn't it the truth that I tell them? Don't they turn all ideas upside down? Don't they stir up right and wrong into one hotchpotch? Don't they call lies everything that I know to be the truth? But the maddest thing of all is to see crowds of grown men, calling themselves liberals, go about persuading themselves and others that they are friends of freedom! Did you ever hear anything like it, Katrina?

MRS. STOCKMANN   Yes, yes, no doubt. But—

[*Petra enters from the sitting room.*]

MRS. STOCKMANN   Back from school already?

PETRA   Yes, I have been dismissed.

MRS. STOCKMANN   Dismissed?

DR. STOCKMANN   You too!

PETRA   Mrs. Busk gave me notice, and so I thought it best to leave there and then.

DR. STOCKMANN   You did perfectly right!

MRS. STOCKMANN   Who could have thought Mrs. Busk was such a bad woman!

PETRA   Oh mother, Mrs. Busk isn't bad at all; I saw clearly how sorry she was. But she dared not do otherwise, she said; and so I am dismissed.

DR. STOCKMANN   [*Laughing and rubbing his hands.*] She dared not do otherwise—just like the rest! Oh, it's delicious.

MRS. STOCKMANN   Oh well, after that frightful scene last night—

PETRA   It wasn't only that. What do you think, father—?

DR. STOCKMANN   Well?

PETRA   Mrs. Busk showed me no fewer than three letters she had received this morning—

DR. STOCKMANN   Anonymous, of course?

PETRA   Yes.

DR. STOCKMANN   They never dare give their names, Katrina!

PETRA   And two of them stated that a gentleman who is often at our house said at the club last night that I held extremely advanced opinions upon various things—

DR. STOCKMANN   Of course you didn't deny it.

PETRA   Of course not. You know Mrs. Busk herself is pretty advanced in her opinions when we're alone together, but now that this has come out about me, she dared not keep me on.

MRS. STOCKMANN   Someone that is often at our house, too. There, you see, Thomas, what comes of all your hospitality.

DR. STOCKMANN   We won't live any longer in such a pigsty! Pack up as quickly as you can, Katrina; let's get away—the sooner the better.

MRS. STOCKMANN   Hush! I think there is some one in the passage. See who it is, Petra.

PETRA   [Opening the door.] Oh, is it you, Captain Horster? Please come in.

HORSTER   [From the hall.] Good morning. I thought I might just look in and ask how you are.

DR. STOCKMANN   [Shaking his hand.] Thanks; that's very good of you.

MRS. STOCKMANN   And thank you for helping us through the crowd last night, Captain Horster.

PETRA   How did you ever get home again?

HORSTER   Oh, that was all right. I am tolerably able-bodied, you know, and those fellows' bark is worse than their bite.

DR. STOCKMANN   Yes, isn't it extraordinary, this piggish cowardice? Come here and let me show you something! Look, here are all the stones they threw in at us. Only look at them! Upon my soul there aren't more than two decent-sized lumps in the whole heap; the rest are nothing but pebbles—mere gravel. They stood down there, and yelled, and swore they'd half kill me—but as for really doing it—no, there's mighty little fear of that in this town!

HORSTER   You may thank your stars for that this time, Doctor.

DR. STOCKMANN   So I do, of course. But it's depressing all the same, for if ever it should come to a serious national struggle, you may be sure public opinion would be for taking to its heels, and the solid majority would scamper for their lives like a flock of sheep, Captain Horster. That is what's so melancholy to think of; it grieves me to the heart. But devil take it—it's foolish of me to feel anything of the sort! They have called me an enemy of the people; well then, let me be an enemy of the people!

MRS. STOCKMANN   That you'll never be, Thomas.

DR. STOCKMANN   You'd better not take your oath of it, Katrina. A bad name may act like a pin scratch in the lung. And that confounded word—I can't get rid of it; it has sunk deep into my heart, and there it lies gnawing and sucking like an acid. And no magnesia can cure me.

PETRA   Pooh, you should only laugh at them, father.

HORSTER   People will think differently yet, Doctor.

MRS. STOCKMANN   Yes, Thomas, that's as certain as that you are standing here.

DR. STOCKMANN   Yes, perhaps, when it is too late. Well, as they make their bed so they must lie! Let them go on wallowing here in their pigsty and learn to repent having driven a patriot into exile. When do you sail, Captain Horster?

HORSTER   Well—that's really what I came to speak to you about—

DR. STOCKMANN   What? Anything wrong with the ship?

HORSTER   No, but the fact is, I won't be sailing in her.

PETRA Surely you have not been dismissed?

HORSTER [*Smiling*] Yes, I have.

PETRA You too!

MRS. STOCKMANN There, you see, Thomas.

DR. STOCKMANN And for the truth's sake! Oh, if I could possibly have imagined such a thing—

HORSTER You mustn't be troubled about this. I shall soon find a berth with some other company, elsewhere.

DR. STOCKMANN And this is that man Vik! A wealthy man, independent of everyone! Bah!

HORSTER Oh, for that matter, he's a very well-meaning man. He said himself he would gladly have kept me on if only he dared—

DR. STOCKMANN But he didn't dare? Of course not!

HORSTER It's not so easy, he said, when you belong to a party—

DR. STOCKMANN My gentleman has hit it there! A party is like a sausage machine; it grinds all the brains together in one mash, and that's why we see nothing but porridge-heads and pulp-heads all around!

MRS. STOCKMANN Now really, Thomas!

PETRA [*To Horster.*] If only you hadn't seem us home, perhaps it would not have come to this.

HORSTER I don't regret it.

PETRA [*Gives him her hand.*] Thank you for that!

HORSTER [*To Dr. Stockmann.*] And then, too, I wanted to tell you this: if you are really determined to go abroad, I've thought of another way—

DR. STOCKMANN That's good—if only we can get off quickly—

MRS. STOCKMANN Hush! Isn't that a knock?

PETRA I believe it is uncle.

DR. STOCKMANN   Aha! [*Calls.*] Come in!

MRS. STOCKMANN   My dear Thomas, now do promise me—

[*The mayor enters from the hall.*]

MAYOR STOCKMANN   [*In the doorway.*] Oh, you are engaged. Then
   I'd better—

DR. STOCKMANN   No, no, come in.

MAYOR STOCKMANN   But I wanted to speak to you alone.

MRS. STOCKMANN   We can go into the sitting room.

HORSTER   And I shall look in again presently.

DR. STOCKMANN   No, no, go with the ladies, Captain Horster. I must
   hear more about—

HORSTER   All right, then I'll wait.

[*He follows Mrs. Stockmann and Petra into the sitting room. The mayor says
nothing, but casts glances at the windows.*]

DR. STOCKMANN   I daresay you find it rather drafty here today? Put on
   your cap.

MAYOR STOCKMANN   Thanks, if I may. [*Does so.*] I fancy I caught cold
   yesterday evening. I stood there shivering—

DR. STOCKMANN   Really. On my soul, now, I found it quite warm enough.

MAYOR STOCKMANN   I regret that it was not in my power to prevent
   these nocturnal excesses.

DR. STOCKMANN   Have you anything else in particular to say to me?

MAYOR STOCKMANN   [*Producing a large letter.*] I have this document
   for you from the directors of the baths.

DR. STOCKMANN   My dismissal?

MAYOR STOCKMANN   Yes, dated from today. [*Places the letter on the table.*]
   We are very sorry—but frankly, we dared not do otherwise, on
   account of public opinion.

DR. STOCKMANN [*Smiling.*] Dared not? I've heard that phrase already today.

MAYOR STOCKMANN I beg you to realize your position clearly. For the future, you cannot count upon any sort of practice in the town.

DR. STOCKMANN Devil take the practice! But how can you be so sure of that?

MAYOR STOCKMANN The Homeowners' Association is sending round a circular from house to house, in which all well-disposed citizens are called upon not to employ you; and I dare swear that not a single head of a family will venture to refuse his signature. He simply dare not.

DR. STOCKMANN Well, well. I don't doubt that. But what then?

MAYOR STOCKMANN If I might advise, I would suggest that you should leave the town for a time—

DR. STOCKMANN Yes, I've had some such idea in my mind already.

MAYOR STOCKMANN Good. And when you have had six months or so for mature deliberation, if you could make up your mind to acknowledge your error, with a few words of regret—

DR. STOCKMANN I might perhaps be reinstated, you think?

MAYOR STOCKMANN Perhaps it's not quite out of the question.

DR. STOCKMANN Yes, but how about public opinion? You dare not, on account of public opinion.

MAYOR STOCKMANN Opinion is extremely variable. And, to speak candidly, it is of the greatest importance for us to have such an admission under your own hand.

DR. STOCKMANN Yes, I daresay it would be mightily convenient for you! But you remember what I've said to you before about such foxes' tricks!

MAYOR STOCKMANN At that time your position was infinitely more favorable. At that time you thought you had the whole town at your back—

DR. STOCKMANN   Yes, and now I have the whole town on my back—
[*Flaring up.*] But no—not if I had the devil and his dam on my
back—! Never—never, I tell you!

MAYOR STOCKMANN   The father of a family has no right to act as you are
doing. You have no right to do it, Thomas.

DR. STOCKMANN   I have no right! There's only one thing in the world
that a free man has no right to do, and do you know what that is?

MAYOR STOCKMANN   No.

DR. STOCKMANN   Of course not, but *I* will tell you. A free man has no
right to wallow in filth like a cur; he has no right to act so that he
ought to spit in his own face!

MAYOR STOCKMANN   That sounds extremely plausible, and if there were
not another explanation of your obstinacy—but we all know there is—

DR. STOCKMANN   What do you mean by that?

MAYOR STOCKMANN   You understand well enough. But as your brother
and as a man who knows the world, I warn you not to build too
confidently upon prospects and expectations that may very likely
come to nothing.

DR. STOCKMANN   Why, what on earth are you driving at?

MAYOR STOCKMANN   Do you really want me to believe that you are
ignorant of the terms of old Morten Kiil's will?

DR. STOCKMANN   I know that the little he has is to go to a home for old
and needy artisans. But what has that got to do with me?

MAYOR STOCKMANN   To begin with, "the little he has" is no trifle.
Morten Kiil is a tolerably wealthy man.

DR. STOCKMANN   I have never had the least notion of that!

MAYOR STOCKMANN   H'm—really? Then I suppose you have no notion
that a not inconsiderable part of his fortune is to go to your children,
you and your wife having a life interest in it. Has he not told you that?

DR. STOCKMANN   No, I'll be hanged if he has! On the contrary, he has
done nothing but grumble about being so preposterously overtaxed.
But are you really sure of this, Peter?

MAYOR STOCKMANN   I have it from a thoroughly trustworthy source.

DR. STOCKMANN   Why, good heavens, then Katrina's provided for—
and the children too! Oh, I must tell her— [*Calls*] Katrina, Katrina!

MAYOR STOCKMANN   [*Holding him back.*] Hush! Don't say anything about
it yet.

MRS. STOCKMANN   [*Opening the door.*] What is it?

DR. STOCKMANN   Nothing my dear; go in again.

[*Mrs. Stockmann closes the door.*]

DR. STOCKMANN   [*Pacing up and down.*] Provided for! Only think—all
of them provided for! And for life! After all, it's a grand thing to
feel yourself secure!

MAYOR STOCKMANN   Yes, but that is just what you are not. Morten Kiil
can revoke his will any day or hour he chooses.

DR. STOCKMANN   But he won't, my good Peter. The Badger is only too
delighted to see me fall foul of you and your wise friends.

MAYOR STOCKMANN   [*Starts and looks searchingly at him.*] Aha! That throws
a new light on a good many things.

DR. STOCKMANN   What things?

MAYOR STOCKMANN   So the whole affair has been a carefully-concocted
intrigue. Your recklessly violent onslaught—in the name of truth—
upon the leading men of the town—

DR. STOCKMANN   Well, what of it?

MAYOR STOCKMANN   It was nothing but a preconcerted requital for that
vindictive old Morten Kiil's will.

DR. STOCKMANN   [*Almost speechless.*] Peter—you are the most abominable
plebeian I have ever known in all my born days.

MAYOR STOCKMANN   All is over between us. Your dismissal is
irrevocable—for now we have a weapon against you. [*He goes out.*]

DR. STOCKMANN   Shame! shame! shame! [*Calls.*] Katrina! The floor must be scrubbed after him! Tell her to come here with a pail—what's her name? Confound it—the girl with the smudge on her nose—

MRS. STOCKMANN   [*In the sitting-room doorway.*] Hush, hush! Thomas!

PETRA   [*Also in the doorway.*] Father, here's grandfather; he wants to know if he can speak to you alone.

DR. STOCKMANN   Yes, of course he can. [*By the door.*] Come in, father-in-law.

[*Morten Kiil enters. Dr. Stockmann closes the door behind him.*]

DR. STOCKMANN   Well, what is it? Sit down.

MORTEN KIIL   I won't sit down. [*Looking about him.*] It looks cheerful here today, Stockmann.

DR. STOCKMANN   Yes, don't you think so?

MORTEN KIIL   Sure enough. And you've plenty of fresh air too; you've got your fill of that oxygen you were talking about yesterday. You must have a rare good conscience today, I should think.

DR. STOCKMANN   Yes, I have.

MORTEN KIIL   So I should suppose. [*Tapping himself on the breast.*] But do you know what *I* have got here?

DR. STOCKMANN   A good conscience too, I hope.

MORTEN KIIL   Pooh! No, something far better than that.

[*Takes out a large pocketbook, opens it, and shows Stockmann a bundle of papers.*]

DR. STOCKMANN   [*Looking at him in astonishment.*] Shares in the baths!

MORTEN KIIL   They weren't difficult to get today.

DR. STOCKMANN   And you've gone and bought these up—?

MORTEN KIIL   All I had the money to pay for.

DR. STOCKMANN   Why, my dear sir—just when things are in such a desperate way at the baths—

MORTEN KIIL If you behave like a reasonable being, you can soon set the baths all right again.

DR. STOCKMANN Well, you can see for yourself I'm doing all I can. But the people of this town are mad!

MORTEN KIIL You said yesterday that the worst filth came from my tannery. Now, if that's true, then my grandfather, and my father before me, and I myself, have forever so many years been poisoning the town with filth, like three destroying angels. Do you think I'm going to sit quiet under such a reproach?

DR. STOCKMANN Unfortunately, you can't help it.

MORTEN KIIL No, thank you. I hold fast to my good name. I've heard that people call me "the Badger." A badger's a sort of a pig, I know, but I'm determined to give them the lie. I will live and die a clean man.

DR. STOCKMANN And how will you manage that?

MORTEN KIIL You shall make me clean, Stockmann.

DR. STOCKMANN I!

MORTEN KIIL Do you know what money I've used to buy these shares with? No, you can't know, but now I'll tell you. It's the money Katrina and Petra and the boys are to have after my death. For, you see, I've laid by something after all.

DR. STOCKMANN [*Flaring up.*] And you've taken Katrina's money and done this with it!

MORTEN KIIL Yes, the whole of it is invested in the baths now. And now I want to see if you're really so stark, staring mad, after all, Stockmann. If you go on making out that these beasts and other abominations dribble down from my tannery, it'll be just as if you were to flay broad stripes of Katrina's skin—and Petra's too, and the boys! No decent father would ever do that—unless he were a madman.

DR. STOCKMANN [*Walking up and down.*] Yes, but I am a madman; I am a madman!

MORTEN KIIL You surely can't be so raving, ramping mad where your wife and children are concerned.

DR. STOCKMANN   [*Stopping in front of him.*] Why couldn't you have spoken to me before you went and bought all that rubbish?

MORTEN KIIL   What's done can't be undone.

DR. STOCKMANN   [*Walking restlessly about.*] If only I weren't so certain about the affair—! But I am absolutely convinced that I'm right.

MORTEN KIIL   [*Weighing the pocketbook in his hand.*] If you stick to this lunacy, these aren't worth much.

[*Puts the book into his pocket.*]

DR. STOCKMANN   But, devil take it! surely science ought to be able to hit upon some antidote, some sort of prophylactic—

MORTEN KIIL   Do you mean something to kill the beasts?

DR. STOCKMANN   Yes, or at least to make them harmless.

MORTEN KIIL   Couldn't you try rat poison?

DR. STOCKMANN   Oh, nonsense, nonsense!—But since everyone declares it's nothing but fancy, why fancy let it be! Let them have it their own way! Haven't the ignorant, narrow-hearted curs reviled me as an enemy of the people? —and weren't they on the point of tearing the clothes off my back?

MORTEN KIIL   And they've smashed all your windows for you too!

DR. STOCKMANN   Yes, and then there's one's duty to one's family! I must talk that over with Katrina; such things are more in her line.

MORTEN KIIL   That's right! You just follow the advice of a sensible woman.

DR. STOCKMANN   [*Turning upon him angrily.*] How could you act so preposterously! Risking Katrina's money and putting me to this horrible torture! When I look at you, I seem to see the devil himself—!

MORTEN KIIL   Then I'd better be off. But I must hear from you, yes or no, by two o'clock. If it's no, all the shares go to the hospital—and that this very day.

DR. STOCKMANN   And what will Katrina get?

MORTEN KIIL   Not a rap.

[*The door leading to the hall opens. Hovstad and Aslaksen are seen outside it.*]

MORTEN KIIL Hullo! look at these two.

DR. STOCKMANN [*Staring at them.*] What! Do you actually venture to come here?

HOVSTAD Why, to be sure we do.

ASLAKSEN You see, we've something to discuss with you.

MORTEN KIIL [*Whispers.*] Yes or no—by two o'clock.

ASLAKSEN [*With a glance at Hovstad.*] Aha!

[*Morten Kiil goes out.*]

DR. STOCKMANN Well, what do you want with me? Be brief.

HOVSTAD I can quite understand that you resent our attitude at the meeting yesterday—

DR. STOCKMANN Your attitude, you say? Yes, it was a pretty attitude! I call it the attitude of cowards—of old women. Shame upon you!

HOVSTAD Call it what you will, but we could not act otherwise.

DR. STOCKMANN You dared not, I suppose? Isn't that so?

HOVSTAD Yes, if you like to put it so.

ASLAKSEN But why didn't you just say a word to us beforehand? The merest hint to Mr. Hovstad or to me—

DR. STOCKMANN A hint? What about?

ASLAKSEN About what was really behind it all.

DR. STOCKMANN I don't in the least understand you.

ASLAKSEN [*Nods confidentially.*] Oh yes, you do, Dr. Stockmann.

HOVSTAD It's no good making a mystery of it any longer.

DR. STOCKMANN [*Looking from one, to the other.*] Why, what in the devil's name—!

ASLAKSEN   May I ask—isn't your father-in-law going about the town buying up all the bath stock?

DR. STOCKMANN   Yes, he has been buying bath stock today but—

ASLAKSEN   It would have been more prudent to let somebody else do that—someone not so closely connected with you.

HOVSTAD   And then you ought not to have appeared in the matter under your own name. No one need have known that the attack on the baths came from you. You should have taken me into your counsels, Dr. Stockmann.

DR. STOCKMANN   [*Stares straight in front of him; a light seems to break in upon him, and he says as though thunderstruck.*] Is this possible? Can such things be?

ASLAKSEN   [*Smiling.*] It's plain enough that they can. But they ought to be managed delicately; you understand.

HOVSTAD   And there ought to be more people in it, for the responsibility always falls more lightly when there are several to share it.

DR. STOCKMANN   [*Calmly.*] In one word, gentlemen—what is it you want?

ASLAKSEN   Mr. Hovstad can best—

HOVSTAD   No, you explain, Aslaksen.

ASLAKSEN   Well, it's this: now that we know how the matter really stands, we believe we can venture to place the *People's Messenger* at your disposal.

DR. STOCKMANN   You can venture to now, eh? But how about public opinion? Aren't you afraid of bringing down a storm upon us?

HOVSTAD   We must manage to ride out the storm.

ASLAKSEN   And you must be ready to put about quickly, Doctor. As soon as your attack has done its work—

DR. STOCKMANN   As soon as my father-in-law and I have bought up the shares at a discount, you mean?

HOVSTAD   I presume it is mainly on scientific grounds that you want to take the management of the baths into your own hands.

DR. STOCKMANN Of course, it was on scientific grounds that I got the old Badger to stand in with me. And then we'll tinker up the water-works a little, and potter about a bit down at the beach, without its costing the town sixpence. That ought to do the business? Eh?

HOVSTAD I think so—if you have the *Messenger* to back you up.

ASLAKSEN In a free community the press is a power, Doctor.

DR. STOCKMANN Yes, indeed, and so is public opinion. And you, Mr. Aslaksen—I suppose you will answer for the Homeowners' Association?

ASLAKSEN Both for the Homeowners' Association and the Temperance Society. You may make your mind easy.

DR. STOCKMANN But, gentlemen—really I'm quite ashamed to mention such a thing—but—what return—?

HOVSTAD Of course, we should prefer to give you our support for nothing. But the *Messenger* is not very firmly established; it's not getting on as it ought to, and I should be very sorry to have to stop the paper just now, when there's so much to be done in general politics.

DR. STOCKMANN Naturally, that would be very hard for a friend of the people like you. [*Flaring up.*] But I—I am an enemy of the people! [*Striding about the room.*] Where's my stick? Where the hell is my stick?

HOVSTAD What do you mean?

ASLAKSEN Surely you wouldn't—

DR. STOCKMANN [*Standing still.*] And suppose I don't give you a single farthing out of all my shares? You must remember we rich folk don't like parting with our money.

HOVSTAD And you must remember that this business of the shares can be represented in two ways.

DR. STOCKMANN Yes, you are the man for that; if I don't come to the rescue of the *Messenger*, you'll manage to put a vile complexion on the affair, you'll hunt me down, I suppose—bait me—try to throttle me as a dog throttles a rabbit!

HOVSTAD That's a law of nature—every animal fights for its own subsistence.

ASLAKSEN   And must take its food where it can find it, you know.

DR. STOCKMANN   Then see if you can't find some out in the gutter; [*Striding about the room.*] for now, by heaven, we shall see which is the strongest animal of us three. [*Finds his umbrella and brandishes it.*] Now, look here—!

HOVSTAD   You surely don't mean to assault us!

ASLAKSEN   I say, be careful with that umbrella!

DR. STOCKMANN   Out at the window with you, Mr. Hovstad!

HOVSTAD   [*By the hall door.*] Are you utterly crazy?

DR. STOCKMANN   Out at the window, Mr. Aslaksen! Jump I tell you! Be quick about it!

ASLAKSEN   [*Running round the writing table.*] Moderation, Doctor. I'm not at all strong; I can't stand much— [*Screams.*] Help! help!

[*Mrs. Stockmann, Petra, and Horster enter from sitting room.*]

MRS. STOCKMANN   Good heavens, Thomas! What can be the matter?

DR. STOCKMANN   [*Brandishing the umbrella.*] Jump! I tell you! Out into the gutter!

HOVSTAD   An unprovoked assault! I call you to witness, Captain Horster.

[*Rushes off through the hall.*]

ASLAKSEN   [*Bewildered.*] If one only knew the local situation—!

[*He slinks out by the sitting-room door.*]

MRS. STOCKMANN   [*Holding back the doctor.*] Now, do restrain yourself, Thomas!

DR. STOCKMANN   [*Throwing down the umbrella.*] I'll be damned if they haven't got off after all.

MRS. STOCKMANN   Why, what can they have wanted with you?

DR. STOCKMANN I'll tell you afterward; I have other things to think of now. [*Goes to the table and writes on a visiting card.*] Look here, Katrina. What's written here?

MRS. STOCKMANN Three big Noes; what does that mean?

DR. STOCKMANN That I'll tell you afterward, too. [*Handing the card.*] There, Petra, let smudgy-face run to the Badger's with this as fast as she can. Be quick!

[*Petra goes out through the hall with the card.*]

DR. STOCKMANN Well, if I haven't had visits today from all the emissaries of the devil! But now I'll sharpen my pen against them till it becomes a goad. I'll dip it in gall and venom; I'll hurl my inkstand straight at their skulls.

MRS. STOCKMANN You forget we are going away, Thomas.

[*Petra returns.*]

DR. STOCKMANN Well?

PETRA She has gone.

DR. STOCKMANN Good. Going away, do you say? No, I'll be damned if we do; we stay where we are, Katrina!

PETRA Stay!

MRS. STOCKMANN Here in the town?

DR. STOCKMANN Yes, here: the field of battle is here; here the fight must be fought; here I will conquer! As soon as my trousers are mended, I shall go out into the town and look for a house; we must have a roof over our heads for the winter.

HORSTER That you can have in my house.

DR. STOCKMANN Can I?

HORSTER Yes, there's no difficulty about that. I have room enough, and I'm hardly ever at home myself.

MRS. STOCKMANN Oh, how kind of you, Captain Horster.

PETRA   Thank you!

DR. STOCKMANN   [*Shaking his hand.*] Thanks, thanks! So that is off my mind. And this very day I shall set to work in earnest. Oh, there's no end of work to be done here, Katrina! It's a good thing I shall have all my time at my disposal now, for you must know I've had notice from the baths—

MRS. STOCKMANN   [*Sighing.*] Oh yes, I was expecting that.

DR. STOCKMANN   —And now they want to take away my practice as well. But let them! The poor I shall keep anyhow—those that can't pay. And, good Lord, it's they that need me most. But by heaven, I'll make them listen to me; I'll preach to them in season and out of season, as the saying goes.

MRS. STOCKMANN   My dear Thomas, I should have thought you had learned what good preaching does.

DR. STOCKMANN   You really are absurd, Katrina. Am I to let myself be beaten off the field by public opinion, and the majority, and all that sort of devilry? No, thank you! Besides, my point is so simple, so clear and straightforward. I only want to drive it into the heads of these curs that the liberals are the craftiest foes free men have to face; that party programs wring the necks of all young and living truths; that considerations of expediency turn justice and morality upside down, until life here becomes simply unlivable. Come, Captain Horster, don't you think I shall be able to make the people understand that?

HORSTER   Maybe, I don't know much about these things myself.

DR. STOCKMANN   Well, you see—this is the way of it! It's the party leaders that must be exterminated. For a party leader is just like a wolf, you see—like a ravening wolf; he must devour a certain number of smaller animals a year, if he's to exist at all. Just look at Hovstad and Aslaksen! How many small animals they polish off—or at least mangle and maim, so that they're fit for nothing else but to be homeowners and subscribers to the *People's Messenger*! [*Sits on the edge of the table.*] Just come here, Katrina—see how bravely the sun shines today! And how the blessed fresh spring air blows in upon me!

MRS. STOCKMANN   Yes, if only we could live on sunshine and spring air, Thomas.

DR. STOCKMANN Well, you'll have to pinch and save to eke them out—
and then we shall get on all right. That's what troubles me least.
No, what does trouble me is that I don't see any man free enough
and high-minded enough to dare to take up my work after me.

PETRA Oh, don't think about that, father; you have time enough before
you—Why, see, there are the boys already.

[*Eilif and Morten enter from the sitting room.*]

MRS. STOCKMANN Have you a holiday today?

MORTEN No, but we had a fight with the other fellows in play-time—

EILIF That's not true; it was the other fellows that fought us.

MORTEN Yes, and then Mr. Rörlund said we had better stop at home
for a few days.

DR. STOCKMANN [*Snapping his fingers and springing down from the table.*]
Now I have it! Now I have it, on my soul! You shall never set foot
in school again!

THE BOYS Never go to school!

MRS. STOCKMANN Why, Thomas—

DR. STOCKMANN Never, I say! I shall teach you myself—that's to say,
I won't teach you any mortal thing—

MORTEN Hurrah!

DR. STOCKMANN —but I shall help you to grow into free, high-minded
men. Look here, you'll have to help me, Petra.

PETRA Yes, father, you may be sure I will.

DR. STOCKMANN And we'll have our school in the room where they
reviled me as an enemy of the people. But we must have more
pupils. I must have at least a dozen boys to begin with.

MRS. STOCKMANN You'll never get them in this town.

DR. STOCKMANN We shall see. [*To the boys.*] Don't you know any street
urchins—any regular ragamuffins—?

MORTEN   Yes, father, I know lots!

DR. STOCKMANN   That's all right; bring me a few of them. I shall experiment with the street curs; there are sometimes excellent heads among them.

MORTEN   But what are we to do when we've grown into free and high-minded men?

DR. STOCKMANN   Drive all the wolves out to the far west, boys!

[*Eilif looks rather doubtful; Morten jumps about shouting "Hurrah!"*]

MRS. STOCKMANN   If only the wolves don't drive you out, Thomas.

DR. STOCKMANN   Are you quite mad, Katrina! Drive me out! Now that I am the strongest man in the town?

MRS. STOCKMANN   The strongest—now?

DR. STOCKMANN   Yes, I venture to say this: that now I am one of the strongest men in the whole world.

MORTEN   I say, what fun!

DR. STOCKMANN   [*In a subdued voice.*] Hush, you mustn't speak about it yet, but I have made a great discovery.

MRS. STOCKMANN   What, another?

DR. STOCKMANN   Yes, of course! [*Gathers them about him, and speaks confidentially.*] This is what I have discovered, you see: the strongest man in the world is he who stands most alone.

MRS. STOCKMANN   [*Shakes her head, smiling.*] Ah, Thomas dear—

PETRA   [*Grasping his hands cheerily.*] Father!

QUESTIONS

1. Why is Dr. Stockmann portrayed as living off his wife's savings?

2. Why doesn't Dr. Stockmann want to confide his suspicions about the baths to his brother (or his wife) before his findings are confirmed and he can make his report?

3. Why does Dr. Stockmann abandon moderation and fall so easily into the hands of Hovstad and Billing, in their effort to foment revolution?

4. Why does Dr. Stockmann give up in his effort to tell the townspeople the truth about the waters that feed the spa, and instead argue to "exterminate them like other noxious animals"? (296)

5. Why does Dr. Stockmann say that "the most dangerous foe to truth and freedom in our midst is the majority," (297) and why does he question "the doctrine that the multitude . . . are the heart of the people"? (299)

6. How does Dr. Stockmann claim to distinguish between "wretched mongrels" and a "poodle"? (300–301)

7. Why does Dr. Stockmann choose words that seem deliberately offensive to the crowd? Was there a way for him to deliver his message and be heard?

8. Why are the liberals, in Dr. Stockmann's view, "the craftiest foes free men have to face"? (325)

9. Why does Dr. Stockmann say "the strongest man in the world is he who stands most alone"? (327) Would he be able to say this if he did not have the support of his wife and children, and Horster?

FOR FURTHER REFLECTION

1. What is the source of conflict between Dr. Stockmann and his brother Peter, the mayor?

2. Are we to see Dr. Stockmann as completely altruistic, or is he motivated by self-interest to some degree like the other characters in the story?

3. Why is the apolitical Horster the only figure who remains loyal in his friendship to Dr. Stockmann and his family?

4. Why does Dr. Stockmann's report fail to convince his brother about the condition of the water at the spa baths?

5. Would the town be better off if Dr. Stockmann, and not Peter, were mayor?

6. Is there a higher wisdom than being right?

7. Does the play throw into question the wisdom of democratic political process?

8. Does the play suggest that there are times when the truth should be moderated or delayed in its telling? Who should decide what those times are?

HENRI POINCARÉ

When Henri Poincaré began his professional career as a mathematician in the 1870s, it was still conceivable that someone of his outstanding ability could master most, if not all, of the existing branches of mathematics. But during his prolific life, the contributions he made to mathematics, analytical physics, theoretical astronomy, the philosophy of science, and the psychology of scientific creativity were central to the development of a far more complex conceptual world than the one he had inherited.

Born Jules Henri Poincaré in Nancy, France, in 1854, to a distinguished family—his brother was president of the French Republic during World War I—Poincaré received early recognition for his outstanding mathematical talent. In 1881, he joined the faculty of the University of Paris, where he remained for the rest of his life. During his long tenure, he lectured and wrote extensively—more than 500 papers and 30 books—both on topics of theoretical and applied mathematics. In a tradition as old as the early Greek astronomers, Poincaré used mathematics to formulate explanatory and predictive models for celestial mechanics. In a 1906 paper on the dynamics of the electron, he independently arrived at many of the same results as Einstein's special theory of relativity, which suggests not only his individual talent but also the ripeness of the time for that momentous discovery.

In the early twentieth century, Poincaré wrote a series of books for the general public that explore the meaning and relationship of mathematics and natural science. These include *Science and Hypothesis, Science and Method*, and *The Value of Science*. Far from being merely popularized explanations of difficult topics, these books are original contributions to the philosophy of science that quickly achieved the status of classics. For his mastery of clear and polished writing in French, in 1908 Poincaré was elected to the Académie Française, an unusual honor for someone in the sciences. In addition to his academic activities, he served the French government as general inspector of mines and was involved in the effort to set universal standards for maps and timekeeping devices. Poincaré died in Paris in 1912, two years before the watershed events of World War I.

Poincaré was very interested in the psychological aspects of mathematical and scientific discovery, and he was a strong proponent of the view that the subconscious is deeply implicated in creativity in these fields. Compatible with this view is his emphasis on the place of convention in scientific method— that is, the communal agreement to base scientific theory on arbitrarily chosen concepts. In the following selection from *The Value of Science*, Poincaré asks us to consider how science arises from the careful selection of significant facts and observations coupled with an inherent desire for intellectual beauty. In addition, Poincaré raises searching questions about the relation of science to ethics.

The Value of Science (selection)

Tolstoy somewhere explains why "science for its own sake" is in his eyes an absurd conception. We cannot know *all* facts, since their number is practically infinite. It is necessary to choose; then we may let this choice depend on the pure caprice of our curiosity. Would it not be better to let ourselves be guided by utility, by our practical and above all by our moral needs; have we nothing better to do than counting the number of ladybugs on our planet?

It is clear the word *utility* has not for him the sense men of affairs give it, and following them most of our contemporaries. Little cares he for industrial applications, for the marvels of electricity or of automobilism, which he regards rather as obstacles to moral progress; *utility* for him is solely what can make man better.

For my part, it need scarce be said, I could never be content with either the one or the other ideal; I want neither that plutocracy grasping and mean, nor that democracy goody and mediocre, occupied solely in turning the other cheek, where would dwell sages without curiosity, who, shunning excess, would not die of disease, but would surely die of ennui. But that is a matter of taste and is not what I wish to discuss.

The question nevertheless remains and should fix our attention; if our choice can only be determined by caprice or by immediate utility, there can be no science for its own sake, and consequently no science. But is that true? That a choice must be made is incontestable; whatever be our activity, facts go quicker than we, and we cannot catch them. While the scientist discovers one fact, there happen milliards of milliards in a cubic millimeter of his body. To wish to comprise nature in science would be to want to put the whole into the part.

This selection is taken from "Author's Essay Prefatory to the Translation"; the introduction, chapter 6, "Astronomy"; and chapter 11, "Science and Reality."

But scientists believe there is a hierarchy of facts and that among them may be made a judicious choice. They are right, since otherwise there would be no science, yet science exists. One need only open the eyes to see that the conquests of industry, which have enriched so many practical men, would never have seen the light, if these practical men alone had existed and if they had not been preceded by unselfish devotees who died poor, who never thought of utility, and yet had a guide far other than caprice.

As Mach says, these devotees have spared their successors the trouble of thinking. Those who might have worked solely in view of an immediate application would have left nothing behind them, and, in face of a new need, all must have been begun over again. Now most men do not love to think, and this is perhaps fortunate when instinct guides them, for most often, when they pursue an aim which is immediate and ever the same, instinct guides them better than reason would guide a pure intelligence. But instinct is routine, and if thought did not fecundate it, it would no more progress in man than in the bee or ant. It is needful then to think for those who love not thinking and, as they are numerous, it is needful that each of our thoughts be as often useful as possible, and this is why a law will be the more precious the more general it is.

This shows us how we should choose: the most interesting facts are those which may serve many times; these are the facts which have a chance of coming up again. We have been so fortunate as to be born in a world where there are such. Suppose that instead of 60 chemical elements there were 60 milliards of them, that they were not, some common, the others rare, but that they were uniformly distributed. Then, every time we picked up a new pebble there would be great probability of its being formed of some unknown substance; all that we knew of other pebbles would be worthless for it; before each new object we should be as the newborn babe; like it we could only obey our caprices or our needs. Biologists would be just as much at a loss if there were only individuals and no species and if heredity did not make sons like their fathers.

In such a world there would be no science; perhaps thought and even life would be impossible, since evolution could not there develop the preservational instincts. Happily it is not so; like all good fortune to which we are accustomed, this is not appreciated at its true worth.

Which then are the facts likely to reappear? They are first the simple facts. It is clear that in a complex fact a thousand circumstances are united by chance, and that only a chance still much less probable could reunite them anew. But are there any simple facts? And if there are, how recognize them? What assurance is there that a thing we think simple does not hide a dreadful complexity? All we can say is that we ought to prefer the facts which *seem* simple to those where our crude eye discerns unlike elements. And then one of two things: either this simplicity is real, or else the elements are so intimately mingled as not to be distinguishable. In the first case, there is chance of our meeting anew this same simple fact, either in all its purity or entering itself as element in a complex manifold. In the second case, this intimate mixture has likewise more chances of recurring than a heterogeneous assemblage. Chance knows how to mix, it knows not how to disentangle; and to make with multiple elements a well-ordered edifice in which something is distinguishable, it must be made expressly. The facts which appear simple, even if they are not so, will therefore be more easily revived by chance. This it is which justifies the method instinctively adopted by the scientist, and what justifies it still better, perhaps, is that oft-recurring facts appear to us simple, precisely because we are used to them.

But where is the simple fact? Scientists have been seeking it in the two extremes, in the infinitely great and in the infinitely small. The astronomer has found it because the distances of the stars are immense, so great that each of them appears but as a point, so great that the qualitative differences are effaced, and because a point is simpler than a body which has form and qualities. The physicist, on the other hand, has sought the elementary phenomenon in fictively cutting up bodies into infinitesimal cubes, because the conditions of the problem, which undergo slow and continuous variation in passing from one point of the body to another, may be regarded as constant in the interior of each of these little cubes. In the same way, the biologist has been instinctively led to regard the cell as more interesting than the whole animal, and the outcome has shown his wisdom, since cells belonging to organisms the most different are more alike, for the one who can recognize their resemblances, than are these organisms themselves. The sociologist is more embarrassed; the elements, which for him are men, are too unlike, too variable, too capricious in a word, too complex; besides, history never begins over again. How then choose the interesting fact, which is that which begins again? Method is precisely the choice of facts; it is needful then to be occupied first with creating a method, and many have been imagined, since none imposes itself, so that sociology is the science which has the most methods and the fewest results.

Therefore, it is by the regular facts that it is proper to begin; but after the rule is well established, after it is beyond all doubt, the facts in full conformity with it are ere long without interest since they no longer teach us anything new. It is then the exception which becomes important. We cease to seek resemblances; we devote ourselves above all to the differences, and among the differences are chosen first the most accentuated, not only because they are the most striking, but because they will be the most instructive. A simple example will make my thought plainer. Suppose one wishes to determine a curve by observing some of its points. The practitioner who concerns himself only with immediate utility would observe only the points he might need for some special object. These points would be badly distributed on the curve; they would be crowded in certain regions, rare in others, so that it would be impossible to join them by a continuous line, and they would be unavailable for other applications. The scientist will proceed differently; as he wishes to study the curve for itself, he will distribute regularly the points to be observed, and when enough are known, he will join them by a regular line and then he will have the entire curve. But for that, how does he proceed? If he has determined an extreme point of the curve, he does not stay near this extremity, but goes first to the other end; after the two extremities the most instructive point will be the midpoint and so on.

So when a rule is established we should first seek the cause where this rule has the greatest chance of failing. Thence, among other reasons, come the interest of astronomic facts and the interest of the geologic past; by going very far away in space or very far away in time, we may find our usual rules entirely overturned, and these grand overturnings aid us the better to see or the better to understand the little changes which may happen nearer to us, in the little corner of the world where we are called to live and act. We shall better know this corner for having traveled in distant countries with which we have nothing to do.

But what we ought to aim at is less the ascertainment of resemblances and differences than the recognition of likenesses hidden under apparent divergences. Particular rules seem at first discordant, but looking more closely we see in general that they resemble each other; different as to matter, they are alike as to form, as to the order of their parts. When we look at them with this bias, we shall see them enlarge and tend to embrace everything. And this it is which makes the value of certain facts which come to complete an assemblage and to show that it is the faithful image of other known assemblages.

I will not further insist, but these few words suffice to show that the scientist does not choose at random the facts he observes. He does not, as Tolstoy says, count the ladybugs, because, however interesting ladybugs may be, their number is subject to capricious variations. He seeks to condense much experience and much thought into a slender volume; and that is why a little book on physics contains so many past experiences and a thousand times as many possible experiences whose result is known beforehand.

But we have as yet looked at only one side of the question. The scientist does not study nature because it is useful; he studies it because he delights in it, and he delights in it because it is beautiful. If nature were not beautiful, it would not be worth knowing, and nature were not worth knowing, life would not be worth living. Of course I do not here speak of that beauty which strikes the senses, the beauty of qualities and of appearances; not that I undervalue such beauty, far from it, but it has nothing to do with science. I mean that profounder beauty which comes from the harmonious order of the parts and which a pure intelligence can grasp. This it is which gives body, a structure so to speak, to the iridescent appearances which flatter our senses, and without this support the beauty of these fugitive dreams would be only imperfect, because it would be vague and always fleeting. On the contrary, intellectual beauty is sufficient unto itself, and it is for its sake, more perhaps than for the future good of humanity, that the scientist devotes himself to long and difficult labors.

It is, therefore, the quest of this especial beauty, the sense of the harmony of the cosmos, which makes us choose the facts most fitting to contribute to this harmony, just as the artist chooses from among the features of his model those which perfect the picture and give it character and life. And we need not fear that this instinctive and unavowed prepossession will turn the scientist aside from the search for the true. One may dream a harmonious world, but how far the real world will leave it behind! The greatest artists that ever lived, the Greeks, made their heavens; how shabby it is beside the true heavens, ours!

And it is because simplicity, because grandeur, is beautiful, that we preferably seek simple facts, sublime facts, that we delight now to follow the majestic course of the stars, now to examine with the microscope that prodigious littleness which is also a grandeur, now to seek in geologic time the traces of a past which attracts because it is far away.

We see too that the longing for the beautiful leads us to the same choice as the longing for the useful. And so it is that this economy of thought, this economy of effort, which is, according to Mach, the constant tendency of science, is at the same time a source of beauty and a practical advantage. The edifices that we admire are those where the architect has known how to proportion the means to the end, where the columns seem to carry gaily, without effort, the weight placed upon them, like the gracious caryatids of the Erechtheion.

Whence comes this concordance? Is it simply that the things which seem to us beautiful are those which best adapt themselves to our intelligence, and that consequently they are at the same time the implement this intelligence knows best how to use? Or is there here a play of evolution and natural selection? Have the peoples whose ideal most conformed to their highest interest exterminated the others and taken their place? All pursued their ideals without reference to consequences, but while this quest led some to destruction, to others it gave empire. One is tempted to believe it. If the Greeks triumphed over the barbarians, and if Europe, heir of Greek thought, dominates the world, it is because the savages loved loud colors and the clamorous tones of the drum which occupied only their senses, while the Greeks loved the intellectual beauty which hides beneath sensuous beauty, and that this intellectual beauty it is which makes intelligence sure and strong.

Doubtless such a triumph would horrify Tolstoy, and he would not like to acknowledge that it might be truly useful. But this disinterested quest of the true for its own beauty is sane also and able to make man better. I well know that there are mistakes, that the thinker does not always draw thence the serenity he should find therein, and even that there are scientists of bad character. Must we, therefore, abandon science and study only morals? What! Do you think the moralists themselves are irreproachable when they come down from their pedestal?

The search for truth should be the goal of our activities; it is the sole end worthy of them. Doubtless we should first bend our efforts to assuage human suffering, but why? Not to suffer is a negative ideal more surely attained by the annihilation of the world. If we wish more and more to free man from material cares, it is that he may be able to employ the liberty obtained in the study and contemplation of truth.

But sometimes truth frightens us. And in fact we know that it is sometimes deceptive, that it is a phantom never showing itself for a moment except to ceaselessly flee, that it must be pursued further and ever further without ever being attained. Yet to work one must stop, as some Greek, Aristotle or another, has said. We also know how cruel the truth often is, and we wonder whether illusion is not more consoling, yea, even more bracing, for illusion it is which gives confidence. When it shall have vanished, will hope remain and shall we have the courage to achieve? Thus would not the horse harnessed to his treadmill refuse to go, were his eyes not bandaged? And then to seek truth it is necessary to be independent, wholly independent. If on the contrary we wish to act, to be strong, we should be united. This is why many of us fear truth; we consider it a cause of weakness. Yet truth should not be feared, for it alone is beautiful.

When I speak here of truth, assuredly I refer first to scientific truth, but I also mean moral truth, of which what we call justice is only one aspect. It may seem that I am misusing words, that I combine thus under the same name two things having nothing in common; that scientific truth, which is demonstrated, can in no way be likened to moral truth, which is felt. And yet I cannot separate them, and whosoever loves the one cannot help loving the other. To find the one, as well as to find the other, it is necessary to free the soul completely from prejudice and from passion; it is necessary to attain absolute sincerity. These two sorts of truth when discovered give the same joy; each when perceived beams with the same splendor, so that we must see it or close our eyes. Lastly, both attract us and flee from us; they are never fixed: when we think to have reached them, we find that we have still to advance, and he who pursues them is condemned never to know repose. It must be added that those who fear the one will also fear the other, for they are the ones who in everything are concerned above all with consequences. In a word, I liken the two truths, because the same reasons make us love them and because the same reasons make us fear them.

If we ought not to fear moral truth, still less should we dread scientific truth. In the first place it cannot conflict with ethics. Ethics and science have their own domains, which touch but do not interpenetrate. The one shows us to what goal we should aspire, the other, given the goal, teaches us how to attain it. So they can never conflict since they can never meet. There can no more be immoral science than there can be scientific morals.

But if science is feared, it is above all because it cannot give us happiness. Of course it cannot. We may even ask whether the beast does not suffer less than man. But can we regret that earthly paradise where man brutelike was really immortal in knowing not that he must die? When we have tasted the apple, no suffering can make us forget its savor. We always come back to it. Could it be otherwise? As well ask if one who has seen and is blind will not long for the light. Man, then, cannot be happy through science, but today he can much less be happy without it.

But if truth be the sole aim worth pursuing, may we hope to attain it? It may well be doubted. Readers of my little book *Science and Hypothesis* already know what I think about the question. The truth we are permitted to glimpse is not altogether what most men call by that name. Does this mean that our most legitimate, most imperative aspiration is at the same time the most vain? Or can we, despite all, approach truth on some side? This it is which must be investigated.

In the first place, what instrument have we at our disposal for this conquest? Is not human intelligence, more specifically the intelligence of the scientist, susceptible of infinite variation? Volumes could be written without exhausting this subject; I, in a few brief pages, have only touched it lightly. That the geometer's mind is not like the physicist's or the naturalist's, all the world would agree; but mathematicians themselves do not resemble each other; some recognize only implacable logic, others appeal to intuition and see in it the only source of discovery. And this would be a reason for distrust. To minds so unlike can the mathematical theorems themselves appear in the same light? Truth which is not the same for all, is it truth? But looking at things more closely, we see how these very different workers collaborate in a common task, which could not be achieved without their cooperation. And that already reassures us.

Next must be examined the frames in which nature seems enclosed and which are called time and space. In *Science and Hypothesis* I have already shown how relative their value is; it is not nature which imposes them upon us, it is we who impose them upon nature because we find them convenient. But I have spoken of scarcely more than space, and particularly quantitative space, so to say, that is of the mathematical relations whose aggregate constitutes geometry. I should have shown that it is the same with time as with space and still the same with "qualitative space"; in particular, I should have investigated why we attribute three dimensions to space. I may be pardoned then for taking up again these important questions.

Is mathematical analysis then, whose principal object is the study of these empty frames, only a vain play of the mind? It can give to the physicist only a convenient language; is this not a mediocre service, which, strictly speaking, could be done without; and even is it not to be feared that this artificial language may be a veil interposed between reality and the eye of the physicist? Far from it; without this language most of the intimate analogies of things would have remained forever unknown to us; and we should forever have been ignorant of the internal harmony of the world, which is, we shall see, the only true objective reality.

The best expression of this harmony is law. Law is one of the most recent conquests of the human mind; there still are people who live in the presence of a perpetual miracle and are not astonished at it. On the contrary, we should be astonished at nature's regularity. Men demand of their gods to prove their existence by miracles; but the eternal marvel is that there are not miracles without cease. The world is divine because it is a harmony. If it were ruled by caprice, what could prove to us it was not ruled by chance?

This conquest of law we owe to astronomy, and just this makes the grandeur of the science rather than the material grandeur of the objects it considers. It was altogether natural then that celestial mechanics should be the first model of mathematical physics, but since then this science has developed; it is still developing, even rapidly developing. And it is already necessary to modify in certain points the scheme I outlined in 1900 and from which I drew two chapters of *Science and Hypothesis*. In an address at the St. Louis exposition in 1904, I sought to survey the road traveled; the result of this investigation the reader shall see farther on.

The progress of science has seemed to imperil the best established principles, those even which were regarded as fundamental. Yet nothing shows they will not be saved; and if this comes about only imperfectly, they will still subsist even though they are modified. The advance of science is not comparable to the changes of a city, where old edifices are pitilessly torn down to give place to new, but to the continuous evolution of zoologic types which develop ceaselessly and end by becoming unrecognizable to the common sight, but where an expert eye finds always traces of the prior work of the centuries past. One must not think then that the old-fashioned theories have been sterile and vain.

Were we to stop there, we should find in these pages some reasons for confidence in the value of science, but many more for distrusting it; an impression of doubt would remain. It is needful now to set things to rights.

Some people have exaggerated the role of convention in science; they have even gone so far as to say that law, that scientific fact itself, was created by the scientist. This is going much too far in the direction of nominalism. No, scientific laws are not artificial creations; we have no reason to regard them as accidental, though it be impossible to prove they are not.

Does the harmony the human intelligence thinks it discovers in nature exist outside of this intelligence? No, beyond doubt, a reality completely independent of the mind which conceives it, sees or feels it, is an impossibility. A world as exterior as that, even if it existed, would for us be forever inaccessible. But what we call objective reality is, in the last analysis, what is common to many thinking beings and could be common to all; this common part, we shall see, can only be the harmony expressed by mathematical laws. It is this harmony then which is the sole objective reality, the only truth we can attain; and when I add that the universal harmony of the world is the source of all beauty, it will be understood what price we should attach to the slow and difficult progress which little by little enables us to know it better.

———————————

Governments and parliaments must find that astronomy is one of the sciences which cost most dear: the least instrument costs hundreds of thousands of dollars; the least observatory costs millions; each eclipse carries with it supplementary appropriations. And all that for stars which are so far away, which are complete strangers to our electoral contests, and in all probability will never take any part in them. It must be that our politicians have retained a remnant of idealism, a vague instinct for what is grand. Truly, I think they have been calumniated; they should be encouraged and shown that this instinct does not deceive them, that they are not dupes of that idealism.

We might indeed speak to them of navigation, of which no one can underestimate the importance, and which has need of astronomy. But this would be to take the question by its smaller side.

Astronomy is useful because it raises us above ourselves; it is useful because it is grand; that is what we should say. It shows us how small is man's body, how great his mind, since his intelligence can embrace the whole of this dazzling immensity, where his body is only an obscure point, and enjoy its silent harmony. Thus we attain the consciousness of our power, and this is something which cannot cost too dear, since this consciousness makes us mightier.

But what I should wish before all to show is, to what point astronomy has facilitated the work of the other sciences, more directly useful, since it has given us a soul capable of comprehending nature.

Think how diminished humanity would be if, under heavens constantly overclouded, as Jupiter's must be, it had forever remained ignorant of the stars. Do you think that in such a world we should be what we are? I know well that under this somber vault we should have been deprived of the light of the sun, necessary to organisms like those which inhabit the earth. But if you please, we shall assume that these clouds are phosphorescent and emit a soft and constant light. Since we are making hypotheses, another will cost no more. Well! I repeat my question: Do you think that in such a world we should be what we are?

The stars send us not only that visible and gross light, which strikes our bodily eyes, but from them also comes to us a light far more subtle, which illuminates our minds and whose effects I shall try to show you. You know what man was on the earth some thousands of years ago, and what he is today. Isolated amidst a nature where everything was a mystery to him, terrified at each unexpected manifestation of incomprehensible forces, he was incapable of seeing in the conduct of the universe anything but caprice; he attributed all phenomena to the action of a multitude of little genii, fantastic and exacting, and to act on the world he sought to conciliate them by means analogous to those employed to gain the good graces of a minister or a deputy. Even his failures did not enlighten him, any more than today a beggar refused is discouraged to the point of ceasing to beg.

Today we no longer beg of nature; we command her, because we have discovered certain of her secrets and shall discover others each day. We command her in the name of laws she cannot challenge because they are hers. These laws we do not madly ask her to change; we are the first to submit to them. Nature can only be governed by obeying her.

What a change must our souls have undergone to pass from the one state to the other! Does anyone believe that, without the lessons of the stars, under the heavens perpetually overclouded that I have just supposed, they would have changed so quickly? Would the metamorphosis have been possible, or at least would it not have been much slower?

And first of all, astronomy it is which taught that there are laws. The Chaldeans, who were the first to observe the heavens with some attention, saw that this multitude of luminous points is not a confused crowd wandering at random, but rather a disciplined army. Doubtless the rules of this discipline escaped them, but the harmonious spectacle of the starry night sufficed to give them the impression of regularity, and that was in itself already a great thing. Besides, these rules were discerned by Hipparchus, Ptolemy, Copernicus, Kepler, one after another, and finally, it is needless to recall that it was Newton who enunciated the oldest, the most precise, the most simple, the most general of all natural laws.

And then, taught by this example, we have seen our little terrestrial world better and, under the apparent disorder, there also we have found again the harmony that the study of the heavens had revealed to us. It also is regular, it also obeys immutable laws, but they are more complicated, in apparent conflict one with another, and an eye untrained by other sights would have seen there only chaos and the reign of chance or caprice. If we had not known the stars, some bold spirits might perhaps have sought to foresee physical phenomena; but their failures would have been frequent, and they would have excited only the derision of the vulgar. Do we not see that even in our day the meteorologists sometimes deceive themselves and that certain persons are inclined to laugh at them.

How often would the physicists, disheartened by so many checks, have fallen into discouragement, if they had not had, to sustain their confidence, the brilliant example of the success of the astronomers! This success showed them that nature obeys laws; it only remained to know what laws; for that they only needed patience, and they had the right to demand that the sceptics should give them credit.

This is not all: astronomy has not only taught us that there are laws, but that from these laws there is no escape, that with them there is no possible compromise. How much time should we have needed to comprehend that fact, if we had known only the terrestrial world, where each elemental force would always seem to us in conflict with other forces? Astronomy has taught us that the laws are infinitely precise and that if those we enunciate are approximative, it is because we do not know them well. Aristotle, the most scientific mind of antiquity, still accorded a part to accident, to chance, and seemed to think that the laws of nature, at least here below, determine only the large features of phenomena. How much has the ever-increasing precision of astronomical predictions contributed to correct such an error, which would have rendered nature unintelligible!

But are these laws not local, varying in different places, like those which men make; does not that which is truth in one corner of the universe, on our globe for instance or in our little solar system, become error a little farther away? And then could it not be asked whether laws depending on space do not also depend upon time, whether they are not simple habitudes, transitory, therefore, and ephemeral? Again it is astronomy that answers this question. Consider the double stars; all describe conics; thus, as far as the telescope carries, it does not reach the limits of the domain which obeys Newton's law.

Even the simplicity of this law is a lesson for us; how many complicated phenomena are contained in the two lines of its enunciation. Persons who do not understand celestial mechanics may form some idea of it at least from the size of the treatises devoted to this science, and then it may be hoped that the complication of physical phenomena likewise hides from us some simple cause still unknown.

It is therefore astronomy which has shown us what are the general characteristics of natural laws; but among these characteristics there is one, the most subtle and the most important of all, which I shall ask leave to stress.

How was the order of the universe understood by the ancients; for instance, by Pythagoras, Plato, or Aristotle? It was either an immutable type fixed once for all or an ideal to which the world sought to approach. Kepler himself still thought thus when, for instance, he sought whether the distances of the planets from the sun had not some relation to the five regular polyhedrons. This idea contained nothing absurd, but it was sterile, since nature is not so made. Newton has shown us that a law is only a necessary relation between the present state of the world and its immediately subsequent state. All the other laws since discovered are nothing else; they are in sum differential equations, but it is astronomy which furnished the first model for them, without which we should doubtless long have erred.

Astronomy has also taught us to set appearances at naught. The day Copernicus proved that what was thought the most stable was in motion, that what was thought moving was fixed, he showed us how deceptive the infantile reasonings could be which spring directly from the immediate data of our senses. True, his ideas did not easily triumph, but since this triumph there is no longer a prejudice so inveterate that we cannot shake it off. How can we estimate the value of the new weapon thus won?

The ancients thought everything was made for man, and this illusion must be very tenacious, since it must ever be combated. Yet it is necessary to divest oneself of it, or else one will be only an eternal myope, incapable of seeing the truth. To comprehend nature one must be able to get out of self, so to speak, and to contemplate her from many different points of view; otherwise we never shall know more than one side. Now, to get out of self is what he who refers everything to himself cannot do. Who delivered us from this illusion? It was those who showed us that the earth is only one of the smallest planets of the solar system, and that the solar system itself is only an imperceptible point in the infinite spaces of the stellar universe.

At the same time astronomy taught us not to be afraid of big numbers. This was needful, not only for knowing the heavens, but to know the earth itself; and was not so easy as it seems to us today. Let us try to go back and picture to ourselves what a Greek would have thought if told that red light vibrates four hundred millions of millions of times per second. Without any doubt, such an assertion would have appeared to him pure madness, and he never would have lowered himself to test it. Today a hypothesis will no longer appear absurd to us because it obliges us to imagine objects much larger or smaller than those our senses are capable of showing us, and we no longer comprehend those scruples which arrested our predecessors and prevented them from discovering certain truths simply because they were afraid of them. But why? It is because we have seen the heavens enlarging and enlarging without cease; because we know that the sun is 150 million kilometers from the earth and that the distances of the nearest stars are hundreds of thousands of times greater yet. Habituated to the contemplation of the infinitely great, we have become apt to comprehend the infinitely small. Thanks to the education it has received, our imagination, like the eagle's eye that the sun does not dazzle, can look truth in the face.

Was I wrong in saying that it is astronomy which has made us a soul capable of comprehending nature; that under heavens always overcast and starless, the earth itself would have been for us eternally unintelligible; that we should there have seen only caprice and disorder; and that, not knowing the world, we should never have been able to subdue it? What science could have been more useful? And in thus speaking I put myself at the point of view of those who only value practical applications. Certainly, this point of view is not mine; as for me, on the contrary, if I admire the conquests of industry, it is above all because, if they free us from material cares, they will one day give to all the leisure to contemplate nature. I do not say: Science is useful, because it teaches us to construct machines. I say: Machines are useful, because in working for us, they will some day leave us more time to make science. But finally it is worth remarking that between the two points of view there is no antagonism, and that man having pursued a disinterested aim, all else has been added unto him.

Auguste Comte has said somewhere that it would be idle to seek to know the composition of the sun, since this knowledge would be of no use to sociology. How could he be so shortsighted? Have we not just seen that it is by astronomy that, to speak his language, humanity has passed from the theological to the positive state? He found an explanation for that because it had happened. But how has he not understood that what remained to do was not less considerable and would be not less profitable? Physical astronomy, which he seems to condemn, has already begun to bear fruit, and it will give us much more, for it only dates from yesterday.

First was discovered the nature of the sun, what the founder of positivism wished to deny us, and there, bodies were found which exist on the earth but had here remained undiscovered; for example, helium, that gas almost as light as hydrogen. That already contradicted Comte. But to the spectroscope we owe a lesson precious in a quite different way; in the most distant stars, it shows us the same substances. It might have been asked whether the terrestrial elements were not due to some chance which had brought together more tenuous atoms to construct of them the more complex edifice that the chemists call atoms; whether, in other regions of the universe, other fortuitous meetings had not engendered edifices entirely different. Now we know that this is not so, that the laws of our chemistry are the general laws of nature, and that they owe nothing to the chance which caused us to be born on the earth.

But, it will be said, astronomy has given to the other sciences all it can give them, and now that the heavens have procured for us the instruments which enable us to study terrestrial nature, they could without danger veil themselves forever. After what we have just said, is there still need to answer this objection? One could have reasoned the same in Ptolemy's time; then also men thought they knew everything, and they still had almost everything to learn.

The stars are majestic laboratories, gigantic crucibles, such as no chemist could dream. There reign temperatures impossible for us to realize. Their only defect is being a little far away; but the telescope will soon bring them near to us, and then we shall see how matter acts there. What good fortune for the physicist and the chemist!

Matter will there exhibit itself to us under a thousand different states, from those rarefied gases, which seem to form the nebula and which are luminous with I know not what glimmering of mysterious origin, even to the incandescent stars and to the planets so near and yet so different.

Perchance even, the stars will someday teach us something about life; that seems an insensate dream and I do not at all see how it can be realized, but, a hundred years ago, would not the chemistry of the stars have also appeared a mad dream?

But limiting our views to horizons less distant, there still will remain to us promises less contingent and yet sufficiently seductive. If the past has given us much, we may rest assured that the future will give us still more.

After all, it could scarce be believed how useful belief in astrology has been to humanity. If Kepler and Tycho Brahe made a living, it was because they sold to naive kings predictions founded on the conjunctions of the stars. If these princes had not been so credulous, we should perhaps continue to believe that nature obeys caprice, and we should still wallow in ignorance.

It is only through science and art that civilization is of value. Some have wondered at the formula: science for its own sake; and yet it is as good as life for its own sake, if life is only misery; and even as happiness for its own sake, if we do not believe that all pleasures are of the same quality, if we do not wish to admit that the goal of civilization is to furnish alcohol to people who love to drink.

Every act should have an aim. We must suffer, we must work, we must pay for our place at the game, but this is for seeing's sake; or at the very least that others may one day see.

All that is not thought is pure nothingness; since we can think only thought, and all the words we use to speak of things can express only thoughts, to say there is something other than thought is therefore an affirmation which can have no meaning.

And yet—strange contradiction for those who believe in time—geologic history shows us that life is only a short episode between two eternities of death, and that, even in this episode, conscious thought has lasted and will last only a moment. Thought is only a gleam in the midst of a long night.

But it is this gleam which is everything.

QUESTIONS

1. Aside from the distinction that Poincaré makes regarding simple and complex facts, what does he mean by a fact per se?

2. According to Poincaré, are all simple facts of equal value to a scientist? How would a scientist create a hierarchy among simple facts?

3. In considering sociology, what does Poincaré mean that among the sciences it has "fewest results"? (348) Do you think that he considers sociology a science in the same sense as biology, astronomy, and physics?

4. What relation does Poincaré show between facts and what he refers to as "a rule"? (335–336)

5. What does Poincaré mean when he says that although rules may be "different as to matter, they are alike as to form"? (336)

6. Do you think Poincaré is implying that a scientist who devotes himself to the labors of science primarily for the future good of humanity is less of a scientist than one who is primarily motivated by the search for intellectual beauty?

7. What are the parts that Poincaré claims are in "harmonious order"? (337) How is the perception of this order related to the scientist's consideration of facts?

8. Is Poincaré claiming that intellectual beauty is discovered or created by the activity of the scientist studying nature? Is the scientist's activity different from that of the artist in the example Poincaré gives?

9. What does Poincaré mean by "the true heavens" in contrast to the heavens "made" by the Greeks? (337)

10. According to Poincaré, what is the "constant tendency of science" that is "at the same time a source of beauty and a practical advantage"? (337)

11. When Poincaré claims that ethics "shows us to what goal we should aspire" and science "teaches us how to attain it," does he allow the possibility that scientific findings might give us important information that would sometimes determine our choice of goals? (339)

12. What does Poincaré mean by saying that space and time are frames that we impose upon nature "because we find them convenient"? (340)

13. What are the "intimate analogies of things [that] would have remained forever unknown to us" that mathematical analysis of the world can provide? (340)

14. For Poincaré, what is the relation of objective reality to scientific truth?

15. According to Poincaré, how did the lawful regularity that astronomy observed in the heavens lead scientists to understand that physical processes on earth were also lawful and regular?

16. What does Poincaré mean when he says that if the laws "we enunciate are approximate, it is because we do not know them well"? (343) What would it mean to know them better?

17. When Poincaré points out that "a law is only a necessary relation between the present state of the world and its immediately subsequent state," is he saying that laws have nothing to do with explaining underlying causes in the physical world? (344)

FOR FURTHER REFLECTION

1. Are there fundamental differences in the scientific investigation of living as opposed to nonliving phenomena?

2. Should scientific investigation be pursued for its own sake, or should it be pursued mainly to alleviate human suffering?

3. Is there some scientific investigation that should be prohibited because of possible dangerous results?

SIGMUND FREUD

For Sigmund Freud, as for so many individuals, the horrors of World War I led to profound questions about the ability of what we call civilization to protect humans from their own destructive aggressiveness. After the long, relatively peaceful era in Europe in the late nineteenth and early twentieth centuries, when it appeared that scientific progress and social reform would continue without interruption, the physical and psychological damage caused by the war led to a sense of widespread disillusionment that Freud speaks to in *Thoughts for the Times on War and Death*.

Born in Moravia (now the Czech Republic) in 1856, Freud began his medical career as a neurological researcher at a time when there was much debate in the scientific community about the sources of human behavior. Freud's earliest mentor, Ernst von Brücke, held that the causes of behavior were to be found solely in the body's chemistry. However, Freud's extensive clinical experience, along with the influence of the psychological theorizing of the French neurologist Jean Charcot, led him to develop the practice of psycho-analysis. Freud's famous case studies published in the 1880s and 1890s of patients such as "Anna O." and "Dora" provide a record of his investigations into the purely psychological causes of behavior. During this period in Vienna, Freud's conversational approach to treating personality disorders—the famous "talking cure"—was viewed with deep skepticism by all but a few other physicians. His growing interest in psychopathology and his emphasis on what he regarded as the fundamental importance of sexuality and unconscious motivation as explanations for human behavior were deeply unsettling to a society that desired to maintain the façade of what it considered civilized respectability. By 1900, Freud had developed a comprehensive theory of psychological structure, detailed in his masterwork, *The Interpretation of Dreams* (1900). Along with a powerful analysis of how dreams function, this book gives definitive expression to many of the concepts that came to form the core of Freudian psychology, including the Oedipus complex and the central importance of infantile life in forming adult personality.

Following the publication of *The Interpretation of Dreams*, Freud began to achieve international recognition, both through his books and through direct contact with a growing number of followers—and dissenters—at the meetings of the Vienna Psychoanalytical Society that he helped found in 1908. Among the psychologists who later broke with Freud were Carl Jung and Alfred Adler. In addition, the popularization and spread of Freudian ideas deeply influenced literature, visual arts, and numerous academic disciplines such as history and political science throughout the rest of the twentieth century.

From 1915, when he wrote *Thoughts for the Times on War and Death*, Freud began to expand the application of his psychological theories from the individual to societies as a whole. He continued until his death in London in 1939, a refugee from the fascist onslaught in Germany and Austria. In books such as *The Future of an Illusion* (1927) and *Civilization and Its Discontents* (1930), Freud repeatedly makes the point that the aggressive instincts of individuals are contained but never eradicated by the social institutions that we refer to collectively as civilization. In *Thoughts for the Times on War and Death*, written before the outcome of World War I was known, Freud claims that times of war unleash the augmented destructiveness of such instincts. He challenges us to consider how this unvarnished view can lead to a mature life without illusion or despair.

SIGMUND FREUD

Thoughts for the Times on War and Death

The Disillusionment of the War

Swept as we are into the vortex of this wartime, our information one-sided, ourselves too near to focus the mighty transformations which have already taken place or are beginning to take place, and without a glimmering of the inchoate future, we are incapable of apprehending the significance of the thronging impressions and know not what value to attach to the judgments we form. We are constrained to believe that never has any event been destructive of so much that is valuable in the commonwealth of humanity, nor so misleading to many of the clearest intelligences, nor so debasing to the highest that we know. Science herself has lost her passionless impartiality; in their deep embitterment her servants seek for weapons from her with which to contribute toward the defeat of the enemy. The anthropologist is driven to declare the opponent inferior and degenerate; the psychiatrist to publish his diagnosis of the enemy's disease of mind or spirit. But probably our sense of these immediate evils is disproportionately strong, and we are not entitled to compare them with the evils of other times of which we have not undergone the experience.

The individual who is not himself a combatant—and so a wheel in the gigantic machinery of war—feels conscious of disorientation and of an inhibition in his powers and activities. I believe that he will welcome any indication, however slight, which may enable him to find out what is wrong with himself at least. I propose to distinguish two among the most potent factors in the mental distress felt by noncombatants, against which it is such a heavy task to struggle and to treat of them here: the disillusionment which this war has evoked; and the altered attitude toward death which this—like every other war—imposes on us.

When I speak of disillusionment, everyone at once knows what I mean. One need not be a sentimentalist; one may perceive the biological and psychological necessity of suffering in the economics of human life, and yet condemn war both in its means and in its aims, and devoutly look forward to the cessation of all wars. True, we have told ourselves that wars can never cease so long as nations live under such widely differing conditions, so long as the value of individual life is in each nation so variously computed, and so long as the animosities which divide them represent such powerful instinctual forces in the mind. And we were prepared to find that wars between the primitive and the civilized peoples, between those races whom a color line divides, nay, wars with and among the undeveloped nationalities of Europe or those whose culture has perished—that for a considerable period such wars would occupy mankind. But we permitted ourselves to have other hopes. We had expected the great ruling powers among the white nations upon whom the leadership of the human species has fallen, who were known to have cultivated worldwide interests, to whose creative powers were due our technical advances in the direction of dominating nature, as well as the artistic and scientific acquisitions of the mind—peoples such as these we had expected to succeed in discovering another way of settling misunderstandings and conflicts of interest. Within each of these nations there prevailed high standards of accepted custom for the individual, to which his manner of life was bound to conform if he desired a share in communal privileges. These ordinances, frequently too stringent, exacted a great deal from him, much self-restraint, much renunciation of instinctual gratification. He was especially forbidden to make use of the immense advantages to be gained by the practice of lying and deception in the competition with his fellow men. The civilized state regarded these accepted standards as the basis of its existence; stern were its proceedings when an impious hand was laid upon them; frequent the pronouncement that to subject them even to examination by a critical intelligence was entirely impracticable. It could be assumed, therefore, that the state itself would respect them, nor would contemplate undertaking any infringement of what it acknowledged as the basis of its own existence. To be sure, it was evident that within these civilized states were mingled remnants of certain other races who were universally unpopular and had therefore been only reluctantly, and even so not to the fullest extent, admitted to participation in the common task of civilization, for which they had shown themselves suitable enough. But the great nations themselves, it might have been supposed, had acquired so much comprehension of their common interests, and enough tolerance for the differences that existed between them, that *foreigner* and *enemy* could no longer, as still in antiquity, be regarded as synonymous.

Relying on this union among the civilized races, countless people have exchanged their native home for a foreign dwelling place, and made their existence dependent on the conditions of intercourse between friendly nations. But he who was not by stress of circumstances confined to one spot, could also confer upon himself, through all the advantages and attractions of these civilized countries, a new, a wider fatherland, wherein he moved unhindered and unsuspected. In this way he enjoyed the blue sea and the gray; the beauty of the snow-clad mountains and of the green pasturelands; the magic of the northern forests and the splendor of the southern vegetation; the emotion inspired by landscapes that recall great historical events, and the silence of nature in her inviolate places. This new fatherland was for him a museum also, filled with all the treasures which the artists among civilized communities had in the successive centuries created and left behind. As he wandered from one gallery to another in this museum, he could appreciate impartially the varied types of perfection that miscegenation, the course of historical events, and the special characteristics of their mother earth had produced among his more remote compatriots. Here he would find a cool inflexible energy developed to the highest point; there, the gracious art of beautifying existence; elsewhere, the sense of order and fixed law—in short, any and all of the qualities which have made mankind the lords of the earth.

Nor must we forget that each of these citizens of culture had created for himself a personal "Parnassus" and "School of Athens." From among the great thinkers and artists of all nations he had chosen those to whom he conceived himself most deeply indebted for what he had achieved in enjoyment and comprehension of life, and in his veneration had associated them with the immortals of old as well as with the more familiar masters of his own tongue. None of these great figures had seemed to him alien because he had spoken another language—not the incomparable investigator of the passions of mankind, nor the intoxicated worshipper of beauty, nor the vehement and threatening prophet, nor the subtle mocking satirist; and never did he on this account rebuke himself as a renegade toward his own nation and his beloved mother tongue.

The enjoyment of this fellowship in civilization was from time to time disturbed by warning voices, which declared that as a result of long-prevailing differences wars were unavoidable, even among the members of a fellowship such as this. We refused to believe it; but if such a war indeed must be, what was our imaginary picture of it? We saw it as an opportunity for demonstrating the progress of mankind in communal feeling since the era when the Greek amphictyonies had proclaimed that no city of the league might be demolished, nor its olive groves hewn down, nor its water cut off. As a chivalrous crusade, which would limit itself to establishing the superiority of one side in the contest, with the least possible infliction of dire sufferings that could contribute nothing to the decision, and with complete immunity for the wounded who must of necessity withdraw from the contest, as well as for the physicians and nurses who devoted themselves to the task of healing. And of course with the utmost precautions for the noncombatant classes of the population—for women who are debarred from war work, and for the children who, grown older, should be enemies no longer but friends and cooperators. And again, with preservation of all the international undertakings and institutions in which the mutual civilization of peacetime had been embodied.

Even a war like this would have been productive of horrors and sufferings enough, but it would not have interrupted the development of ethical relations between the greater units of mankind, between the peoples and the states.

Then the war in which we had refused to believe broke out, and brought—disillusionment. Not only is it more sanguinary and more destructive than any war of other days, because of the enormously increased perfection of weapons of attack and defense; but it is at least as cruel, as embittered, as implacable as any that has preceded it. It sets at naught all those restrictions known as international law, which in peacetime the states had bound themselves to observe; it ignores the prerogatives of the wounded and the medical service, the distinction between civil and military sections of the population, the claims of private property. It tramples in blind fury on all that comes in its way, as though there were to be no future and no goodwill among men after it has passed. It rends all bonds of fellowship between the contending peoples, and threatens to leave such a legacy of embitterment as will make any renewal of such bonds impossible for a long time to come.

Moreover, it has brought to light the almost unbelievable phenomenon of a mutual comprehension between the civilized nations so slight that the one can turn with hate and loathing upon the other. Nay, more—that one of the great civilized nations is so universally unpopular that the attempt can actually be made to exclude it from the civilized community as "barbaric," although it long has proved its fitness by the most magnificent cooperation in the work of civilization. We live in the hope that the impartial decision of history will furnish the proof that precisely this nation, this in whose tongue we now write, this for whose victory our dear ones are fighting, was the one which least transgressed the laws of civilization—but at such a time who shall dare present himself as the judge of his own cause?

Nations are in a measure represented by the states which they have formed; these states, by the governments which administer them. The individual in any given nation has in this war a terrible opportunity to convince himself of what would occasionally strike him in peacetime— that the state has forbidden to the individual the practice of wrongdoing, not because it desired to abolish it, but because it desires to monopolize it, like salt and tobacco. The warring state permits itself every such misdeed, every such act of violence, as would disgrace the individual man. It practices not only the accepted stratagems, but also deliberate lying and deception against the enemy; and this, too, in a measure which appears to surpass the usage of former wars. The state exacts the utmost degree of obedience and sacrifice from its citizens, but at the same time treats them as children by maintaining an excess of secrecy, and a censorship of news and expressions of opinion that renders the spirits of those thus intellectually oppressed defenseless against every unfavorable turn of events and every sinister rumor. It absolves itself from the guarantees and contracts it had formed with other states, and makes unabashed confession of its rapacity and lust for power, which the private individual is then called upon to sanction in the name of patriotism.

Nor may it be objected that the state cannot refrain from wrongdoing, since that would place it at a disadvantage. It is no less disadvantageous, as a general rule, for the individual man to conform to the customs of morality and refrain from brutal and arbitrary conduct; and the state but seldom proves able to indemnify him for the sacrifices it exacts. It cannot be a matter for astonishment, therefore, that this relaxation of all the moral ties between the greater units of mankind should have had a seducing influence on the morality of individuals; for our conscience is not the inflexible judge that ethical teachers are wont to declare it, but in its origin is "dread of the community" and nothing else. When the community has no rebuke to make, there is an end of all suppression of the baser passions, and men perpetrate deeds of cruelty, fraud, treachery, and barbarity so incompatible with their civilization that one would have held them to be impossible.

Well may that civilized cosmopolitan, therefore, of whom I spoke, stand helpless in a world grown strange to him—his all-embracing patrimony disintegrated, the common estates in it laid waste, the fellow citizens embroiled and debased!

In criticism of his disillusionment, nevertheless, certain things must be said. Strictly speaking, it is not justified, for it consists in the destruction of—an illusion! We welcome illusions because they spare us emotional distress and enable us instead to indulge in gratification. We must not then complain if now and again they come into conflict with some portion of reality and are shattered against it.

Two things in this war have evoked our sense of disillusionment: the destitution shown in moral relations externally by the states, which in their interior relations pose as the guardians of accepted moral usage, and the brutality in behavior shown by individuals, whom, as partakers in the highest form of human civilization, one would not have credited with such a thing.

Let us begin with the second point and endeavor to formulate, as succinctly as may be, the point of view which it is proposed to criticize. How do we imagine the process by which an individual attains to a higher plane of morality? The first answer is sure to be: he is good and noble from his very birth, his very earliest beginnings. We need not consider this any further. A second answer will suggest that we are concerned with a developmental process and will probably assume that this development consists in eradicating from him the evil human tendencies and, under the influence of education and a civilized environment, replacing them by good ones. From that standpoint it is certainly astonishing that evil should show itself to have such power in those who have been thus nurtured.

But this answer implies the thesis from which we propose to dissent. In reality, there is no such thing as "eradicating" evil tendencies. Psychological—more strictly speaking, psychoanalytic—investigation shows instead that the inmost essence of human nature consists of elemental instincts, which are common to all men and aim at the satisfaction of certain primal needs. These instincts in themselves are neither good nor evil. We but classify them and their manifestations in that fashion, according as they meet the needs and demands of the human community. It is admitted that all those instincts which society condemns as evil—let us take as representatives the selfish and the cruel—are of this primitive type.

These primitive instincts undergo a lengthy process of development before they are allowed to become active in the adult being. They are inhibited, directed toward other aims and departments, become commingled, alter their objects, and are to some extent turned back upon their possessor. Reaction-formations against certain instincts take the deceptive form of a change in content, as though egoism had changed into altruism, or cruelty into pity. These reaction-formations are facilitated by the circumstance that many instincts are manifested almost from the first in pairs of opposites, a very remarkable phenomenon—and one strange to the lay public—which is termed the "ambivalence of feeling." The most easily observable and comprehensible instance of this is the fact that intense love and intense hatred are so often to be found together in the same person. Psychoanalysis adds that the conflicting feelings not infrequently have the same person for their object.

It is not until all these "vicissitudes to which instincts are subject" have been surmounted that what we call the character of a human being is formed, and this, as we know, can only very inadequately be classified as "good" or "bad." A human being is seldom altogether good or bad; he is usually "good" in one relation and "bad" in another, or "good" in certain external circumstances and in others decidedly "bad." It is interesting to learn that the existence of strong "bad" impulses in infancy is often the actual condition for an unmistakable inclination toward "good" in the adult person. Those who as children have been the most pronounced egoists may well become the most helpful and self-sacrificing members of the community; most of our sentimentalists, friends of humanity, champions of animals have been evolved from little sadists and animal-tormentors.

The transformation of "bad" instincts is brought about by two cooperating factors, an internal and an external. The internal factor consists in an influence on the bad—say, the egoistic—instincts exercised by erotism, that is, by the human need for love, taken in its widest sense. By the admixture of *erotic* components the egoistic instincts are transmuted into social ones. We learn to value being loved as an advantage for which we are willing to sacrifice other advantages. The external factor is the force exercised by upbringing, which advocates the claims of our cultural environment, and this is furthered later by the direct pressure of that civilization by which we are surrounded. Civilization is the fruit of renunciation of instinctual satisfaction, and from each newcomer in turn it exacts the same renunciation. Throughout the life of the individual there is a constant replacement of the external compulsion by the internal. The influences of civilization cause an ever-increasing transmutation of egoistic trends into altruistic and social ones, and this by an admixture of erotic elements. In the last resort it may be said that every internal compulsion which has been of service in the development of human beings was originally, that is, in the evolution of the human race, nothing but an external one. Those who are born today bring with them as an inherited constitution some degree of a tendency (disposition) toward transmutation of egoistic into social instincts, and this disposition is easily stimulated to achieve that effect. A further measure of this transformation must be accomplished during the life of the individual himself. And so the human being is subject not only to the pressure of his immediate environment, but also to the influence of the cultural development attained by his forefathers.

If we give the name of *cultural adaptability* to a man's personal capacity for transformation of the egoistic impulses under the influence of the erotic, we may further affirm that this adaptability is made up of two parts, one innate and the other acquired through experience, and that the relation of the two to each other and to that portion of the instinctual life which remains untransformed is a very variable one.

Generally speaking, we are apt to attach too much importance to the innate part, and in addition to this we run the risk of overestimating the general adaptability to civilization in comparison with those instincts which have remained in their primitive state—by which I mean that in this way we are led to regard human nature as "better" than it actually is. For there is, besides, another factor which obscures our judgment and falsifies the issue in too favorable a sense.

The impulses of another person are naturally hidden from our observation. We deduce them from his actions and behavior, which we trace to motives born of his instinctual life. Such a conclusion is bound to be, in many cases, erroneous. This or that action which is "good" from the civilized point of view may in one instance be born of a "noble" motive, in another not so. Ethical theorists class as "good" actions only those which are the outcome of good impulses; to the others they refuse their recognition. But society, which is practical in its aims, is little troubled on the whole by this distinction; it is content if a man regulates his behavior and actions by the precepts of civilization, and is little concerned with his motives.

We have seen that the external compulsion exercised on a human being by his upbringing and environment produces a further transformation toward good in his instinctual life—a turning from egoism toward altruism. But this is not the regular or necessary effect of the external compulsion. Education and environment offer benefits not only in the way of love, but also employ another kind of premium system, namely, reward and punishment. In this way their effect may turn out to be that he who is subjected to their influence will choose to "behave well" in the civilized sense of the phrase, although no ennoblement of instinct, no transformation of egoistic into altruistic inclinations, has taken place within. The result will, roughly speaking, be the same; only a particular concatenation of circumstances will reveal that one man always acts rightly because his instinctual inclination compels him so to do, and the other is "good" only in so far and for so long as such civilized behavior is advantageous for his own egoistic purposes. But superficial acquaintance with an individual will not enable us to distinguish between the two cases, and we are certainly misled by our optimism into grossly exaggerating the number of human beings who have been transformed in a civilized sense.

Civilized society, which exacts good conduct and does not trouble itself about the impulses underlying it, has thus won over to obedience a great many people who are not thereby following the dictates of their own natures. Encouraged by this success, society has suffered itself to be led into straining the moral standard to the highest possible point, and thus it has forced its members into a yet greater estrangement from their instinctual dispositions. They are consequently subjected to an unceasing suppression of instinct, the resulting strain of which betrays itself in the most remarkable phenomena of reaction and compensation formations. In the domain of sexuality, where such suppression is most difficult to enforce, the result is seen in the reaction-phenomena of neurotic disorders. Elsewhere the pressure of civilization brings in its train no pathological results, but is shown in malformations of character, and in the perpetual readiness of the inhibited instincts to break through to gratification at any suitable opportunity. Anyone thus compelled to act continually in the sense of precepts which are not the expression of instinctual inclinations, is living, psychologically speaking, beyond his means, and might objectively be designated a hypocrite, whether this difference be clearly known to him or not. It is undeniable that our contemporary civilization is extraordinarily favorable to the production of this form of hypocrisy. One might venture to say that it is based upon such hypocrisy, and that it would have to submit to far-reaching modifications if people were to undertake to live in accordance with the psychological truth. Thus there are very many more hypocrites than truly civilized persons—indeed, it is a debatable point whether a certain degree of civilized hypocrisy be not indispensable for the maintenance of civilization, because the cultural adaptability so far attained by those living today would perhaps not prove adequate to the task. On the other hand, the maintenance of civilization even on so questionable a basis offers the prospect of each new generation achieving a farther-reaching transmutation of instinct and becoming the pioneer of a higher form of civilization.

From the foregoing observations we may already derive this consolation—that our mortification and our grievous disillusionment regarding the uncivilized behavior of our world-compatriots in this war are shown to be unjustified. They were based on an illusion to which we had abandoned ourselves. In reality our fellow citizens have not sunk so low as we feared, because they had never risen so high as we believed. That the greater units of humanity, the peoples and states, have mutually abrogated their moral restraints naturally prompted these individuals to permit themselves relief for a while from the heavy pressure of civilization and to grant a passing satisfaction to the instincts it holds in check. This probably caused no breach in the relative morality within their respective national frontiers.

We may, however, obtain insight deeper than this into the change brought about by the war in our former compatriots, and at the same time receive a warning against doing them an injustice. For the evolution of the mind shows a peculiarity which is present in no other process of development. When a village grows into a town, a child into a man, the village and the child become submerged in the town and the man. Memory alone can trace the earlier features in the new image; in reality the old materials or forms have been superseded and replaced by new ones. It is otherwise with the development of the mind. Here one can describe the state of affairs, which is a quite peculiar one, only by saying that in this case every earlier stage of development persists alongside the later stage which has developed from it; the successive stages condition a coexistence, although it is in reference to the same materials that the whole series of transformations has been fashioned. The earlier mental state may not have manifested itself for years, but nonetheless it is so far present that it may at any time again become the mode of expression of the forces in the mind, and that exclusively, as though all later developments had been annulled, undone. This extraordinary plasticity of the evolution that takes place in the mind is not unlimited in its scope; it might be described as a special capacity for retroversion—for regression—since it may well happen that a later and higher stage of evolution, once abandoned, cannot be reached again. But the primitive stages can always be reestablished; the primitive mind is, in the fullest meaning of the word, imperishable.

What are called mental diseases inevitably impress the layman with the idea of destruction of the life of mind and soul. In reality, the destruction relates only to later accretions and developments. The essence of mental disease lies in a return to earlier conditions of affective life and functioning. An excellent example of the plasticity of mental life is afforded by the state of sleep, which every night we desire. Since we have learned to interpret even absurd and chaotic dreams, we know that whenever we sleep we cast off our hard-won morality like a garment, only to put it on again next morning. This divestiture is naturally unattended by any danger because we are paralysed, condemned to inactivity, by the state of sleep. Only through a dream can we learn of the regression of our emotional life to one of the earliest stages of development. For instance, it is noteworthy that all our dreams are governed by purely egoistic motives. One of my English friends put forward this proposition at a scientific meeting in America, whereupon a lady who was present remarked that that might be the case in Austria, but she could maintain for herself and her friends that *they* were altruistic even in their dreams. My friend, although himself of English race, was obliged to contradict the lady emphatically on the ground of his personal experience in dream analysis, and to declare that in their dreams high-minded American ladies were quite as egoistical as the Austrians.

Thus the transformations of instinct on which our cultural adaptability is based, may also be permanently or temporarily undone by the experiences of life. Undoubtedly the influences of war are among the forces that can bring about such regression; therefore we need not deny adaptability for culture to all who are at the present time displaying uncivilized behavior, and we may anticipate that the refinement of their instincts will be restored in times of peace.

There is, however, another symptom in our world-compatriots which has perhaps astonished and shocked us no less than the descent from their ethical nobility which has so greatly distressed us. I mean the narrow-mindedness shown by the best intellects, their obduracy, their inaccessibility to the most forcible arguments, their uncritical credulity for the most disputable assertions. This indeed presents a lamentable picture, and I wish to say emphatically that in this I am by no means a blind partisan who finds all the intellectual shortcomings on one side. But this phenomenon is much easier to account for and much less disquieting than that which we have just considered. Students of human nature and philosophers have long taught us that we are mistaken in regarding our intelligence as an independent force and in overlooking its dependence upon the emotional life. Our intelligence, they teach us, can function reliably only when it is removed from the influences of strong emotional impulses; otherwise it behaves merely as an instrument of the will and delivers the inference which the will requires. Thus, in their view, logical arguments are impotent against affective interests, and that is why reasons, which in Falstaff's phrase are "as plenty as blackberries," produce so few victories in the conflict with interests. Psychoanalytic experience has, if possible, further confirmed this statement. It daily shows that the shrewdest persons will all of a sudden behave like imbeciles as soon as the needful insight is confronted by an emotional resistance, but will completely regain their wonted acuity once that resistance has been overcome. The logical infatuations into which this war has deluded our fellow citizens, many of them the best of their kind, are therefore a secondary phenomenon, a consequence of emotional excitement, and are destined, we may hope, to disappear with it.

Having in this way come to understand once more our fellow citizens who are now so greatly alienated from us, we shall the more easily endure the disillusionment which the nations, those greater units of the human race, have caused us, for we shall perceive that the demands we make upon them ought to be far more modest. Perhaps they are reproducing the course of individual evolution, and still today represent very primitive phases in the organization and formation of higher unities. It is in agreement with this that the educative factor of an external compulsion toward morality, which we found to be so effective for the individual, is barely discernible in them. True, we had hoped that the extensive community of interests established by commerce and production would constitute the germ of such a compulsion, but it would seem that nations still obey their immediate passions far more readily than their interests. Their interests serve them, at most, as rationalizations for their passions; they parade their interests as their justification for satisfying their passions. Actually why the national units should disdain, detest, abhor one another, and that even when they are at peace, is indeed a mystery. I cannot tell why it is. It is just as though when it becomes a question of a number of people, not to say millions, all individual moral acquirements were obliterated, and only the most primitive, the oldest, the crudest mental attitudes were left. Possibly only future stages in development will be able in any way to alter this regrettable state of affairs. But a little more truthfulness and upright dealing on all sides, both in the personal relations of men to one another and between them and those who govern them, should also do something toward smoothing the way for this transformation.

Our Attitude Toward Death

The second factor to which I attribute our present sense of estrangement in this once lovely and congenial world is the disturbance that has taken place in our attitude toward death, an attitude to which hitherto we have clung so fast.

This attitude was far from straightforward. We were of course prepared to maintain that death was the necessary outcome of life, that everyone owes a debt to nature and must expect to pay the reckoning—in short, that death was natural, undeniable, and unavoidable. In reality, however, we were accustomed to behave as if it were otherwise. We displayed an unmistakable tendency to "shelve" death, to eliminate it from life. We tried to hush it up; indeed we even have the saying, "To think of something as we think of death."[1] That is our own death, of course. Our own death is indeed unimaginable, and whenever we make the attempt to imagine it we can perceive that we really survive as spectators. Hence the psychoanalytic school could venture on the assertion that at bottom no one believes in his own death, or to put the same thing in another way, in the unconscious every one of us is convinced of his own immortality.

As to the death of another, the civilized man will carefully avoid speaking of such a possibility in the hearing of the person concerned. Children alone disregard this restriction; unabashed they threaten one another with the eventuality of death, and even go so far as to talk of it before one whom they love, as for instance: "Dear Mamma, it will be a pity when you are dead but then I shall do this or that." The civilized adult can hardly even entertain the thought of another's death without seeming to himself hard- or evil-hearted; unless, of course, as a physician, lawyer, or something of the sort, he has to deal with death professionally. Least of all will he permit himself to think of the death of another if with that event some gain to himself in freedom, means, or position is connected. This sensitiveness of ours is, of course, impotent to arrest the hand of death; when it has fallen, we are always deeply affected, as if we were prostrated by the overthrow of our expectations. Our habit is to lay stress on the fortuitous causation of the death—accident, disease, infection, advanced age; in this way we betray our endeavor to modify the significance of death from a necessity to an accident. A multitude of simultaneous deaths appears to us exceedingly terrible. Toward the dead person himself we take up a special attitude, something like admiration for one who has accomplished a very difficult task. We suspend criticism of him, overlook his possible misdoings, issue the command, *De mortuis nil nisi bene*, and regard it as justifiable to set forth in the funeral oration and upon the tombstone only that which is most favorable to his memory. Consideration for the dead, who no longer need it, is dearer to us than the truth, and certainly, for most of us, is dearer also than consideration for the living.

The culmination of this conventional attitude toward death among civilized persons is seen in our complete collapse when death has fallen on some person whom we love—a parent or a partner in marriage, a brother or sister, a child, a dear friend. Our hopes, our pride, our happiness, lie in the grave with him, we will not be consoled, we will not fill the loved one's place. We behave then as if we belonged to the tribe of the Asra, who must die too when those die whom they love.

---

1. [The German saying is used as an equivalent for *incredible* or *unlikely*.—Trans.]

But this attitude of ours toward death has a powerful effect upon our lives. Life is impoverished, it loses in interest, when the highest stake in the game of living, life itself, may not be risked. It becomes as flat, as superficial, as one of those American flirtations in which it is from the first understood that nothing is to happen, contrasted with a Continental love affair in which both partners must constantly bear in mind the serious consequences. Our ties of affection, the unbearable intensity of our grief, make us disinclined to court danger for ourselves and for those who belong to us. We dare not contemplate a great many undertakings which are dangerous but quite indispensable, such as attempts at mechanical flight, expeditions to far countries, experiments with explosive substances. We are paralyzed by the thought of who is to replace the son with his mother, the husband with his wife, the father with his children, if there should come disaster. The tendency to exclude death from our calculations brings in its train a number of other renunciations and exclusions. And yet the motto of the Hanseatic League declared, *Navigare necesse est, vivere non necesse!* (It is necessary to sail the seas, it is not necessary to live.)

It is an inevitable result of all this that we should seek in the world of fiction, of general literature, and of the theater compensation for the impoverishment of life. There we still find people who know how to die, indeed, who are even capable of killing someone else. There alone too we can enjoy the condition which makes it possible for us to reconcile ourselves with death—namely, that behind all the vicissitudes of life we preserve our existence intact. For it is indeed too sad that in life it should be as it is in chess, when one false move may lose us the game, but with the difference that we can have no second game, no return match. In the realm of fiction, we discover that plurality of lives for which we crave. We die in the person of a given hero, yet we survive him and are ready to die again with the next hero just as safely.

It is evident that the war is bound to sweep away this conventional treatment of death. Death will no longer be denied; we are forced to believe in him. People really are dying, and now not one by one, but many at a time, often ten thousand in a single day. Nor is it any longer an accident. To be sure, it still seems a matter of chance whether a particular bullet hits this man or that. But the survivor may easily be hit by another bullet, and the accumulation puts an end to the impression of accident. Life has, in truth, become interesting again; it has regained its full significance.

Here a distinction should be made between two groups—those who personally risk their lives in battle and those who have remained at home and have only to wait for the loss of their dear ones by wounds, disease, or infection. It would indeed be very interesting to study the changes in the psychology of the combatants, but I know too little about it. We must stop short at the second group, to which we ourselves belong. I have said already that in my opinion the bewilderment and the paralysis of energies, now so generally felt by us, are essentially determined in part by the circumstance that we cannot maintain our former attitude toward death, and have not yet discovered a new one. Perhaps it will assist us to do this if we direct our psychological inquiry toward two other relations with death—the one which we may ascribe to primitive, prehistoric peoples, and that other which in every one of us still exists, but which conceals itself, invisible to consciousness, in the deepest-lying strata of our mental life.

The attitude of prehistoric man toward death is known to us, of course, only by inferences and reconstruction, but I believe that these processes have furnished us with tolerably trustworthy information.

Primitive man assumed a very remarkable attitude toward death. It was far from consistent, was indeed extremely contradictory. On the one hand, he took death seriously, recognized it as the termination of life, and used it to that end; on the other hand, he also denied death, reduced it to nothingness. This contradiction arose from the circumstance that he took up radically different attitudes toward the death of another man, of a stranger, of an enemy, and toward his own. The death of the other man he had no objection to; it meant the annihilation of a creature hated, and primitive man had no scruples against bringing it about. He was, in truth, a very violent being, more cruel and more malign than other animals. He liked to kill and killed as a matter of course. That instinct which is said to restrain the other animals from killing and devouring their own species we need not attribute to him.

Hence the primitive history of mankind is filled with murder. Even today, the history of the world which our children learn in school is essentially a series of race-murders. The obscure sense of guilt, which has been common to man since prehistoric times and which in many religions has been condensed into the doctrine of original sin, is probably the outcome of a blood-guiltiness incurred by primitive man. In my book *Totem und Tabu* (1913) I have, following clues given by W. Robertson Smith, Atkinson, and Charles Darwin, attempted to surmise the nature of this primal guilt, and I think that even the contemporary Christian doctrine enables us to deduce it. If the Son of God was obliged to sacrifice his life to redeem mankind from original sin, then by the law of the talion, the requital of like for like, that sin must have been a killing, a murder. Nothing else could call for the sacrifice of a life in expiation. And if the original sin was an offense against God the Father, the primal crime of mankind must have been a parricide, the killing of the primal father of the primitive human horde, whose image in memory was later transfigured into a deity.

His own death was for primitive man certainly just as unimaginable and unreal as it is for any one of us today. But there was for him a case in which the two opposite attitudes toward death came into conflict and joined issue; and this case was momentous and productive of far-reaching results. It occurred when primitive man saw someone who belonged to him die—his wife, his child, his friend, whom assuredly he loved as we love ours, for love cannot be much younger than the lust to kill. Then, in his pain, he had to learn that one can indeed die oneself, an admission against which his whole being revolted; for each of these loved ones was, in very truth, a part of his own beloved ego. But even so, on the other hand, such deaths had a rightfulness for him, since in each of the loved persons something of the hostile stranger had resided. The law of ambivalence of feeling, which to this day governs our emotional relations with those whom we love most, had assuredly a very much wider validity in primitive periods. Thus, these beloved dead had also been enemies and strangers who had aroused in him a measure of hostile feeling.

Philosophers have declared that the intellectual enigma presented to primitive man by the picture of death was what forced him to reflection, and thus that it became the starting point of all speculation. I believe that here the philosophers think too philosophically, and give too little consideration to the primarily effective motives. I would therefore limit and correct this assertion: by the body of his slain enemy primitive man would have triumphed, without racking his brains about the enigma of life and death. Not the intellectual enigma, and not every death, but the conflict of feeling at the death of loved, yet withal alien and hated persons was what disengaged the spirit of inquiry in man. Of this conflict of feeling psychology was the direct offspring. Man could no longer keep death at a distance, for he had tasted of it in his grief for the dead; but still he did not consent entirely to acknowledge it, for he could not conceive of himself as dead. So he devised a compromise; he conceded the fact of death, even his own death, but denied it the significance of annihilation, which he had had no motive for contesting where the death of his enemy had been concerned. During his contemplation of his loved one's corpse he invented ghosts, and it was his sense of guilt at the satisfaction mingled with his sorrow that turned these newborn spirits into evil, dreaded demons. The changes wrought by death suggested to him the disjunction of the individuality into a body and a soul—first of all into several souls; in this way his train of thought ran parallel with the process of disintegration which sets in with death. The enduring remembrance of the dead became the basis for assuming other modes of existence, gave him the conception of life continued after apparent death.

These subsequent modes of existence were at first no more than appendages to that life which death had brought to a close—shadowy, empty of content, and until later times but slightly valued; they showed as yet a pathetic inadequacy. We may recall the answer made to Odysseus by the soul of Achilles:

> Erst in the life on the earth, no less than a god we revered thee,
> We the Achaeans; and now in the realm of the dead as a monarch
> Here dost thou rule; then why should death thus grieve thee, Achilles?
> Thus did I speak: forthwith then answering thus he addressed me,
> Speak not smoothly of death, I beseech, O famous Odysseus,
> Better by far to remain on the earth as the thrall of another;
> E'en of a portionless man that hath means right scanty of living,
> Rather than reign sole king in the realm of the bodiless phantoms.[2]

Or in the powerful, bitterly burlesque rendering by Heine, where he makes Achilles say that the most insignificant little Philistine at Stuckert-on-the-Neckar, in being alive, is far happier than he, the son of Peleus, the dead hero, the prince of shadows in the nether world.

It was not until much later that the different religions devised the view of this afterlife as the more desirable, the truly valid one, and degraded the life which is ended by death to a mere preparation. It was then but consistent to extend life backward into the past, to conceive of former existences, transmigrations of the soul and reincarnation, all with the purpose of depriving death of its meaning as the termination of life. So early did the denial of death, which above we designated a convention of civilization, actually originate.

Beside the corpse of the beloved were generated not only the idea of the soul, the belief in immortality, and a great part of man's deep-rooted sense of guilt, but also the earliest inkling of ethical law. The first and most portentous prohibition of the awakening conscience was, thou shalt not kill. It was born of the reaction against that hate-gratification which lurked behind the grief for the loved dead, and was gradually extended to unloved strangers and finally even to enemies.

This final extension is no longer experienced by civilized man. When the frenzied conflict of this war shall have been decided, every one of the victorious warriors will joyfully return to his home, his wife, and his children, undelayed and undisturbed by any thought of the enemy he has slain either at close quarters or by distant weapons of destruction. It is worthy of note that such primitive races as still inhabit the earth, who are

---

2. [*Odyssey*, xi.484–491; translated by H. B. Cotterill.—Eds.]

undoubtedly closer than we to primitive man, act differently in this respect, or did so act until they came under the influence of our civilization. The savage—Australian, Bushman, Tierra del Fuegan—is by no means a remorseless murderer; when he returns victorious from the warpath he may not set foot in his village nor touch his wife until he has atoned for the murders committed in war by penances which are often prolonged and toilsome. This may be presumed, of course, to be the outcome of superstition; the savage still goes in fear of the avenging spirits of the slain. But the spirits of the fallen enemy are nothing but the expression of his own conscience, uneasy on account of his blood-guiltiness; behind this superstition lurks a vein of ethical sensitiveness, which has been lost by us civilized men.

Pious souls, who cherish the thought of our remoteness from whatever is evil and base, will be quick to draw from the early appearance and the urgency of the prohibition of murder gratifying conclusions in regard to the force of these ethical stirrings, which must consequently have been implanted in us. Unfortunately this argument proves even more for the opposite contention. So powerful a prohibition can only be directed against an equally powerful impulse. What no human soul desires there is no need to prohibit; it is automatically excluded. The very emphasis of the commandment thou shall not kill makes it certain that we spring from an endless ancestry of murderers, with whom the lust for killing was in the blood, as possibly it is to this day with ourselves. The ethical strivings of mankind, of which we need not in the least depreciate the strength and the significance, are an acquisition accompanying evolution; they have then become the hereditary possession of those human beings alive today, though unfortunately only in a very variable measure.

Let us now leave primitive man, and turn to the unconscious in our own mental life. Here we depend entirely upon the psychoanalytic method of investigation, the only one which plumbs such depths. We ask what is the attitude of our unconscious toward the problem of death. The answer must be: almost exactly the same as primitive man's. In this respect, as in many others, the man of prehistoric ages survives unchanged in our unconscious. Thus, our unconscious does not believe in its own death; it behaves as if immortal. What we call our unconscious (the deepest strata of our minds, made up of instinctual impulses) knows nothing whatever of negatives or of denials—contradictories coincide in it—and so it knows nothing whatever of our own death, for to that we can give only a negative purport. It follows that no instinct we possess is ready for a belief in death. This is even perhaps the secret of heroism. The rational explanation for heroism is that it consists in the decision that the personal life cannot be so precious as certain abstract general ideals. But more frequent, in my view, is that instinctive and impulsive heroism which knows no such motivation, and flouts danger in the spirit of Anzengruber's Hans the Road-Mender: "Nothing can happen to *me*." Or else that motivation serves but to clear away the hesitation which might delay a heroic reaction in accord with the unconscious. The dread of death, which dominates us oftener than we know, is on the other hand something secondary, being usually the outcome of the sense of guilt.

On the other hand, for strangers and for enemies, we do acknowledge death, and consign them to it quite as readily and unthinkingly as did primitive man. Here there does, indeed, appear a distinction, which in practice shows for a decisive one. Our unconscious does not carry out the killing; it merely thinks it and wishes it. But it would be wrong entirely to depreciate this psychical reality as compared with actual reality. It is significant and pregnant enough. In our unconscious we daily and hourly deport all who stand in our way, all who have offended or injured us. The expression, "Devil take him!" which so frequently comes to our lips in joking anger, and which really means, "Death take him!" is in our unconscious an earnest deliberate death wish. Indeed, our unconscious will murder even for trifles; like the ancient Athenian law of Draco, it knows no other punishment for crime than death; and this has a certain consistency, for every injury to our almighty and autocratic ego is at bottom a crime of *lèse-majesté*.

And so, if we are to be judged by the wishes in our unconscious, we are, like primitive man, simply a gang of murderers. It is well that all these wishes do not possess the potency which was attributed to them by primitive men; in the crossfire of mutual maledictions mankind would long since have perished, the best and wisest of men and the loveliest and fairest of women with the rest.

Psychoanalysis finds little credence among laymen for assertions such as these. They reject them as calumnies which are confuted by conscious experience, and adroitly overlook the faint indications through which the unconscious is apt to betray itself even to consciousness. It is therefore relevant to point out that many thinkers who could not have been influenced by psychoanalysis have quite definitely accused our unspoken thoughts of a readiness, heedless of the murder-prohibition, to get rid of anyone who stands in our way. From many examples of this I will choose one very famous one.

In *Le Père Goriot*, Balzac alludes to a passage in the works of J. J. Rousseau where that author asks the reader what he would do if—without leaving Paris and of course without being discovered—he could kill, with great profit to himself, an old mandarin in Peking by a mere act of the will. Rousseau implies that he would not give much for the life of this dignitary. *Tuer son mandarin* has passed into a proverb for this secret readiness even on the part of ourselves today.

There is as well a whole array of cynical jests and anecdotes which testify in the same sense, such as, for instance, the remark attributed to a husband: "If one of us dies, I shall go and live in Paris." Such cynical jokes would not be possible unless they contained an unacknowledged verity which could not be countenanced if seriously and baldly expressed. In joke, as we know, even the truth may be told.

As for primitive man, so also for us in our unconscious, there arises a case in which the two contrasted attitudes toward death, that which acknowledges it as the annihilation of life and the other which denies it as ineffectual to that end, conflict and join issue—and this case is the same as in primitive ages—the death, or the endangered life, of one whom we love, a parent or partner in marriage, a brother or sister, a child or dear friend. These loved ones are on the one hand an inner possession, an ingredient of our personal ego, but on the other hand are partly strangers, even enemies. With the exception of only a very few situations, there adheres to the tenderest and closest of our affections a vestige of hostility which can excite an unconscious death wish. But this conflict of ambivalence does not now, as it did then, find issue in theories of the soul and of ethics, but in neuroses, which afford us deep insight into normal mental life as well. How often have those physicians who practice psychoanalysis had to deal with the symptom of an exaggeratedly tender care for the well-being of relatives, or with entirely unfounded self-reproaches after the death of a loved person. The study of these cases has left them in no doubt about the extent and the significance of unconscious death wishes.

The layman feels an extraordinary horror at the possibility of such feelings, and takes this repulsion as a legitimate ground for disbelief in the assertions of psychoanalysis. I think, mistakenly. No depreciation of our love is intended, and none is actually contained in it. It is indeed foreign to our intelligence as also to our feelings thus to couple love and hate, but nature, by making use of these twin opposites, contrives to keep love ever vigilant and fresh, so as to guard it against the hate which lurks behind it. It might be said that we owe the fairest flowers of our love life to the reaction against the hostile impulse which we divine in our breasts.

To sum up, our unconscious is just as inaccessible to the idea of our own death, as murderously minded toward the stranger, as divided or ambivalent toward the loved, as was man in earliest antiquity. But how far we have moved from this primitive state in our conventionally civilized attitude toward death!

It is easy to see the effect of the impact of war on this duality. It strips us of the later accretions of civilization and lays bare the primal man in each of us. It constrains us once more to be heroes who cannot believe in their own death; it stamps the alien as the enemy, whose death is to be brought about or desired; it counsels us to rise above the death of those we love. But war is not to be abolished; so long as the conditions of existence among the nations are so varied, and the repulsions between peoples so intense, there will be, must be, wars. The question then arises: is it not we who must give in, who must adapt ourselves to them? Is it not for us to confess that in our civilized attitude toward death we are once more living psychologically beyond our means and must reform and give truth its due? Would it not be better to give death the place in actuality and in our thoughts which properly belongs to it and to yield a little more prominence to that unconscious attitude toward death which we have hitherto so carefully suppressed? This hardly seems indeed a greater achievement, but rather a backward step in more than one direction, a regression; but it has the merit of taking somewhat more into account the true state of affairs and of making life again more endurable for us. To endure life remains, when all is said, the first duty of all living beings. Illusion can have no value if it makes this more difficult for us.

We remember the old saying, *Si vis pacem, para bellum*. If you desire peace, prepare for war.

It would be timely thus to paraphrase it, *Si vis vitam, para mortem*. If you would endure life, be prepared for death.

QUESTIONS

1. According to Freud, what makes someone truly civilized? Is he saying that some individuals or races are inherently more civilized than others?

2. Does Freud believe people's behavior is completely predetermined by the "internal and external factors" he cites? (359)

3. Why does Freud say that primitive man's attitude toward death was "very remarkable"? (367) How is it different from our reluctance to believe in our own death?

4. Why is Freud convinced that life only has "its full significance" when people are willing to risk death? (366)

5. According to Freud, is art's function merely to give us, vicariously, experiences we forbid ourselves?

6. What is the "vein of ethical sensitiveness" that Freud says has been lost by civilized men? (370)

7. In his discussion of heroism and its motives, is Freud suggesting that heroism as it is usually thought of does not exist?

8. Why does Freud assert that "there will be, must be, wars" and suggest that it may be necessary to "adapt ourselves to them"? (373)

9. Why does Freud say that the first duty of all living beings is "to endure life"? (373) Why does he believe that being prepared for death is necessary to enduring life?

FOR FURTHER REFLECTION

1. Do you find Freud's explanations of disillusionment and the avoidance of death consoling? How applicable do you think Freud's ideas are to the world today?

2. Do you believe that "future stages in development" are likely to end nations' hating and fighting each other? (364)

3. Is a certain degree of hypocrisy necessary to civilization?

4. How would you compare Freud's and Jung's attitudes toward civilization and the afterlife?

JOSEPH CONRAD

Regarded in his own day as a writer of seafaring action and adventure tales set in exotic locales, Joseph Conrad (1857–1924) is today considered one of the most important modernist writers in the English language. Many of his novels use multiple points of view or intermediate narrators, such as Marlow in "Heart of Darkness" (1902), Conrad's famous story of the European colonial experiment gone bad in Africa. The overall effect of these literary devices is to highlight the ambiguity of experience, memory, and motive, not to mention the resulting difficulty of making meaningful moral judgments about human actions once those actions have been established.

Conrad was born Józef Teodor Konrad (Nalecz) Korzeniowski in 1857 to parents who were Polish aristocrats and ardent nationalists living in what was then Russian Poland (now Ukraine). Both parents died of tuberculosis before Conrad was a teenager, and he became the ward of his rich maternal uncle, Tadeusz Bobrowski, who educated him in Krakow. In 1874, Conrad expressed his desire to go to sea and, with his uncle's permission, traveled to Marseille, where he began his career in the French merchant marine. He made three trips to the West Indies over the next three years. The details of Conrad's life during this period are as fantastic as some of his fiction. He assisted in a gunrunning adventure for the Carlist rebels in Spain, and shot himself in the chest in an unsuccessful suicide attempt. In 1878, he signed on with a British merchant vessel and, in 1886, obtained his master mariner's certificate in the British Merchant Service as well as British citizenship papers, taking the English name "Joseph Conrad." He made command of his own ship, *Otago*, in 1888.

By the early 1890s, Conrad was writing fiction in English (his third language, after Polish and French) based on his travels throughout the Far East. While serving as first mate aboard a ship, he met the English novelist John Galsworthy, who encouraged Conrad in this new vocational direction. After publication of *Almayer's Folly* in 1895, Conrad married and settled in Kent,

England. There he steadily produced novels and short stories for nearly three decades, notable among them *Lord Jim* (1900), *Nostromo* (1904), and *The Secret Agent* (1907). The latter work is perhaps the most penetrating study written about the politics and psychology of a suicide bomber.

"The Secret Sharer" is one of the English language's great sea stories because it is more than just a sea story. Conrad's narrator, recounting his first command of a vessel far from home, must make critical decisions that will either make or break his standing with a veteran crew that eyes him with considerable suspicion. Conrad also explores one of his recurring obsessions, the need for strict moral codes of conduct at sea in order to maintain discipline, as well as the enigmatic occurrences that at times may cause rational men to violate such codes and risk everything.

JOSEPH CONRAD

The Secret Sharer

I

On my right hand there were lines of fishing stakes resembling a mysterious system of half-submerged bamboo fences, incomprehensible in its division of the domain of tropical fishes, and crazy of aspect as if abandoned forever by some nomad tribe of fishermen now gone to the other end of the ocean; for there was no sign of human habitation as far as the eye could reach. To the left a group of barren islets, suggesting ruins of stone walls, towers, and blockhouses, had its foundations set in a blue sea that itself looked solid, so still and stable did it lie below my feet; even the track of light from the westering sun shone smoothly, without that animated glitter which tells of an imperceptible ripple. And when I turned my head to take a parting glance at the tug which had just left us anchored outside the bar, I saw the straight line of the flat shore joined to the stable sea, edge to edge, with a perfect and unmarked closeness, in one leveled floor half brown, half blue under the enormous dome of the sky. Corresponding in their insignificance to the islets of the sea, two small clumps of trees, one on each side of the only fault in the impeccable joint, marked the mouth of the river Meinam we had just left on the first preparatory stage of our homeward journey; and, far back on the inland level, a larger and loftier mass, the grove surrounding the great Paknam pagoda, was the only thing on which the eye could rest from the vain task of exploring the monotonous sweep of the horizon. Here and there gleams as of a few scattered pieces of silver marked the windings of the great river; and on the nearest of them, just within the bar, the tug steaming right into the land became lost to my sight, hull and funnel and masts, as though the impassive earth had swallowed her up without an effort, without a tremor. My eye followed the light cloud of her smoke, now here, now there, above the plain, according to the devious curves of the stream, but always fainter and farther away, till I lost it at last behind the miter-shaped hill of the great pagoda. And then I was left alone with my ship, anchored at the head of the Gulf of Siam.

She floated at the starting point of a long journey, very still in an immense stillness, the shadows of her spars flung far to the eastward by the setting sun. At that moment I was alone on her decks. There was not a sound in her—and around us nothing moved, nothing lived, not a canoe on the water, not a bird in the air, not a cloud in the sky. In this breathless pause at the threshold of a long passage we seemed to be measuring our fitness for a long and arduous enterprise, the appointed task of both our existences to be carried out, far from all human eyes, with only sky and sea for spectators and for judges.

There must have been some glare in the air to interfere with one's sight, because it was only just before the sun left us that my roaming eyes made out beyond the highest ridge of the principal islet of the group something which did away with the solemnity of perfect solitude. The tide of darkness flowed on swiftly; and with tropical suddenness a swarm of stars came out above the shadowy earth, while I lingered yet, my hand resting lightly on my ship's rail as if on the shoulder of a trusted friend. But, with all that multitude of celestial bodies staring down at one, the comfort of quiet communion with her was gone for good. And there were also disturbing sounds by this time—voices, footsteps forward; the steward flitted along the main deck, a busily ministering spirit; a hand bell tinkled urgently under the poop deck. . . .

I found my two officers waiting for me near the supper table, in the lighted cuddy. We sat down at once, and as I helped the chief mate, I said:

"Are you aware that there is a ship anchored inside the islands? I saw her mastheads above the ridge as the sun went down."

He raised sharply his simple face, overcharged by a terrible growth of whisker, and emitted his usual ejaculations: "Bless my soul, sir! You don't say so!"

My second mate was a round-cheeked, silent young man, grave beyond his years, I thought; but as our eyes happened to meet I detected a slight quiver on his lips. I looked down at once. It was not my part to encourage sneering on board my ship. It must be said, too, that I knew very little of my officers. In consequence of certain events of no particular significance, except to myself, I had been appointed to the command only a fortnight before. Neither did I know much of the hands forward. All these people had been together for eighteen months or so, and my position was that of the only stranger on board. I mention this because it has some bearing on what is to follow. But what I felt most was my being a stranger to the ship; and if all the truth must be told, I was somewhat of a stranger to myself. The youngest man on board (barring the second mate), and untried as yet by a position of the fullest responsibility, I was willing to take the adequacy of the others for granted. They had simply to be equal to their tasks; but I wondered how far I should turn out faithful to that ideal conception of one's own personality every man sets up for himself secretly.

Meantime the chief mate, with an almost visible effect of collaboration on the part of his round eyes and frightful whiskers, was trying to evolve a theory of the anchored ship. His dominant trait was to take all things into earnest consideration. He was of a painstaking turn of mind. As he used to say, he "liked to account to himself" for practically everything that came in his way, down to a miserable scorpion he had found in his cabin a week before. The why and the wherefore of that scorpion—how it got on board and came to select his room rather than the pantry (which was a dark place and more what a scorpion would be partial to), and how on earth it managed to drown itself in the inkwell of his writing desk— had exercised him infinitely. The ship within the islands was much more easily accounted for; and just as we were about to rise from the table he made his pronouncement. She was, he doubted not, a ship from home lately arrived. Probably she drew too much water to cross the bar except at the top of spring tides. Therefore she went into that natural harbor to wait for a few days in preference to remaining in an open roadstead.

"That's so," confirmed the second mate, suddenly, in his slightly hoarse voice. "She draws over twenty feet. She's the Liverpool ship *Sephora* with a cargo of coal. Hundred and twenty-three days from Cardiff."

We looked at him in surprise.

"The tugboat skipper told me when he came on board for your letters, sir," explained the young man. "He expects to take her up the river the day after tomorrow."

After thus overwhelming us with the extent of his information he slipped out of the cabin. The mate observed regretfully that he "could not account for that young fellow's whims." What prevented him telling us all about it at once, he wanted to know.

I detained him as he was making a move. For the last two days the crew had had plenty of hard work, and the night before they had very little sleep. I felt painfully that I—a stranger—was doing something unusual when I directed him to let all hands turn in without setting an anchor watch. I proposed to keep on deck myself till one o'clock or thereabouts. I would get the second mate to relieve me at that hour.

"He will turn out the cook and the steward at four," I concluded, "and then give you a call. Of course at the slightest sign of any sort of wind we'll have the hands up and make a start at once."

He concealed his astonishment. "Very well, sir." Outside the cuddy he put his head in the second mate's door to inform him of my unheard-of caprice to take a five hours' anchor watch on myself. I heard the other raise his voice incredulously: "What? The captain himself?" Then a few more murmurs, a door closed, then another. A few moments later I went on deck.

My strangeness, which had made me sleepless, had promoted that unconventional arrangement, as if I had expected in those solitary hours of the night to get on terms with the ship of which I knew nothing, manned by men of whom I knew very little more. Fast alongside a wharf, littered like any ship in port with a tangle of unrelated things, invaded by unrelated shore people, I had hardly seen her yet properly. Now, as she lay cleared for sea, the stretch of her main deck seemed to me very fine under the stars. Very fine, very roomy for her size, and very inviting. I descended the poop and paced the waist, my mind picturing to myself the coming passage through the Malay Archipelago, down the Indian Ocean, and up the Atlantic. All its phases were familiar enough to me, every characteristic, all the alternatives which were likely to face me on the high seas—everything! . . . except the novel responsibility of command. But I took heart from the reasonable thought that the ship was like other ships, the men like other men, and that the sea was not likely to keep any special surprises expressly for my discomfiture.

Arrived at that comforting conclusion, I bethougt myself of a cigar and went below to get it. All was still down there. Everybody at the after end of the ship was sleeping profoundly. I came out again on the quarter-deck, agreeably at ease in my sleeping suit on that warm breathless night, barefooted, a glowing cigar in my teeth, and, going forward, I was met by the profound silence of the fore end of the ship. Only as I passed the door of the forecastle I heard a deep, quiet, trustful sigh of some sleeper inside. And suddenly I rejoiced in the great security of the sea as compared with the unrest of the land, in my choice of that untempted life presenting no disquieting problems, invested with an elementary moral beauty by the absolute straightforwardness of its appeal and by the singleness of its purpose.

The riding light in the fore-rigging burned with a clear, untroubled, as if symbolic, flame, confident and bright, in the mysterious shades of the night. Passing on my way aft along the other side of the ship, I observed that the rope side ladder, put over, no doubt, for the master of the tug when he came to fetch away our letters, had not been hauled in as it should have been. I became annoyed at this, for exactitude in small matters is the very soul of discipline. Then I reflected that I had myself peremptorily dismissed, my officers from duty, and by my own act had prevented the anchor watch being formally set and things properly attended to. I asked myself whether it was wise ever to interfere with the established routine of duties even from the kindest of motives. My action might have made me appear eccentric. Goodness only knew how that absurdly whiskered mate would "account" for my conduct, and what the whole ship thought of that informality of their new captain. I was vexed with myself.

Not from compunction certainly, but, as it were mechanically, I proceeded to get the ladder in myself. Now a side ladder of that sort is a light affair and comes in easily, yet my vigorous tug, which should have brought it flying on board, merely recoiled upon my body in a totally unexpected jerk. What the devil! . . . I was so astounded by the immovableness of that ladder that I remained stock-still, trying to account for it to myself like that imbecile mate of mine. In the end, of course, I put my head over the rail.

The side of the ship made an opaque belt of shadow on the darkling glassy shimmer of the sea. But I saw at once something elongated and pale floating very close to the ladder. Before I could form a guess a faint flash of phosphorescent light, which seemed to issue suddenly from the naked body of a man, flicked in the sleeping water with the elusive, silent play of summer lightning in a night sky. With a gasp I saw revealed to my stare a pair of feet, the long legs, a broad livid back immersed right up to the neck in a greenish cadaverous glow. One hand, awash, clutched the bottom rung of the ladder. He was complete but for the head. A headless corpse! The cigar dropped out of my gaping mouth with a tiny plop and a short hiss quite audible in the absolute stillness of all things under heaven. At that I suppose he raised up his face, a dimly pale oval in the shadow of the ship's side. But even I could only barely make out down there the shape his black-haired head. However, it was enough for the horrid, frost-bound sensation which had gripped me about chest to pass off. The movement of vain exclamations was past, too. I only climbed on the spare spar and leaned over the rail as far as I could, to bring my eyes nearer to that mystery floating alongside.

As he hung by the ladder, like a resting swimmer, the sea lightning played about his limbs at every stir; and he appeared in it ghastly, silvery, fishlike. He remained as mute as a fish, too. He made no motion to get out of the water, either. It was inconceivable that he should not attempt to come on board, and strangely troubling to suspect that perhaps he did not want to. And my first words were prompted by just that troubled incertitude.

"What's the matter?" I asked in my ordinary tone, speaking down to the face upturned exactly under mine.

"Cramp," it answered, no louder. Then slightly anxious, "I say, no need to call anyone."

"I was not going to," I said.

"Are you alone on deck?"

"Yes."

I had somehow the impression that he was on the point of letting go the ladder to swim away beyond my ken—mysterious as he came. But, for the moment, this being appearing as if he had risen from the bottom of the sea (it was certainly the nearest land to the ship) wanted only to know the time. I told him. And he, down there, tentatively:

"I suppose your captain's turned in?"

"I am sure he isn't," I said.

He seemed to struggle with himself, for I heard something like the low, bitter murmur of doubt. "What's the good?" His next words came out with a hesitating effort.

"Look here, my man. Could you call him out quietly?"

I thought the time had come to declare myself.

"*I* am the captain."

I heard a "By Jove!" whispered at the level of the water. The phosphorescence flashed in the swirl of the water all about his limbs, his other hand seized the ladder.

"My name's Leggatt."

The voice was calm and resolute. A good voice. The self-possession of that man had somehow induced a corresponding state in myself. It was very quietly that I remarked:

"You must be a good swimmer."

"Yes. I've been in the water practically since nine o'clock. The question for me now is whether I am to let go this ladder and go on swimming till I sink from exhaustion, or—to come on board here."

I felt this was no mere formula of desperate speech, but a real alternative in the view of a strong soul. I should have gathered from this that he was young; indeed, it is only the young who are ever confronted by such clear issues. But at the time it was pure intuition on my part. A mysterious communication was established already between us two—in the face of that silent, darkened tropical sea. I was young, too; young enough to make no comment. The man in the water began suddenly to climb up the ladder, and I hastened away from the rail to fetch some clothes.

Before entering the cabin I stood still, listening in the lobby at the foot of the stairs; A faint snore came through the closed door of the chief mate's room. The second mate's door was on the hook, but the darkness in there was absolutely soundless. He, too, was young and could sleep like a stone. Remained the steward, but he was not likely to wake up before he was called. I got a sleeping suit out of my room and, coming back on deck, saw the naked man from the sea sitting on the main hatch, glimmering white in the darkness, his elbows on his knees and his head in his hands. In a moment he had concealed his damp body in a sleeping suit of the same gray-stripe pattern as the one I was wearing and followed me like my double on the poop. Together we moved right aft, barefooted, silent.

"What is it?" I asked in a deadened voice, taking the lighted lamp out of the binnacle, and raising it to his face.

"An ugly business."

He had rather regular features; a good mouth; light eyes under some-what heavy, dark eyebrows; a smooth, square forehead; no growth on his cheeks; a small, brown mustache, and a well-shaped, round chin. His expression was concentrated, meditative, under the inspecting light of the lamp I held up to his face; such as a man thinking hard in solitude might wear. My sleeping suit was just right for his size. A well-knit young fellow of twenty-five at most. He caught his lower lip with the edge of white, even teeth.

"Yes," I said, replacing the lamp in the binnacle. The warm, heavy tropical night closed upon his head again.

"There's a ship over there," he murmured.

"Yes, I know. The *Sephora*. Did you know of us?"

"Hadn't the slightest idea. I am the mate of her—" He paused and corrected himself. "I should say I *was*."

"Aha! Something wrong?"

"Yes. Very wrong indeed. I've killed a man."

"What do you mean? Just now?"

"No, on the passage. Weeks ago. Thirty-nine south. When I say a man—"

"Fit of temper," I suggested, confidently.

The shadowy, dark head, like mine, seemed to nod imperceptibly above the ghostly gray of my sleeping suit. It was, in the night, as though I had been faced by my own reflection in the depths of a somber and immense mirror.

"A pretty thing to have to own up to for a Conway boy," murmured my double, distinctly.

"You're a Conway boy?"

"I am," he said, as if startled. Then, slowly . . . "Perhaps you too—"

It was so; but being a couple of years older I had left before he joined. After a quick interchange of dates a silence fell; and I thought suddenly of my absurd mate with his terrific whiskers and the "Bless my soul—you don't say so" type of intellect. My double gave me an inkling of his thoughts by saying:

"My father's a parson in Norfolk. Do you see me before a judge and jury on that charge? For myself I can't see the necessity. There are fellows that an angel from heaven—And I am not that. He was one of those creatures that are just simmering all the time with a silly sort of wickedness. Miserable devils that have no business to live at all. He wouldn't do his duty and wouldn't let anybody else do theirs. But what's the good of talking! You know well enough the sort of ill-conditioned snarling cur—"

He appealed to me as if our experiences had been as identical as our clothes. And I knew well enough the pestiferous danger of such a character where there are no means of legal repression. And I knew well enough also that my double there was no homicidal ruffian. I did not think of asking him for details, and he told me the story roughly in brusque, disconnected sentences. I needed no more. I saw it all going on as though I were myself inside that other sleeping suit.

"It happened while we were setting a reefed foresail, at dusk. Reefed foresail! You understand the sort of weather. The only sail we had left to keep the ship running; so you may guess what it had been like for days. Anxious sort of job, that. He gave me some of his cursed insolence at the sheet. I tell you I was overdone with this terrific weather that seemed to have no end of it. Terrific, I tell you—and a deep ship. I believe the fellow himself was half crazed with funk. It was no time for gentlemanly reproof, so I turned round and felled him like an ox. He up and at me. We closed just as an awful sea made for the ship. All hands saw it coming and took to the rigging, but I had him by the throat, and went on shaking him like a rat, the men above us yelling, 'Look out! Look out!' Then a crash as if the sky had fallen on my head. They say that for over ten minutes hardly anything was to be seen of the ship—just the three masts and a bit of the forecastle head and of the poop all awash driving along in a smother of foam. It was a miracle that they found us, jammed together behind the forebits. It's clear that I meant business, because I was holding him by the throat still when they picked us up. He was black in the face. It was too much for them. It seems they rushed us aft together, gripped as we were, screaming 'Murder!' like a lot of lunatics, and broke into the cuddy. And the ship running for her life, touch and go all the time, any minute her last in a sea fit to turn your hair gray only a-looking at it. I understand that the skipper, too, started raving like the rest of them. The man had been deprived of sleep for more than a week, and to have this sprung on him at the height of a furious gale nearly drove him out of his mind. I wonder they didn't fling me overboard after getting the carcass of their precious shipmate out of my fingers. They had rather a job to separate us, I've been told. A sufficiently fierce story to make an old judge and a respectable jury sit up a bit. The first thing I heard when I came to myself was the maddening howling of that endless gale, and on that the voice of the old man. He was hanging on to my bunk, staring into my face out of his sou'wester.

"'Mr. Leggatt, you have killed a man. You can act no longer as chief mate of this ship.'"

His care to subdue his voice made it sound monotonous. He rested a hand on the end of the skylight to steady himself with, and all that time did not stir a limb, so far as I could see. "Nice little tale for a quiet tea party," he concluded in the same tone.

One of my hands, too, rested on the end of the skylight; neither did I stir a limb, so far as I knew. We stood less than a foot from each other. It occurred to me that if old "Bless my soul—you don't say so" were to put his head up the companion and catch sight of us, he would think he was seeing double, or imagine himself come upon a scene of weird witchcraft; the strange captain having a quiet confabulation by the wheel with his own gray ghost. I became very much concerned to prevent anything of the sort. I heard the other's soothing undertone.

"My father's a parson in Norfolk," it said. Evidently he had forgotten he had told me this important fact before. Truly a nice little tale.

"You had better slip down into my stateroom now," I said, moving off stealthily. My double followed my movements; our bare feet made no sound; I let him in, closed the door with care, and, after giving a call to the second mate, returned on deck for my relief.

"Not much sign of any wind yet," I remarked when be approached.

"No, sir. Not much," he assented, sleepily, in his hoarse voice, with just enough deference, no more, and barely supressing a yawn.

"Well, that's all you have to look out for. You have got your orders."

"Yes, sir."

I paced a turn or two on the poop and saw him take up his position face forward with his elbow in the ratlines of the mizzen rigging before I went below. The mate's faint snoring was still going on peacefully. The cuddy lamp was burning over the table on which stood a vase with flowers, a polite attention from the ships' provision merchant—the last flowers we should see for the next three months at the very least. Two bunches of bananas hung from the beam symmetrically, one on each side of the rudder casing. Everything was as before in the ship—except that two of her captain's sleeping suits were simultaneously in use, one motionless in the cuddy, the other keeping very still in the captain's stateroom.

It must be explained here that my cabin had the form of the capital letter *L*, the door being within the angle and opening into the short part of the letter. A couch was to the left, the bed-place to the right; my writing desk and the chronometers' table faced the door. But anyone opening it, unless he stepped right inside, had no view of what I call the long (or vertical) part of the letter. It contained some lockers surmounted by a bookcase; and a few clothes, a thick jacket or two, caps, oilskin coat, and such like, hung on hooks. There was at the bottom of that part a door opening into my bathroom, which could be entered also directly from the saloon. But that way was never used.

The mysterious arrival had discovered the advantage of this particular shape. Entering my room, lighted strongly by a big bulkhead lamp swung on gimbals above my writing desk, I did not see him anywhere till he stepped out quietly from behind the coats hung in the recessed part.

"I heard somebody moving about, and went in there at once," he whispered.

I, too, spoke under my breath.

"Nobody is likely to come in here without knocking and getting permission."

He nodded. His face was thin and the sunburn faded, as though he had been ill. And no wonder. He had been, I heard presently, kept under arrest in his cabin for nearly seven weeks. But there was nothing sickly in his eyes or in his expression. He was not a bit like me, really; yet, as we stood leaning over my bed-place, whispering side by side, with our dark heads together and our backs to the door, anybody bold enough to open it stealthily would have been treated to the uncanny sight of a double captain busy talking in whispers with his other self.

"But all this doesn't tell me how you came to hang on to our side ladder," I inquired, in the hardly audible murmurs we used, after he had told me something more of the proceedings on board the *Sephora* once the bad weather was over.

"When we sighted Java Head I had had time to think all those matters out several times over. I had six weeks of doing nothing else, and with only an hour or so every evening for a tramp on the quarterdeck."

He whispered, his arms folded on the side of my bed-place, staring through the open port. And I could imagine perfectly the manner of this thinking out—a stubborn if not a steadfast operation; something of which I should have been perfectly incapable.

"I reckoned it would be dark before we closed with the land," he continued, so low that I had to strain my hearing, near as we were to each other, shoulder touching shoulder almost. "So I asked to speak to the old man. He always seemed very sick when he came to see me—as if he could not look me in the face. You know, that foresail saved the ship. She was too deep to have run long under the bare poles. And it was I that managed to set it for him. Anyway, he came. When I had him in my cabin—he stood by the door looking at me as if I had the halter around my neck already—I asked him right away to leave my cabin door unlocked at night while the ship was going through Sunda Straits. There would be the Java coast within two or three miles, off Angier Point. I wanted nothing more. I've had a prize for swimming my second year in the Conway."

"I can believe it," I breathed out.

"God only knows why they locked me in every night. To see some of their faces you'd have thought they were afraid I'd go about at night strangling people. Am I a murdering brute? Do I look it? By Jove! If I had been he wouldn't have trusted himself like that into my room. You'll say I might have chucked him aside and bolted out, there and then—it was dark already. Well, no. And for the same reason I wouldn't think of trying to smash the door. There would have been a rush to stop me at the noise, and I did not mean to get into a confounded scrimmage. Somebody else might have got killed—for I would not have broken out only to get chucked back, and I did not want any more of that work. He refused, looking more sick than ever. He was afraid of the men, and also of that old second mate of his who had been sailing with him for years— a gray-headed old humbug; and his steward, too, had been with him devil knows how long—seventeen years or more—a dogmatic sort of loafer who hated me like poison, just because I was the chief mate. No chief mate ever made more than one voyage in the *Sephora*, you know. Those two old chaps ran the ship. Devil only knows what the skipper wasn't afraid of (all his nerve went to pieces altogether in that hellish spell of bad weather we had)—of what the law would do to him—of his wife, perhaps. Oh, yes! She's on board. Though I don't think she would have meddled. She would have been only too glad to have me out of the ship in any way. The 'brand of Cain' business, don't you see. That's all right. I was ready enough to go off wandering on the face of the earth—and that was price enough to pay for an Abel of that sort. Anyhow, he wouldn't listen to me. 'This thing must take its course. I represent the law here.' He was shaking like a leaf. 'So you won't?' 'No!' 'Then I hope you will be able to sleep on that,' I said, and turned my back on him. 'I wonder that *you* can,' cries he, and locks the door.

"Well, after that, I couldn't. Not very well. That was three weeks ago. We have had a slow passage through the Java Sea; drifted about Carimata for ten days. When we anchored here they thought, I suppose, it was all right. The nearest land (and that's five miles) is the ship's destination; the consul would soon set about catching me; and there would have been no object in bolting to these islets there. I don't suppose there's a drop of water on them. I don't know how it was, but tonight that steward, after bringing me my supper, went out to let me eat it, and left the door unlocked. And I ate it—all there was, too. After I had finished I strolled out on the quarterdeck. I don't know that I meant to do anything. A breath of fresh air was all I wanted, I believe. Then a sudden temptation came over me. I kicked off my slippers and was in the water before I had made up my mind fairly. Somebody heard the splash and they raised an awful hullabaloo. 'He's gone! Lower the boats! He's committed suicide! No, he's swimming.' Certainly I was swimming. It's not so easy for a swimmer like me to commit suicide by drowning. I landed on the nearest islet before the boat left the ship's side. I heard them pulling about in the dark, hailing, and so on, but after a bit they gave up. Everything quieted down and the anchorage became as still as death. I sat down on a stone and began to think. I felt certain they would start searching for me at daylight. There was no place to hide on those stony things—and if there had been, what would have been the good? But now I was clear of that ship, I was not going back. So after a while I took off all my clothes, tied them up in a bundle with a stone inside, and dropped them in the deep water on the outer side of that islet. That was suicide enough for me. Let them think what they liked, but I didn't mean to drown myself. I meant to swim till I sank—but that's not the same thing. I struck out for another of these little islands, and it was from that one that I first saw your riding light. Something to swim for. I went on easily, and on the way I came upon a flat rock a foot or two above water. In the daytime, I dare say, you might make it out with a glass from your poop. I scrambled up on it and rested myself for a bit. Then I made another start. That last spell must have been over a mile."

His whisper was getting fainter and fainter, and all the time he stared straight out through the porthole, in which there was not even a star to be seen. I had not interrupted him. There was something that made comment impossible in his narrative, or perhaps in himself; a sort of feeling, a quality, which I can't find a name for. And when he ceased, all I found was a futile whisper: "So you swam for our light?"

"Yes—straight for it. It was something to swim for. I couldn't see any stars low down because the coast was in the way, and I couldn't see the land, either. The water was like glass. One might have been swimming in a confounded thousand-feet deep cistern with no place for scrambling out anywhere; but what I didn't like was the notion of swimming round and round like a crazed bullock before I gave out; and as I didn't mean to go back . . . No. Do you see me being hauled back, stark naked, off one of these little islands by the scruff of the neck and fighting like a wild beast? Somebody would have got killed for certain, and I did not want any of that. So I went on. Then your ladder—"

"Why didn't you hail the ship?" I asked, a little louder.

He touched my shoulder lightly. Lazy footsteps came right over our heads and stopped. The second mate had crossed from the other side of the poop and might have been hanging over the rail, for all we knew.

"He couldn't hear us talking—could he?" My double breathed into my very war, anxiously.

His anxiety was an answer, a sufficient answer, to the question I had put to him. An answer containing all the difficulty of that situation. I closed the porthole quietly, to make sure. A louder word might have been overheard.

"Who's that?" he whispered then.

"My second mate. But I don't know much more of the fellow than you do."

And I told him a little about myself. I had been appointed to take charge while I least expected anything of the sort, not quite a fortnight ago. I didn't know either the ship or the people. Hadn't had the time in port to look about me or size anybody up. And as to the crew, all they knew was that I was appointed to take the ship home. For the rest, I was almost as much of a stranger on board as himself, I said. And at the moment I felt it most acutely. I felt that it would take very little to make me a suspect person in the eyes of the ship's company.

He had turned about meantime; and we, the two strangers in the ship, faced each other in identical attitudes.

"Your ladder—" he murmured, after a silence. "Who'd have thought of finding a ladder hanging over at night in a ship anchored out here! I felt just then a very unpleasant faintness. After the life I've been leading for nine weeks, anybody would have got out of condition. I wasn't capable of swimming round as far as your rudder chains. And, lo and behold! There was a ladder to get hold of. After I gripped it I said to myself, 'What's the good?' When I saw a man's head looking over I thought I would swim away presently and leave him shouting—in whatever language it was. I didn't mind being looked at. I—I liked it. And then you speaking to me so quietly—as if you had expected me—made me hold on a little longer. It had been a confounded lonely time—I don't mean while swimming. I was glad to talk a little to somebody that didn't belong to the *Sephora*. As to asking for the captain, that was a mere impulse. It could have been no use, with all the ship knowing about me and the other people pretty certain to be round here in the morning. I don't know—I wanted to be seen, to talk with somebody, before I went on. I don't know what I would have said. . . . 'Fine night, isn't it?' or something of the sort."

"Do you think they will be round here presently?" I asked with some incredulity.

"Quite likely," he said, faintly.

He looked extremely haggard all of a sudden. His head rolled on his shoulders.

"H'm. We shall see then. Meantime get into that bed," I whispered. "Want help? There."

It was a rather high bed-place with a set of drawers underneath. This amazing swimmer really needed the lift I gave him by seizing his leg. He tumbled in, rolled over on his back, and flung one arm across his eyes. And then, with his face nearly hidden, he must have looked exactly as I used to look in that bed. I gazed upon my other self for a while before drawing across carefully the two green serge curtains which ran on a brass rod. I thought for a moment of pinning them together for greater safety, but I sat down on the couch, and once there I felt unwilling to rise and hunt for a pin. I would do it in a moment. I was extremely tired, in a peculiarly intimate way, by the strain of stealthiness, by the effort of whispering and the general secrecy of this excitement. It was three o'clock by now and I had been on my feet since nine, but I was not sleepy; I could not have gone to sleep. I sat there, fagged out, looking at the curtains, trying to clear my mind of the confused sensation of being in two places at once, and greatly bothered by an exasperating knocking in my head. It was a relief to discover suddenly that it was not in my head at all, but on the outside of the door. Before I could collect myself the words "Come in" were out of my mouth, and the steward entered with a tray, bringing in my morning coffee. I had slept, after all, and I was so frightened that I shouted, "This way! I am here, steward," as though he had been miles away. He put down the tray on the table next the couch and only then said, very quietly, "I can see you are here, sir." I felt him give me a keen look, but I dared not meet his eyes just then. He must have wondered why I had drawn the curtains of my bed before going to sleep on the couch. He went out, hooking the door open as usual.

I heard the crew washing decks above me. I knew I would have been told at once if there had been any wind. Calm, I thought, and I was doubly vexed. Indeed, I felt dual more than ever. The steward reappeared suddenly in the doorway. I jumped up from the couch so quickly that he gave a start.

"What do you want here?"

"Close your port, sir—they are washing decks."

"It is closed," I said, reddening.

"Very well, sir." But he did not move from the doorway and returned my stare in an extraordinary, equivocal manner for a time. Then his eyes wavered, all his expression changed, and in a voice unusually gentle, almost coaxingly:

"May I come in to take the empty cup away, sir?"

"Of course!" I turned my back on him while he popped in and out. Then I unhooked and closed the door and even pushed the bolt. This sort of thing could not go on very long. The cabin was as hot as an oven, too. I took a peep at my double, and discovered that he had not moved, his arm was still over his eyes; but his chest heaved; his hair was wet; his chin glistened with perspiration. I reached over him and opened the port.

"I must show myself on deck," I reflected.

Of course, theoretically, I could do what I liked, with no one to say nay to me within the whole circle of the horizon; but to lock my cabin door and take the key away I did not dare. Directly I put my head out of the companion I saw the group of my two officers, the second mate bare-footed, the chief mate in long india-rubber boots, near the break of the poop, and the steward halfway down the poop ladder talking to them eagerly. He happened to catch sight of me and dived, the second ran down on the main deck shouting some order or other, and the chief mate came to meet me, touching his cap.

There was a sort of curiosity in his eye that I did not like. I don't know whether the steward had told them that I was "queer" only, or downright drunk, but I know the man meant to have a good look at me. I watched him coming with a smile which, as he got into point-blank range, took effect and froze his very whiskers. I did not give him time to open his lips.

"Square the yards by lifts and braces before the hands go to breakfast."

It was the first particular order I had given on board that ship; and I stayed on deck to see it executed, too. I had felt the need of asserting myself without loss of time. That sneering young cub got taken down a peg or two on that occasion, and I also seized the opportunity of having a good look at the face of every foremast man as they filed past me to go to the after braces. At breakfast time, eating nothing myself, I presided with such frigid dignity that the two mates were only too glad to escape from the cabin as soon as decency permitted; and all the time the dual working of my mind distracted me almost to the point of insanity. I was constantly watching myself, my secret self, as dependent on my actions as my own personality, sleeping in that bed, behind that door which faced me as I sat at the head of the table. It was very much like being mad, only it was worse because one was aware of it.

I had to shake him for a solid minute, but when at last he opened his eyes it was in the full possession of his senses, with an inquiring look.

"All's well so far," I whispered. "Now you must vanish into the bathroom."

He did so, as noiseless as a ghost, and then I rang for the steward, and facing him boldly, directed him to tidy up my stateroom while I was having my bath—"and be quick about it." As my tone admitted of no excuses, he said, "Yes, sir," and ran off to fetch his dustpan and brushes. I took a bath and did most of my dressing, splashing, and whistling softly for the steward's edification, while the secret sharer of my life stood drawn up bolt upright in that little space, his face looking very sunken in daylight, his eyelids lowered under the stern, dark line of his eyebrows drawn together by a slight frown.

When I left him there to go back to my room the steward was finishing dusting. I sent for the mate and engaged him in some insignificant conversation. It was, as it were, trifling with the terrific character of his whiskers; but my object was to give him an opportunity for a good look at my cabin. And then I could at last shut, with a clear conscience, the door of my stateroom and get my double back into the recessed part. There was nothing else for it. He had to sit still on a small folding stool, half smothered by the heavy coats hanging there. We listened to the steward going into the bathroom out of the saloon, filling the water bottles there, scrubbing the bath, setting things to rights, whisk, bang, clatter—out again into the saloon—turn the key—click. Such was my scheme for keeping my second self invisible. Nothing better could be contrived under the circumstances. And there we sat; I at my writing desk ready to appear busy with some papers, he behind me, out of sight of the door. It would not have been prudent to talk in daytime; and I could not have stood the excitement of that queer sense of whispering to myself. Now and then, glancing over my shoulder, I saw him far back there, sitting rigidly on the low stool, his bare feet close together, his arms folded, his head hanging on his breast—and perfectly still. Anybody would have taken him for me.

I was fascinated by it myself. Every moment I had to glance over my shoulder. I was looking at him when a voice outside the door said:

"Beg pardon, sir."

"Well!" . . . I kept my eyes on him, and so, when the voice outside the door announced, "There's a ship's boat coming our way, sir," I saw him give a start—the first movement he had made for hours. But he did not raise his bowed head.

"All right. Get the ladder over."

I hesitated. Should I whisper something to him? But what? His immobility seemed to have been never disturbed. What could I tell him he did not know already? . . . Finally I went on deck.

II

The skipper of the *Sephora* had a thin red whisker all round his face, and the sort of complexion that goes with hair of that color; also the particular, rather smeary shade of blue in the eyes. He was not exactly a showy figure; his shoulders were high, his statute but middling—one leg slightly more bandy than the other. He shook hands, looking vaguely around. A spiritless tenacity was his main characteristic, I judged. I behaved with a politeness which seemed to disconcert him. Perhaps he was shy. He mumbled to me as if he were ashamed of what he was saying; gave his name (it was something like Archbold—but at this distance of years I hardly am sure), his ship's name, and a few other particulars of that sort, in the manner of a criminal making a reluctant and doleful confession. He had had terrible weather on the passage out—terrible—terrible—wife aboard, too.

By this time we were seated in the cabin and the steward brought in a tray with a bottle and glasses. "Thanks! No." Never took liquor. Would have some water, though. He drank two tumblerfuls. Terrible thirsty work. Ever since daylight had been exploring the islands round his ship.

"What was that for—fun?" I asked, with an appearance of polite interest.

"No!" He sighed. "Painful duty."

As he persisted in his mumbling and I wanted my double to hear every word, I hit upon the notion of informing him that I regretted to say I was hard of hearing.

"Such a young man, too!" he nodded, keeping his smeary blue, unintelligent eyes fastened upon me. What was the cause of it—some disease? he inquired, without the least sympathy and as if he thought that, if so, I'd got no more than I deserved.

"Yes; disease," I admitted in a cheerful tone which seemed to shock him. But my point was gained, because he had to raise his voice to give me his tale. It is not worthwhile to record that version. It was just over two months since all this had happened, and he had thought so much about it that he seemed completely muddled as to its bearings, but still immensely impressed.

"What would you think of such a thing happening on board your own ship? I've had the *Sephora* for these fifteen years. I am a well-known shipmaster."

He was densely distressed—and perhaps I should have sympathized with him if I had been able to detach my mental vision from the unsuspected sharer of my cabin as though he were my second self. There he was on the other side of the bulkhead, four or five feet from us, no more, as we sat in the saloon. I looked politely at Captain Archbold (if that was his name), but it was the other I saw, in a gray sleeping suit, seated on a low stool, his bare feet close together, his arms folded, and every word said between us falling into the ears of his dark head bowed on his chest.

"I have been at sea now, man and boy, for seven-and-thirty years, and I've never heard of such a thing happening in an English ship. And that it should be my ship. Wife on board, too."

I was hardly listening to him.

"Don't you think," I said, "that the heavy sea which, you told me, came aboard just then might have killed the man? I have seen the sheer weight of a sea kill a man very neatly, by simply breaking his neck."

"Good God!" he uttered impressively, fixing his smeary blue eyes on me. "The sea! No man killed by the sea ever looked like that." He seemed positively scandalized at my suggestion. And as I gazed at him, certainly not prepared for anything original on his part, he advanced his head close to mine and thrust his tongue out at me so suddenly that I couldn't help starting back.

After scoring over my calmness in this graphic way he nodded wisely. If I had seen the sight, he assured me, I would never forget it as long as I lived. The weather was too bad to give the corpse a proper sea burial. So next day at dawn they took it up on the poop, covering its face with a bit of bunting; he read a short prayer, and then, just as it was, in its oilskins and long boots, they launched it amongst those mountainous seas that seemed ready every moment to swallow up the ship herself and the terrified lives on board of her.

"That reefed foresail saved you," I threw in.

"Under God—it did," he exclaimed fervently. "It was by a special mercy, I firmly believe, that it stood some of those hurricane squalls."

"It was the setting of that sail which—" I began.

"God's own hand in it," he interrupted me. "Nothing less could have done it. I don't mind telling you that I hardly dared give the order. It seemed impossible that we could touch anything without losing it, and then our last hope would have been gone."

The terror of that gale was on him yet. I let him go on for a bit, then said, casually—as if returning to a minor subject:

"You were very anxious to give up your mate to the shore people, I believe?"

He was. To the law. His obscure tenacity on that point had in it something incomprehensible and a little awful; something, as it were, mystical, quite apart from his anxiety that he should not be suspected of "countenancing any doings of that sort." Seven-and-thirty virtuous years at sea, of which over twenty of immaculate command, and the last fifteen in the *Sephora*, seemed to have laid him under some pitiless obligation.

"And you know," he went on, groping shamefacedly amongst his feelings, "I did not engage that young fellow. His people had some interest with my owners. I was in a way forced to take him on. He looked very smart, very gentlemanly, and all that. But do you know—I never liked him, somehow. I am a plain man. You see, he wasn't exactly the sort for the chief mate of a ship like the *Sephora*."

I had become so connected in thoughts and impressions with the secret sharer of my cabin that I felt as if I, personally, were being given to understand that I, too, was not the sort that would have done for the chief mate of a ship like the *Sephora*. I had no doubt of it in my mind.

"Not at all the style of man. You understand," he insisted, superfluously, looking hard at me.

I smiled urbanely. He seemed at a loss for a while.

"I suppose I must report a suicide."

"Beg pardon?"

"Sui-cide! That's what I'll have to write to my owners directly I get in."

"Unless you manage to recover him before tomorrow," I assented, dispassionately. . . . I mean, alive."

He mumbled something which I really did not catch, and I turned my ear to him in a puzzled manner. He fairly bawled:

"The land—I say, the mainland is at least seven miles off my anchorage."

"About that."

My lack of excitement, of curiosity, of surprise, of any sort of pronounced interest, began to arouse his distrust. But except for the felicitous pretense of deafness I had not tried to pretend anything. I had felt utterly incapable of playing the part of ignorance properly, and therefore was afraid to try. It is also certain that he had brought some ready-made suspicions with him, and that he viewed my politeness as a strange and unnatural phenomenon. And yet how else could I have received him? Not heartily! That was impossible for psychological reasons, which I need not state here. My only object was to keep off his inquiries. Surlily? Yes, but surliness might have provoked a point-blank question. From its novelty to him and from its nature, punctilious courtesy was the manner best calculated to restrain the man. But there was the danger of his breaking through my defense bluntly. I could not, I think, have met him by a direct lie, also for psychological (not moral) reasons. If he had only known how afraid I was of his putting my feeling of identity with the other to the test! But, strangely enough—(I thought of it only afterward)—I believe that he was not a little disconcerted by the reverse side of that weird situation, by something in me that reminded him of the man he was seeking—suggested a mysterious similitude to the young fellow he had distrusted and disliked from the first.

However that might have been, the silence was not very prolonged. He took another oblique step.

"I reckon I had no more than a two-mile pull to your ship. Not a bit more."

"And quite enough, too, in this awful heat," I said.

Another pause full of mistrust followed. Necessity, they say, is mother of invention, but fear, too, is not barren of ingenious suggestions. And I was afraid he would ask me point-blank for news of my other self.

"Nice little saloon, isn't it?" I remarked, as if noticing for the first time the way his eyes roamed from one closed door to the other. "And very well fitted out, too. Here, for instance," I continued, reaching over the back of my seat negligently and flinging the door open, "is my bathroom."

He made an eager movement, but hardly gave it a glance. I got up, shut the door of the bathroom, and invited him to have a look round, as if I were very proud of my accommodation. He had to rise and be shown round, but he went through the business without any raptures whatever.

"And now we'll have a look at my stateroom," I declared, in a voice as loud as I dared to make it, crossing the cabin to the starboard side with purposely heavy steps.

He followed me in and gazed around. My intelligent double had vanished. I played my part.

"Very convenient—isn't it?"

"Very nice. Very comf . . ." He didn't finish, and went out brusquely as if to escape from some unrighteous wiles of mine. But it was not to be. I had been too frightened not to feel vengeful; I felt I had him on the run, and I meant to keep him on the run. My polite insistence must have had something menacing in it, because he gave in suddenly. And I did not let him off a single item; mate's room, pantry, storerooms, the very sail locker which was also under the poop—he had to look into them all. When at last I showed him out on the quarterdeck he drew a long, spiritless sigh, and mumbled dismally that he must really be going back to his ship now. I desired my mate, who had joined us, to see to the captain's boat.

The man of whiskers gave a blast on the whistle which he used to wear hanging round his neck, and yelled, "*Sephora*'s away!" My double down there in my cabin must have heard, and certainly could not feel more relieved than I. Four fellows came running out from somewhere forward and went over the side, while my own men, appearing on deck too, lined the rail. I escorted my visitor to the gangway ceremoniously, and nearly overdid it. He was a tenacious beast. On the very ladder he lingered, and in that unique, guiltily conscientious manner of sticking to the point:

"I say . . . you . . . you don't think that—"

I covered his voice loudly:

"Certainly not. . . . I am delighted. Good-bye."

I had an idea of what he meant to say, and just saved myself by the privilege of defective hearing. He was too shaken generally to insist, but my mate, close witness of this parting, looked mystified and his face took on a thoughtful cast. As I did not want to appear as if I wished to avoid all communication with my officers, he had the opportunity to address me.

"Seems a very nice man. His boat's crew told our chaps a very extraordinary story, if what I am told by the steward is true. I suppose you had it from the captain, sir?"

"Yes. I had a story from the captain."

"A very horrible affair—isn't it, sir?"

"It is."

"Beats all these tales we hear about murders in Yankee ships."

"I don't think it beats them. I don't think it resembles them in the least."

"Bless my soul—you don't say so! But of course I've no acquaintance whatever with American ships, not I, so I couldn't go against your knowledge. It's horrible enough for me. . . . But the queerest part is that those fellows seemed to have some idea the man was hidden aboard here. They had really. Did you ever hear of such a thing?"

"Preposterous—isn't it?"

We were walking to and fro athwart the quarterdeck. No one of the crew forward could be seen (the day was Sunday), and the mate pursued:

"There was some little dispute about it. Our chaps took offense. 'As if we would harbor a thing like that,' they said. 'Wouldn't you like to look for him in our coal hole?' Quite a tiff. But they made it up in the end. I suppose he did drown himself. Don't you, sir?"

"I don't suppose anything."

"You have no doubt in the matter, sir?"

"None whatever."

I left him suddenly. I felt I was producing a bad impression, but with my double down there it was most trying to be on deck. And it was almost as trying to be below. Altogether a nerve-trying situation. But on the whole I felt less torn in two when I was with him. There was no one in the whole ship whom I dared take into my confidence. Since the hands had got to know his story, it would have been impossible to pass him off for anyone else, and an accidental discovery was to be dreaded now more than ever. . . .

The steward being engaged in laying the table for dinner, we could talk only with our eyes when I first went down. Later in the afternoon we had a cautious try at whispering. The Sunday quietness of the ship was against us; the stillness of air and water around her was against us; the elements, the men were against us—everything was against us in our secret partnership; time itself—for this could not go on forever. The very trust in Providence was, I suppose, denied to his guilt. Shall I confess that this thought cast me down very much? And as to the chapter of accidents which counts for so much in the book of success, I could only hope that it was closed. For what favorable accident could be expected?

"Did you hear everything?" were my first words as soon as we took up our position side by side, leaning over my bed-place.

He had. And the proof of it was his earnest whisper, "The man told you he hardly dared to give the order."

I understood the reference to be to that saving foresail.

"Yes. He was afraid of it being lost in the setting."

"I assure you he never gave the order. He may think he did, but he never gave it. He stood there with me on the break of the poop after the maintopsail blew away, and whimpered about our last hope—positively whimpered about it and nothing else—and the night coming on! To hear one's skipper go on like that in such weather was enough to drive any fellow out of his mind. It worked me up into a sort of desperation. I just took it into my own hands and went away from him, boiling, and—. But what's the use telling you? You know! . . . Do you think that if I had not been pretty fierce with them I should have got the men to do anything? Not it! The bosun perhaps? Perhaps! It wasn't a heavy sea—it was a sea gone mad! I suppose the end of the world will be something like that; and a man may have the heart to see it coming once and be done with it—but to have to face it day after day—I don't blame anybody. I was precious little better than the rest. Only—I was an officer of that old coal wagon, anyhow—"

"I quite understand," I conveyed that sincere assurance into his ear. He was out of breath with whispering; I could hear him pant slightly. It was all very simple. The same strung-up force which had given twenty-four men a chance, at least, for their lives, had, in a sort of recoil, crushed an unworthy mutinous existence.

But I had no leisure to weigh the merits of the matter—footsteps in the saloon, a heavy knock. "There's enough wind to get under way with, sir." Here was the call of a new claim upon my thoughts and even upon my feelings.

"Turn the hands up," I cried through the door. "I'll be on deck directly."

I was going out to make the acquaintance of my ship. Before I left the cabin our eyes met—the eyes of the only two strangers on board. I pointed to the recessed part where the little campstool awaited him and laid my finger on my lips. He made a gesture—somewhat vague—a little mysterious, accompanied by a faint smile, as if of regret.

This is not the place to enlarge upon the sensations of a man who feels for the first time a ship move under his feet to his own independent word. In my case they were not unalloyed. I was not wholly alone with my command; for there was that stranger in my cabin. Or rather, I was not completely and wholly with her. Part of me was absent. That mental feeling of being in two places at once affected me physically as if the mood of secrecy had penetrated my very soul. Before an hour had elapsed since the ship had begun to move, having occasion to ask the mate (he stood by my side) to take a compass bearing of the Pagoda, I caught myself reaching up to his ear in whispers. I say I caught myself, but enough had escaped to startle the man. I can't describe it otherwise than by saying that he shied. A grave, preoccupied manner, as though he were in possession of some perplexing intelligence, did not leave him henceforth. A little later I moved away from the rail to look at the compass with such a stealthy gait that the helmsman noticed it—and I could not help noticing the unusual roundness of his eyes. These are trifling instances, though it's to no commander's advantage to be suspected of ludicrous eccentricities. But I was also more seriously affected. There are to a seaman certain words, gestures, that should in given conditions come as naturally, as instinctively as the winking of a menaced eye. A certain order should spring onto his lips without thinking; a certain sign should get itself made, so to speak, without reflection. But all unconscious alertness had abandoned me. I had to make an effort of will to recall myself back (from the cabin) to the conditions of the moment. I felt that I was appearing an irresolute commander to those people who were watching me more or less critically.

And, besides, there were the scares. On the second day out, for instance, coming off the deck in the afternoon (I had straw slippers on my bare feet) I stopped at the open pantry door and spoke to the steward. He was doing something there with his back to me. At the sound of my voice he nearly jumped out of his skin, as the saying is, and incidentally broke a cup.

"What on earth's the matter with you?" I asked, astonished.

He was extremely confused. "Beg your pardon, sir. I made sure you were in your cabin."

"You see I wasn't."

"No, sir. I could have sworn I had heard you moving in there not a moment ago. It's most extraordinary . . . very sorry, sir."

I passed on with an inward shudder. I was so identified with my secret double that I did not even mention the fact in those scanty, fearful whispers we exchanged. I suppose he had made some slight noise of some kind or other. It would have been miraculous if he hadn't at one time or another. And yet, haggard as he appeared, he looked always perfectly self-controlled, more than calm—almost invulnerable. On my suggestion he remained almost entirely in the bathroom, which, upon the whole, was the safest place. There could be really no shadow of an excuse for anyone ever wanting to go in there, once the steward had done with it. It was a very tiny place. Sometimes he reclined on the floor, his legs bent, his head sustained on one elbow. At others I would find him on the campstool, sitting in his gray sleeping suit and with his cropped dark hair like a patient, unmoved convict. At night I would smuggle him into my bed-place, and we would whisper together, with the regular footfalls of the officer of the watch passing and repassing over our heads. It was an infinitely miserable time. It was lucky that some tins of fine preserves were stowed in a locker in my stateroom; hard bread I could always get hold of; and so he lived on stewed chicken, pâté de foie gras, asparagus, cooked oysters, sardines—on all sorts of abominable sham delicacies out of tins. My early morning coffee he always drank; and it was all I dared do for him in that respect.

Every day there was the horrible maneuvering to go through so that my room and then the bathroom should be done in the usual way. I came to hate the sight of the steward, to abhor the voice of that harmless man. I felt that it was he who would bring on the disaster of discovery. It hung like a sword over our heads.

The fourth day out, I think (we were then working down the east side of the Gulf of Siam, tack for tack, in light winds and smooth water)—the fourth day, I say, of this miserable juggling with the unavoidable, as we sat at our evening meal, that man, whose slightest movement I dreaded, after putting down the dishes ran up on deck busily. This could not be dangerous. Presently he came down again; and then it appeared that he had remembered a coat of mine which I had thrown over a rail to dry after having been wetted in a shower which had passed over the ship in the afternoon. Sitting stolidly at the head of the table I became terrified at the sight of the garment on his arm. Of course he made for my door. There was no time to lose.

"Steward," I thundered. My nerves were so shaken that I could not govern my voice and conceal my agitation. This was the sort of thing that made my terrifically whiskered mate tap his forehead with his forefinger. I had detected him using that gesture while talking on deck with a confidential air to the carpenter. It was too far to hear a word, but I had no doubt that this pantomime could only refer to the strange new captain.

"Yes, sir," the pale-faced steward turned resignedly to me. It was this maddening course of being shouted at, checked without rhyme or reason, arbitrarily chased out of my cabin, suddenly called into it, sent flying out of his pantry on incomprehensible errands, that accounted for the growing wretchedness of his expression.

"Where are you going with that coat?"

"To your room, sir."

"Is there another shower coming?"

"I'm sure I don't know, sir. Shall I go up again and see, sir?"

"No! Never mind."

My object was attained, as of course my other self in there would have heard everything that passed. During this interlude my two officers never raised their eyes off their respective plates; but the lip of that confounded cub, the second mate, quivered visibly.

I expected the steward to hook my coat on and come out at once. He was very slow about it; but I dominated my nervousness sufficiently not to shout after him. Suddenly I became aware (it could be heard plainly enough) that the fellow for some reason or other was opening the door of the bathroom. It was the end. The place was literally not big enough to swing a cat in. My voice died in my throat and I went stony all over. I expected to hear a yell of surprise and terror, and made a movement, but had not the strength to get on my legs. Everything remained still. Had my second self taken the poor wretch by the throat? I don't know what I would have done next moment if I had not seen the steward come out of my room, close the door, and then stand quietly by the sideboard.

Saved, I thought. But, no! Lost! Gone! He was gone!

I laid my knife and fork down and leaned back in my chair. My head swam. After a while, when sufficiently recovered to speak in a steady voice, I instructed my mate to put the ship round at eight o'clock himself.

"I won't come on deck," I went on. "I think I'll turn in, and unless the wind shifts I don't want to be disturbed before midnight. I feel a bit seedy."

"You did look middling bad a little while ago," the chief mate remarked without showing any great concern.

They both went out, and I stared at the steward clearing the table. There was nothing to be read on that wretched man's face. But why did he avoid my eyes I asked myself. Then I thought I should like to hear the sound of his voice.

"Steward!"

"Sir!" Startled as usual.

"Where did you hang up the coat?"

"In the bathroom, sir." The usual anxious tone. "It's not quite dry yet, sir—"

For some time longer I sat in the cuddy. Had my double vanished as he had come? But of his coming there was an explanation, whereas his disappearance would be inexplicable. . . . I went slowly into my dark room, shut the door, lighted the lamp, and for a time dared not turn round. When at last I did I saw him standing bolt upright in the narrow recessed part. It would not be true to say I had a shock, but an irresistible doubt of his bodily existence flitted through my mind. Can it be, I asked myself, that he is not visible to other eyes than mine? It was like being haunted. Motionless, with a grave face, he raised his hands slightly at me in a gesture which meant clearly, "Heavens! What a narrow escape!" Narrow indeed. I think I had come creeping quietly as near insanity as any man who has not actually gone over the border. That gesture restrained me, so to speak.

The mate with the terrific whiskers was now putting the ship on the other tack. In the moment of profound silence which follows upon the hands going to their stations I heard on the poop his raised voice: "Hard alee!" and the distant shout of the order repeated on the main deck. The sails, in that light breeze, made but a faint fluttering noise. It ceased. The ship was coming round slowly; I held my breath in the renewed stillness of expectation; one wouldn't have thought that there was a single living soul on her decks. A sudden brisk shout, "Mainsail haul!" broke the spell, and in the noisy cries and rush overhead of the men running away with the main brace we two, down in my cabin, came together in our usual position by the bed-place.

He did not wait for my question. "I heard him fumbling here and just managed to squat myself down in the bath," he whispered to me. "The fellow only opened the door and put his arm in to hang the coat up. All the same—"

"I never thought of that," I whispered back, even more appalled than before at the closeness of the shave, and marveling at that something unyielding in his character which was carrying him through so finely. There was no agitation in his whisper. Whoever was being driven distracted, it was not he. He was sane. And the proof of his sanity was continued when he took up the whispering again.

"It would never do for me to come to life again."

It was something that a ghost might have said. But what he was alluding to was his old captain's reluctant admission of the theory of suicide. It would obviously serve his turn—if I had understood at all the view which seemed to govern the unalterable purpose of his action.

"You must maroon me as soon as ever you can get amongst these islands off the Cambodje shore," he went on.

"Maroon you! We are not living in a boy's adventure tale," I protested. His scornful whispering took me up.

"We aren't indeed! There's nothing of a boy's tale in this. But there's nothing else for it. I want no more. You don't suppose I am afraid of what can be done to me? Prison or gallows or whatever they may please. But you don't see me coming back to explain such things to an old fellow in a wig and twelve respectable tradesmen, do you? What can they know whether I am guilty or not—or of *what* I am guilty, either? That's my affair. What does the Bible say? 'Driven off the face of the earth now. As I came at night so I shall go."

"Impossible!" I murmured. "You can't."

"Can't? . . . Not naked like a soul on the Day of Judgment. I shall freeze onto this sleeping suit. The Last Day is not yet—and . . . you have understood thoroughly. Didn't you?"

I felt suddenly ashamed of myself. I may say truly that I understood—and my hesitation in letting that man swim away from my ship's side had been a mere sham sentiment, a sort of cowardice.

"It can't be done now till next night," I breathed out. "The ship is on the offshore tack and the wind may fail us."

"As long as I know that you understand," he whispered. "But of course you do. It's a great satisfaction to have got somebody to understand. You seem to have been there on purpose." And in the same whisper, as if we two whenever we talked had to say things to each other which were not fit for the world to hear, he added, "It's very wonderful."

We remained side by side talking in our secret way—but sometimes silent or just exchanging a whispered word or two at long intervals. And as usual he stared through the port. A breath of wind came now and again into our faces. The ship might have been moored in dock, so gently and on an even keel she slipped through the water, that did not murmur even at our passage, shadowy and silent like a phantom sea.

At midnight I went on deck, and to my mate's great surprise put the ship round on the other tack. His terrible whiskers flitted round me in silent criticism. I certainly should not have done it if it had been only a question of getting out of that sleepy gulf as quickly as possible. I believe he told the second mate, who relieved him, that it was a great want of judgment. The other only yawned. That intolerable cub shuffled about so sleepily and lolled against the rails in such a slack, improper fashion that I came down on him sharply.

"Aren't you properly awake yet?"

"Yes, sir! I am awake."

"Well, then, be good enough to hold yourself as if you were. And keep a lookout. If there's any current we'll be closing with some islands before daylight."

The east side of the gulf is fringed with islands, some solitary, others in groups. On the blue background of the high coast they seem to float on silvery patches of calm water, arid and gray, or dark green and rounded like clumps of evergreen bushes, with the larger ones, a mile or two long, showing the outlines of ridges, ribs of gray rock under the dark mantle of matted leafage. Unknown to trade, to travel, almost to geography, the manner of life they harbor is an unsolved secret. There must be villages—settlements of fishermen at least—on the largest of them, and some communication with the world is probably kept up by native craft. But all that forenoon, as we headed for them, fanned along by the faintest of breezes, I saw no sign of man or canoe in the field of the telescope I kept on pointing at the scattered group.

At noon I gave no orders for a change of course, and the mate's whiskers became much concerned and seemed to be offering themselves unduly to my notice. At last I said:

"I am going to stand right in. Quite in—as far as I can take her."

The stare of extreme surprise imparted an air of ferocity also to his eyes, and he looked truly terrific for a moment.

"We're not doing well in the middle of the gulf," I continued, casually. "I am going to look for the land breezes tonight."

"Bless my soul! Do you mean, sir, in the dark amongst the lot of all them islands and reefs and shoals?"

"Well—if there are any regular land breezes at all on this coast one must get close inshore to find them, mustn't one?"

"Bless my soul!" he exclaimed again under his breath. All that afternoon he wore a dreamy, contemplative appearance which in him was a mark of perplexity. After dinner I went into my stateroom as if I meant to take some rest. There we two bent our dark heads over a half-unrolled chart lying on my bed.

"There," I said. "It's got to be Koh-ring. I've been looking at it ever since sunrise. It has got two hills and a low point. It must be inhabited. And on the coast opposite there is what looks like the mouth of a biggish river—with some town, no doubt, not far up. It's the best chance for you that I can see."

"Anything. Koh-ring let it be."

He looked thoughtfully at the chart as if surveying chances and distances from a lofty height—and following with his eyes his own figure wandering on the blank land of Cochin China, and then passing off that piece of paper clean out of sight into uncharted regions. And it was as if the ship had two captains to plan her course for her. I had been so worried and restless running up and down that I had not had the patience to dress that day. I had remained in my sleeping suit, with straw slippers and a soft floppy hat. The closeness of the heat in the gulf had been most oppressive, and the crew were used to see me wandering in that airy attire.

"She will clear the south point as she heads now," I whispered into his ear. "Goodness only knows when, though, but certainly after dark. I'll edge her in to half a mile, as far as I may be able to judge in the dark—"

"Be careful," he murmured, warningly—and I realized suddenly that all my future, the only future for which I was fit, would perhaps go irretrievably to pieces in any mishap to my first command.

I could not stop a moment longer in the room. I motioned him to get out of sight and made my way on the poop. That unplayful cub had the watch. I walked up and down for a while thinking things out, then beckoned him over.

"Send a couple of hands to open the two quarterdeck ports," I said, mildly.

He actually had the impudence, or else so forgot himself in his wonder at such an incomprehensible order, as to repeat:

"Open the quarterdeck ports! What for, sir?"

"The only reason you need concern yourself about is because I tell you to do so. Have them open wide and fastened properly."

He reddened and went off, but I believe made some jeering remark to the carpenter as to the sensible practice of ventilating a ship's quarterdeck. I know he popped into the mate's cabin to impart the fact to him because the whiskers came on deck, as it were by chance, and stole glances at me from below—for signs of lunacy or drunkenness, I suppose.

A little before supper, feeling more restless than ever, I rejoined, for a moment, my second self. And to find him sitting so quietly was surprising, like something against nature, inhuman.

I developed my plan in a hurried whisper.

"I shall stand in as close as I dare and then put her round. I shall presently find means to smuggle you out of here into the sail locker, which communicates with the lobby. But there is an opening, a sort of square for hauling the sails out, which gives straight on the quarterdeck and which is never closed in fine weather, so as to give air to the sails. When the ship's way is deadened in stays and all the hands are aft at the main braces you shall have a clear road to slip out and get overboard through the open quarterdeck port. I've had them both fastened up. Use a rope's end to lower yourself into the water so as to avoid a splash—you know. It could be heard and cause some beastly complication."

He kept silent for a while, then whispered, "I understand."

"I won't be there to see you go," I began with an effort. "The rest . . . I only hope I have understood, too."

"You have. From first to last," and for the first time there seemed to be a faltering, something strained in his whisper. He caught hold of my arm, but the ringing of the supper bell made me start. He didn't, though; he only released his grip.

After supper I didn't come below again till well past eight o'clock. The faint, steady breeze was loaded with dew; and the wet, darkened sails held all there was of propelling power in it. The night, clear and starry, sparkled darkly, and the opaque, lightless patches shifting slowly against the low stars were the drifting islets. On the port bow there was a big one more distant and shadowily imposing by the great space of sky it eclipsed.

On opening the door I had a back view of my very own self looking at a chart. He had come out of the recess and was standing near the table.

"Quite dark enough," I whispered.

He stepped back and leaned against my bed with a level, quiet glance. I sat on the couch. We had nothing to say to each other. Over our heads the officer of the watch moved here and there. Then I heard him move quickly. I knew what that meant. He was making for the companion; and presently his voice was outside my door.

"We are drawing in pretty fast, sir. Land looks rather close."

"Very well," I answered. "I am coming on deck directly."

I waited till he was gone out of the cuddy, then rose. My double moved too. The time had come to exchange our last whispers, for neither of us was ever to hear each other's natural voice.

"Look here!" I opened a drawer and took out three sovereigns. "Take this, anyhow. I've got six and I'd give you the lot, only I must keep a little money to buy some fruit and vegetables for the crew from native boats as we go through Sunda Straits."

He shook his head.

"Take it," I urged him, whispering desperately. "No one can tell what—"

He smiled and slapped meaningly the only pocket of the sleeping jacket. It was not safe, certainly. But I produced a large old silk handkerchief of mine, and tying the three pieces of gold in a corner, pressed it on him. He was touched, I suppose, because he took it at last and tied it quickly round his waist under the jacket, on his bare skin.

Our eyes met; several seconds elapsed, till, our glances still mingled, I extended my hand and turned the lamp out. Then I passed through the cuddy, leaving the door of my room wide open. . . . "Steward!"

He was still lingering in the pantry in the greatness of his zeal, giving a rub-up to a plated cruet stand the last thing before going to bed. Being careful not to awake up the mate, whose room was opposite, I spoke in an undertone.

He looked round anxiously. "Sir!"

"Can you get me a little hot water from the galley?"

"I am afraid, sir, the galley fire's been out for some time now."

"Go and see."

He fled up the stairs.

"Now," I whispered, loudly, into the saloon—too loudly, perhaps, but I was afraid I couldn't make a sound. He was by my side in an instant—the double captain slipped past the stairs—through the tiny dark passage . . . a sliding door. We were in the sail locker, scrambling on our knees over the sails. A sudden thought struck me. I saw myself wandering barefooted, bareheaded, the sun beating on my dark poll. I snatched off my floppy hat and tried hurriedly in the dark to ram it on my other self. He dodged and fended off silently. I wonder what he thought had come to me before he understood and suddenly desisted. Our hands met gropingly, lingered united in a steady, motionless clasp for second. . . . No word was breathed by either of us when they separated.

I was standing quietly by the pantry door when the steward returned.

"Sorry, sir. Kettle barely warm. Shall I light the spirit lamp?"

"Never mind."

I came out on deck slowly. It was now a matter of conscience to shave the land as close as possible—for now he must go overboard whenever the ship was put in stays. Must! There could be no going back for him. After a moment I walked over to leeward and my heart flew into my mouth at the nearness of the land on the bow. Under any other circumstances I would not have held on a minute longer. The second mate had followed me anxiously.

I looked on till I felt I could command my voice.

"She will weather," I said then in a quiet tone.

"Are you going to try that, sir?" he stammered out incredulously.

I took no notice of him and raised my tone just enough to be heard by the helmsman.

"Keep her good full."

"Good full, sir."

The wind fanned my cheek, the sails slept, the world was silent. The strain of watching the dark loom of the land grow bigger and denser was too much for me. I had shut my eyes—because the ship must go closer. She must! The stillness was intolerable. Were we standing still?

When I opened my eyes the second view started my heart with a thump. The black southern hill of Koh-ring seemed to hang right over the ship like a towering fragment of the everlasting night. On that enormous mass of blackness there was not a gleam to be seen, not a sound to be heard. It was gliding irresistibly toward us and yet seemed already within reach of the hand. I saw the vague figures of the watch grouped in the waist, gazing in awed silence.

"Are you going on, sir?" inquired an unsteady voice at my elbow.

I ignored it. I had to go on.

"Keep her full. Don't check her way. That won't do now," I said warningly.

"I can't see the sails very well," the helmsman answered me, in strange, quavering tones.

Was she close enough? Already she was, I won't say in the shadow of the land, but in the very blackness of it, already swallowed up as it were, gone too close to be recalled, gone from me altogether.

"Give the mate a call," I said to the young man who stood at my elbow as still as death. "And turn all hands up."

My tone had a borrowed loudness reverberated from the height of the land. Several voices cried out together: "We are all on deck, sir."

Then stillness again, with the great shadow gliding closer, towering higher, without a light, without a sound. Such a hush had fallen on the ship that she might have been a bark of the dead floating in slowly under the very gate of Erebus.

"My God! Where are we?"

It was the mate moaning at my elbow. He was thunderstruck, and as it were deprived of the moral support of his whiskers. He clapped his hands and absolutely cried out, "Lost!"

"Be quiet," I said sternly.

He lowered his tone, but I saw the shadowy gesture of his despair. "What are we doing here?"

"Looking for the land wind."

He made as if to tear his hair, and addressed me recklessly.

"She will never get out. You have done it, sir. I knew it'd end in something like this. She will never weather, and you are too close now to stay. She'll drift ashore before she's round. O my God!"

I caught his arm as he was raising it to batter his poor devoted head, and shook it violently.

"She's ashore already," he wailed, trying to tear himself away.

"Is she? . . . Keep good full there!"

"Good full, sir," cried the helmsman in a frightened, thin, childlike voice.

I hadn't let go the mate's arm and went on shaking it. "Ready about, do you hear? You go forward"—shake—"and stop there"—shake—"and hold your noise"—shake—"and see these head sheets properly overhauled"—shake, shake—shake.

And all the time I dared not look toward the land lest my heart should fail me. I released my grip at last and he ran forward as if fleeing for dear life.

I wondered what my double there in the sail locker thought of this commotion. He was able to hear everything—and perhaps he was able to understand why, on my conscience, it had to be thus close—no less. My first order "Hard alee!" re-echoed ominously under the towering shadow of Koh-ring as if I had shouted in a mountain gorge. And then I watched the land intently. In that smooth water and light wind it was impossible to feel the ship coming-to. No! I could not feel her. And my second self was making now ready to slip out and lower himself overboard. Perhaps he was gone already . . . ?

The great black mass brooding over our very mastheads began to pivot away from the ship's side silently. And now I forgot the secret stranger ready to depart, and remembered only that I was a total stranger to the ship. I did not know her. Would she do it? How was she to be handled?

I swung the mainyard and waited helplessly. She was perhaps stopped, and her very fate hung in the balance, with the black mass of Koh-ring like the gate of the everlasting night towering over her taffrail. What would she do now? Had she way on her yet? I stepped to the side swiftly, and on the shadowy water I could see nothing except a faint phosphorescent flash revealing the glassy smoothness of the sleeping surface. It was impossible to tell—and I had not learned yet the feel of my ship. Was she moving? What I needed was something easily seen, a piece of paper, which I could throw overboard and watch. I had nothing on me. To run down for it I didn't dare. There was no time. All at once my strained, yearning stare distinguished a white object floating within a yard of the ship's side. White on the black water. A phosphorescent flash passed under it. What was that thing? . . . I recognized my own floppy hat. It must have fallen off his head . . . and he didn't bother. Now I had what I wanted—the saving mark for my eyes. But I hardly thought of my other self, now gone from the ship, to be hidden forever from all friendly faces, to be a fugitive and a vagabond on the earth, with no brand of the curse on his sane forehead to stay a slaying hand . . . too proud to explain.

And I watched the hat—the expression of my sudden pity for his mere flesh. It had been meant to save his homeless head from the dangers of the sun. And now—behold—it was saving the ship, by serving me for a mark to help out the ignorance of my strangeness. Ha! It was drifting forward, warning me just in time that the ship had gathered sternway.

"Shift the helm," I said in a low voice to the seaman standing still like a statue.

The man's eyes glistened wildly in the binnacle light as he jumped round to the other side and spun round the wheel.

I walked to the break of the poop. On the overshadowed deck all hands stood by the forebraces waiting for my order. The stars ahead seemed to be gliding from right to left. And all was so still in the world that I heard the quiet remark "She's round," passed in a tone of intense relief between two seamen.

"Let go and haul."

The foreyards ran round with a great noise, amidst cheery cries. And now the frightful whiskers made themselves heard giving various orders. Already the ship was drawing ahead. And I was alone with her. Nothing! No one in the world should stand now between us, throwing a shadow on the way of silent knowledge and mute affection, the perfect communion of a seaman with his first command.

Walking to the taffrail, I was in time to make out, on the very edge of a darkness thrown by a towering black mass like the very gateway of Erebus—yes, I was in time to catch an evanescent glimpse of my white hat left behind to mark the spot where the secret sharer of my cabin and of my thoughts, as though he were my second self, had lowered himself into the water to take his punishment; a free man, a proud swimmer striking out for a new destiny.

QUESTIONS

1. What does the narrator mean when he says, "I was somewhat of a stranger to myself"? (380–381)

2. When the narrator sees the naked body of a man clinging to the ladder at the side of the ship, why does he ask, "What's the matter?" in an "ordinary tone" and tell the swimmer that he didn't intend to call anyone? (384)

3. Why does Leggatt admit to the narrator that he killed a man?

4. What is the significance of Leggatt repeating twice that his father is a parson in Norfolk?

5. Why does the narrator secretly hide Leggatt in his cabin?

6. How do we explain that the narrator claims Leggatt "was not a bit like me, really," but subsequently suggests it would be easy for an observer to mistake Leggatt as his "other self"? (388)

7. After Captain Archbold tells his story, why does the narrator still choose to hide Leggatt?

8. Why does the narrator say he can't be sure about the name of the captain of the *Sephora*?

9. Why does the narrator say, "I had felt utterly incapable of playing the part of ignorance properly, and therefore was afraid to try"? (397)

10. Why does the narrator feel distracted "almost to the point of insanity," while Leggatt "looked always perfectly self-controlled, more than calm—almost invulnerable"? (393, 401–402)

11. Why does the narrator endanger the entire ship and the lives of the crew to help Leggatt swim ashore?

FOR FURTHER REFLECTION

1. Does the new captain gain the respect and loyalty of his crew?

2. Does the young captain's ability to deceive his crew about what is going on in the cabin suggest deception is an important quality, essential for command?

3. How does the older narrator view the actions of his younger self?

4. Do you view the narrator's actions as the folly of a green commander, or as the bold, independent actions that will make him a strong commander?

5. Do you believe Leggatt's story?

6. What do the narrator and Leggatt share?

THORSTEIN VEBLEN

Economist Thorstein Veblen (1857–1929) is difficult to categorize. Although he earned a doctorate in philosophy, at times he sounds like a social satirist in the vein of Jonathan Swift, or a cultural anthropologist writing thickly detailed description. Whether investigating how college presidents resemble captains of industry or the kind of consumer behavior that defines the "leisure class," Veblen seldom limits his observations to what can be strictly understood as "economic laws." Rather, he expands the domain of economic theory by situating both rational and irrational choices in the context of imitative human behavior and evolutionary development.

The son of a Norwegian farmer in Wisconsin, Veblen attended Carleton College with the intention of entering the Lutheran ministry. Instead, his immersion in the classics of philosophy took him to graduate school at Johns Hopkins and Yale universities. Unable to find an academic job after receiving his degree from Yale in 1884, Veblen returned to the family farm for several years before enrolling as a student at Cornell in 1891. There he obtained a fellowship and, one year later, followed a mentor to the University of Chicago, where he taught for more than a decade and wrote his best-known work, *The Theory of the Leisure Class, an Economic Study in the Evolution of Institutions* (1899). Later, Veblen taught at Stanford University, the University of Missouri, and the New School for Social Research in New York City, and published several more books including *Imperial Germany and the Industrial Revolution* (1915) and *The Higher Learning in America* (1918). Though he enjoyed a brief period of public recognition in the early 1920s—as an intellectual featured in the pages of leading national magazines—his iconoclastic outlook put him more and more at odds with the booming economic optimism of the decade. He died just a month before the U.S. stock market crash of 1929.

The Theory of the Leisure Class is one of the most incisive studies ever written about capitalist consumer culture. But Veblen delivers his observations about America's engines of commerce and consumption in the context of a wider sweep that demonstrates his vast understanding of human history and anthropology. Veblen shows how the leisure class in any culture or time period establishes the forms of "wasteful" behavior likely to be emulated by the rest of society. Even more provocatively, he suggests how "conspicuous consumption" becomes associated with other values perceived as being of a "higher" or even "spiritual" nature. Although this book can be read alongside other classics that investigate specifically American habits of mind, it is also clear that Veblen is speaking to what he perceives as universals.

THORSTEIN VEBLEN

The Theory of the Leisure Class (selection)

T he institution of a leisure class is found in its best development at
the higher stages of the barbarian culture; as, for instance, in feudal
Europe or feudal Japan. In such communities the distinction
between classes is very rigorously observed; and the feature of most
striking economic significance in these class differences is the distinction
maintained between the employments proper to the several classes.
The upper classes are by custom exempt or excluded from industrial
occupations, and are reserved for certain employments to which a degree
of honor attaches. Chief among the honorable employments in any
feudal community is warfare; and priestly service is commonly second to
warfare. If the barbarian community is not notably warlike, the priestly
office may take the precedence, with that of the warrior second. But the
rule holds with but slight exceptions that, whether warriors or priests, the
upper classes are exempt from industrial employments, and this exemption is the economic expression of their superior rank. Brahman India
affords a fair illustration of the industrial exemption of both these
classes. In the communities belonging to the higher barbarian culture
there is a considerable differentiation of subclasses within what may be
comprehensively called the leisure class; and there is a corresponding differentiation of employments between these subclasses. The leisure class
as a whole comprises the noble and the priestly classes, together with
much of their retinue. The occupations of the class are correspondingly
diversified, but they have the common economic characteristic of being
nonindustrial. These nonindustrial upper-class occupations may be
roughly comprised under government, warfare, religious observances,
and sports.

*This selection is taken from chapter 1 and chapter 4, "Conspicuous
Consumption."*

At an earlier, but not the earliest, stage of barbarism, the leisure class is found in a less differentiated form. Neither the class distinctions nor the distinctions between leisure-class occupations are so minute and intricate. The Polynesian islanders generally show this stage of the development in good form, with the exception that, owing to the absence of large game, hunting does not hold the usual place of honor in their scheme of life. The Icelandic community in the time of the Sagas also affords a fair instance. In such a community there is a rigorous distinction between classes and between the occupations peculiar to each class. Manual labor, industry, whatever has to do directly with the everyday work of getting a livelihood, is the exclusive occupation of the inferior class. This inferior class includes slaves and other dependents, and ordinarily also all the women. If there are several grades of aristocracy, the women of high rank are commonly exempt from industrial employment, or at least, from the more vulgar kinds of manual labor. The men of the upper classes are not only exempt, but by prescriptive custom they are debarred, from all industrial occupations. The range of employments open to them is rigidly defined. As on the higher plane already spoken of, these employments are government, warfare, religious observances, and sports. These four lines of activity govern the scheme of life of the upper classes, and for the highest rank—the kings or chieftains—these are the only kinds of activity that custom or the common sense of the community will allow. Indeed, where the scheme is well developed even sports are accounted doubtfully legitimate for the members of the highest rank. To the lower grades of the leisure class certain other employments are open, but they are employments that are subsidiary to one or another of these typical leisure-class occupations. Such are, for instance, the manufacture and care of arms and accoutrements and of war canoes, the dressing and handling of horses, dogs, and hawks, the preparation of sacred apparatus, etc. The lower classes are excluded from these secondary honorable employments, except from such as are plainly of an industrial character and are only remotely related to the typical leisure-class occupations.

If we go a step back of this exemplary barbarian culture, into the lower stages of barbarism, we no longer find the leisure class in fully developed form. But this lower barbarism shows the usages, motives, and circumstances of which the institution of a leisure class has arisen, and indicates the steps of its early growth. Nomadic hunting tribes in various parts of the world illustrate these more primitive phases of the differentiation. Any one of the North American hunting tribes may be taken as a convenient illustration. These tribes can scarcely be said to have a defined leisure class. There is a differentiation of function, and there is a distinction between classes on the basis of this difference of function, but the exemption of the superior class from work has not gone far enough to make the designation "leisure class" altogether applicable. The tribes belonging on this economic level have carried the economic differentiation to the point at which a marked distinction is made between the occupations of men and women, and this distinction is of an invidious character. In nearly all these tribes the women are, by prescriptive custom, held to those employments out of which the industrial occupations proper develop at the next advance. The men are exempt from these vulgar employments and are reserved for war, hunting, sports, and devout observances. A very nice discrimination is ordinarily shown in this matter.

This division of labor coincides with the distinction between the working and the leisure class as it appears in the higher barbarian culture. As the diversification and specialization of employments proceed, the line of demarcation so drawn comes to divide the industrial from the nonindustrial employments. The man's occupation as it stands at the earlier barbarian stage is not the original out of which any appreciable portion of later industry has developed. In the later development it survives only in employments that are not classed as industrial—war, politics, sports, learning, and the priestly office. The only notable exceptions are a portion of the fishery industry and certain slight employments that are doubtfully to be classed as industry; such as the manufacture of arms, toys, and sporting goods. Virtually the whole range of industrial employments is an outgrowth of what is classed as woman's work in the primitive barbarian community.

The work of the men in the lower barbarian culture is no less indispensable to the life of the group than the work done by the women. It may even be that the men's work contributes as much to the food supply and the other necessary consumption of the group. Indeed, so obvious is this "productive" character of the men's work that in the conventional economic writings the hunter's work is taken as the type of primitive industry. But such is not the barbarian's sense of the matter. In his own eyes he is not a laborer, and he is not to be classed with the women in this respect; nor is his effort to be classed with the women's drudgery, as labor or industry, in such a sense as to admit of its being confounded with the latter. There is in all barbarian communities a profound sense of the disparity between man's and woman's work. His work may conduce to the maintenance of the group, but it is felt that it does so through an excellence and an efficacy of a kind that cannot without derogation be compared with the uneventful diligence of the women.

At a farther step backward in the cultural scale—among savage groups—the differentiation of employments is still less elaborate and the invidious distinction between classes and employments is less consistent and less rigorous. Unequivocal instances of a primitive savage culture are hard to find. Few of those groups or communities that are classed as "savage" show no traces of regression from a more advanced cultural stage. But there are groups—some of them apparently not the result of retrogression—which show the traits of primitive savagery with some fidelity. Their culture differs from that of the barbarian communities in the absence of a leisure class and the absence, in great measure, of the animus or spiritual attitude on which the institution of a leisure class rests. These communities of primitive savages in which there is no hierarchy of economic classes make up but a small and inconspicuous fraction of the human race. As good an instance of this phase of culture as may be had is afforded by the tribes of the Andamans, or by the Todas of the Nilgiri Hills. The scheme of life of these groups at the time of their earliest contact with Europeans seems to have been nearly typical, so far as regards the absence of a leisure class. As a further instance might be cited the Ainu of Yezo, and, more doubtfully, also some Bushman and Eskimo groups. Some Pueblo communities are less confidently to be included in the same class. Most, if not all, of the communities here cited may well be cases of degeneration from a higher barbarism, rather than bearers of a culture that has never risen above its present level. If so, they are for the present purpose to be taken with allowance, but they may serve none the less as evidence to the same effect as if they were really "primitive" populations.

The evidence afforded by the usages and cultural traits of communities that are without a defined leisure class resemble one another also in certain other features of their social structure and manner of life. They are small groups and of a simple (archaic) structure; they are commonly peaceable and sedentary; they are poor; and individual ownership is not a dominant feature of their economic system. At the same time, it does not follow that these are the smallest of existing communities, or that their social structure is in all respects the least differentiated; nor does the class necessarily include all primitive communities which have no defined system of individual ownership. But it is to be noted that the class seems to include the most peaceable—perhaps all the characteriztically peaceable primitive groups of men. Indeed, the most notable trait common to members of such communities is a certain amiable inefficiency when confronted with force or fraud.

The evidence afforded by the usages and cultural traits of communities at a low stage of development indicates that the institution of a leisure class has emerged gradually during the transition from primitive savagery to barbarism; or more precisely, during the transition from a peaceable to a consistently warlike habit of life. The conditions apparently necessary to its emergence in a consistent form are: (1) the community must be of a predatory habit of life (war or the hunting of large game or both); that is to say, the men, who constitute the inchoate leisure class in these cases, must be habituated to the infliction of injury by force and stratagem; (2) subsistence must be obtainable on sufficiently easy terms to admit of the exemption of a considerable portion of the community from steady application to a routine of labor. The institution of a leisure class is the outgrowth of an early discrimination between employments, according to which some employments are worthy and others unworthy. Under this ancient distinction the worthy employments are those which may be classed as exploit; unworthy are those necessary everyday employments into which no appreciable element of exploit enters.

This distinction has but little obvious significance in a modern industrial community, and it has, therefore, received but slight attention at the hands of economic writers. When viewed in the light of that modern common sense which has guided economic discussion, it seems formal and insubstantial. But it persists with great tenacity as a commonplace preconception even in modern life, as is shown, for instance, by our habitual aversion to menial employments. It is a distinction of a personal kind—of superiority and inferiority. In the earlier stages of culture, when the personal force of the individual counted more immediately and obviously in shaping the course of events, the element of exploit counted for more in the everyday scheme of life. Interest centered about this fact to a greater degree. Consequently a distinction proceeding on this ground seemed more imperative and more definitive than is the case today. As a fact in the sequence of development, therefore, the distinction is a substantial one and rests on sufficiently valid and cogent grounds.

The ground on which a discrimination between facts is habitually made changes as the interest from which the facts are habitually viewed changes. Those features of the facts at hand are salient and substantial upon which the dominant interest of the time throws its light. Any given ground of distinction will seem insubstantial to anyone who habitually apprehends the facts in question from a different point of view and values them for a different purpose. The habit of distinguishing and classifying the various purposes and directions of activity prevails of necessity always and everywhere; for it is indispensable in reaching a working theory or scheme of life. The particular point of view, or the particular characteristic that is pitched upon as definitive in the classification of the facts of life depends upon the interest from which a discrimination of the facts is sought. The grounds of discrimination, and the norm of procedure in classifying the facts, therefore, progressively change as the growth of culture proceeds; for the end for which the facts of life are apprehended changes, and the point of view consequently changes also. So that what are recognized as the salient and decisive features of a class of activities or of a social class at one stage of culture will not retain the same relative importance for the purposes of classification at any subsequent stage.

But the change of standards and points of view is gradual only, and it seldom results in the subversion or entire suppression of a standpoint once accepted. A distinction is still habitually made between industrial and nonindustrial occupations; and this modern distinction is a transmuted form of the barbarian distinction between exploit and drudgery. Such employments as warfare, politics, public worship, and public merrymaking are felt, in the popular apprehension, to differ intrinsically from the labor that has to do with elaborating the material means of life. The precise line of demarcation is not the same as it was in the early barbarian scheme, but the broad distinction has not fallen into disuse.

The tacit, commonsense distinction today is, in effect, that any effort is to be accounted industrial only so far as its ultimate purpose is the utilization of nonhuman things. The coercive utilization of man by man is not felt to be an industrial function, but all effort directed to enhance human life by taking advantage of the nonhuman environment is classed together as industrial activity. By the economists who have best retained and adapted the classical tradition, man's "power over nature" is currently postulated as the characteristic fact of industrial productivity. This industrial power over nature is taken to include man's power over the life of the beasts and over all the elemental forces. A line is in this way drawn between mankind and brute creation.

In other times and among men imbued with a different body of preconceptions, this line is not drawn precisely as we draw it today. In the savage or the barbarian scheme of life it is drawn in a different place and in another way. In all communities under the barbarian culture there is an alert and pervading sense of antithesis between two comprehensive groups of phenomena, in one of which barbarian man includes himself, and in the other, his victual. There is a felt antithesis between economic and noneconomic phenomena, but it is not conceived in the modern fashion; it lies not between man and brute creation, but between animate and inert things.

It may be an excess of caution at this day to explain that the barbarian notion which it is here intended to convey by the term *animate* is not the same as would be conveyed by the word *living*. The term does not cover all living things, and it does cover a great many others. Such a striking natural phenomenon as a storm, a disease, a waterfall, are recognized as "animate"; while fruits and herbs, and even inconspicuous animals, such as houseflies, maggots, lemmings, sheep, are not ordinarily apprehended as "animate" except when taken collectively. As here used the term does not necessarily imply an indwelling soul or spirit. The concept includes such things as in the apprehension of the animistic savage or barbarian are formidable by virtue of a real or imputed habit of initiating action. This category comprises a large number and range of natural objects and phenomena. Such a distinction between the inert and the active is still present in the habits of thought of unreflecting persons, and it still profoundly affects the prevalent theory of human life and of natural processes; but it does not pervade our daily life to the extent or with the far-reaching practical consequences that are apparent at earlier stages of culture and belief.

To the mind of the barbarian, the elaboration and utilization of what is afforded by inert nature is activity on quite a different plane from his dealings with "animate" things and forces. The line of demarcation may be vague and shifting, but the broad distinction is sufficiently real and cogent to influence the barbarian scheme of life. To the class of things apprehended as animate, the barbarian fancy imputes an unfolding of activity directed to some end. It is this teleological unfolding of activity that constitutes any object or phenomenon an "animate" fact. Wherever the unsophisticated savage or barbarian meets with activity that is at all obtrusive, he construes it in the only terms that are ready to hand—the terms immediately given in his consciousness of his own actions. Activity is, therefore, assimilated to human action, and active objects are insofar assimilated to the human agent. Phenomena of this character—especially those whose behavior is notably formidable or baffling—have to be met in a different spirit and with proficiency of a different kind from what is required in dealing with inert things. To deal successfully with such phenomena is a work of exploit rather than of industry. It is an assertion of prowess, not of diligence.

Under the guidance of this naive discrimination between the inert and the animate, the activities of the primitive social group tend to fall into two classes, which would in modern phrase be called exploit and industry. Industry is effort that goes to create a new thing, with a new purpose given it by the fashioning hand of its maker out of passive ("brute") material; while exploit, so far as it results in an outcome useful to the agent, is the conversion to his own ends of energies previously directed to some other end by another agent. We still speak of "brute matter" with something of the barbarian's realization of a profound significance in the term.

The distinction between exploit and drudgery coincides with a difference between the sexes. The sexes differ, not only in stature and muscular force, but perhaps even more decisively in temperament, and this must early have given rise to a corresponding division of labor. The general range of activities that come under the head of exploit falls to the males as being the stouter, more massive, better capable of a sudden and violent strain, and more readily inclined to self-assertion, active emulation, and aggression. The difference in mass, in physiological character, and in temperament may be slight among the members of the primitive group; it appears, in, fact, to be relatively slight and inconsequential in some of the more archaic communities with which we are acquainted—as for instance the tribes of the Andamans. But so soon as a differentiation of function has well begun on the lines marked out by this difference in physique and animus, the original difference between the sexes will itself widen. A cumulative process of selective adaptation to the new distribution of employments will set in, especially if the habitat or the fauna with which the group is in contact is such as to call for a considerable exercise of the sturdier virtues. The habitual pursuit of large game requires more of the manly qualities of massiveness, agility, and ferocity, and it can therefore scarcely fail to hasten and widen the differentiation of functions between the sexes. And so soon as the group comes into hostile contact with other groups, the divergence of function will take on the developed form of a distinction between exploit and industry.

In such a predatory group of hunters it comes to be the able-bodied men's office to fight and hunt. The women do what other work there is to do—other members who are unfit for man's work being for this purpose classed with the women. But the men's hunting and fighting are both of the same general character. Both are of a predatory nature; the warrior and the hunter alike reap where they have not strewn. Their aggressive assertion of force and sagacity differs obviously from the women's assiduous and uneventful shaping of materials; it is not to be accounted productive labor, but rather an acquisition of substance by seizure. Such being the barbarian man's work, in its best development and widest divergence from women's work, any effort that does not involve an assertion of prowess comes to be unworthy of the man. As the tradition gains consistency, the common sense of the community erects it into a canon of conduct; so that no employment and no acquisition is morally possible to the self-respecting man at this cultural stage, except such as proceeds on the basis of prowess—force or fraud. When the predatory habit of life has been settled upon the group by long habituation, it becomes the able-bodied man's accredited office in the social economy to kill, to destroy such competitors in the struggle for existence as attempt to resist or elude him, to overcome and reduce to subservience those alien forces that assert themselves refractorily in the environment. So tenaciously and with such nicety is this theoretical distinction between exploit and drudgery adhered to that in many hunting tribes the man must not bring home the game which he has killed, but must send his woman to perform that baser office.

As has already been indicated, the distinction between exploit and drudgery is an invidious distinction between employments. Those employments which are to be classed as exploit are worthy, honorable, noble; other employments, which do not contain this element of exploit, and especially those which imply subservience or submission, are unworthy, debasing, ignoble. The concept of dignity, worth, or honor, as applied either to persons or conduct, is of first-rate consequence in the development of classes and of class distinctions, and it is therefore necessary to say something of its derivation and meaning. Its psychological ground may be indicated in outline as follows.

As a matter of selective necessity, man is an agent. He is, in his own apprehension, a center of unfolding impulsive activity—"teleological" activity. He is an agent seeking in every act the accomplishment of some concrete, objective, impersonal end. By force of his being such an agent he is possessed of a taste for effective work, and a distaste for futile effort. He has a sense of the merit of serviceability or efficiency and of the demerit of futility, waste, or incapacity. This aptitude or propensity may be called the instinct of workmanship. Wherever the circumstances or traditions of life lead to a habitual comparison of one person with another in point of efficiency, the instinct of workmanship works out in an emulative or invidious comparison of persons. The extent to which this result follows depends in some considerable degree on the temperament of the population. In any community where such an invidious comparison of persons is habitually made, visible success becomes an end sought for its own utility as a basis of esteem. Esteem is gained and dispraise is avoided by putting one's efficiency in evidence. The result is that the instinct of workmanship works out in an emulative demonstration of force.

During that primitive phase of social development, when the community is still habitually peaceable, perhaps sedentary, and without a developed system of individual ownership, the efficiency of the individual can be shown chiefly and most consistently in some employment that goes to further the life of the group. What emulation of an economic kind there is between the members of such a group will be chiefly emulation in industrial serviceability. At the same time the incentive to emulation is not strong, nor is the scope for emulation large.

When the community passes from peaceable savagery to a predatory phase of life, the conditions of emulation change. The opportunity and the incentive to emulation increase greatly in scope and urgency. The activity of the men more and more takes on the character of exploit; and an invidious comparison of one hunter or warrior with another grows continually easier and more habitual. Tangible evidences of prowess—trophies—find a place in men's habits of thought as an essential feature of the paraphernalia of life. Booty, trophies of the chase or of the raid, come to be prized as evidence of preeminent force. Aggression becomes the accredited form of action, and booty serves as prima facie evidence of successful aggression. As accepted at this cultural stage, the accredited, worthy form of self-assertion is contest; and useful articles or services obtained by seizure or compulsion serve as a conventional evidence of successful contest. Therefore, by contrast, the obtaining of goods by other methods than seizure comes to be accounted unworthy of man in his best estate. The performance of productive work, or employment in personal service, falls under the same odium for the same reason. An invidious distinction in this way arises between exploit and acquisition by seizure on the one hand and industrial employment on the other hand. Labor acquires a character of irksomeness by virtue of the indignity imputed to it.

With the primitive barbarian, before the simple content of the notion has been obscured by its own ramifications and by a secondary growth of cognate ideas, "honorable" seems to connote nothing else than assertion of superior force. "Honorable" is "formidable"; "worthy" is "prepotent." A honorific act is in the last analysis little if anything else than a recognized successful act of aggression; and where aggression means conflict with men and beasts, the activity which comes to be especially and primarily honorable is the assertion of the strong hand. The naive, archaic habit of construing all manifestations of force in terms of personality or "will power" greatly fortifies this conventional exaltation of the strong hand. Honorific epithets, in vogue among barbarian tribes as well as among peoples of a more advanced culture, commonly bear the stamp of this unsophisticated sense of honor. Epithets and titles used in addressing chieftains, and in the propitiation of kings and gods, very commonly impute a propensity for overbearing violence and an irresistible devastating force to the person who is to be propitiated. This holds true to an extent also in the more civilized communities of the present day. The predilection shown in heraldic devices for the more rapacious beasts and birds of prey goes to enforce the same view.

Under this commonsense barbarian appreciation of worth or honor, the taking of life—the killing of formidable competitors, whether brute or human—is honorable in the highest degree. And this high office of slaughter, as an expression of the slayer's prepotence, casts a glamour of worth over every act of slaughter and over all the tools and accessories of the act. Arms are honorable, and the use of them, even in seeking the life of the meanest creatures of the fields, becomes an honorific employment. At the same time, employment in industry becomes correspondingly odious, and, in the commonsense apprehension, the handling of the tools and implements of industry falls beneath the dignity of able-bodied men. Labor becomes irksome.

It is here assumed that in the sequence of cultural evolution primitive groups of men have passed from an initial peaceable stage to a subsequent stage at which fighting is the avowed and characteristic employment of the group. But it is not implied that there has been an abrupt transition from unbroken peace and goodwill to a later or higher phase of life in which the fact of combat occurs for the first time. Neither is it implied that all peaceful industry disappears on the transition to the predatory phase of culture. Some fighting, it is safe to say, would be met with at any early stage of social development. Fights would occur with more or less frequency through sexual competition. The known habits of primitive groups, as well as the habits of the anthropoid apes, argue to that effect, and the evidence from the well-known promptings of human nature enforces the same view.

It may therefore be objected that there can have been no such initial stage of peaceable life as is here assumed. There is no point in cultural evolution prior to which fighting does not occur. But the point in question is not as to the occurrence of combat, occasional or sporadic, or even more or less frequent and habitual; it is a question as to the occurrence of a habitual bellicose frame of mind—a prevalent habit of judging facts and events from the point of view of the fight. The predatory phase of culture is attained only when the predatory attitude has become the habitual and accredited spiritual attitude for the members of the group; when the fight has become the dominant note in the current theory of life; when the commonsense appreciation of men and things has come to be an appreciation with a view to combat.

The substantial difference between the peaceable and the predatory phases of culture, therefore, is a spiritual difference, not a mechanical one. The change in spiritual attitude is the outgrowth of a change in the material facts of the life of the group, and it comes on gradually as the material circumstances favorable to a predatory attitude supervene. The inferior limit of the predatory culture is an industrial limit. Predation cannot become the habitual, conventional resource of any group or any class until industrial methods have been developed to such a degree of efficiency as to leave a margin worth fighting for, above the subsistence of those engaged in getting a living. The transition from peace to predation therefore depends on the growth of technical knowledge and the use of tools. A predatory culture is similarly impracticable in early times, until weapons have been developed to such a point as to make man a formidable animal. The early development of tools and of weapons is of course the same fact seen from two different points of view.

The life of a given group would be characterized as peaceable so long as habitual recourse to combat has not brought the fight into the foreground in men's everyday thoughts, as a dominant feature of the life of man. A group may evidently attain such a predatory attitude with a greater or lesser degree of completeness, so that its scheme of life and canons of conduct may be controlled to a greater or lesser extent by the predatory animus. The predatory phase of culture is therefore conceived to come on gradually, through a cumulative growth of predatory aptitudes, habits, and traditions, this growth being due to a change in the circumstances of the group's life of such a kind as to develop and conserve those traits of human nature and those traditions and norms of conduct that make for a predatory rather than a peaceable life.

The evidence for the hypothesis that there has been such a peaceable stage of primitive culture is in great part drawn from psychology rather than from ethnology and cannot be detailed here. It will be recited in part in a later chapter, in discussing the survival of archaic traits of human nature under the modern culture.

In what has been said of the evolution of the vicarious leisure class and its differentiation from the general body of the working classes, reference has been made to a further division of labor—that between different servant classes. One portion of the servant class, chiefly those persons whose occupation is vicarious leisure, come to undertake a new, subsidiary range of duties—the vicarious consumption of goods. The most obvious form in which this consumption occurs is seen in the wearing of liveries and the occupation of spacious servants' quarters. Another, scarcely less obtrusive or less effective form of vicarious consumption, and a much more widely prevalent one, is the consumption of food, clothing, dwelling, and furniture by the lady and the rest of the domestic establishment.

But already at a point in economic evolution far antedating the emergence of the lady, specialized consumption of goods as an evidence of pecuniary strength had begun to work out in a more or less elaborate system. The beginning of a differentiation in consumption even antedates the appearance of anything that can fairly be called pecuniary strength. It is traceable back to the phase of predatory culture, and there is even a suggestion that an incipient differentiation in this respect lies back of the beginnings of the predatory life. This most primitive differentiation in the consumption of goods is like the later differentiation with which we are all so intimately familiar, in that it is largely of a ceremonial character, but unlike the latter it does not rest on a difference in accumulated wealth. The utility of consumption as an evidence of wealth is to be classed as a derivative growth. It is an adaptation to a new end, by a selective process, of a distinction previously existing and well established in men's habits of thought.

In the earlier phases of the predatory culture the only economic differentiation is a broad distinction between an honorable superior class made up of the able-bodied men on the one side, and a base inferior class of laboring women on the other. According to the ideal scheme of life in force at that time, it is the office of the men to consume what the women produce. Such consumption as falls to the women is merely incidental to their work; it is a means to their continued labor, and not a consumption directed to their own comfort and fullness of life. Unproductive consumption of goods is honorable, primarily as a mark of prowess and a perquisite of human dignity; secondarily it becomes substantially honorable in itself, especially the consumption of the more desirable things. The consumption of choice articles of food, and frequently also of rare articles of adornment, becomes taboo to the women and children; and if there is a base (servile) class of men, the taboo holds also for them. With a further advance in culture this taboo may change into simple custom of a more or less rigorous character; but whatever be the theoretical basis of the distinction which is maintained, whether it be a taboo or a larger conventionality, the features of the conventional scheme of consumption do not change easily. When the quasi-peaceable stage of industry is reached, with its fundamental institution of chattel slavery, the general principle, more or less rigorously applied, is that the base, industrious class should consume only what may be necessary to their subsistence. In the nature of things, luxuries and the comforts of life belong to the leisure class. Under the taboo, certain victuals, and more particularly certain beverages, are strictly reserved for the use of the superior class.

The ceremonial differentiation of the dietary is best seen in the use of intoxicating beverages and narcotics. If these articles of consumption are costly, they are felt to be noble and honorific. Therefore the base classes, primarily the women, practice an enforced continence with respect to these stimulants, except in countries where they are obtainable at a very low cost. From archaic times down through all the length of the patriarchal regime it has been the office of the women to prepare and administer these luxuries, and it has been the perquisite of the men of gentle birth and breeding to consume them. Drunkenness and the other pathological consequences of the free use of stimulants therefore tend in their turn to become honorific, as being a mark, at the second remove, of the superior status of those who are able to afford the indulgence. Infirmities induced by overindulgence are among some peoples freely recognized as manly attributes. It has even happened that the name for certain diseased conditions of the body arising from such an origin has passed into everyday speech as a synonym for "noble" or "gentle." It is only at a relatively early stage of culture that the symptoms of expensive vice are conventionally accepted as marks of a superior status, and so tend to become virtues and command the deference of the community; but the reputability that attaches to certain expensive vices long retains so much of its force as to appreciably lessen the disapprobation visited upon the men of the wealthy or noble class for any excessive indulgence. The same invidious distinction adds force to the current disapproval of any indulgence of this kind on the part of women, minors, and inferiors. This invidious traditional distinction has not lost its force even among the more advanced peoples of today. Where the example set by the leisure class retains its imperative force in the regulation of the conventionalities, it is observable that the women still in great measure practice the same traditional continence with regard to stimulants.

This characterization of the greater continence in the use of stimulants practiced by the women of the reputable classes may seem an excessive refinement of logic at the expense of common sense. But facts within easy reach of anyone who cares to know them go to say that the greater abstinence of women is in some part due to an imperative conventionality; and this conventionality is, in a general way, strongest where the patriarchal tradition—the tradition that the woman is a chattel—has retained its hold in greatest vigor. In a sense which has been greatly qualified in scope and rigor, but which has by no means lost its meaning even yet, this tradition says that the woman, being a chattel, should consume only what is necessary to her sustenance—except so far as her further consumption contributes to the comfort or the good repute of her master. The consumption of luxuries, in the true sense, is a consumption directed to the comfort of the consumer himself, and is, therefore, a mark of the master. Any such consumption by others can take place only on a basis of sufferance. In communities where the popular habits of thought have been profoundly shaped by the patriarchal tradition we may accordingly look for survivals of the taboo on luxuries at least to the extent of a conventional deprecation of their use by the unfree and dependent class. This is more particularly true as regards certain luxuries, the use of which by the dependent class would detract sensibly from the comfort or pleasure of their masters, or which are held to be of doubtful legitimacy on other grounds. In the apprehension of the great conservative middle class of Western civilization the use of these various stimulants is obnoxious to at least one, if not both, of these objections; and it is a fact too significant to be passed over that it is precisely among these middle classes of the Germanic culture, with their strong surviving sense of the patriarchal proprieties, that the women are to the greatest extent subject to a qualified taboo on narcotics and alcoholic beverages. With many qualifications—with more qualifications as the patriarchal tradition gradually weakened—the general rule is felt to be right and binding that women should consume only for the benefit of their masters. The objection of course presents itself that expenditure on women's dress and household paraphernalia is an obvious exception to this rule; but it will appear in the sequel that this exception is much more obvious than substantial.

During the earlier stages of economic development, consumption of goods without stint, especially consumption of the better grades of goods—ideally all consumption in excess of the subsistence minimum—pertains normally to the leisure class. This restriction tends to disappear, at least formally, after the later peaceable stage has been reached, with private ownership of goods and an industrial system based on wage labor or on the petty household economy. But during the earlier quasi-peaceable stage, when so many of the traditions through which the institution of a leisure class has affected the economic life of later times were taking form and consistency, this principle has had the force of a conventional law. It has served as the norm to which consumption has tended to conform, and any appreciable departure from it is to be regarded as an aberrant form, sure to be eliminated sooner or later in the further course of development.

The quasi-peaceable gentleman of leisure, then, not only consumes of the staff of life beyond the minimum required for subsistence and physical efficiency, but his consumption also undergoes a specialization as regards the quality of the goods consumed. He consumes freely and of the best, in food, drink, narcotics, shelter, services, ornaments, apparel, weapons and accoutrements, amusements, amulets, and idols or divinities. In the process of gradual amelioration which takes place in the articles of his consumption, the motive principle and the proximate aim of innovation is no doubt the higher efficiency of the improved and more elaborate products for personal comfort and well-being. But that does not remain the sole purpose of their consumption. The canon of reputability is at hand and seizes upon such innovations as are, according to its standard, fit to survive. Since the consumption of these more excellent goods is an evidence of wealth, it becomes honorific; and conversely, the failure to consume in due quantity and quality becomes a mark of inferiority and demerit.

This growth of punctilious discrimination as to qualitative excellence in eating, drinking, etc., presently affects not only the manner of life, but also the training and intellectual activity of the gentleman of leisure. He is no longer simply the successful, aggressive male—the man of strength, resource, and intrepidity. In order to avoid stultification he must also cultivate his tastes, for it now becomes incumbent on him to discriminate with some nicety between the noble and the ignoble in consumable goods. He becomes a connoisseur in creditable viands of various degrees of merit, in manly beverages and trinkets, in seemly apparel and architecture, in weapons, games, dancers, and the narcotics. This cultivation of the aesthetic faculty requires time and application, and the demands made upon the gentleman in this direction therefore tend to change his life of leisure into a more or less arduous application to the business of learning how to live a life of ostensible leisure in a becoming way. Closely related to the requirement that the gentleman must consume freely and of the right kind of goods, there is the requirement that he must know how to consume them in a seemly manner. His life of leisure must be conducted in due form. Hence arise good manners in the way pointed out in an earlier chapter. High-bred manners and ways of living are items of conformity to the norm of conspicuous leisure and conspicuous consumption.

Conspicuous consumption of valuable goods is a means of reputability to the gentleman of leisure. As wealth accumulates on his hands, his own unaided effort will not avail to sufficiently put his opulence in evidence by this method. The aid of friends and competitors is therefore brought in by resorting to the giving of valuable presents and expensive feasts and entertainments. Presents and feasts had probably another origin than that of naive ostentation, but they acquired their utility for this purpose very early, and they have retained that character to the present; so that their utility in this respect has now long been the substantial ground on which these usages rest. Costly entertainments, such as the potlatch or the ball, are peculiarly adapted to serve this end. The competitor with whom the entertainer wishes to institute a comparison is, by this method, made to serve as a means to the end. He consumes vicariously for his host at the same time that he is a witness to the consumption of that excess of good things which his host is unable to dispose of single-handed, and he is also made to witness his host's facility in etiquette.

In the giving of costly entertainments other motives, of a more genial kind, are of course also present. The custom of festive gatherings probably originated in motives of conviviality and religion; these motives are also present in the later development, but they do not continue to be the sole motives. The latter-day leisure-class festivities and entertainments may continue in some slight degree to serve the religious need and in a higher degree the needs of recreation and conviviality, but they also serve an invidious purpose; and they serve it nonetheless effectually for having a colorable noninvidious ground in these more avowable motives. But the economic effect of these social amenities is not therefore lessened, either in the vicarious consumption of goods or in the exhibition of difficult and costly achievements in etiquette.

As wealth accumulates, the leisure class develops further in function and structure, and there arises a differentiation within the class. There is a more or less elaborate system of rank and grades. This differentiation is furthered by the inheritance of wealth and the consequent inheritance of gentility. With the inheritance of gentility goes the inheritance of obligatory leisure; and gentility of a sufficient potency to entail a life of leisure may be inherited without the complement of wealth required to maintain a dignified leisure. Gentle blood may be transmitted without goods enough to afford a reputably free consumption at one's ease. Hence results a class of impecunious gentlemen of leisure, incidentally referred to already. These half-caste gentlemen of leisure fall into a system of hierarchical gradations. Those who stand near the higher and the highest grades of the wealthy leisure class, in point of birth, or in point of wealth, or both, outrank the remoter-born and the pecuniarily weaker. These lower grades, especially the impecunious, or marginal, gentlemen of leisure, affiliate themselves by a system of dependence or fealty to the great ones; by so doing they gain an increment of repute, or of the means with which to lead a life of leisure, from their patron. They become his courtiers or retainers, servants; and being fed and countenanced by their patron they are indices of his rank and vicarious consumers of his superfluous wealth. Many of these affiliated gentlemen of leisure are at the same time lesser men of substance in their own right; so that some of them are scarcely at all, others only partially, to be rated as vicarious consumers. So many of them, however, as make up the retainers and hangers-on of the patron may be classed as vicarious consumers without qualification. Many of these again, and also many of the other aristocracy of lesser degree, have in turn attached to their persons a more or less comprehensive group of vicarious consumers in the persons of their wives and children, their servants, retainers, etc.

Throughout this graduated scheme of vicarious leisure and vicarious consumption the rule holds that these offices must be performed in some such manner, or under some such circumstance or insignia, as shall point plainly to the master to whom this leisure or consumption pertains, and to whom therefore the resulting increment of good repute of right inures. The consumption and leisure executed by these persons for their master or patron represents an investment on his part with a view to an increase of good fame. As regards feasts and largesses this is obvious enough, and the imputation of repute to the host or patron here takes place immediately, on the ground of common notoriety. Where leisure and consumption is performed vicariously by henchmen and retainers, imputation of the resulting repute to the patron is effected by their residing near his person so that it may be plain to all men from what source they draw. As the group whose good esteem is to be secured in this way grows larger, more patent means are required to indicate the imputation of merit for the leisure performed, and to this end uniforms, badges, and liveries come into vogue. The wearing of uniforms or liveries implies a considerable degree of dependence, and may even be said to be a mark of servitude, real or ostensible. The wearers of uniforms and liveries may be roughly divided into two classes—the free and the servile, or the noble and the ignoble. The services performed by them are likewise divisible into noble and ignoble. Of course the distinction is not observed with strict consistency in practice; the less debasing of the base services and the less honorific of the noble functions are not infrequently merged in the same person. But the general distinction is not on that account to be overlooked. What may add some perplexity is the fact that this fundamental distinction between noble and ignoble, which rests on the nature of the ostensible service performed, is traversed by a secondary distinction into honorific and humiliating, resting on the rank of the person for whom the service is performed or whose livery is worn. So, those offices which are by right the proper employment of the leisure class are noble; such are government, fighting, hunting, the care of arms and accoutrements, and the like—in short, those which may be classed as ostensibly predatory employments. On the other hand, those employments which properly fall to the industrious class are ignoble; such as handicraft or other productive labor, menial services, and the like. But a base service performed for a person of very high degree may become a very honorific office; as for instance the office of a maid of honor or of a lady in waiting to the queen, or the king's master of the horse or his keeper of the hounds. The two offices last named suggest a principle of some general bearing. Whenever, as in these cases, the menial service in question has to do directly with the primary leisure employments of fighting and hunting, it easily acquires a reflected honorific character. In this way great honor may come to attach to an employment which in its own nature belongs to the baser sort.

In the later development of peaceable industry, the usage of employing an idle corps of uniformed men-at-arms gradually lapses. Vicarious consumption by dependents bearing the insignia of their patron or master narrows down to a corps of liveried menials. In a heightened degree, therefore, the livery comes to be a badge of servitude, or rather of servility. Something of an honorific character always attached to the livery of the armed retainer, but this honorific character disappears when the livery becomes the exclusive badge of the menial. The livery becomes obnoxious to nearly all who are required to wear it. We are yet so little removed from a state of effective slavery as still to be fully sensitive to the sting of any imputation of servility. This antipathy asserts itself even in the case of the liveries or uniforms which some corporations prescribe as the distinctive dress of their employees. In this country the aversion even goes the length of discrediting—in a mild and uncertain way—those government employments, military and civil, which require the wearing of a livery or uniform.

With the disappearance of servitude, the number of vicarious consumers attached to any one gentleman tends, on the whole, to decrease. The like is of course true, and perhaps in a still higher degree, of the number of dependents who perform vicarious leisure for him. In a general way, though not wholly nor consistently, these two groups coincide. The dependent who was first delegated for these duties was the wife, or the chief wife; and, as would be expected, in the later development of the institution, when the number of persons by whom these duties are customarily performed gradually narrows, the wife remains the last. In the higher grades of society a large volume of both these kinds of service is required; and here the wife is of course still assisted in the work by a more or less numerous corps of menials. But as we descend the social scale, the point is presently reached where the duties of vicarious leisure and consumption devolve upon the wife alone. In the communities of the Western culture, this point is at present found among the lower middle class.

And here occurs a curious inversion. It is a fact of common observation that in this lower middle class there is no pretense of leisure on the part of the head of the household. Through force of circumstances it has fallen into disuse. But the middle-class wife still carries on the business of vicarious leisure, for the good name of the household and its master. In descending the social scale in any modern industrial community, the primary fact—the conspicuous leisure of the master of the household—disappears at a relatively high point. The head of the middle-class household has been reduced by economic circumstances to turn his hand to gaining a livelihood by occupations which often partake largely of the character of industry, as in the case of the ordinary business man of today. But the derivative fact—the vicarious leisure and consumption rendered by the wife and the auxiliary vicarious performance of leisure by menials—remains in vogue as a conventionality which the demands of reputability will not suffer to be slighted. It is by no means an uncommon spectacle to find a man applying himself to work with the utmost assiduity, in order that his wife may in due form render for him that degree of vicarious leisure which the common sense of the time demands.

The leisure rendered by the wife in such cases is, of course, not a simple manifestation of idleness or indolence. It almost invariably occurs disguised under some form of work or household duties or social amenities, which prove on analysis to serve little or no ulterior end beyond showing that she does not and need not occupy herself with anything that is gainful or that is of substantial use. As has already been noticed under the head of manners, the greater part of the customary round of domestic cares to which the middle-class housewife gives her time and effort is of this character. Not that the results of her attention to household matters, of a decorative and mundificatory character, are not pleasing to the sense of men trained in middle-class proprieties; but the taste to which these effects of household adornment and tidiness appeal is a taste which has been formed under the selective guidance of a canon of propriety that demands just these evidences of wasted effort. The effects are pleasing to us chiefly because we have been taught to find them pleasing. There goes into these domestic duties much solicitude for a proper combination of form and color, and for other ends that are to be classed as aesthetic in the proper sense of the term; and it is not denied that effects having some substantial aesthetic value are sometimes attained. Pretty much all that is here insisted on is that, as regards these amenities of life, the housewife's efforts are under the guidance of traditions that have been shaped by the law of conspicuously wasteful expenditure of time and substance. If beauty or comfort is achieved—and it is a more or less fortuitous circumstance if they are—they must be achieved by means and methods that commend themselves to the great economic law of wasted effort. The more reputable, "presentable" portion of middle-class household paraphernalia are, on the one hand, items of conspicuous consumption, and on the other hand, apparatus for putting in evidence the vicarious leisure rendered by the housewife.

The requirement of vicarious consumption at the hands of the wife continues in force even at a lower point in the pecuniary scale than the requirement of vicarious leisure. At a point below which little if any pretense of wasted effort, in ceremonial cleanness and the like, is observable, and where there is assuredly no conscious attempt at ostensible leisure, decency still requires the wife to consume some goods conspicuously for the reputability of the household and its head. So that, as the latter-day outcome of this evolution of an archaic institution, the wife, who was at the outset the drudge and chattel of the man, both in fact and in theory— the producer of goods for him to consume—has become the ceremonial consumer of goods which he produces. But she still quite unmistakably remains his chattel in theory; for the habitual rendering of vicarious leisure and consumption is the abiding mark of the unfree servant.

This vicarious consumption practiced by the household of the middle and lower classes cannot be counted as a direct expression of the leisure-class scheme of life, since the household of this pecuniary grade does not belong within the leisure class. It is rather that the leisure-class scheme of life here comes to an expression at the second remove. The leisure class stands at the head of the social structure in point of reputability; and its manner of life and its standards of worth therefore afford the norm of reputability for the community. The observance of these standards, in some degree of approximation, becomes incumbent upon all classes lower in the scale. In modern civilized communities the lines of demarcation between social classes have grown vague and transient, and wherever this happens the norm of reputability imposed by the upper class extends its coercive influence with but slight hindrance down through the social structure to the lowest strata. The result is that the members of each stratum accept as their ideal of decency the scheme of life in vogue in the next higher stratum, and bend their energies to live up to that ideal. On pain of forfeiting their good name and their self-respect in case of failure, they must conform to the accepted code, at least in appearance.

The basis on which good repute in any highly organized industrial community ultimately rests is pecuniary strength; and the means of showing pecuniary strength, and so of gaining or retaining a good name, are leisure and a conspicuous consumption of goods. Accordingly, both of these methods are in vogue as far down the scale as it remains possible; and in the lower strata in which the two methods are employed, both offices are in great part delegated to the wife and children of the household. Lower still, where any degree of leisure, even ostensible, has become impracticable for the wife, the conspicuous consumption of goods remains and is carried on by the wife and children. The man of the household also can do something in this direction, and, indeed, he commonly does; but with a still lower descent into the levels of indigence—along the margin of the slums—the man, and presently also the children, virtually cease to consume valuable goods for appearances, and the woman remains virtually the sole exponent of the household's pecuniary decency. No class of society, not even the most abjectly poor, forgoes all customary conspicuous consumption. The last items of this category of consumption are not given up except under stress of the direst necessity. Very much of squalor and discomfort will be endured before this last trinket or the last pretense of pecuniary decency is put away. There is no class and no country that has yielded so abjectly before the pressure of physical want as to deny themselves all gratification of this higher or spiritual need.

From the foregoing survey of the growth of conspicuous leisure and consumption, it appears that the utility of both alike for the purposes of reputability lies in the element of waste that is common to both. In the one case it is a waste of time and effort, in the other it is a waste of goods. Both are methods of demonstrating the possession of wealth, and the two are conventionally accepted as equivalents. The choice between them is a question of advertising expediency simply, except so far as it may be affected by other standards of propriety, springing from a different source. On grounds of expediency the preference may be given to the one or the other at different stages of the economic development. The question is, which of the two methods will most effectively reach the persons whose convictions it is desired to affect? Usage has answered this question in different ways under different circumstances.

So long as the community or social group is small enough and compact enough to be effectually reached by common notoriety alone—that is to say, so long as the human environment to which the individual is required to adapt himself in respect of reputability is comprised within his sphere of personal acquaintance and neighborhood gossip—so long the one method is about as effective as the other. Each will therefore serve about equally well during the earlier stages of social growth. But when the differentiation has gone farther and it becomes necessary to reach a wider human environment, consumption begins to hold over leisure as an ordinary means of decency. This is especially true during the later, peaceable economic stage. The means of communication and the mobility of the population now expose the individual to the observation of many persons who have no other means of judging of his reputability than the display of goods (and perhaps of breeding) which he is able to make while he is under their direct observation.

The modern organization of industry works in the same direction also by another line. The exigencies of the modern industrial system frequently place individuals and households in juxtaposition between whom there is little contact in any other sense than that of juxtaposition. One's neighbors, mechanically speaking, often are socially not one's neighbors, or even acquaintances; and still their transient good opinion has a high degree of utility. The only practicable means of impressing one's pecuniary ability on these unsympathetic observers of one's everyday life is an unremitting demonstration of ability to pay. In the modern community there is also a more frequent attendance at large gatherings of people to whom one's everyday life is unknown; in such places as churches, theaters, ballrooms, hotels, parks, shops, and the like. In order to impress these transient observers, and to retain one's self-complacency under their observation, the signature of one's pecuniary strength should be written in characters which he who runs may read. It is evident, therefore, that the present trend of the development is in the direction of heightening the utility of conspicuous consumption as compared with leisure.

It is also noticeable that the serviceability of consumption as a means of repute, as well as the insistence on it as an element of decency, is at its best in those portions of the community where the human contact of the individual is widest and the mobility of the population is greatest. Conspicuous consumption claims a relatively larger portion of the income of the urban than of the rural population, and the claim is also more imperative. The result is that, in order to keep up a decent appearance, the former habitually live hand-to-mouth to a greater extent than the latter. So it comes, for instance, that the American farmer and his wife and daughters are notoriously less modish in their dress, as well as less urbane in their manners, than the city artisan's family with an equal income. It is not that the city population is by nature much more eager for the peculiar complacency that comes of a conspicuous consumption, nor has the rural population less regard for pecuniary decency. But the provocation to this line of evidence, as well as its transient effectiveness, are more decided in the city. This method is therefore more readily resorted to, and in the struggle to outdo one another the city population push their normal standard of conspicuous consumption to a higher point, with the result that a relatively greater expenditure in this direction is required to indicate a given degree of pecuniary decency in the city. The requirement of conformity to this higher conventional standard becomes mandatory. The standard of decency is higher, class for class, and this requirement of decent appearance must be lived up to on pain of losing caste.

Consumption becomes a larger element in the standard of living in the city than in the country. Among the country population its place is to some extent taken by savings and home comforts known through the medium of neighborhood gossip sufficiently to serve the like general purpose of pecuniary repute. These home comforts and the leisure indulged in—where the indulgence is found—are of course also in great part to be classed as items of conspicuous consumption; and much the same is to be said of the savings. The smaller amount of the savings laid by, by the artisan class is no doubt due, in some measure, to the fact that in the case of the artisan the savings are a less effective means of advertisement, relative to the environment in which he is placed, than are the savings of the people living on farms and in the small villages. Among the latter, everybody's affairs, especially everybody's pecuniary status, are known to everybody else. Considered by itself simply—taken in the first degree—this added provocation to which the artisan and the urban laboring classes are exposed may not very seriously decrease the amount of savings; but in its cumulative action, through raising the standard of decent expenditure, its deterrent effect on the tendency to save cannot but be very great.

A felicitous illustration of the manner in which this canon of reputability works out its results is seen in the practice of dram-drinking, "treating," and smoking in public places, which is customary among the laborers and handicraftsmen of the towns, and among the lower middle class of the urban population generally. Journeymen printers may be named as a class among whom this form of conspicuous consumption has a great vogue, and among whom it carries with it certain well-marked consequences that are often deprecated. The peculiar habits of the class in this respect are commonly set down to some kind of an ill-defined moral deficiency with which this class is credited, or to a morally deleterious influence which their occupation is supposed to exert, in some unascertainable way, upon the men employed in it. The state of the case for the men who work in the composition and press rooms of the common run of printing houses may be summed up as follows. Skill acquired in any printing house or any city is easily turned to account in almost any other house or city; that is to say, the inertia due to special training is slight. Also, this occupation requires more than the average of intelligence and general information, and the men employed in it are therefore ordinarily more ready than many others to take advantage of any slight variation in the demand for their labor from one place to another. The inertia due to the home feeling is consequently also slight. At the same time the wages in the trade are high enough to make movement from place to place relatively easy. The result is a great mobility of the labor employed in printing; perhaps greater than in any other equally well-defined and considerable body of workmen. These men are constantly thrown in contact with new groups of acquaintances, with whom the relations established are transient or ephemeral, but whose good opinion is valued nonetheless for the time being. The human proclivity to ostentation, reenforced by sentiments of goodfellowship, leads them to spend freely in those directions which will best serve these needs. Here as elsewhere prescription seizes upon the custom as soon as it gains a vogue, and incorporates it in the accredited standard of decency. The next step is to make this standard of decency the point of departure for a new move in advance in the same direction—for there is no merit in simple spiritless conformity to a standard of dissipation that is lived up to as a matter of course by everyone in the trade.

The greater prevalence of dissipation among printers than among the average of workmen is accordingly attributable, at least in some measure, to the greater ease of movement and the more transient character of acquaintance and human contact in this trade. But the substantial ground of this high requirement in dissipation is in the last analysis no other than that same propensity for a manifestation of dominance and pecuniary decency which makes the French peasant-proprietor parsimonious and frugal, and induces the American millionaire to found colleges, hospitals, and museums. If the canon of conspicuous consumption were not offset to a considerable extent by other features of human nature, alien to it, any saving should logically be impossible for a population situated as the artisan and laboring classes of the cities are at present, however high their wages or their income might be.

But there are other standards of repute and other, more or less imperative, canons of conduct, besides wealth and its manifestation, and some of these come in to accentuate or to qualify the broad, fundamental canon of conspicuous waste. Under the simple test of effectiveness for advertising, we should expect to find leisure and the conspicuous consumption of goods dividing the field of pecuniary emulation pretty evenly between them at the outset. Leisure might then be expected gradually to yield ground and tend to obsolescence as the economic development goes forward, and the community increases in size; while the conspicuous consumption of goods should gradually gain in importance, both absolutely and relatively, until it had absorbed all the available product, leaving nothing over beyond a bare livelihood. But the actual course of development has been somewhat different from this ideal scheme. Leisure held the first place at the start, and came to hold a rank very much above wasteful consumption of goods, both as a direct exponent of wealth and as an element in the standard of decency, during the quasi-peaceable culture. From that point onward, consumption has gained ground, until, at present, it unquestionably holds the primacy, though it is still far from absorbing the entire margin of production above the subsistence minimum.

The early ascendency of leisure as a means of reputability is traceable to the archaic distinction between noble and ignoble employments. Leisure is honorable and becomes imperative partly because it shows exemption from ignoble labor. The archaic differentiation into noble and ignoble classes is based on an invidious distinction between employments as honorific, or debasing; and this traditional distinction grows into an imperative canon of decency during the early quasi-peaceable stage. Its ascendency is furthered by the fact that leisure is still fully as effective an evidence of wealth as consumption. Indeed, so effective is it in the relatively small and stable human environment to which the individual is exposed at that cultural stage, that, with the aid of the archaic tradition which deprecates all productive labor, it gives rise to a large impecunious leisure class, and it even tends to limit the production of the community's industry to the subsistence minimum. This extreme inhibition of industry is avoided because slave labor, working under a compulsion more rigorous than that of reputability, is forced to turn out a product in excess of the subsistence minimum of the working class. The subsequent relative decline in the use of conspicuous leisure as a basis of repute is due partly to an increasing relative effectiveness of consumption as an evidence of wealth; but in part it is traceable to another force, alien, and in some degree antagonistic, to the usage of conspicuous waste.

This alien factor is the instinct of workmanship. Other circumstances permitting, that instinct disposes men to look with favor upon productive efficiency and on whatever is of human use. It disposes them to deprecate waste of substance or effort. The instinct of workmanship is present in all men, and asserts itself even under very adverse circumstances. So that however wasteful a given expenditure may be in reality, it must at least have some colorable excuse in the way of an ostensible purpose. The manner in which, under special circumstances, the instinct eventuates in a taste for exploit and an invidious discrimination between noble and ignoble classes has been indicated in an earlier chapter. Insofar as it comes into conflict with the law of conspicuous waste, the instinct of workmanship expresses itself not so much in insistence on substantial usefulness as in an abiding sense of the odiousness and aesthetic impossibility of what is obviously futile. Being of the nature of an instinctive affection, its guidance touches chiefly and immediately the obvious and apparent violations of its requirements. It is only less promptly and with less constraining force that it reaches such substantial violations of its requirements as are appreciated only upon reflection.

So long as all labor continues to be performed exclusively or usually by slaves, the baseness of all productive effort is too constantly and deterrently present in the mind of men to allow the instinct of workmanship seriously to take effect in the direction of industrial usefulness; but when the quasi-peaceable stage (with slavery and status) passes into the peaceable stage of industry (with wage labor and cash payment) the instinct comes more effectively into play. It then begins aggressively to shape men's views of what is meritorious, and asserts itself at least as an auxiliary canon of self-complacency. All extraneous considerations apart, those persons (adults) are but a vanishing minority today who harbor no inclination to the accomplishment of some end, or who are not impelled of their own motion to shape some object or fact or relation for human use. The propensity may in large measure be overborne by the more immediately constraining incentive to a reputable leisure and an avoidance of indecorous usefulness, and it may therefore work itself out in make-believe only; as for instance in "social duties," and in quasi-artistic or quasi-scholarly accomplishments, in the care and decoration of the house, in sewing-circle activity or dress reform, in proficiency at dress, cards, yachting, golf, and various sports. But the fact that it may under stress of circumstances eventuate in inanities no more disproves the presence of the instinct than the reality of the brooding instinct is disproved by inducing a hen to sit on a nestful of china eggs.

This latter-day uneasy reaching-out for some form of purposeful activity that shall at the same time not be indecorously productive of either individual or collective gain marks a difference of attitude between the modern leisure class and that of the quasi-peaceable stage. At the earlier stage, as was said above, the all-dominating institution of slavery and status acted resistlessly to discountenance exertion directed to other than naively predatory ends. It was still possible to find some habitual employment for the inclination to action in the way of forcible aggression or repression directed against hostile groups or against the subject classes within the group; and this served to relieve the pressure and draw off the energy of the leisure class without a resort to actually useful, or even ostensibly useful employments. The practice of hunting also served the same purpose in some degree. When the community developed into a peaceful industrial organization, and when fuller occupation of the land had reduced the opportunities for the hunt to an inconsiderable residue, the pressure of energy seeking purposeful employment was left to find an outlet in some other direction. The ignominy which attaches to useful effort also entered upon a less acute phase with the disappearance of compulsory labor; and the instinct of workmanship then came to assert itself with more persistence and consistency.

The line of least resistance has changed in some measure, and the energy which formerly found a vent in predatory activity, now in part takes the direction of some ostensibly useful end. Ostensibly purposeless leisure has come to be deprecated, especially among that large portion of the leisure class whose plebeian origin acts to set them at variance with the tradition of the otium cum dignitate. But that canon of reputability which discountenances all employment that is of the nature of productive effort is still at hand, and will permit nothing beyond the most transient vogue to any employment that is substantially useful or productive. The consequence is that a change has been wrought in the conspicuous leisure practiced by the leisure class; not so much in substance as in form. A reconciliation between the two conflicting requirements is effected by a resort to make-believe. Many and intricate polite observances and social duties of a ceremonial nature are developed; many organizations are founded, with some specious object of amelioration embodied in their official style and title; there is much coming and going, and a deal of talk, to the end that the talkers may not have occasion to reflect on what is the effectual economic value of their traffic. And along with the make-believe of purposeful employment, and woven inextricably into its texture, there is commonly, if not invariably, a more or less appreciable element of purposeful effort directed to some serious end.

In the narrower sphere of vicarious leisure a similar change has gone forward. Instead of simply passing her time in visible idleness, as in the best days of the patriarchal regime, the housewife of the advanced peaceable stage applies herself assiduously to household cares. The salient features of this development of domestic service have already been indicated.

Throughout the entire evolution of conspicuous expenditure, whether of goods or of services or human life, runs the obvious implication that in order to effectually mend the consumer's good fame it must be an expenditure of superfluities. In order to be reputable it must be wasteful. No merit would accrue from the consumption of the bare necessaries of life, except by comparison with the abjectly poor who fall short even of the subsistence minimum; and no standard of expenditure could result from such a comparison, except the most prosaic and unattractive level of decency. A standard of life would still be possible which should admit of invidious comparison in other respects than that of opulence; as, for instance, a comparison in various directions in the manifestation of moral, physical, intellectual, or aesthetic force. Comparison in all these directions is in vogue today; and the comparison made in these respects is commonly so inextricably bound up with the pecuniary comparison as to be scarcely distinguishable from the latter. This is especially true as regards the current rating of expressions of intellectual and aesthetic force or proficiency; so that we frequently interpret as aesthetic or intellectual a difference which in substance is pecuniary only.

The use of the term *waste* is in one respect an unfortunate one. As used in the speech of everyday life the word carries an undertone of deprecation. It is here used for want of a better term that will adequately describe the same range of motives and of phenomena, and it is not to be taken in an odious sense, as implying an illegitimate expenditure of human products or of human life. In the view of economic theory, the expenditure in question is no more and no less legitimate than any other expenditure. It is here called *waste* because this expenditure does not serve human life or human well-being on the whole, not because it is waste or misdirection of effort or expenditure as viewed from the standpoint of the individual consumer who chooses it. If he chooses it, that disposes of the question of its relative utility to him, as compared with other forms of consumption that would not be deprecated on account of their wastefulness. Whatever form of expenditure the consumer chooses, or whatever end he seeks in making his choice, has utility to him by virtue of his preference. As seen from the point of view of the individual consumer, the question of wastefulness does not arise within the scope of economic theory proper. The use of the word *waste* as a technical term, therefore, implies no deprecation of the motives or of the ends sought by the consumer under this canon of conspicuous waste.

But it is, on other grounds, worth noting that the term *waste* in the language of everyday life implies deprecation of what is characterized as wasteful. This commonsense implication is itself an outcropping of the instinct of workmanship. The popular reprobation of waste goes to say that in order to be at peace with himself the common man must be able to see in any and all human effort and human enjoyment an enhancement of life and well-being on the whole. In order to meet with unqualified approval, any economic fact must approve itself under the test of impersonal usefulness—usefulness as seen from the point of view of the generically human. Relative or competitive advantage of one individual in comparison with another does not satisfy the economic conscience, and therefore competitive expenditure has not the approval of this conscience.

In strict accuracy nothing should be included under the head of conspicuous waste but such expenditure as is incurred on the ground of an invidious pecuniary comparison. But in order to bring any given item or element in under this head it is not necessary that it should be recognized as waste in this sense by the person incurring the expenditure. It frequently happens that an element of the standard of living which set out with being primarily wasteful, ends with becoming, in the apprehension of the consumer, a necessary of life; and it may in this way become as indispensable as any other item of the consumer's habitual expenditure. As items which sometimes fall under this head, and are therefore available as illustrations of the manner in which this principle applies, may be cited carpets and tapestries, silver table service, waiter's services, silk hats, starched linen, many articles of jewelry and of dress. The indispensability of these things after the habit and the convention have been formed, however, has little to say in the classification of expenditures as waste or not waste in the technical meaning of the word. The test to which all expenditure must be brought in an attempt to decide that point is the question whether it serves directly to enhance human life on the whole—whether it furthers the life process taken impersonally. For this is the basis of award of the instinct of workmanship, and that instinct is the court of final appeal in any question of economic truth or adequacy. It is a question as to the award rendered by a dispassionate common sense. The question is, therefore, not whether, under the existing circumstances of individual habit and social custom, a given expenditure conduces to the particular consumer's gratification or peace of mind; but whether, aside from acquired tastes and from the canons of usage and conventional decency, its result is a net gain in comfort or in the fullness of life. Customary expenditure must be classed under the head of waste insofar as the custom on which it rests is traceable to the habit of making an invidious pecuniary comparison—insofar as it is conceived that it could not have become customary and prescriptive without the backing of this principle of pecuniary reputability or relative economic success.

It is obviously not necessary that a given object of expenditure should be exclusively wasteful in order to come in under the category of conspicuous waste. An article may be useful and wasteful both, and its utility to the consumer may be made up of use and waste in the most varying proportions. Consumable goods, and even productive goods, generally show the two elements in combination, as constituents of their utility; although, in a general way, the element of waste tends to predominate in articles of consumption, while the contrary is true of articles designed for productive use. Even in articles which appear at first glance to serve for pure ostentation only, it is always possible to detect the presence of some, at least ostensible, useful purpose; and on the other hand, even in special machinery and tools contrived for some particular industrial process, as well as in the rudest appliances of human industry, the traces of conspicuous waste, or at least of the habit of ostentation, usually become evident on a close scrutiny. It would be hazardous to assert that a useful purpose is ever absent from the utility of any article or of any service, however obviously its prime purpose and chief element is conspicuous waste; and it would be only less hazardous to assert of any primarily useful product that the element of waste is in no way concerned in its value, immediately or remotely.

QUESTIONS

1. Why are warriors and priests in a feudal society considered to be part of the leisure class?

2. Why does Veblen assert that "virtually the whole range of industrial employments is an outgrowth of what is classed as woman's work in the primitive barbarian community"? (419)

3. Does Veblen view development of a leisure class as progress?

4. Why is the institution of a leisure class predicated on "a predatory habit of life" (war or hunting)? (421)

5. What features of their temperament make women more suitable for drudgery, according to Veblen?

6. Why does the division of productive labor result in man's work being deemed "worthy, honorable, noble" and woman's work, "unworthy, debasing"? (425)

7. How does "an invidious distinction" arise "between exploit and acquisition by seizure on the one hand and industrial employment on the other hand"? (426)

8. Why does Veblen say, "The substantial difference between the peaceable and the predatory phases of culture . . . is a spiritual difference"? (427)

9. What makes the unproductive consumption of goods "honorable"? (429)

10. Why does Veblen denigrate the efforts of the lower middle-class housewife to beautify the home?

11. If women have historically been burdened with doing the menial work, how does Veblen explain the "curious inversion" in which men assume the burden of work and their women become idle? (435)

12. What does Veblen mean by "the great economic law of wasted effort"? (436)

13. Who is the audience for the mandatory show of "pecuniary strength"? (437)

14. Why does Veblen equate "conspicuous consumption," or the "pretense of pecuniary decency," with a "higher or spiritual need"? (437)

15. Why does Veblen see the demands of leisure and of conspicuous consumption as competitive rather than complementary? Why does he see consumption as winning out over leisure as a means to impress others?

16. Does Veblen believe that some forms of "wasteful" behavior can "enhance human life on the whole," or are all such behaviors examples of the way we delude ourselves into thinking our activity serves some higher purpose? (445)

17. Why does Veblen introduce the notion of "useful" consumption (versus "wasteful" consumption) relatively late in this chapter? (444–446) How does he distinguish the two?

FOR FURTHER REFLECTION

1. Are the professions with the highest status still those that are the least productive?

2. Are the activities of human culture such as art, literature, and music "wasteful" expenditures of behavior, or are they, in Veblen's view, "useful"?

3. Would Veblen see laborsaving devices in the kitchen as "generically human" or as something new?

4. Can married women still be viewed as "chattel in theory"? (437)

CARL JUNG

When Carl Jung resigned as president of the International Psychoanalytical Association in 1914, it marked both a personal and professional break from Sigmund Freud, the man who was most responsible for setting the course of early modern psychology. Although Freud was the dominant figure in the psychoanalytic movement in the early twentieth century, other powerful thinkers such as Jung and Alfred Adler—both one-time close working associates of Freud—were already forming deeply divergent psychological theories and therapeutic practices. Among these constructive dissenters, Jung was personally closest to Freud and the one whose separation caused his mentor the most distress.

Jung was born in Switzerland in 1875, the son of a pastor. There were clergymen on both sides of his family, and Jung's early interest in religion seemed to point the way toward a career in the ministry. However, a stronger interest in psychology drew him to the study of medicine, and in 1902, he joined the psychiatric staff of the Burghölzli Asylum in Zurich. His clinical research and practice led him to develop a way of explaining the apparently illogical behavior of mental patients using patterns of richly linked associations of meaning that he termed "complexes." Jung already had earned an international reputation when he met Freud around 1907, and his own work seemed to further confirm Freud's theories.

The first major rift between Jung and Freud resulted from Jung's growing dissatisfaction with Freud's insistence that neuroses could be primarily understood and treated by addressing sexual problems. Jung's much broader view led him to develop his highly compelling theories of human "types," which include the now-familiar categories of *introvert* and *extrovert*. Jung postulated that, to flourish, the individual human being must come to terms with deep-seated areas of the unconscious mind that find their overt expression in dreams, myths, and symbols.

Jung believed that, to find life meaningful, an individual must find a strong relationship between his temperamental type and the rich array of transpersonal material in this "collective unconscious." He called this accomplishment *individuation*. Moving farther than ever from Freud, Jung pursued his lifelong interest in religion. He wrote a series of books that explored what he perceived to be connections of fundamental importance between religious ideas and modern psychology.

Through the 1920s and 1930s, Jung developed psychotherapies based on having patients reflectively explore the life of their dreams and imaginations in order to find their own personal myths. To assist this research, he often appealed to esoteric spiritual texts from both Western and Eastern traditions.

For many years, Jung was a professor of psychology at the Federal Polytechnical University in Zurich, where, over the years, more and more of his followers gathered. These followers became participants in an international Jungian movement that still remains very strong. Jung died in 1961 at the age of 85 at his home near Zurich.

In the following selection, Jung asks us to consider whether there is an inherent pattern to the advancing years of human life, and what we can discern about the significance of such a pattern. Drawing on his pioneering work with people in middle age who thought their lives had lost meaning, Jung addresses the perennial question of what constitutes happiness.

The Stages of Life

To discuss the problems connected with the stages of human development is an exacting task, for it means nothing less than unfolding a picture of psychic life in its entirety from the cradle to the grave. Within the narrow frame of this essay the task can be carried out only on the broadest lines, and it must be well understood that no attempt will be made to describe the normal psychic occurrences within the various stages. We shall rather restrict ourselves and deal only with certain "problems"; that is, with things that are difficult, questionable, or ambiguous; in a word, with questions which allow of more than one answer—and, moreover, answers that are always open to doubt. For this reason there will be much to which we must add a question mark in our thoughts. And—worse still—there will be some things which we must accept on faith, while now and then we must even indulge in speculations.

If psychic life consisted only of overt happenings—which on a primitive level is still the case—we could content ourselves with a sturdy empiricism. The psychic life of civilized man, however, is full of problems; we cannot even think of it except in terms of problems. Our psychic processes are made up to a large extent of reflections, doubts, and experiments, all of which are almost completely foreign to the unconscious, instinctive mind of primitive man. It is the growth of consciousness that we must thank for the existence of problems; they are the dubious gift of civilization. It is just man's turning away from instinct—his opposing himself to instinct—that creates consciousness. Instinct is nature and seeks to perpetuate nature; while consciousness can only seek culture or its denial. Even when we turn back to nature, inspired by a Rousseauesque longing, we "cultivate" nature. As long as we are still submerged in nature we are unconscious, and we live in the security of instinct that knows no problems. Everything in us that still belongs to nature shrinks away from a problem; for its name is doubt, and wherever doubt holds sway, there is uncertainty and the possibility of divergent ways. And where several ways seem possible, there we have turned away from the certain guidance of instinct and are handed over to fear. For consciousness is now called upon to do that which nature has always done for her children—namely, to give a certain, unquestionable, and unequivocal decision. And here we are beset by an all-too-human fear that consciousness—our Promethean conquest—may in the end not be able to serve us in the place of nature.

Problems thus draw us into an orphaned and isolated state where we are abandoned by nature and are driven to consciousness. There is no other way open to us; we are forced to resort to decisions and solutions where we formerly trusted ourselves to natural happenings. Every problem, therefore, brings the possibility of a widening of consciousness—but also the necessity of saying good-bye to childlike unconsciousness and trust in nature. This necessity is a psychic fact of such importance that it constitutes one of the essential symbolic teachings of the Christian religion. It is the sacrifice of the merely natural man—of the unconscious, ingenuous being whose tragic career began with the eating of the apple in Paradise. The biblical fall of man presents the dawn of consciousness as a curse. And as a matter of fact it is in this light that we first look upon every problem that forces us to greater consciousness and separates us even further from the paradise of unconscious childhood. Every one of us gladly turns away from his problems; if possible, they must not be mentioned, or, better still, their existence is denied. We wish to make our lives simple, certain, and smooth—and for that reason problems are taboo. We choose to have certainties and no doubts—results and no experiments—without even seeing that certainties can arise only through doubt, and results through experiment. The artful denial of a problem will not produce conviction; on the contrary, a wider and higher consciousness is called for to give us the certainty and clarity we need.

This introduction, long as it is, seemed to me necessary in order to make clear the nature of our subject. When we must deal with problems, we instinctively refuse to try the way that leads through darkness and obscurity. We wish to hear only of unequivocal results, and completely forget that these results can only be brought about when we have ventured into and emerged again from the darkness. But to penetrate the darkness we must summon all the powers of enlightenment that consciousness can offer; as I have already said, we must even indulge in speculations. For in treating of the problems of psychic life we perpetually stumble over questions of principle belonging to the private domains of the most different branches of knowledge. We disturb and anger the theologian no less than the philosopher, the physician no less than the educator; we even grope about in the field of the biologist and of the historian. This extravagant behavior is not to be charged to our arrogance, but to the circumstance that man's psyche is a unique combination of factors which also make up the special subjects of far-reaching lines of research. For it is out of himself and out of his peculiar constitution that man produced his sciences. They are symptoms of his psyche.

If, therefore, we ask ourselves the unavoidable question "Why does man, in obvious contrast to the animal world, have problems?" we run into that inextricable tangle of thoughts which many thousands of incisive minds have brought about in the course of centuries. I shall not perform the labors of a Sisyphus upon this masterpiece of confusion, but will try to present quite simply my contribution toward man's attempt to answer this basic question.

There are no problems without consciousness. We must therefore put the question in another way: In what way does consciousness arise? Nobody can say with certainty; but we can observe small children in the process of becoming conscious. Every parent can see it, if he pays attention. And this is what we are able to observe: when the child recognizes someone or something—when he "knows" a person or a thing—then we feel that the child has consciousness. That, no doubt, is also why in Paradise it was the tree of knowledge which bore such fateful fruit.

But what is recognition or knowledge in this sense? We speak of "knowing" something when we succeed in linking a new perception to an already established context in such a way that we hold in consciousness not only the new perception but this context as well. "Knowing" is based, therefore, upon a conscious connection between psychic contents. We cannot have knowledge of disconnected contents, and we cannot even be conscious of them. The first stage of consciousness, then, which we can observe consists in a mere connection between two or more psychic contents. At this level, consciousness is merely sporadic, being limited to the representation of a few connections, and the content is not remembered later on. It is a fact that in the early years of life there is no continuous memory; at the most there are islands of consciousness which are like single lamps or lighted objects in the far-flung darkness. But these islands of memory are not the same as those initial connections between psychic contents; they contain something more and something new. This something is that highly important series of related contents which constitutes the so-called ego. The ego—quite like the initial content series—is an object in consciousness, and for this reason the child speaks of itself at first objectively, in the third person. Only later, when the ego-contents have been charged with energy of their own (very likely as a result of exercise), does the feeling of subjectivity or "I-ness" arise. This is no doubt the moment when the child begins to speak of itself in the first person. At this level the continuity of memory has its beginning. Essentially, therefore, it is a continuity in the ego-memories.

In the childish stage of consciousness there are as yet no problems; nothing depends upon the subject, for the child itself is still wholly dependent upon its parents. It is as though it were not yet completely born, but were still enclosed in the psychic atmosphere of its parents. Psychic birth, and with it the conscious distinction of the ego from the parents, takes place in the normal course of things at the age of puberty with the eruption of sexual life. The physiological change is attended by a psychic revolution. For the various bodily manifestations give such an emphasis to the ego that it often asserts itself without stint or measure. This is sometimes called "the unbearable age."

Until this period is reached the psychic life of the individual is essentially governed by impulse, and few or no problems are met with. Even when external limitations oppose the subjective impulses, these restraints do not put the individual at variance with himself. He submits to them or circumvents them, remaining quite at one with himself. He does not yet know the state of inner tension which a problem brings about. This state only arises when what was an external limitation becomes an inner obstacle; when one impulse opposes itself to another. Resorting to psychological terms we would say: the state induced by a problem—the state of being at variance with oneself—arises when, side by side with the series of ego-contents, a second series of equal intensity comes into being. This second series, because of its energy value, has a functional significance equal to that of the ego-complex; we might call it another, second ego which in a given case can wrest the leadership from the first. This brings about an estrangement from oneself—the state that betokens a problem.

With reference to what was said above we can epitomize as follows: the first stage of consciousness which consists of recognizing or "knowing" is an anarchic or chaotic state. The second—that of the developed ego-complex—is a monarchic or monistic phase. The third is another step forward in consciousness, and consists in the awareness of one's divided state; it is a dualistic phase.

And here we take up our actual theme, namely the question of the stages of life. First of all we must deal with the period of youth. It extends roughly from the years just after puberty to middle life, which itself begins between the thirty-fifth and fortieth year.

I might well be asked why I choose to begin with the second period of human existence. Are there no difficult questions connected with childhood? The complex psychic life of the child is of course a problem of the first magnitude to parents, educators, and physicians; but when normal, the child has no real problems of its own. It is only when a human being has grown up that he can have doubts about himself and be at variance with himself.

We are all thoroughly familiar with the sources of the problems which arise in the period of youth. For most people it is the demands of life which harshly put an end to the dream of childhood. If the individual is sufficiently well prepared, the transition to a professional career may take place smoothly. But if he clings to illusions that contradict reality, then problems will surely arise. No one takes the step into life without making certain presuppositions—and occasionally they are false. That is, they may not fit the conditions into which one is thrown. It is often a question of exaggerated expectations, of underestimation of difficulties, of unjustified optimism or of a negative attitude. One could compile quite a list of the false presuppositions which give rise to the earliest, conscious problems.

But it is not always the contrast of subjective presuppositions with external facts that gives rise to problems; it may as often be inner, psychic disturbances. They may exist even when things run smoothly enough in the outer world. Very often it is the disturbance of the psychic equilibrium by the sexual impulse; and perhaps just as often it is the feeling of inferiority which springs from an unbearable sensitivity. These inner difficulties may exist even when adaptation to the outer world has been achieved without apparent effort. It even seems as if young people who have had to struggle hard for their existence are spared inner problems, while those for whom adaptation for some reason or other is made easy, run into problems of sex or conflicts growing from the sense of inferiority.

People whose own temperaments offer problems are often neurotic, but it would be a serious misunderstanding to confuse the existence of problems with neurosis. There is a marked distinction between the two in that the neurotic is ill because he is unconscious of his problems; while the man with a difficult temperament suffers from his conscious problems without being ill.

If we try to extract the common and essential factors from the almost inexhaustible variety of individual problems found in the period of youth, we meet in nearly all cases with a particular feature: a more or less patent clinging to the childhood level of consciousness—a rebellion against the fateful forces in and around us which tend to involve us in the world. Something in us wishes to remain a child; to be unconscious, or, at most, conscious only of the ego; to reject everything foreign, or at least subject it to our will; to do nothing, or in any case indulge our own craving for pleasure or power. In this leaning we observe something like the inertia of matter; it is persistence in a hitherto existing state whose level of consciousness is smaller, narrower, and more egoistic than that of the dualistic stage. For in the latter the individual finds himself compelled to recognize and to accept what is different and strange as a part of his own life—as a kind of "also-I."

It is the extension of the horizon of life which is the essential feature of the dualistic stage—and to which resistance is offered. To be sure, this enlargement—or this diastole, to use Goethe's expression—had started long before this. It begins at birth, when the child abandons the narrow confinement of the mother's womb; and from then on it gains steadily until it reaches a critical point in that phase when, beset by problems, the individual begins to struggle against it.

What would happen to him if he simply changed himself into that other, foreign "also-I," and allowed the earlier ego to vanish into the past? We might suppose this to be a quite practicable course. The very aim of religious education, from the exhortation to put off the old Adam, backward in time to the rebirth rituals of primitive races, is to transform a human being into a new—a future—man, and to allow the old forms of life to die away.

Psychology teaches us that, in a certain sense, there is nothing in the psyche that is old; nothing that can really, definitively die away. Even Paul was left with a sting in his flesh. Whoever protects himself against what is new and strange, and thereby regresses to the past, falls into the same neurotic condition as the man who identifies himself with the new and runs away from the past. The only difference is that the one has estranged himself from the past, and the other from the future. In principle both are doing the same thing; they are salvaging a narrow state of consciousness. The alternative is to shatter it with the tension inherent in the play of opposites—in the dualistic stage—and thereby to build up a state of wider and higher consciousness.

This outcome would be ideal if it could be brought about in the second stage of life—but here is the rub. For one thing, nature cares nothing whatsoever about a higher level of consciousness; quite the contrary. And then society does not value these feats of the psyche very highly; its prizes are always given for achievement and not for personality—the latter being rewarded, for the most part, posthumously. This being so, a particular solution of the difficulty becomes compulsive: we are forced to limit ourselves to the attainable and to differentiate particular aptitudes, for in this way the capable individual discovers his social being.

Achievement, usefulness, and so forth are the ideals which appear to guide us out of the confusion of crowding problems. They may be our lodestars in the adventure of extending and solidifying our psychic existences—they may help us in striking our roots in the world; but they cannot guide us in the development of that wider consciousness to which we give the name of culture. In the period of youth, at any rate, this course is the normal one and in all circumstances preferable to merely tossing about in the welter of problems.

The dilemma is often solved, therefore, in this way: whatever is given to us by the past is adapted to the possibilities and the demands of the future. We limit ourselves to the attainable, and this means the renunciation of all other potentialities. One man loses a valuable piece of his past, another a valuable piece of his future. Everyone can call to mind friends or schoolmates who were promising and idealistic youngsters, but who, when met with years later, seemed to have grown dry and cramped in a narrow mold. These are examples of the solution given above.

The serious problems of life, however, are never fully solved. If it should for once appear that they are, this is the sign that something has been lost. The meaning and design of a problem seem not to lie in its solution, but in our working at it incessantly. This alone preserves us from stultification and petrifaction. So also with that solution of the problems of the period of youth which consists in restricting ourselves to the attainable: it is only temporarily valid and not lasting in a deeper sense. Of course, to win for oneself a place in society and so to transform one's nature that it is more or less fitted to this existence, is in every instance an important achievement. It is a fight waged within oneself as well as outside, comparable to the struggle of the child to defend his ego. This struggle, we must grant, is for the most part unobserved because it happens in the dark; but when we see how stubbornly childish illusions, presuppositions, and egoistic habits are still clung to in later years we are able to realize the energy it took to form them. And so it is also with the ideals, convictions, guiding ideas, and attitudes which in the period of youth lead us out into life—for which we struggle, suffer, and win victories: they grow together with our own beings, we apparently change into them, and we therefore perpetuate them at pleasure and as a matter of course, just as the child asserts its ego in the face of the world and in spite of itself—occasionally even to spite itself.

The nearer we approach to the middle of life, and the better we have succeeded in entrenching ourselves in our personal standpoints and social positions, the more it appears as if we had discovered the right course and the right ideals and principles of behavior. For this reason we suppose them to be eternally valid, and make a virtue of unchangeably clinging to them. We wholly overlook the essential fact that the achievements which society rewards are won at the cost of a diminution of personality. Many—far too many—aspects of life which should also have been experienced lie in the lumberroom among dusty memories. Sometimes, even, they are glowing coals under gray ashes.

Statistical tables show a rise in the frequency of cases of mental depression in men about forty. In women the neurotic difficulties generally begin somewhat earlier. We see that in this phase of life—between thirty-five and forty—a significant change in the human psyche is in preparation. At first it is not a conscious and striking change; it is rather a matter of indirect signs of a change which seems to take its rise from the unconscious. Often it is something like a slow change in a person's character; in another case certain traits may come to light which had disappeared in childhood; or again, inclinations and interests begin to weaken and others arise to take their places. It also frequently happens that the convictions and principles which have hitherto been accepted—especially the moral principles—commence to harden and to grow increasingly rigid until, somewhere toward the age of fifty, a period of intolerance and fanaticism is reached. It is then as if the existence of these principles were endangered, and it were therefore necessary to emphasize them all the more.

The wine of youth does not always clear with advancing years; often-times it grows turbid. All the manifestations mentioned above can be most clearly seen in rather one-sided people, turning up sometimes sooner and sometimes later. In my opinion, their appearance is often delayed by the fact that a person's parents are still alive. It is then as if the period of youth were unduly continued. I have seen this especially in the cases of men whose fathers were long lived. The death of the father then has the effect of an overhurried—an almost catastrophic—ripening.

I know of a pious man who was a churchwarden and who, from the age of forty onward, showed a growing and finally unbearable intolerance in things of morality and religion. At the same time his disposition grew visibly worse. At last he was nothing more than a darkly lowering "pillar of the church." In this way he got along until his fifty-fifth year, when suddenly, one night, sitting up in bed, he said to his wife: " Now at last I've got it! As a matter of fact I'm just a plain rascal." Nor did this self-realization remain without results. He spent his declining years in riotous living and in wasting a goodly part of his fortune. Obviously quite a likeable person capable of both extremes!

The very frequent neurotic disturbances of adult years have this in common, that they betray the attempt to carry the psychic dispositions of youth beyond the threshold of the so-called years of discretion. Who does not know those touching old gentlemen who must always warm up the dish of their student days, who can fan the flames of life only by reminiscences of their heroic youth—and who, for the rest, are stuck in a hopelessly wooden philistinism? As a rule, to be sure, they have this one merit which it would be wrong to undervalue: they are not neurotic, but only boring or stereotyped. The neurotic is rather a person who can never have things as he would like them in the present, and who can therefore never enjoy the past.

As formerly the neurotic could not escape from childhood, so now he cannot part with his youth. He shrinks from the gray thoughts of approaching age; and, feeling the prospect before him unbearable, is always straining to look behind him. Just as a childish person shrinks back from the unknown in the world and in human existence, so the grown man shrinks back from the second half of life. It is as if unknown and dangerous tasks were expected of him; or as if he were threatened with sacrifices and losses which he does not wish to accept; or as if his life up to now seemed to him so fair and so precious that he could not do without it.

Is it perhaps at bottom the fear of death ? That does not seem to me very probable, because as a rule death is still far in the distance, and is therefore regarded somewhat in the light of an abstraction. Experience shows us rather that the basis and cause of all the difficulties of this transition are to be found in a deep-seated and peculiar change within the psyche. In order to characterize it I must take for comparison the daily course of the sun—but a sun that is endowed with human feeling and man's limited consciousness. In the morning it arises from the nocturnal sea of unconsciousness and looks upon the wide, bright world which lies before it in an expanse that steadily widens the higher it climbs in the firmament. In this extension of its field of action caused by its own rising, the sun will discover its significance; it will see the attainment of the greatest possible height—the widest possible dissemination of its blessings—as its goal. In this conviction the sun pursues its unforeseen course to the zenith; unforeseen, because its career is unique and individual, and its culminating point could not be calculated in advance. At the stroke of noon the descent begins. And the descent means the reversal of all the ideals and values that were cherished in the morning. The sun falls into contradiction with itself. It is as though it should draw in its rays, instead of emitting them. Light and warmth decline and are at last extinguished.

All comparisons are lame, but this simile is at least not lamer than others. A French aphorism sums it up with cynical resignation: *Si jeunesse savait, si vieillesse pouvait.*

Fortunately we men are not rising and setting suns, for then it would fare badly with our cultural values. But there is something sunlike within us; and to speak of the morning and spring, of the evening and autumn of life is not mere sentimental jargon. We thus give expression to a psychological truth, even more, to physiological facts; for the reversal at noon changes even bodily characteristics. Especially among southern races one can observe that older women develop rough and deep voices, incipient moustaches, hard facial expressions, and other masculine traits.

On the other hand, the masculine physique is toned down by feminine features, as for instance adiposity and softer facial expressions.

There is an interesting report in ethnological literature about an Indian warrior chief to whom in middle age the Great Spirit appeared in a dream. The spirit announced to him that from then on he must sit among the women and children, wear women's clothes, and eat the food of women. He obeyed the dream without suffering a loss of prestige. This vision is a true expression of the psychic revolution of life's noon——of the beginning of life's decline. Man's values and even his body tend to undergo a reversal into the opposite.

We might compare masculinity and femininity with their psychic components to a particular store of substances of which, in the first half of life, unequal use is made. A man consumes his large supply of masculine substance and has left over only the smaller amount of feminine substance, which he must now put to use. It is the other way round with a woman; she allows her unused supply of masculinity to become active.

This transformation weighs more heavily still in the psychic realm than in the physical. How often it happens that a man of forty or fifty years winds up his business, and that his wife then dons the trousers and opens a little shop where he sometimes performs the duties of handyman. There are many women who only awake to social responsibility and to social consciousness after their fortieth year. In modern business life— especially in the United States—nervous breakdown in the forties or after is a very common occurrence. If one studies the victims a little closely one sees that the thing which has broken down is the masculine style of life which held the field up to now; what is left over is an effeminate man. Contrariwise, one can observe women in these selfsame business spheres who have developed in the second half of life an uncommon masculinity and an incisiveness which push the feelings and the heart aside. Very often the reversal is accompanied by all sorts of catastrophes in marriage; for it is not hard to imagine what may happen when the husband discovers his tender feelings, and the wife her sharpness of mind.

The worst of it all is that intelligent and cultivated people have these leanings without even knowing of the possibility of such transformations. Wholly unprepared, they embark upon the second half of life. Or are there perhaps colleges for forty-year-olds which prepare them for their coming life and its demands as the ordinary colleges introduce our young people to a knowledge of the world and of life? No, there are none. Thoroughly unprepared we take the step into the afternoon of life; worse still, we take this step with the false presupposition that our truths and ideals will serve us as hitherto. But we cannot live the afternoon of life according to the program of life's morning—for what was great in the morning will be little at evening, and what in the morning was true will at evening have become a lie. I have given psychological treatment to too many people of advancing years, and have looked too often into the secret chambers of their souls, not to be moved by this fundamental truth.

Aging people should know that their lives are not mounting and unfolding, but that an inexorable inner process forces the contraction of life. For a young person it is almost a sin—and certainly a danger—to be too much occupied with himself; but for the aging person it is a duty and a necessity to give serious attention to himself. After having lavished its light upon the world, the sun withdraws its rays in order to illumine itself. Instead of doing likewise, many old people prefer to be hypochondriacs, niggards, doctrinaires, applauders of the past, or eternal adolescents— all lamentable substitutes for the illumination of the self, but inevitable consequences of the delusion that the second half of life must be governed by the principles of the first.

I said just now that we have no schools for forty-year-olds. That is not quite true. Our religions were always such schools in the past, but how many people regard them as such today? How many of us older persons have really been brought up in such a school and prepared for the second half of life, for old age, death, and eternity?

A human being would certainly not grow to be seventy or eighty years old if this longevity had no meaning for the species to which he belongs. The afternoon of human life must also have a significance of its own and cannot be merely a pitiful appendage to life's morning. The significance of the morning undoubtedly lies in the development of the individual, our entrenchment in the outer world, the propagation of our kind, and the care of our children. This is the obvious purpose of nature. But when this purpose has been attained—and even more than attained—shall the earning of money, the extension of conquests, and the expansion of life go steadily on beyond the bounds of all reason and sense? Whoever carries over into the afternoon the law of the morning— that is, the aims of nature—must pay for so doing with damage to his soul just as surely as a growing youth who tries to salvage his childish egoism must pay for this mistake with social failure. Moneymaking, social existence, family, and posterity are nothing but plain nature—not culture. Culture lies beyond the purpose of nature. Could by any chance culture be the meaning and purpose of the second half of life?

In primitive tribes we observe that the old people are almost always the guardians of the mysteries and the laws, and it is in these that the cultural heritage of the tribe is expressed. How does the matter stand with us? Where is the wisdom of our old people—where are their precious secrets and their visions? For the most part our old people try to compete with the young. In the United States it is almost an ideal for the father to be the brother of his sons, and for the mother if possible to be the younger sister of her daughter.

I do not know how much of this confusion comes as a reaction to an earlier exaggeration of the dignity of age, and how much is to be charged to false ideals. These undoubtedly exist, and the goal of those who hold them lies behind, and not in front. Therefore they are always striving to turn back. We have to grant to these persons that it is hard to see what other goal the second half of life can offer than the well-known goal of the first. Expansion of life, usefulness, efficiency, the cutting of a figure in social life, the shrewd steering of offspring into suitable marriages and good positions—are not these purposes enough? Unfortunately this is not enough meaning or purpose for many persons who see in the approach of old age a mere diminution of life, and who look upon their earlier ideals only as something faded and worn out. Of course, if these persons had filled up the beaker of life earlier and emptied it to the lees, they would feel quite differently about everything now; had they kept nothing back, all that wanted to catch fire would have been consumed, and the quiet of old age would be very welcome to them. But we must not forget that only a very few people are artists in life; that the art of life is the most distinguished and rarest of all the arts. Who ever succeeded in draining the whole cup with grace? So for many people all too much unlived life remains over—sometimes potentialities which they could never have lived with the best of wills; and so they approach the threshold of old age with unsatisfied claims which inevitably turn their glances backward.

It is particularly fatal for such people to look backward. For them a prospect and a goal in the future are indispensable. This is why all great religions hold the promise of a life beyond; it makes it possible for mortal man to live the second half of life with as much perseverance and aim as the first. For the man of today the enlargement of life and its culmination are plausible goals; but the idea of life after death seems to him questionable or beyond belief. And yet life's cessation, that is, death, can only be accepted as a goal when existence is so wretched that we are glad for it to end, or when we are convinced that the sun strives to its setting——"to illumine distant races"—with the same perseverance it showed in rising to the zenith. But to believe has become today such a difficult art, that people, and particularly the educated part of humanity, can hardly find their way there. They have become too accustomed to the thought that, with regard to immortality and such questions, there are many contradictory opinions and no convincing proofs. Since "science" has become the catchword which carries the weight of conviction in the contemporary world, we ask for "scientific" proofs. But educated people who can think know that proof of this kind is out of the question. We simply know nothing whatever about it.

May I remark that, for the same reasons, we cannot know whether anything happens to a person after he is dead? The answer is neither yes nor no. We simply have no definite scientific proofs about it one way or another, and are therefore in the same position as when we ask whether the planet Mars is inhabited or not. And the inhabitants of Mars, if there are any, are certainly not concerned whether we affirm or deny their existence. They may exist or not. And that is how it stands with so-called immortality—with which we may shelve the problem.

But here my physician's conscience awakes and urges me to say a word which is essential to this question. I have observed that a directed life is in general better, richer, and healthier than an aimless one, and that it is better to go forward with the stream of time than backward against it. To the psychotherapist an old man who cannot bid farewell to life appears as feeble and sickly as a young man who is unable to embrace it. And as a matter of fact, in many cases it is a question of the selfsame childish covetousness, of the same fear, the same obstinacy, and willfulness, in the one as in the other. As a physician I am convinced that it is hygienic—if I may use the word—to discover in death a goal toward which one can strive; and that shrinking away from it is something unhealthy and abnormal which robs the second half of life of its purpose. I therefore consider the religious teaching of a life hereafter consonant with the standpoint of psychic hygiene. When I live in a house which I know will fall about my head within the next two weeks, all my vital functions will be impaired by this thought; but if on the contrary I feel myself to be safe, I can dwell there in a normal and comfortable way. From the standpoint of psychotherapy it would therefore be desirable to think of death as only a transition—one part of a life process whose extent and duration escape our knowledge.

In spite of the fact that by far the larger part of mankind does not know why the body needs salt, everyone demands it nonetheless because of an instinctive need. It is the same in the things of the psyche. A large majority of people have from time immemorial felt the need of believing in a continuance of life. The demands of therapy, therefore, do not lead us into any by-paths, but down the middle of the roadway trodden by humankind. And therefore we are thinking correctly with respect to the meaning of life, even though we do not understand what we think.

Do we ever understand what we think? We only understand that thinking which is a mere equation, and from which nothing comes out but what we have put in. That is the working of the intellect. But beyond that there is a thinking in primordial images—in symbols which are older than historical man; which have been ingrained in him from earliest times, and, eternally living, outlasting all generations, still make up the groundwork of the human psyche. It is only possible to live the fullest life when we are in harmony with these symbols; wisdom is a return to them. It is neither a question of belief nor of knowledge, but of the agreement of our thinking with the primordial images of the unconscious. They are the source of all our conscious thoughts, and one of these primordial thoughts is the idea of life after death. Science and these symbols are incommensurables. They are indispensable conditions of the imagination; they are primary data—the materials whose expediency and warrant to exist science cannot deny offhand. It can only treat of them as given facts, much as it can explore a function like that of the thyroid gland, for example. Before the nineteenth century the thyroid was regarded as a meaningless organ, merely because it was not understood. It would be equally shortsighted of us today to call the primordial images senseless. For me these images are something like psychic organs, and I treat them with the very greatest care. It happens sometimes that I must say to an older patient: "Your picture of God or your idea of immortality is atrophied; consequently your psychic metabolism is out of gear." The ancient *pharmakon athanasias*, the medicament of immortality, is more profound and meaningful than we supposed.

In this place I would like to return again for a moment to the comparison with the sun. The 180 degrees of the arc of life are divisible into four parts. The first quarter, lying to the east, is childhood—that state in which we are a problem for others, but are not yet conscious of any problems of our own. Conscious problems fill out the second and third quarters; while in the last—in extreme old age—we descend again into that condition where, unworried by our state of consciousness, we again become something of a problem for others. Childhood and extreme old age, to be sure, are utterly different, and yet they have one thing in common: submersion in unconscious psychic happenings. Since the mind of a child grows out of the unconscious, its psychic processes—though not easily accessible—are not as difficult to discern as those of a very old person who has plunged again into the unconscious, and who progressively vanishes within it. Childhood and old age are the stages of life without any conscious problems, for which reason I have not taken them into consideration here.

QUESTIONS

1. Why does Jung believe that we can only think of "the psychic life of civilized man" in terms of its problems? Why does Jung conclude that the growth of consciousness is responsible for them? (451)

2. Why does Jung call the various sciences "symptoms" of the human psyche? (453)

3. Why does Jung say that we are drawn "into an orphaned and isolated state where we are abandoned by nature and are driven to consciousness"? (452) Who or what is responsible for this?

4. Why does Jung believe that a child has a "complex psychic life" but "no real problems of its own"? Why does he locate "psychic birth" at puberty? (454)

5. Why does Jung say that the achievements that society rewards "are won at the cost of a diminution of personality"? (457)

6. What point is Jung making in the story of the church warden who turns into "a plain rascal"? (458)

7. For Jung, why is the neurotic defined as someone who cannot part with his or her youth?

8. Is Jung saying that the middle-aged person's fears of being confronted with "unknown and dangerous tasks" are unfounded? (459)

9. How does Jung distinguish the fear of death from the "deep-seated and peculiar change within the psyche" that causes people to shrink back from the second half of life? (459)

10. How does Jung think people should respond to the changes in masculinity and femininity that he describes occurring in middle age? Why does he include the story of the Indian warrior chief?

11. Why is Jung sure that "the afternoon of human life must also have a significance of its own and cannot be merely a pitiful appendage to life's morning"? (461)

12. Why does Jung define "moneymaking, social existence, family, and posterity" as "nothing but plain nature—not culture"? (461)

13. Does Jung believe that life after death is real, or merely that belief in it is "hygienic"? (463)

14. Why does Jung repeatedly use the metaphor of "the afternoon of human life"? (460–461) What limitations does Jung recognize in this metaphor?

15. Why does Jung assert that to live the fullest life one must live in harmony with the "symbols which are older than historical man" that "make up the groundwork of the human psyche"? (463–464) How does one achieve this, according to Jung?

FOR FURTHER REFLECTION

1. Why do people often do foolish or extravagant things when they reach middle age?

2. Do you agree that it is healthy to "discover in death a goal toward which one can strive"?

3. In your experience, do middle-aged people undergo the changes in masculinity and femininity that Jung describes?

4. What do you consider most healthy and unhealthy in our society's attitude toward aging and death?

5. Why, according to Jung, are the serious problems of life never fully solved?

6. How does Jung think we should prepare for "the afternoon of life"?

TILLIE OLSEN

The daughter of Samuel and Ida Lerner, working-class Jewish immigrants from Russia, Tillie Olsen was born in either 1912 or 1913 (her birth was not formally recorded). Her parents had joined the failed 1905 Russian revolution, and Samuel was imprisoned for his part in it. He and Ida, his common-law wife, left for Nebraska after he managed to escape from prison. Her parents' continuing socialist activism and constant battle with poverty profoundly influenced Olsen, whose writing explores the tension between the struggle for basic survival and the human need to create beauty and meaning. Olsen has not only written about but also has lived this struggle, spending many years working at factory and clerical jobs, largely supporting her four daughters, and engaging in political activism, with very little time to write.

The second oldest of six children, Olsen helped support her family from an early age: at ten, she worked shelling peanuts after school. In the free time she could find, she read the revolutionary pamphlets and magazines her parents kept and began reading her way through the Omaha Public Library's fiction section. One of a few from her neighborhood chosen to attend an "academic" high school, Olsen dropped out of school in eleventh grade to earn money for her family. She joined the Young Communist League at 18 and, soon afterward, was briefly jailed for distributing leaflets to packinghouse workers. In 1932, she moved to Minnesota and began a novel, *Yonnondio*. She became pregnant and was soon raising her daughter Karla alone.

Olsen's story "The Iron Throat," published in 1934 in *The Partisan Review*, led to a contract with Random House to finish *Yonnondio*. Because she needed to be separated from her daughter to finish the book on schedule, Olsen decided to forfeit the contract. She married Jack Olsen in 1936, had three more daughters, and devoted her time to motherhood, work to support her family, and political causes, including the fledging women's movement. She did not begin writing again until 1953, when she enrolled in a creative writing class at San Francisco State College. She was awarded a Stanford University writing fellowship in 1955 and 1956, which enabled her to write the four stories collected in *Tell Me A Riddle*. The title story won the O. Henry Award for best short story of the year in 1961. In 1974, she published the fragmentary *Yonnondio*. Her nonfiction book *Silences,* which explores the economic and social pressures that prevent writers from creating or finishing fiction, appeared in 1978. "Tell Me a Riddle" powerfully unites the themes characteristic of her work: economic hardship, political struggle, and the barriers to self-expression experienced especially by women.

TILLIE OLSEN
Tell Me a Riddle
"These Things Shall Be"

1

For forty-seven years they had been married. How deep back the stubborn, gnarled roots of the quarrel reached, no one could say—but only now, when tending to the needs of others no longer shackled them together, the roots swelled up visible, split the earth between them, and the tearing shook even to the children, long since grown.

Why now, why now? wailed Hannah.

As if when we grew up weren't enough, said Paul.

Poor Ma. Poor Dad. It hurts so for both of them, said Vivi. They never had very much; at least in old age they should be happy.

Knock their heads together, insisted Sammy; tell 'em: you're too old for this kind of thing; no reason not to get along now.

Lennie wrote to Clara: They've lived over so much together; what could possibly tear them apart?

Something tangible enough.

Arthritic hands, and such work as he got, occasional. Poverty all his life, and there was little breath left for running. He could not, could not turn away from this desire: to have the troubling of responsibility, the fretting with money, over and done with; to be free, to be *care*free where success was not measured by accumulation, and there was use for the vitality still in him.

There was a way. They could sell the house, and with the money join his lodge's Haven, cooperative for the aged. Happy communal life, and was he not already an official; had he not helped organize it, raise funds, served as a trustee?

But she—would not consider it.

"What do we need all this for?" he would ask loudly, for her hearing aid was turned down and the vacuum was shrilling. "Five rooms" (pushing the sofa so she could get into the corner) "furniture" (smoothing down the rug) "floors and surfaces to make work. Tell me, why do we need it?" And he was glad he could ask in a scream.

"Because I'm use't."

"Because you're use't. This is a reason, Mrs. Word Miser? Used to can get unused!"

"Enough unused I have to get used to already.... Not enough words?" turning off the vacuum a moment to hear herself answer. "Because soon enough we'll need only a little closet, no windows, no furniture, nothing to make work, but for worms. Because now I want room.... Screech and blow like you're doing, you'll need that closet even sooner. . . . Ha, again!" for the vacuum bag wailed, puffed half up, hung stubbornly limp. "This time fix it so it stays; quick before the phone rings and you get too important-busy."

But while he struggled with the motor, it seethed in him. Why fix it? Why have to bother? And if it can't be fixed, have to wring the mind with how to pay the repair? At the Haven they come in with their own machines to clean your room or your cottage; you fish, or play cards, or make jokes in the sun, not with knotty fingers fight to mend vacuums.

Over the dishes, coaxingly: "For once in your life, to be free, to have everything done for you, like a queen."

"I never liked queens."

"No dishes, no garbage, no towel to sop, no worry what to buy, what to eat."

"And what else would I do with my empty hands? Better to eat at my own table when I want, and to cook and eat how I want."

"In the cottages they buy what you ask, and cook it how you like. *You* are the one who always used to say: better mankind born without mouths and stomachs than always to worry for money to buy, to shop, to fix, to cook, to wash, to clean."

"How cleverly you hid that you heard. I said it then because eighteen hours a day I ran. And you never scraped a carrot or knew a dish towel sops. Now—for you and me—who cares? A herring out of a jar is enough. But when *I* want, and nobody to bother." And she turned off her ear button, so she would not have to hear.

But as *he* had no peace, juggling and rejuggling the money to figure: how will I pay for this now?; prying out the storm windows (there they take care of this); jolting in the streetcar on errands (there I would not have to ride to take care of this or that); fending the patronizing relatives just back from Florida (at the Haven it matters what one is, not what one can afford), he gave *her* no peace.

"Look! In their bulletin. A reading circle. Twice a week it meets."

"Haumm," her answer of not listening.

"A reading circle. Chekhov they read that you like, and Peretz. Cultured people at the Haven that you would enjoy."

"Enjoy!" She tasted the word. "Now, when it pleases you, you find a reading circle for me. And forty years ago when the children were morsels and there was a Circle, did you stay home with them once so I could go? Even once? You trained me well. I do not need others to enjoy. Others!" Her voice trembled. "Because *you* want to be there with others. Already it makes me sick to think of you always around others. Clown, grimacer, floormat, yes man, entertainer, whatever they want of you."

And now it was he who turned on the television loud so he need not hear.

Old scar tissue ruptured and the wounds festered anew. Chekhov indeed. She thought without softness of that young wife, who in the deep night hours while she nursed the current baby, and perhaps held another in her lap, would try to stay awake for the only time there was to read. She would feel again the weather of the outside on his cheek when, coming late from a meeting, he would find her so, and stimulated and ardent, sniffing her skin, coax: "I'll put the baby to bed, and you—put the book away, don't read, don't read."

That had been the most beguiling of all the "don't read, put your book away" her life had been. Chekhov indeed!

"Money?" She shrugged him off. "Could we get poorer than once we were? And in America, who starves?"

But as still he pressed:

"Let me alone about money. Was there ever enough? Seven little ones—for every penny I had to ask—and sometimes, remember, there was nothing. But always *I* had to manage. Now *you* manage. Rub your nose in it good."

But from those years she had had to manage, old humiliations and terrors rose up, lived again, and forced her to relive them. The children's needings; that grocer's face or this merchant's wife she had had to beg credit from when credit was a disgrace; the scenery of the long blocks walked around when she could not pay; school coming, and the desperate going over the old to see what could yet be remade; the soups of meat bones begged "for-the-dog" one winter. . . .

Enough. Now they had no children. Let *him* wrack his head for how they would live. She would not exchange her solitude for anything. *Never again to be forced to move to the rhythms of others.*

For in this solitude she had won to a reconciled peace.

Tranquillity from having the empty house no longer an enemy, for it stayed clean—not as in the days when it was her family, the life in it, that had seemed the enemy: tracking, smudging, littering, dirtying, engaging her in endless defeating battle—and on whom her endless defeat had been spewed.

The few old books, memorized from rereading; the pictures to ponder (the magnifying glass superimposed on her heavy eyeglasses). Or if she wishes, when he is gone, the phonograph, that if she turns up very loud and strains, she can hear: the ordered sounds and the struggling.

Out in the garden, growing things to nurture. Birds to be kept out of the pear tree, and when the pears are heavy and ripe, the old fury of work, for all must be canned, nothing wasted.

And her one social duty (for she will not go to luncheons or meetings) the boxes of old clothes left with her, as with a life-practiced eye for finding what is still wearable within the worn (again the magnifying glass superimposed on the heavy glasses) she scans and sorts—this for rag or rummage, that for mending and cleaning, and this for sending away.

Being able at last to live within, and not move to the rhythms of others, as life had forced her to: denying; removing; isolating; taking the children one by one; then deafening, half-blinding—and at last, presenting her solitude.

And in it she had won to a reconciled peace.

Now he was violating it with his constant campaigning: *Sell the house and move to the Haven.* (You sit, you sit—there too you could sit like a stone.) He was making of her a battleground where old grievances tore. (Turn on your ear button—I am talking.) And stubbornly she resisted—so that from wheedling, reasoning, manipulation, it was bitterness he now started with.

And it came to where every happening lashed up a quarrel.

"I will sell the house anyway," he flung at her one night. "I am putting it up for sale. There will be a way to make you sign."

The television blared, as always it did on the evenings he stayed home, and as always it reached her only as noise. She did not know if the tumult was in her or outside. Snap! she turned the sound off. "Shadows," she whispered to him, pointing to the screen, "look, it is only shadows." And in a scream: "Did you say that you will sell the house? Look at me, not at that. I am no shadow. You cannot sell without me."

"Leave on the television. I am watching."

"Like Paulie, like Jenny, a four-year-old. Staring at shadows. *You cannot sell the house.*"

"I will. We are going to the Haven. There you would not hear the television when you do not want it. I could sit in the social room and watch. You could lock yourself up to smell your unpleasantness in a room by yourself—for who would want to come near you?"

"No, no selling." A whisper now.

"The television is shadows. Mrs. Enlightened! Mrs. Cultured! A world comes into your house—and it is shadows. People you would never meet in a thousand lifetimes. Wonders. When you were four years old, yes, like Paulie, like Jenny, did you know of Indian dances, alligators, how they use bamboo in Malaya? No, you scratched in your dirt with the chickens and thought Olshana was the world. Yes, Mrs. Unpleasant, I will sell the house, for there better can we be rid of each other than here."

She did not know if the tumult was outside, or in her. Always a ravening inside, a pull to the bed, to lie down, to succumb.

"Have you thought maybe Ma should let a doctor have a look at her?" asked their son Paul after Sunday dinner, regarding his mother crumpled on the couch, instead of, as was her custom, busying herself in Nancy's kitchen.

"Why not the President too?"

"Seriously, Dad. This is the third Sunday she's lain down like that after dinner. Is she that way at home?"

"A regular love affair with the bed. Every time I start to talk to her."

Good protective reaction, observed Nancy to herself. The workings of hos-til-ity.

"Nancy could take her. I just don't like how she looks. Let's have Nancy arrange an appointment."

"You think she'll go?" regarding his wife gloomily. "All right, we have to have doctor bills, we have to have doctor bills." Loudly: "Something hurts you?"

She startled, looked to his lips. He repeated: "Mrs. Take It Easy, something hurts?"

"Nothing. . . . Only you."

"A woman of honey. That's why you're lying down?"

"Soon I'll get up to do the dishes, Nancy."

"Leave them, Mother, I like it better this way."

"Mrs. Take It Easy, Paul says you should start ballet. You should go to see a doctor and ask: how soon can you start ballet?"

"A doctor?" she begged. "Ballet?"

"We were talking, Ma," explained Paul, "you don't seem any too well. It would be a good idea for you to see a doctor for a checkup."

"I get up now to do the kitchen. Doctors are bills and foolishness, my son. I need no doctors."

"At the Haven," he could not resist pointing out, "a doctor is *not* bills. He lives beside you. You start to sneeze, he is there before you open up a Kleenex. You can be sick there for free, all you want."

"Diarrhea of the mouth, is there a doctor to make you dumb?"

"Ma. Promise me you'll go. Nancy will arrange it."

"It's all of a piece when you think of it," said Nancy, "the way she attacks my kitchen, scrubbing under every cup hook, doing the inside of the oven so I can't enjoy Sunday dinner, knowing that half-blind or not, she's going to find every speck of dirt. . . ."

"Don't, Nancy, I've told you—it's the only way she knows to be useful. What did the *doctor* say?"

"A real fatherly lecture. Sixty-nine is young these days. Go out, enjoy life, find interests. Get a new hearing aid, this one is antiquated. Old age is sickness only if one makes it so. Geriatrics, Inc."

"So there was nothing physical."

"Of course there was. How can you live to yourself like she does without there being? Evidence of a kidney disorder, and her blood count is low. He gave her a diet, and she's to come back for follow-up and lab work. . . . But he was clear enough: Number One prescription—start living like a human being. . . . When I think of your dad, who could really play the invalid with that arthritis of his, as active as a teenager, and twice as much fun. . . ."

"You didn't tell me the doctor says your sickness is in you, how you live." He pushed his advantage. "Life and enjoyments you need better than medicine. And this diet, how can you keep it? To weigh each morsel and scrape away each bit of fat, to make this soup, that pudding. There, at the Haven, they have a dietician, they would do it for you."

She is silent.

"You would feel better there, I know it," he says gently. "There there is life and enjoyments all around."

"What is the matter, Mr. Importantbusy, you have no card game or meeting you can go to?"—turning her face to the pillow.

For a while he cut his meetings and going out, fussed over her diet, tried to wheedle her into leaving the house, brought in visitors:

"I should come to a fashion tea. I should sit and look at pretty babies in clothes I cannot buy. This is pleasure?"

"Always you are better than everyone else. The doctor said you should go out. Mrs. Brem comes to you with goodness and you turn her away."

"Because *you* asked her to, she asked me."

"They won't come back. People you need, the doctor said. Your own cousins I asked; they were willing to come and make peace as if nothing had happened. . . ."

"No more crushers of people, pushers, hypocrites, around me. No more in *my* house. You go to them if you like."

"Kind he is to visit. And you, like ice."

"A babbler. All my life around babblers. Enough!"

"She's even worse, Dad? Then let her stew a while," advised Nancy. "You can't let it destroy you; it's a psychological thing, maybe too far gone for any of us to help."

So he let her stew. More and more she lay silent in bed, and sometimes did not even get up to make the meals. No longer was the tongue-lashing inevitable if he left the coffee cup where it did not belong, or forgot to take out the garbage or mislaid the broom. The birds grew bold that summer and for once pocked the pears, undisturbed.

A bellyful of bitterness and every day the same quarrel in a new way and a different old grievance the quarrel forced her to enter and relive. And the new torment: I am not really sick, the doctor said it, then why do I feel so sick?

One night she asked him: "You have a meeting tonight? Do not go. Stay . . . with me."

He had planned to watch "This Is Your Life," but half-sick himself from the heavy heat, and sickening therefore the more after the brooks and woods of the Haven, with satisfaction he grated:

"Hah, Mrs. Live Alone And Like It wants company all of a sudden. It doesn't seem so good the time of solitary when she was a girl exile in Siberia. 'Do not go. Stay with me.' A new song for Mrs. Free As A Bird. Yes, I am going out, and while I am gone chew this aloneness good, and think how you keep us both from where if you want people, you do not need to be alone."

"Go, go. All your life you have gone without me."

After him she sobbed curses he had not heard in years, old-country curses from their childhood: Grow, oh shall you grow like an onion, with your head in the ground. Like the hide of a drum shall you be, beaten in life, beaten in death. Oh shall you be like a chandelier, to hang, and to burn. . . .

She was not in their bed when he came back. She lay on the cot on the sun porch. All week she did not speak or come near him; nor did he try to make peace or care for her.

He slept badly, so used to her next to him. After all the years, old harmonies and dependencies deep in their bodies; she curled to him, or he coiled to her, each warmed, warming, turning as the other turned, the nights a long embrace.

It was not the empty bed or the storm that woke him, but a faint singing. *She* was singing. Shaking off the drops of rain, the lightning riving her lifted face, he saw her so; the cot covers on the floor.

"This is a private concert?" he asked. "Come in, you are wet."

"I can breathe now," she answered; "my lungs are rich." Though indeed the sound was hardly a breath.

"Come in, come in." Loosing the bamboo shades. "Look how wet you are." Half helping, half carrying her, still faint-breathing her song.

A Russian love song of fifty years ago.

He had found a buyer, but before he told her, he called together those children who were close enough to come. Paul, of course, Sammy from New Jersey, Hannah from Connecticut, Vivi from Ohio.

With a kindling of energy for her beloved visitors, she arrayed the house, cooked and baked. She was not prepared for the solemn after-dinner conclave, they too probing in and tearing. Her frightened eyes watched from mouth to mouth as each spoke.

His stories were eloquent and funny of her refusal to go back to the doctor; of the scorned invitations; of her stubborn silence or the bile "like a Niagara"; of her contrariness: "If I clean it's no good how I cleaned; if I don't clean, I'm still a master who thinks he has a slave."

(Vinegar he poured on me all his life; I am well marinated; how can I be honey now?)

Deftly he marched in the rightness for moving to the Haven; their money from social security free for visiting the children, not sucked into daily needs and into the house; the activities in the Haven for him; but mostly the Haven for *her*: her health, her need of care, distraction, amusement, friends who shared her interests.

"This does offer an outlet for Dad," said Paul; "he's always been an active person. And economic peace of mind isn't to be sneezed at, either. I could use a little of that myself."

But when they asked: "And you, Ma, how do you feel about it?" could only whisper:

"For him it is good. It is not for me. I can no longer live between people."

"You lived all your life *for* people," Vivi cried.

"Not with." Suffering doubly for the unhappiness on her children's faces.

"You have to find some compromise," Sammy insisted. "Maybe sell the house and buy a trailer. After forty-seven years there's surely some way you can find to live in peace."

"There is no help, my children. Different things we need."

"Then live alone!" He could control himself no longer. "I have a buyer for the house. Half the money for you, half for me. Either alone or with me to the Haven. You think I can live any longer as we are doing now?"

"Ma doesn't have to make a decision this minute, however you feel, Dad," Paul said quickly, "and you wouldn't want her to. Let's let it lay a few months, and then talk some more."

"I think I can work it out to take Mother home with me for a while," Hannah said. "You both look terrible, but especially you, Mother. I'm going to ask Phil to have a look at you."

"Sure," cracked Sammy. "What's the use of a doctor husband if you can't get free service out of him once in a while for the family? And absence might make the heart . . . you know."

"There was something after all," Paul told Nancy in a colorless voice. "That was Hannah's Phil calling. Her gall bladder. . . . Surgery."

"Her *gall* bladder. If that isn't classic. 'Bitter as gall'—talk of psycho-som——"

He stepped closer, put his hand over her mouth, and said in the same colorless, plodding voice. "We have to get Dad. They operated at once. The cancer was everywhere, surrounding the liver, everywhere. They did what they could . . . at best she has a year. Dad . . . we have to tell him."

2

Honest in his weakness when they told him, and that she was not to know. "I'm not an actor. She'll know right away by how I am. Oh that poor woman. I am old too, it will break me into pieces. Oh that poor woman. She will spit on me: 'So my sickness was how I live.' Oh Paulie, how she will be, that poor woman. Only she should not suffer. . . . I can't stand sickness, Paulie, I can't go with you."

But went. And play-acted.

"A grand opening and you did not even wait for me. . . . A good thing Hannah took you with her."

"Fashion teas I needed. They cut out what tore in me; just in my throat something hurts yet. . . . Look! so many flowers, like a funeral. Vivi called, did Hannah tell you? And Lennie from San Francisco, and Clara; and Sammy is coming." Her gnome's face pressed happily into the flowers.

It is impossible to predict in these cases, but once over the immediate effects of the operation, she should have several months of comparative well-being.

The money, where will come the money?

Travel with her, Dad. Don't take her home to the old associations. The other children will want to see her.

The money, where will I wring the money?

Whatever happens, she is not to know. No, you can't ask her to sign papers to sell the house; nothing to upset her. Borrow instead, then after. . . .

I had wanted to leave you each a few dollars to make life easier, as other fathers do. There will be nothing left now. (Failure! you and your "business is exploitation." Why didn't you make it when it could be made?—Is that what you're thinking, Sammy?)

Sure she's unreasonable, Dad—but you have to stay with her; if there's to be any happiness in what's left of her life, it depends on you.

Prop me up, children, think of me, too. Shuffled, chained with her, bitter woman. No Haven, and the little money going. . . . How happy she looks, poor creature.

The look of excitement. The straining to hear everything (the new hearing aid turned full). Why are you so happy, dying woman?

How the petals are, fold on fold, and the gladioli color. The autumn air.

Stranger grandsons, tall above the little gnome grandmother, the little spry grandfather. Paul in a frenzy of picture-taking before going.

She, wandering the great house. Feeling the books; laughing at the maple shoemaker's bench of a hundred years ago used as a table. The ear turned to music.

"Let us go home. See how good I walk now." "One step from the hospital," he answers, "and she wants to fly. Wait till Doctor Phil says."

"Look—the birds too are flying home. Very good Phil is and will not show it, but he is sick of sickness by the time he comes home."

"Mrs. Telepathy, to read minds," he answers; "read mine what it says: when the trunks of medicines become a suitcase, then we will go."

The grandboys, they do not know what to say to us. . . . Hannah, she runs around here, there, when is there time for herself?

Let us go home. Let us go home.

Musing; gentleness—*but for the incidents of the rabbi in the hospital, and of the candles of benediction.*

Of the rabbi in the hospital:

Now tell me what happened, Mother.

From the sleep I awoke, Hannah's Phil, and he stands there like a devil in a dream and calls me by name. I cannot hear. I think he prays. Go away, please, I tell him, I am not a believer. Still he stands, while my heart knocks with fright.

You scared *him*, Mother. He thought you were delirious.

Who sent him? Why did he come to me?

It is a custom. The men of God come to visit those of their religion they might help. The hospital makes up the list for them—race, religion—and you are on the Jewish list.

Not for rabbis. At once go and make them change. Tell them to write: Race, human; Religion, none.

And of the candles of benediction:

Look how you have upset yourself, Mrs. Excited Over Nothing. Pleasant memories you should leave.

Go in, go back to Hannah and the lights. Two weeks I saw candles and said nothing. But she asked me.

So what was so terrible? She forgets you never did, she asks you to light the Friday candles and say the benediction like Phil's mother when she visits. If the candles give her pleasure, why shouldn't she have the pleasure?

Not for pleasure she does it. For emptiness. Because his family does. Because all around her do.

That is not a good reason too? But you did not hear her. For heritage, she told you. For the boys, from the past they should have tradition.

Superstition! From our ancestors, savages, afraid of the dark, of themselves: mumbo words and magic lights to scare away ghosts.

She told you: how it started does not take away the goodness. For centuries, peace in the house it means.

Swindler! Does she look back on the dark centuries? Candles bought instead of bread and stuck into a potato for a candlestick? Religion that stifled and said: in Paradise, woman, you will be the footstool of your husband, and in life—poor chosen Jew—ground under, despised, trembling in cellars. And cremated. And cremated.

This is religion's fault? You think you are still an orator of the 1905 revolution? Where are the pills for quieting? Which are they?

Heritage. How have we come from our savage past, how no longer to be savages—this to teach. To look back and learn what humanizes—this to teach. To smash all ghettos that divide us—not to go back, not to go back—this to teach. Learned books in the house, will humankind live or die, and she gives to her boys—superstition.

Hannah that is so good to you. Take your pill, Mrs. Excited For Nothing, swallow.

Heritage! But when did I have time to teach? Of Hannah I asked only hands to help.

Swallow.

Otherwise—musing; gentleness.

Not to travel. To go home.

The children want to see you. We have to show them you are as thorny a flower as ever.

Not to travel.

Vivi wants you should see her new baby. She sent the tickets—airplane tickets—a Mrs. Roosevelt she wants to make of you. To Vivi's we have to go.

A new baby. How many warm, seductive babies. She holds him stiffly, *away* from her, so that he wails. And a long shudder begins, and the sweat beads on her forehead.

"Hush, shush," croons the grandfather, lifting him back. "You should forgive your grandmamma, little prince, she has never held a baby before, only seen them in glass cases. Hush, shush."

"You're tired, Ma," says Vivi. "The travel and the noisy dinner. I'll take you to lie down."

(*A long travel from, to, what the feel of a baby evokes.*)

In the airplane, cunningly designed to encase from motion (no wind, no feel of flight), she had sat severely and still, her face turned to the sky through which they cleaved and left no scar.

So this was how it looked, the determining, the crucial sky, and this was how man moved through it, remote above the dwindled earth, the concealed human life. Vulnerable life, that could scar.

There was a steerage ship of memory that shook across a great, circular sea: clustered, ill human beings; and through the thick-stained air, tiny fretting waters in a window round like the airplane's—sun round, moon round. (The round thatched roofs of Olshana.) Eye round—like the smaller window that framed distance the solitary year of exile when only her eyes could travel, and no voice spoke. And the polar winds hurled themselves across snows trackless and endless and white—like the clouds which had closed together below and hidden the earth.

Now they put a baby in her lap. Do not ask me, she would have liked to beg. Enough the worn face of Vivi, the remembered grandchildren. I cannot, cannot. . . .

Cannot what? Unnatural grandmother, not able to make herself embrace a baby.

She lay there in the bed of the two little girls, her new hearing aid turned full, listening to the sound of the children going to sleep, the baby's fretful crying and hushing, the clatter of dishes being washed and put away. They thought she slept. Still she rode on.

It was not that she had not loved her babies, her children. The love—the passion of tending—had risen with the need like a torrent; and like a torrent drowned and immolated all else. But when the need was done—oh the power that was lost in the painful damming back and drying up of what still surged, but had nowhere to go. Only the thin pulsing left that could not quiet, suffering over lives one felt, but could no longer hold nor help.

On that torrent she had borne them to their own lives, and the riverbed was desert long years now. Not there would she dwell, a memoried wraith. Surely that was not all, surely there was more. Still the springs, the springs were in her seeking. Somewhere an older power that beat for life. Somewhere coherence, transport, meaning. If they would but leave her in the air now stilled of clamor, in the reconciled solitude, to journey on.

And they put a baby in her lap. Immediacy to embrace, and the breath of *that* past: warm flesh like this that had claims and nuzzled away all else and with lovely mouths devoured; hot-living like an animal—intensely and now; the turning maze; the long drunkenness; the drowning into needing and being needed. Severely she looked back—and the shudder seized her again, and the sweat. Not that way. Not there, not now could she, not yet. . . .

And all that visit, she could not touch the baby.

"Daddy, is it the . . . sickness she's like that?" asked Vivi. "I was so glad to be having the baby—for her. I told Tim, it'll give her more happiness than anything, being around a baby again. And she hasn't played with him once."

He was not listening, "Aahh little seed of life, little charmer," he crooned, "Hollywood should see you. A heart of ice you would melt. Kick, kick. The future you'll have for a ball. In 2050 still kick. Kick for your grandaddy then."

Attentive with the older children; sat through their performances (command performance; we command you to be the audience); helped Ann sort autumn leaves to find the best for a school program; listened gravely to Richard tell about his rock collection, while her lips mutely formed the words to remember: *igneous, sedimentary, metamorphic*; looked for missing socks, books, and bus tickets; watched the children whoop after their grandfather who knew how to tickle, chuck, lift, toss, do tricks, tell secrets, make jokes, match riddle for riddle. (Tell me a riddle, Grammy. I know no riddles, child.) Scrubbed sills and woodwork and furniture in every room; folded the laundry; straightened drawers; emptied the heaped baskets waiting for ironing (while he or Vivi or Tim nagged: You're supposed to rest here, you've been sick) but to none tended or gave food—and could not touch the baby.

After a week she said: "Let us go home. Today call about the tickets."

"You have important business, Mrs. Inahurry? The President waits to consult with you?" He shouted, for the fear of the future raced in him. "The clothes are still warm from the suitcase, your children cannot show enough how glad they are to see you, and you want home. There is plenty of time for home. We cannot be with the children at home."

"Blind to around you as always: the little ones sleep four in a room because we take their bed. We are two more people in a house with a new baby, and no help."

"Vivi is happy so. The children should have their grandparents a while, she told to me. I should have my mommy and daddy. . . ."

"Babbler and blind. Do you look at her so tired? How she starts to talk and she cries? I am not strong enough yet to help. Let us go home."

(To reconciled solitude.)

For it seemed to her the crowded noisy house was listening to her, listening for her. She could feel it like a great ear pressed under her heart. And everything knocked: quick constant raps: let me in, let me in.

How was it that soft reaching tendrils also became blows that knocked?

C'mon, Grandma, I want to show you. . . .

Tell me a riddle, Grandma. (*I know no riddles.*)

Look, Grammy, he's so dumb he can't even find his hands. (Dody and the baby on a blanket over the fermenting autumn mold.)

I made them—for you. (Ann) (Flat paper dolls with aprons that lifted on scalloped skirts that lifted on flowered pants; hair of yarn and great ringed questioning eyes.)

Watch me, Grandma. (Richard snaking up the tree, hanging exultant, free, with one hand at the top. Below Dody hunching over in pretend-cooking.)

(*Climb too, Dody, climb and look.*)

Be my nap bed, Grammy. (The "No!" too late.)

Morty's abandoned heaviness, while his fingers ladder up and down her hearing-aid cord to his drowsy chant: eentsiebeentsiespider. (*Children trust.*)

It's to start off your own rock collection, Grandma. That's a trilobite fossil, 200 million years old (millions of years on a boy's mouth) and that one's obsidian, black glass.

Knocked and knocked.

Mother, I *told* you the teacher said we had to bring it back all filled out this morning. Didn't you even ask Daddy? Then tell *me* which plan and I'll check it: evacuate or stay in the city or wait for you to come and take me away. (Seeing the look of straining to hear.) It's for Disaster, Grandma. (*Children trust.*)

Vivi in the maze of the long, the lovely drunkenness. The old old noises: baby sounds; screaming of a mother flayed to exasperation; children quarreling; children playing; singing; laughter.

And Vivi's tears and memories, spilling so fast, half the words not understood.

She had started remembering out loud deliberately, so her mother would know the past was cherished, still lived in her.

Nursing the baby: My friends marvel, and I tell them, oh it's easy to be such a cow. I remember how beautiful my mother seemed nursing my brother, and the milk just flows. . . . Was that Davy? It must have been Davy. . . .

Lowering a hem: How did you ever . . . when I think how you made everything we wore . . . Tim, just think, seven kids and Mommy sewed everything . . . do I remember you sang while you sewed? That white dress with the red apples on the skirt you fixed over for me, was it Hannah's or Clara's before it was mine?

Washing sweaters: Ma, I'll never forget, one of those days so nice you washed clothes outside; one of the first spring days it must have been. The bubbles just danced while you scrubbed, and we chased after, and you stopped to show us how to blow our own bubbles with green onion stalks . . . you always. . . .

"Strong onion, to still make you cry after so many years," her father said, to turn the tears into laughter.

While Richard bent over his homework: Where is it now, do we still have it, the Book of the Martyrs? It always seemed so, well—exalted, when you'd put it on the round table and we'd all look at it together; there was even a halo from the lamp. The lamp with the beaded fringe you could move up and down; they're in style again, pulley lamps like that, but without the fringe. You know the book I'm talking about, Daddy, the Book of the Martyrs, the first picture was a bust of Spartacus . . . Socrates? I wish there was something like that for the children, Mommy, to give them what you. . . . (And the tears splashed again.)

(What I intended and did not? Stop it, daughter, stop it, leave that time. And he, the hyprocrite, sitting there with tears in his eyes—it was nothing to you then, nothing.)

. . . The time you came to school and I almost died of shame because of your accent and because I knew you knew I was ashamed; how could I? . . . Sammy's harmonica and you danced to it once, yes you did, you and Davy squealing in your arms. . . . That time you bundled us up and walked us down to the railway station to stay the night 'cause it was heated and we didn't have any coal, that winter of the strike, you didn't think I remembered that, did you, Mommy? . . . How you'd call us out to see the sunsets. . . .

Day after day, the spilling memories. Worse now, questions, too. Even the grandchildren: Grandma, in the olden days, when you were little. . . .

It was the afternoons that saved.

While they thought she napped, she would leave the mosaic on the wall (of children's drawings, maps, calendars, pictures, Ann's cardboard dolls with their great ringed questioning eyes) and hunch in the girls' closet on the low shelf where the shoes stood, and the girls' dresses covered.

For that while she would painfully sheathe against the listening house, the tendrils and noises that knocked, and Vivi's spilling memories. Sometimes it helped to braid and unbraid the sashes that dangled, or to trace the pattern on the hoop slips.

Today she had jacks and children under jet trails to forget. Last night, Ann and Dody silhouetted in the window against a sunset of flaming man-made clouds of jet trail, their jacks ball accenting the peaceful noise of dinner being made. Had she told them, yes she had told them of how they played jacks in her village though there was no ball, no jacks. Six stones, round and flat, toss them out, the seventh on the back of the hand, toss, catch, and swoop up as many as possible, toss again. . . .

Of stones (repeating Richard) there are three kinds: earth's fire jetting; rock of layered centuries; crucibled new out of the old (*igneous, sedimentary, metamorphic*). But there was that other—frozen to black glass, never to transform or hold the fossil memory . . . (let not my seed fall on stone). There was an ancient man who fought to heights a great rock that crashed back down eternally—eternal labor, freedom, labor . . . (stone will perish, but the word remain). And you, David, who with a stone slew, screaming: Lord, take my heart of stone and give me flesh

Who was screaming? Why was she back in the common room of the prison, the sun motes dancing in the shafts of light, and the informer being brought in, a prisoner now, like themselves. And Lisa leaping, yes, Lisa, the gentle and tender, biting at the betrayer's jugular. Screaming and screaming.

No, it is the children screaming. Another of Paul and Sammy's terrible fights?

In Vivi's house. Severely: you are in Vivi's house.

Blows, screams, a call: "Grandma!" For her? Oh please not for her. Hide, hunch behind the dresses deeper. But a trembling little body hurls itself beside her—surprised, smothered laughter, arms surround her neck, tears rub dry on her cheek, and words too soft to understand whisper into her ear (Is this where you hide too, Grammy? It's my secret place, we have a secret now).

And the sweat beads, and the long shudder seizes.

It seemed the great ear pressed inside now, and the knocking. "We have to go home," she told him, "I grow ill here."

"It's your own fault, Mrs. Bodybusy, you do not rest, you do too much." He raged, but the fear was in his eyes. "It was a serious operation, they told you to take care. . . . All right, we will go to where you can rest."

But where? Not home to death, not yet. He had thought to Lennie's, to Clara's; beautiful visits with each of the children. She would have to rest first, be stronger. If they could but go to Florida—it glittered before him, the never-realized promise of Florida. California: of course. (The money, the money, dwindling!) Los Angeles first for sun and rest, then to Lennie's in San Francisco.

He told her the next day. "You saw what Nancy wrote: snow and wind back home, a terrible winter. And look at you—all bones and a swollen belly. I called Phil: he said: 'A prescription, Los Angeles sun and rest.'"

She watched the words on his lips. "You have sold the house," she cried, "that is why we do not go home. That is why you talk no more of the Haven, why there is money for travel. After the children you will drag me to the Haven."

"The Haven! Who thinks of the Haven any more? Tell her, Vivi, tell Mrs. Suspicious: a prescription, sun and rest, to make you healthy. . . . And how could I sell the house without *you?*"

At the place of farewells and greetings, of winds of coming and winds of going, they say their good-byes.

They look back at her with the eyes of others before them: Richard with her own blue blaze; Ann with the nordic eyes of Tim; Morty's dreaming brown of a great-grandmother he will never know; Dody with the laughing eyes of him who had been her springtide love (who stand beside her now); Vivi's, all tears.

The baby's eyes are closed in sleep.

Good-bye, my children.

3

It is to the back of the great city he brought her, to the dwelling places of the cast-off old. Bounded by two lines of amusement piers to the north and to the south, and between a long straight paving rimmed with black benches facing the sand—sands so wide the ocean is only a far fluting.

In the brief vacation season, some of the boarded stores fronting the sands open, and families, young people and children, may be seen. A little tasseled tram shuttles between the piers, and the lights of roller coasters prink and tweak over those who come to have sensation made in them.

The rest of the year it is abandoned to the old, all else boarded up and still; seemingly empty, except the occasional days and hours when the sun, like a tide, sucks them out of the low rooming houses, casts them onto the benches and sandy rim of the walk—and sweeps them into decaying enclosures once again.

A few newer apartments glint among the low bleached squares. It is in one of these Lennie's Jeannie has arranged their rooms. "Only a few miles north and south people pay hundreds of dollars a month for just this gorgeous air, Grandaddy, just this ocean closeness."

She had been ill on the plane, lay ill for days in the unfamiliar room. Several times the doctor came by—left medicine she would not take. Several times Jeannie drove in the twenty miles from work, still in her Visiting Nurse uniform, the lightness and brightness of her like a healing.

"Who can believe it is winter?" he asked one morning. "Beautiful it is outside like an ad. Come, Mrs. Invalid, come to taste it. You are well enough to sit in here, you are well enough to sit outside. The doctor said it too."

But the benches were encrusted with people, and the sands at the sidewalk's edge. Besides, she had seen the far ruffle of the sea: "there take me," and though she leaned against him, it was she who led.

Plodding and plodding, sitting often to rest, he grumbling. Patting the sand so warm. Once she scooped up a handful, cradling it close to her better eye; peered, and flung it back. And as they came almost to the brink and she could see the glistening wet, she sat down, pulled off her shoes and stockings, left him and began to run. "You'll catch cold," he screamed, but the sand in his shoes weighed him down—he who had always been the agile one—and already the white spray creamed her feet.

He pulled her back, took a handkerchief to wipe off the wet and the sand. "Oh no," she said, "the sun will dry," seized the square and smoothed it flat, dropped on it a mound of sand, knotted the kerchief corners and tied it to a bag—"to look at with the strong glass" (for the first time in years explaining an action of hers)—and lay down with the little bag against her cheek, looking toward the shore that nurtured life as it first crawled toward consciousness the millions of years ago.

He took her one Sunday in the evil-smelling bus, past flat miles of blister houses, to the home of relatives. Oh what is this? she cried as the light began to smoke and the houses to dim and recede. Smog, he said, everyone knows but you. . . . Outside he kept his arms about her, but she walked with hands pushing the heavy air as if to open it, whispered: who has done this? sat down suddenly to vomit at the curb and for a long while refused to rise.

One's age as seen on the altered face of those known in youth. Is this they he has come to visit? This Max and Rose, smooth and pleasant, introducing them to polite children, disinterested grandchildren, "the whole family, once a month on Sundays. And why not? We have the room, the help, the food."

Talk of cars, of houses, of success: this son that, that daughter this. And *your* children? Hastily skimped over, the intermarriages, the obscure work—"my doctor son-in-law, Phil"—all he has to offer. She silent in a corner. (Carsick like a baby, he explains.) Years since he has taken her to visit anyone but the children, and old apprehensions prickle: "no incidents," he silently begs, "no incidents." He itched to tell them. "A very sick woman," significantly, indicating her with his eyes, "a very sick woman." Their restricted faces did not react. "Have you thought maybe she'd do better at Palm Springs?" Rose asked. "Or at least a nicer section of the beach, nicer people, a pool." Not to have to say "money" he said instead: "would she have sand to look at through a magnifying glass?" and went on, detail after detail, the old habit betraying of parading the queerness of her for laughter.

After dinner—the others into the living room in men- or women-clusters, or into the den to watch TV—the four of them alone. She sat close to him, and did not speak. Jokes, stories, people they had known, beginning of reminiscence, Russia fifty-sixty years ago. Strange words across the Duncan Phyfe table: *hunger; secret meetings; human rights; spies; betrayals; prison; escape*—interrupted by one of the grandchildren: "Commercial's on; any Coke left? Gee, you're missing a real hair-raiser." And then a granddaughter (Max proudly: "look at her, an American queen") drove them home on her way back to UCLA. No incident—except that there had been no incidents.

The first few mornings she had taken with her the magnifying glass, but he would sit only on the benches, so she rested at the foot, where slatted bench shadows fell, and unless she turned her hearing aid down, other voices invaded.

Now on the days when the sun shone and she felt well enough, he took her on the tram to where the benches ranged in oblongs, some with tables for checkers or cards. Again the blanket on the sand in the striped shadows, but she no longer brought the magnifying glass. He played cards, and she lay in the sun and looked toward the waters; or they walked—two blocks down to the scaling hotel, two blocks back—past chili-hamburger stands, open-doored bars, Next-to-New and perpetual rummage sale stores.

Once, out of the aimless walkers, slow and shuffling like themselves, someone ran unevenly toward them, embraced, kissed, wept: "dear friends, old friends." A friend of *hers*, not his: Mrs. Mays who had lived next door to them in Denver when the children were small.

Thirty years are compressed into a dozen sentences; and the present, not even in three. All is told: the children scattered; the husband dead; she lives in a room two blocks up from the sing hall—and points to the domed auditorium jutting before the pier. The leg? phlebitis; the heavy breathing? that, one does not ask. She, too, comes to the benches each day to sit. And tomorrow, tomorrow, are they going to the community sing? Of course he would have heard of it, everybody goes—the big doings they wait for all week. They have never been? She will come to them for dinner tomorrow and they will all go together.

So it is that she sits in the wind of the singing, among the thousand various faces of age.

She had turned off her hearing aid at once they came into the auditorium—as she would have wished to turn off sight.

One by one they streamed by and imprinted on her—and though the savage zest of their singing came voicelessly soft and distant, the faces still roared—the faces densened the air—chorded into

children-chants, mother-croons, singing of the chained love serenades, Beethoven storms, mad Lucia's scream drunken joy-songs, keens for the dead, work-singing

> *while from floor to balcony to dome a bare-footed sore-covered little girl threaded the sound-thronged tumult, danced her ecstasy of grimace to flutes that scratched at a crossroads village wedding*

Yes, faces became sound, and the sound became faces; and faces and sound became weight—pushed, pressed

"Air"—her hands claw his.

"Whenever I enjoy myself. . . ." Then he saw the gray sweat on her face. "Here. Up. Help me, Mrs. Mays," and they support her out to where she can gulp the air in sob after sob.

"A doctor, we should get for her a doctor."

"Tch, it's nothing," says Ellen Mays, "I get it all the time. You've missed the tram; come to my place. Fix your hearing aid, honey . . . close . . . tea. My view. See, she *wants* to come. Steady now, that's how." Adding mysteriously: "Remember your advice, easy to keep your head above water, empty things float. Float."

The singing a fading march for them, tall woman with a swollen leg, weaving little man, and the swollen thinness they help between.

The stench in the hall: mildew? decay? "We sit and rest then climb. My gorgeous view. We help each other and here   we   are."

The stench along into the slab of room. A washstand for a sink, a box with oilcloth tacked around for a cupboard, a three-burner gas plate. Artificial flowers, colorless with dust. Everywhere pictures foaming: wedding, baby, party, vacation, graduation, family pictures. From the narrow couch under a slit of window, sure enough the view: lurching rooftops and a scallop of ocean heaving, preening, twitching under the moon.

"While the water heats. Excuse me . . . down the hall." Ellen Mays has gone.

"You'll live?" he asks mechanically, sat down to feel his fright; tried to pull her alongside.

She pushed him away. "For air," she said; stood clinging to the dresser. Then, in a terrible voice:

After a lifetime of room. Of many rooms.

Shhh.

You remember how she lived. Eight children. And now one room   like a coffin.

She pays rent!

Shrinking the life of her   into one room   like a coffin   Rooms and rooms like this   I lie on the quilt and hear them talk

Please, Mrs. Orator-without-Breath.

Once you went for coffee   I walked   I saw   A Balzac   a Chekhov to write it   Rummage   Alone   On scraps

Better old here than in the old country!

On scraps   Yet they sang like   like   Wondrous!

Humankind   one has to believe   So strong   for what? To rot   not grow?

Your poor lungs beg you. They   sob   between   each   word.

Singing.   Unused   the life in them. She   in this poor room   with her pictures Max   You   The children   Everywhere unused the life   And who has meaning?   Century after century   still all in us   not   to grow?

Coffins, rummage, plants: sick woman. Oh lay down. We will get for you the doctor.

"And when will it end. Oh, *the end.*" *That* nightmare thought, and this time she writhed, crumpled against him, seized his hand (for a moment again the weight, the soft distant roaring of humanity) and on the strangled-for breath, begged: "Man . . . we'll destroy ourselves?"

And looking for answer—in the helpless pity and fear for her (for *her*) that distorted his face—she understood the last months, and knew that she was dying.

4

"Let us go home," she said after several days.

"You are in training for a cross-country run? That is why you do not even walk across the room? Here, like a prescription Phil said, till you are stronger from the operation. You want to break doctor's orders?"

She saw the fiction was necessary to him, was silent; then: "At home I will get better. If the doctor here says?"

"And winter? And the visits to Lennie and to Clara? All right," for he saw the tears in her eyes, "I will write Phil, and talk to the doctor."

Days passed. He reported nothing. Jeannie came and took her out for air, past the boarded concessions, the hooded and tented amusement rides, to the end of the pier. They watched the spent waves feeding the new, the gulls in the clouded sky; even up where they sat, the windblown sand stung.

She did not ask to go down the crooked steps to the sea.

Back in her bed, while he was gone to the store, she said: "Jeannie, this doctor, he is not one I can ask questions. Ask him for me, can I go home?"

Jeannie looked at her, said quickly: "Of course, poor Granny. You want your own things around you, don't you? I'll call him tonight. . . . Look, I've something to show you," and from her purse unwrapped a large cookie, intricately shaped like a little girl. "Look at the curls—can you hear me well, Granny?—and the darling eyelashes. I just came from a house where they were baking them."

"The dimples, there in the knees," she marveled, holding it to the better light, turning, studying, "like art. Each singly they cut, or a mold?"

"Singly," said Jeannie, "and if it is a child only the mother can make them. Oh Granny, it's the likeness of a real little girl who died yesterday—

Rosita. She was three years old. Pan del Muerto, the Bread of the Dead. It was the custom in the part of Mexico they came from."

Still she turned and inspected. "Look, the hollow in the throat, the little cross necklace. . . . I think for the mother it is a good thing to be busy with such bread. You know the family?"

Jeannie nodded. "On my rounds. I nursed. . . . Oh Granny, it is like a party; they play songs she liked to dance to. The coffin is lined with pink velvet and she wears a white dress. There are candles. . . ."

"In the house?" Surprised, "They keep her in the house?"

"Yes," said Jeannie, "and it is against the health law. The father said it will be sad to bury her in this country; in Oaxaca they have a feast night with candles each year; everyone picnics on the graves of those they loved until dawn."

"Yes, Jeannie, the living must comfort themselves." And closed her eyes.

"You want to sleep, Granny?"

"Yes, tired from the pleasure of you. I may keep the Rosita? There stand it, on the dresser, where I can see; something of my own around me."

In the kitchenette, helping her grandfather unpack the groceries, Jeannie said in her light voice:

"I'm resigning my job, Grandaddy."

"Ah, the lucky young man. Which one is he?"

"Too late. You're spoken for." She made a pyramid of cans, unstacked, and built again.

"Something is wrong with the job?"

"With me. I can't be"—she searched for the word—"What they call professional enough. I let myself feel things. And tomorrow I have to report a family. . . ." The cans clicked again. "It's not that, either. I just don't know what I want to do, maybe go back to school, maybe go to art school. I thought if you went to San Francisco I'd come along and talk it over with Momma and Daddy. But I don't see how you can go. She wants to go home. She asked me to ask the doctor."

The doctor told her himself. "Next week you may travel, when you are a little stronger." But next week there was the fever of an infection, and by the time that was over, she could not leave the bed—a rented hospital bed that stood beside the double bed he slept in alone now.

Outwardly the days repeated themselves. Every other afternoon and evening he went out to his newfound cronies, to talk and play cards. Twice a week, Mrs. Mays came. And the rest of the time, Jeannie was there.

By the sickbed stood Jeannie's FM radio. Often into the room the shapes of music came. She would lie curled on her side, her knees drawn up, intense in listening (Jeannie sketched her so, coiled, convoluted like an ear), then thresh her hand out and abruptly snap the radio mute—still to lie in her attitude of listening, concealing tears.

Once Jeannie brought in a young Marine to visit, a friend from high-school days she had found wandering near the empty pier. Because Jeannie asked him to, gravely, without self-consciousness, he sat himself cross-legged on the floor and performed for them a dance of his native Samoa.

Long after they left, a tiny thrumming sound could be heard where, in her bed, she strove to repeat the beckon, flight, surrender of his hands, the fluttering footbeats, and his low plaintive calls.

Hannah and Phil sent flowers. To deepen her pleasure, he placed one in her hair. "Like a girl," he said, and brought the hand mirror so she could see. She looked at the pulsing red flower, the yellow skull face; a desolate, excited laugh shuddered from her, and she pushed the mirror away—but let the flower burn.

The week Lennie and Helen came, the fever returned. With it the excited laugh, and incessant words. She, who in her life had spoken but seldom and then only when necessary (never having learned the easy, social uses of words), now in dying, spoke incessantly.

In a half-whisper: "Like Lisa she is, your Jeannie. Have I told you of Lisa who taught me to read? Of the highborn she was, but noble in herself. I was sixteen; they beat me; my father beat me so I would not go to her. It was forbidden, she was a Tolstoyan. At night, past dogs that howled, terrible dogs, my son, in the snows of winter to the road, I to ride in her carriage like a lady, to books. To her, life was holy, knowledge was holy, and she taught me to read. They hung her. Everything that happens one must try to understand why. She killed one who betrayed many. Because of betrayal, betrayed all she lived and believed. In one minute she killed, before my eyes (there is so much blood in a human being, my son), in prison with me. All that happens, one must try to understand.

"The name?" Her lips would work. "The name that was their pole star; the doors of the death houses fixed to open on it; I read of it my year of penal servitude. Thuban!" very excited, "Thuban, in ancient Egypt the pole star. Can you see, look out to see it, Jeannie, if it swings around *our* pole star that seems to *us* not to move.

"Yes, Jeannie, at your age my mother and grandmother had already buried children . . . yes, Jeannie, it is more than oceans between Olshana and you . . . yes, Jeannie, they danced, and for all the bodies they had they might as well be chickens, and indeed, they scratched and flapped their arms and hopped.

"And Andrei Yefimitch, who for twenty years had never known of it and never wanted to know, said as if he wanted to cry: but why my dear friend this malicious laughter?" Telling to herself half-memorized phrases from her few books. "Pain I answer with tears and cries, baseness with indignation, meanness with repulsion . . . for life may be hated or wearied of, but never despised."

Delirious: "Tell me, my neighbor, Mrs. Mays, the pictures never lived, but what of the flowers? Tell them who ask: no rabbis, no ministers, no priests, no speeches, no ceremonies: ah, false—let the living comfort themselves. Tell Sammy's boy, he who flies, tell him to go to Stuttgart and see where Davy has no grave. And what? . . . And what? Where millions have no graves—save air."

In delirium or not, wanting the radio on; not seeming to listen, the words still jetting, wanting the music on. Once, silencing it abruptly as of old, she began to cry, unconcealed tears this time. "You have pain, Granny?" Jeannie asked.

"The music," she said, "still it is there and we do not hear; knocks, and our poor human ears too weak. What else, what else we do not hear?"

Once she knocked his hand aside as he gave her a pill, swept the bottles from her bedside table: "no pills, let me feel what I feel," and laughed as on his hands and knees he groped to pick them up.

Nighttimes her hand reached across the bed to hold his.

A constant retching began. Her breath was too faint for sustained speech now, but still the lips moved:

When no longer necessary   to injure others
Pick   pick pick   Blind chicken
As a human being   responsibility

"David!" imperious, "Basin!" and she would vomit, rinse her mouth, the wasted throat working to swallow, and begin the chant again.

She will be better off in the hospital now, the doctor said.

He sent the telegrams to the children, was packing her suitcase, when her hoarse voice startled. She had roused, was pulling herself to sitting.

"Where now?" she asked. "Where now do you drag me?"

"You do not even have to have a baby to go this time," he soothed, looking for the brush to pack. "Remember, after Davy you told me—worthy to have a baby for the pleasure of the ten-day rest in the hospital?"

"Where now? Not home yet?" Her voice mourned. "Where *is* my home?"

He rose to ease her back. "The doctor, the hospital," he started to explain, but deftly, like a snake, she had slithered out of bed and stood swaying, propped behind the night table.

"Coward," she hissed, "runner."

"You stand," he said senselessly.

"To take me there and run. Afraid of a little vomit."

He reached her as she fell. She struggled against him, half slipped from his arms, pulled herself up again.

"Weakling," she taunted, "to leave me there and run. Betrayer. All your life you have run."

He sobbed, telling Jeannie. "A Marilyn Monroe to run for her virtue. Fifty-nine pounds she weighs, the doctor said, and she beats at me like a Dempsey. Betrayer, she cries, and I running like a dog when she calls; day and night, running to her, her vomit, the bedpan. . . ."

"She needs you, Grandaddy," said Jeannie. "Isn't that what they call love? I'll see if she sleeps, and if she does, poor worn-out darling, we'll have a party, you and I: I brought us rum babas."

They did not move her. By her bed now stood the tall hooked pillar that held the solutions—blood and dextrose—to feed her veins. Jeannie moved down the hall to take over the sickroom, her face so radiant, her grandfather asked her once: "you are in love?" (Shameful the joy, the pure overwhelming joy from being with her grandmother; the peace, the serenity that breathed.) "My darling escape," she answered incoherently, "my darling Granny"—as if that explained.

Now one by one the children came, those that were able. Hannah, Paul, Sammy. Too late to ask: and what did you learn with your living, Mother, and what do we need to know?

Clara, the eldest, clenched:

> *Pay me back, Mother, pay me back for all you took from me. Those others you crowded into your heart. The hands I needed to be for you, the heaviness, the responsibility.*
>
> *Is this she? Noises the dying make, the crablike hands crawling over the covers. The ethereal singing.*
>
> *She hears that music, that singing from childhood; forgotten sound—not heard since, since. . . . And the hardness breaks like a cry:*

Where did we lose each other, first mother, singing mother?
    Annulled: the quarrels, the gibing, the harshness between; the fall into silence and the withdrawal.
    I do not know you, Mother. Mother, I never knew you.

Lennie, suffering not alone for her who was dying, but for that in her which never lived (for that which in him might never live). From him too, unspoken words: *good-bye Mother who taught me to mother myself.*

Not Vivi, who must stay with her children; not Davy, but he is already here, having to die again with *her* this time, for the living take their dead with them when they die.

Light she grew, like a bird, and, like a bird, sound bubbled in her throat while the body fluttered in agony. Night and day, asleep or awake (though indeed there was no difference now) the songs and the phrases leaping.

And he, who had once dreaded a long dying (from fear of himself, from horror of the dwindling money) now desired her quick death profoundly, for *her* sake. He no longer went out, except when Jeannie forced him; no longer laughed, except when, in the bright kitchenette, Jeannie coaxed his laughter (and she, who seemed to hear nothing else, would laugh too, conspiratorial wisps of laughter).

Light, like a bird, the fluttering body, the little claw hands, the beaked shadow on her face; and the throat, bubbling, straining.

He tried not to listen, as he tried not to look on the face in which only the forehead remained familiar, but trapped with her the long nights in that little room, the sounds worked themselves into his consciousness, with their punctuation of death swallows, whimpers, gurglings.

Even in reality (swallow) *life's lack of it*
Slaveships   deathtrains clubs   eeenough
The bell   summon what enables
78,000 in one minute   (whisper of a scream)   *78,000 human beings   we'll destroy ourselves?*

"Aah, Mrs. Miserable," he said, as if she could hear, "all your life working, and now in bed you lie, servants to tend, you do not even need to call to be tended, and still you work. Such hard work it is to die? Such hard work?"

The body threshed, her hand clung in his. A melody, ghost-thin, hovered on her lips, and like a guilty ghost, the vision of her bent in listening to it, silencing the record instantly he was near. Now, heedless of his presence, she floated the melody on and on.

"Hid it from me," he complained, "how many times you listened to remember it so?" And tried to think when she had first played it, or first begun to silence her few records when he came near—but could reconstruct nothing. There was only this room with its tall hooked pillar and its swarm of sounds.

No man one   except through others
Strong   with the not yet   in the now
Dogma dead   war dead   one country

"It helps, Mrs. Philosopher, words from books? It helps?" And it seemed to him that for seventy years she had hidden a tape recorder, infinitely microscopic, within her, that it had coiled infinite mile on mile, trapping every song, every melody, every word read, heard, and spoken—and that maliciously she was playing back only what said nothing of him, of the children, of their intimate life together.

"Left us indeed, Mrs. Babbler," he reproached, "you who called others babbler and cunningly saved your words. A lifetime you tended and loved, and now not a word of us, for us. Left us indeed? Left me."

And he took out his solitaire deck, shuffled the cards loudly, slapped them down.

Lift high   banner of reason   (tatter of an orator's voice)
justice   freedom   light
    Humankind   life worthy   capacities
    Seeks (blur of shudder) *belong   human being*

"Words, words," he accused, "and what human beings did *you* seek around you, Mrs. Live Alone, and what humankind think worthy?"

Though even as he spoke, he remembered she had not always been isolated, had not always wanted to be alone (as he knew there had been a voice before this gossamer one; before the hoarse voice that broke from silence to lash, make incidents, shame him—a girl's voice of eloquence that spoke their holiest dreams). But again he could reconstruct, image, nothing of what had been before, or when, or how, it had changed.

Ace, queen, jack. The pillar shadow fell, so, in two tracks; in the mirror depths glistened a moonlike blob, the empty solution bottle. And it worked in him: *of reason and justice and freedom* . . . *Dogma dead:* he remembered the full quotation, laughed bitterly. "Hah, good you do not know what you say; good Victor Hugo died and did not see it, his twentieth century."

Deuce, ten, five. Dauntlessly she began a song of their youth of belief:

These things shall be, a loftier race
than e'er the world hath known shall rise
with flame of freedom in their souls
and light of knowledge in their eyes

King, four, jack "In the twentieth century, hah!"

They shall be gentle, brave, and strong
to spill no drop of blood, but dare all . . .
on earth and fire and sea and air

"To spill no drop of blood, hah! So, cadaver, and you too, cadaver Hugo, 'in the twentieth century ignorance will be dead, dogma will be dead, war will be dead, and for all mankind one country—of fulfillment?' Hah!"

And every life (long strangling cough) *shall be a song*

The cards fell from his fingers. Without warning, the bereavement and betrayal he had sheltered—compounded through the years—hidden even from himself—revealed itself,
    uncoiled,
    released,
    sprung

and with it the monstrous shapes of what had actually happened in the century.

A ravening hunger or thirst seized him. He groped into the kitchenette, switched on all three lights, piled a tray—"you have finished your night snack, Mrs. Cadaver, now I will have mine." And he was shocked at the tears that splashed on the tray.

"Salt tears. For free. I forgot to shake on salt?"

Whispered: "Lost, how much I lost."

Escaped to the grandchildren whose childhoods were childish, who had never hungered, who lived unravaged by disease in warm houses of many rooms, had all the school for which they cared, could walk on any street, stood a head taller than their grandparents, towered above—beautiful skins, straight backs, clear straightforward eyes. "Yes, you in Olshana," he said to the town of sixty years ago, "they would be nobility to you."

And was this not the dream then, come true in ways undreamed? he asked.

And are there no other children in the world? he answered, as if in her harsh voice.

And the flame of freedom, the light of knowledge?

And the drop, to spill no drop of blood?

And he thought that at six Jeannie would get up and it would be his turn to go to her room and sleep, that he could press the buzzer and she would come now; that in the afternoon Ellen Mays was coming, and this time they would play cards and he could marvel at how rouge can stand half an inch on the cheek; that in the evening the doctor would come, and he could beg him to be merciful, to stop the feeding solutions, to let her die.

To let her die, and with her their youth of belief out of which her bright, betrayed words foamed; stained words, that on her working lips came stainless.

Hours yet before Jeannie's turn. He could press the buzzer and wake her to come now; he could take a pill, and with it sleep; he could pour more brandy into his milk glass, though what he had poured was not yet touched.

Instead he went back, checked her pulse, gently tended with his knotty fingers as Jeannie had taught.

She was whimpering; her hand crawled across the covers for his. Compassionately he enfolded it, and with his free hand gathered up the cards again. Still was there thirst or hunger ravening in him.

That world of their youth—dark, ignorant, terrible with hate and disease—how was it that living in it, in the midst of corruption, filth, treachery, degradation, they had not mistrusted man nor themselves; had believed so beautifully, so . . . falsely?

"Aaah, children," he said out loud, "how we believed, how we belonged." And he yearned to package for each of the children, the grandchildren, for everyone, *that joyous certainty, that sense of mattering, of moving and being moved, of being one and indivisible with the great of the past, with all that freed, ennobled.* Package it, stand on corners, in front of stadiums and on crowded beaches, knock on doors, give it as a fabled gift.

"And why not in cereal boxes, in soap packages?" he mocked himself. "Aah. You have taken my senses, cadaver."

Words foamed, died unsounded. Her body writhed; she made kissing motions with her mouth. (Her lips moving as she read, poring over the Book of the Martyrs, the magnifying glass superimposed over the heavy eyeglasses.) *Still she believed?* "Eva!" he whispered. "Still you believed? You lived by it? These Things Shall Be?" "One pound soup meat," she answered distinctly, "one soup bone."

"My ears heard you. Ellen Mays was witness: 'Humankind . . . one has to believe.'" Imploringly: "Eva!"

"Bread, day-old." She was mumbling. "Please, in a wooden box . . . for kindling. The thread, hah, the thread breaks. Cheap thread"—and a gurgling, enormously loud, began in her throat.

"I ask for stone; she gives me bread—day-old." He pulled his hand away, shouted: "Who wanted questions? Everything you have to wake?" Then dully, "Ah, let me help you turn, poor creature."

Words jumbled, cleared. In a voice of crowded terror:

"Paul, Sammy, don't fight."

"Hannah, have I ten hands?"

"How can I give it, Clara, how can I give it if I don't have?"

"You lie," he said sturdily, "there was joy too." Bitterly: "Ah how cheap you speak of us at the last."

As if to rebuke him, as if her voice had no relationship with her flailing body, she sang clearly, beautifully, a school song the children had taught her when they were little; begged:

"Not look   my hair   where they cut . . . ."

(The crown of braids shorn.) And instantly he left the mute old woman poring over the Book of the Martyrs; went past the mother treading at the sewing machine, singing with the children; past the girl in her wrinkled prison dress, hiding her hair with scarred hands, lifting to him her awkward, shamed, imploring eyes of love; and took her in his arms, dear, personal, fleshed, in all the heavy passion he had loved to rouse from her.

"Eva!"

Her little claw hand beat the covers. How much, how much can a man stand? He took up the cards, put them down, circled the beds, walked to the dresser, opened, shut drawers, brushed his hair, moved his hand bit by bit over the mirror to see what of the reflection he could blot out with each move, and felt that at any moment he would die of what was unendurable. Went to press the buzzer to wake Jeannie, looked down, saw on Jeannie's sketch pad the hospital bed, with *her*; the double bed alongside, with him; the tall pillar feeding into her veins, and their hands, his and hers, clasped, feeding each other. And as if he had been instructed he went to his bed, lay down, holding the sketch (as if it could shield against the monstrous shapes of loss, of betrayal, of death) and with his free hand took hers back into his.

So Jeannie found them in the morning.

That last day the agony was perpetual. Time after time it lifted her almost off the bed, so they had to fight to hold her down. He could not endure and left the room; wept as if there never would be tears enough.

Jeannie came to comfort him. In her light voice she said: Grandaddy, Grandaddy don't cry. She is not there, she promised me. On the last day, she said she would go back to when she first heard music, a little girl on the road of the village where she was born. She promised me. It is a wedding and they dance, while the flutes so joyous and vibrant tremble in the air. Leave her there, Grandaddy, it is all right. She promised me. Come back, come back and help her poor body to die.

For two of that generation
Seevya and Genya
Infinite, dauntless, incorruptible

Death deepens the wonder

QUESTIONS

1. Why is Eva's greatest wish "never again to be forced to move to the rhythms of others"? How does it compare to David's wish "to be free, to be carefree" at the Haven? (471, 469)

2. Why does Eva go out singing in the rain after the week in which she and David slept apart and did not speak?

3. Why is Eva happy in the hospital after the surgery?

4. Why is Eva so opposed to Hannah's observance of Jewish traditions? Why is she convinced that religion is part of "our savage past"? (480)

5. While she was raising her children, what was lost in Eva's "painful damming back and drying up of what still surged, but had nowhere to go"? (481)

6. Why can't Eva bear to touch her baby grandson after holding him once?

7. Why does Eva think "I know no riddles" when one of her grandchildren asks her to tell one? (483)

8. Why are Vivi's memories and the grandchildren's questions such a torment to Eva?

9. Why does seeing Mrs. Mays again and going to the community sing upset Eva so much? After escaping the community sing, why does Eva realize that she is dying?

10. When Lennie and Helen visit, why does Eva suddenly talk so freely? Why does Eva find it easier to talk to Jeannie than to Vivi?

11. Why, after seeing Jeannie's sketch, does David lie down beside Eva and recreate the pose in it?

12. While she is dying, why does Eva sing "These Things Shall Be"?

FOR FURTHER REFLECTION

1. Why does David give Eva so many nicknames (Mrs. Babbler, Mrs. Cadaver, etc.)?

2. What makes Eva change from being an orator in the 1905 Russian revolution to a woman who rarely speaks?

3. How much responsibility does David bear for Eva's bitterness?

4. Is the story suggesting that belief in human progress is an illusion? Are we intended to see Eva and David's children as better or worse off than their parents?

5. Is it selfish to wish to live for oneself rather than for others?

6. When Eva sings "These Things Shall Be," David is overcome with grief at the wars and suffering the twentieth century produced. Do you think it is possible to have hope for human progress after the events of the twentieth and twenty-first centuries?

7. Can a woman spend a great deal of time nurturing others without losing herself?

ALICE MUNRO

Alice Munro, a three-time winner of the Governor General's Literary Award for fiction in Canada and a preeminent master of the short story in the English-speaking world, was born Alice Laidlaw in 1931 in the small rural town of Wingham, Ontario. She began writing short stories when she was fifteen. She did this during her lunch hour, isolating herself in a schoolroom and not showing the work to anyone she knew, for writing wasn't considered typical for teenage girls in Wingham. Munro has told one interviewer: "We lived outside the whole social structure because we didn't live in the town and we didn't live in the country. We lived in this kind of little ghetto where all the bootleggers and prostitutes and hangers-on lived. Those were the people I knew. It was a community of outcasts. I had that feeling about myself." Many of Munro's narrators and protagonists exhibit the tension displayed by Munro's own early awareness: they understand that they are individually *different* from anyone around them, but they are also quite preoccupied with questions of social harmony, with how they fit their society's immediate expectations.

Munro published her first story when she was eighteen, in the student literary magazine *Folio* at the University of Western Ontario. At the university on a two-year scholarship, she left at the end of that time because she was out of money. During the 1950s, shortly after marrying James Munro, she moved with him to a Vancouver suburb, where she gave birth to two daughters and continued to write fiction. In 1963, the family moved to Victoria, where she and her husband opened a bookstore, Munro's Books, and had another daughter. The stories Munro was writing soon began to find markets in small literary magazines, and, in 1968, she published her first collection, *Dance of the Happy Shades*. The book won the Governor General's Award for fiction in 1968 and marked the start of Munro's literary recognition and success. She has published ten collections of stories since.

"Boys and Girls," one of the stories in this first collection, was written when Munro was thirty-five. It shows Munro beginning to extensively use early childhood experience as material for her fiction, including the hardscrabble economics of the Depression—her father, Robert Laidlaw, was for a time an unsuccessful fox farmer—and her feelings of isolation growing up within the Huron County milieu. The expectations of gender weigh heavily in this story, and the narrator's preoccupation with events freighted with ritualistic meaning is characteristic of Munro's best work. This viewpoint continues in her next collection of stories, *Lives of Girls and Women* (1971). If the coming-of-age story or rite-of-passage story has traditionally been a male preserve, Munro corrects such a view with a vengeance—not by arguing with it, but by creating in her stories unforgettable girls and women whose narrative voices compel us to listen.

Boys and Girls

My father was a fox farmer. That is, he raised silver foxes, in pens; and in the fall and early winter, when their fur was prime, he killed them and skinned them and sold their pelts to the Hudson's Bay Company or the Montreal Fur Traders. These companies supplied us with heroic calendars to hang, one on each side of the kitchen door. Against a background of cold blue sky and black pine forests and treacherous northern rivers, plumed adventurers planted the flags of England or of France; magnificent savages bent their backs to the portage.

For several weeks before Christmas, my father worked after supper in the cellar of our house. The cellar was whitewashed, and lit by a hundred-watt bulb over the worktable. My brother Laird and I sat on the top step and watched. My father removed the pelt inside-out from the body of the fox, which looked surprisingly small, mean, and ratlike, deprived of its arrogant weight of fur. The naked, slippery bodies were collected in a sack and buried at the dump. One time the hired man, Henry Bailey, had taken a swipe at me with this sack, saying, "Christmas present!" My mother thought that was not funny. In fact she disliked the whole pelting operation—that was what the killing, skinning, and preparation of the furs was called—and wished it did not have to take place in the house. There was the smell. After the pelt had been stretched inside-out on a long board my father scraped away delicately, removing the little clotted webs of blood vessels, the bubbles of fat; the smell of blood and animal fat, with the strong primitive odor of the fox itself, penetrated all parts of the house. I found it reassuringly seasonal, like the smell of oranges and pine needles.

Henry Bailey suffered from bronchial troubles. He would cough and cough until his narrow face turned scarlet, and his light blue, derisive eyes filled up with tears; then he took the lid off the stove and, standing well back, shot out a clot of phlegm—hsss—straight into the heart of the flames. We admired him for this performance and for his ability to make his stomach growl at will, and for his laughter, which was full of high whistlings and gurglings and involved the whole faulty machinery of his chest. It was sometimes hard to tell what he was laughing at, and always possible that it might be us.

After we had been sent to bed we could still smell fox and still hear Henry's laugh, but these things, reminders of the warm, safe, brightly lit downstairs world, seemed lost and diminished, floating on the stale cold air upstairs. We were afraid at night in the winter. We were not afraid of *outside* though this was the time of year when snowdrifts curled around our house like sleeping whales and the wind harassed us all night, coming up from the buried fields, the frozen swamp, with its old bugbear chorus of threats and misery. We were afraid of *inside*, the room where we slept. At this time the upstairs of our house was not finished. A brick chimney went up one wall. In the middle of the floor was a square hole, with a wooden railing around it; that was where the stairs came up. On the other side of the stairwell were the things that nobody had any use for any more—a soldiery roll of linoleum, standing on end, a wicker baby carriage, a fern basket, china jugs and basins with cracks in them, a picture of the Battle of Balaclava, very sad to look at. I had told Laird, as soon as he was old enough to understand such things, that bats and skeletons lived over there; whenever a man escaped from the county jail, twenty miles away, I imagined that he had somehow let himself in the window and was hiding behind the linoleum. But we had rules to keep us safe. When the light was on, we were safe as long as we did not step off the square of worn carpet which defined our bedroom-space; when the light was off no place was safe but the beds themselves. I had to turn out the light kneeling on the end of my bed, and stretching as far as I could to reach the cord.

In the dark we lay on our beds, our narrow life rafts, and fixed our eyes on the faint light coming up the stairwell, and sang songs. Laird sang "Jingle Bells," which he would sing any time, whether it was Christmas or not, and I sang "Danny Boy." I loved the sound of my own voice, frail and supplicating, rising in the dark. We could make out the tall frosted shapes of the windows now, gloomy and white. When I came to the part, *When I am dead, as dead I well may be*—a fit of shivering caused not by the cold sheets but by pleasurable emotion almost silenced me. *You'll kneel and say, an Ave there above me*—What was an Ave? Every day I forgot to find out.

Laird went straight from singing to sleep. I could hear his long, satisfied, bubbly breaths. Now for the time that remained to me, the most perfectly private and perhaps the best time of the whole day, I arranged myself tightly under the covers and went on with one of the stories I was telling myself from night to night. These stories were about myself, when I had grown a little older; they took place in a world that was recognizably mine, yet one that presented opportunities for courage, boldness and self-sacrifice, as mine ever did. I rescued people from a bombed building (it discouraged me that the real war had gone on so far away from Jubilee). I shot two rabid wolves who were menacing the schoolyard (the teachers cowered terrified at my back). I rode a fine horse spiritedly down the main street of Jubilee, acknowledging the townspeople's gratitude for some yet-to-be-worked-out piece of heroism (nobody ever rode a horse there, except King Billy in the Orangemen's Day parade). There was always riding and shooting in these stories, though I had only been on a horse twice—bareback because we did not own a saddle—and the second time I had slid right around and dropped under the horse's feet; it had stepped placidly over me. I really was learning to shoot, but I could not hit anything yet, not even tin cans on fence posts.

Alive, the foxes inhabited a world my father made for them. It was surrounded by a high guard fence, like a medieval town, with a gate that was padlocked at night. Along the streets of this town were ranged large, sturdy pens. Each of them had a real door that a man could go through, a wooden ramp along the wire, for the foxes to run up and down on, and a kennel—something like a clothes chest with airholes—where they slept and stayed in winter and had their young. There were feeding and watering dishes attached to the wire in such a way that they could be emptied and cleaned from the outside. The dishes were made of old tin cans, and the ramps and kennels of odds and ends of old lumber. Everything was tidy and ingenious; my father was tirelessly inventive and his favorite book in the world was *Robinson Crusoe*. He had fitted a tin drum on a wheelbarrow, for bringing water down to the pens. This was my job in summer, when the foxes had to have water twice a day. Between nine and ten o'clock in the morning, and again after supper, I filled the drum at the pump and trundled it down through the barnyard to the pens, where I parked it, and filled my watering can and went along the streets. Laird came too, with his little cream and green gardening can, filled too full and knocking against his legs and slopping water on his canvas shoes. I had the real watering can, my father's, though I could only carry it three-quarters full.

The foxes all had names, which were printed on a tin plate and hung beside their doors. They were not named when they were born, but when they survived the first year's pelting and were added to the breeding stock. Those my father had named were called names like Prince, Bob, Wally, and Betty. Those I had named were called Star or Turk, or

Maureen or Diana. Laird named one Maud after a hired girl we had when he was little, one Harold after a boy at school, and one Mexico, he did not say why.

Naming them did not make pets out of them, or anything like it. Nobody but my father ever went into the pens, and he had twice had blood poisoning from bites. When I was bringing them their water they prowled up and down on the paths they had made inside their pens, barking seldom—they saved that for nighttime, when they might get up a chorus of community frenzy—but always watching me, their eyes burning, clear gold, in their pointed, malevolent faces. They were beautiful for their delicate legs and heavy, aristocratic tails and the bright fur sprinkled on dark down their backs—which gave them their name—but especially for their faces, drawn exquisitely sharp in pure hostility, and their golden eyes.

Besides carrying water I helped my father when he cut the long grass, and the lamb's quarter and flowering money-musk, that grew between the pens. He cut with the scythe and I raked into piles. Then he took a pitchfork and threw fresh-cut grass all over the top of the pens, to keep the foxes cooler and shade their coats, which were browned by too much sun. My father did not talk to me unless it was about the job we were doing. In this he was quite different from my mother, who, if she was feeling cheerful, would tell me all sorts of things—the name of a dog she had had when she was a little girl, the names of boys she had gone out with later on when she was grown up, and what certain dresses of hers had looked like—she could not imagine now what had become of them. Whatever thoughts and stories my father had were private, and I was shy of him and would never ask him questions. Nevertheless I worked willingly under his eyes, and with a feeling of pride. One time a feed salesman came down into the pens to talk to him and my father said, "Like to have you meet my new hired man." I turned away and raked furiously, red in the face with pleasure.

"Could of fooled me," said the salesman. "I thought it was only a girl."

After the grass was cut, it seemed suddenly much later in the year. I walked on stubble in the earlier evening, aware of the reddening skies, the entering silences, of fall. When I wheeled the tank out of the gate and put the padlock on, it was almost dark. One night at this time I saw my mother and father standing talking on the little rise of ground we called the gangway, in front of the barn. My father had just come from the meathouse; he had his stiff bloody apron on, and a pail of cut-up meat in his hand.

It was an odd thing to see my mother down at the barn. She did not often come out of the house unless it was to do something—hang out the wash or dig potatoes in the garden. She looked out of place, with her bare lumpy legs, not touched by the sun, her apron still on and damp across the stomach from the supper dishes. Her hair was tied up in a kerchief, wisps of it falling out. She would tie her hair up like this in the morning, saying she did not have time to do it properly, and it would stay tied up all day. It was true, too; she really did not have time. These days our back porch was piled with baskets of peaches and grapes and pears, bought in town, and onions and tomatoes and cucumbers grown at home, all waiting to be made into jelly and jam and preserves, pickles, and chili sauce. In the kitchen there was a fire in the stove all day, jars clinked in boiling water, sometimes a cheesecloth bag was strung on a pole between two chairs straining blue-black grape pulp for jelly. I was given jobs to do and I would sit at the table peeling peaches that had been soaked in the hot water, or cutting up onions, my eyes smarting and streaming. As soon as I was done I ran out of the house, trying to get out of earshot before my mother thought of what she wanted me to do next. I hated the hot dark kitchen in summer, the green blinds and the flypapers, the same old oilcloth table and wavy mirror and bumpy linoleum. My mother was too tired and preoccupied to talk to me, she had no heart to tell about the Normal School Graduation Dance; sweat trickled over her face and she was always counting, under her breath, pointing at jars, dumping cups of sugar. It seemed to me that work in the house was endless, dreary, and peculiarly depressing; work done out of doors, and in my father's service, was ritualistically important.

I wheeled the tank up to the barn, where it was kept, and I heard my mother saying, "Wait till Laird gets a little bigger, then you'll have a real help."

What my father said I did not hear. I was pleased by the way he stood listening, politely as he would to a salesman or a stranger, but with an air of wanting to get on with his real work. I felt my mother had no business down here and I wanted him to feel the same way. What did she mean about Laird? He was no help to anybody. Where was he now? Swinging himself sick on the swing, going around in circles, or trying to catch caterpillars. He never once stayed with me till I was finished.

"And then I can use her more in the house," I heard my mother say. She had a dead-quiet, regretful way of talking about me that always made me uneasy. "I just get my back turned and she runs off. It's not like I had a girl in the family at all."

I went and sat on a feed bag in the corner of the barn, not wanting to appear when this conversation was going on. My mother, I felt, was not to be trusted. She was kinder than my father and more easily fooled, but you could not depend on her, and the real reasons for the things she said and did were not to be known. She loved me, and she sat up late at night making a dress of the difficult style I wanted, for me to wear when school started, but she was also my enemy. She was always plotting. She was plotting now to get me to stay in the house more, although she knew I hated it (*because* she knew I hated it) and keep me from working for my father. It seemed to me she would do this simply out of perversity, and to try her power. It did not occur to me that she could be lonely, or jealous. No grownup could be; they were too fortunate. I sat and kicked my heels monotonously against a feedbag, raising dust, and did not come out till she was gone.

At any rate, I did not expect my father to pay any attention to what she said. Who could imagine Laird doing my work—Laird remembering the padlock and cleaning out the watering dishes with a leaf on the end of a stick, or even wheeling the tank without it tumbling over? It showed how little my mother knew about the way things really were.

I have forgotten to say what the foxes were fed. My father's bloody apron reminded me. They were fed horsemeat. At this time most farmers still kept horses, and when a horse got too old to work, or broke a leg or got down and would not get up, as they sometimes did, the owner would call my father, and he and Henry went out to the farm in the truck. Usually they shot and butchered the horse there, paying the farmer from five to twelve dollars. If they had already too much meat on hand, they would bring the horse back alive, and keep it for a few days or weeks in our stable, until the meat was needed. After the war the farmers were buying tractors and gradually getting rid of horses altogether, so it sometimes happened that we got a good healthy horse, that there was just no use for any more. If this happened in the winter we might keep the horse in our stable till spring, for we had plenty of hay and if there was a lot of snow— and the plow did not always get our road cleared—it was convenient to be able to go to town with a horse and cutter.

The winter I was eleven years old we had two horses in the stable. We did not know what names they had had before, so we called them Mack and Flora. Mack was an old black workhorse, sooty and indifferent. Flora was a sorrel mare, a driver. We took them both out in the cutter. Mack was slow and easy to handle. Flora was given to fits of violent alarm, veering at cars and even at other horses, but we loved her speed and high stepping, her general air of gallantry and abandon. On

Saturdays we went down to the stable and as soon as we opened the door on its cozy, animal-smelling darkness Flora threw up her head, rolled her eyes, whinnied despairingly, and pulled herself through a crisis of nerves on the spot. It was not safe to go into her stall; she would kick.

This winter also, I began to hear a great deal more on the theme my mother had sounded when she had been talking in front of the barn. I no longer felt safe. It seemed that in the minds of the people around me there was a steady undercurrent of thought, not to be deflected, on this one subject. The word *girl* had formerly seemed to me innocent and unburdened, like the word *child*; now it appeared that it was no such thing. A girl was not, as I had supposed, simply what I was; it was what I had to become. It was a definition, always touched with emphasis, with reproach and disappointment. Also it was a joke on me. Once Laird and I were fighting, and for the first time ever I had to use all my strength against him; even so, he caught and pinned my arm for a moment, really hurting me. Henry saw this and laughed, saying, "Oh, that there Laird's gonna show you, one of these days!" Laird was getting a lot bigger. But I was getting bigger too.

My grandmother came to stay with us for a few weeks and I heard other things. "Girls don't slam doors like that." "Girls keep their knees together when they sit down." And worse still, when I asked some questions, "That's none of girls' business." I continued to slam the doors and sit as awkwardly as possible, thinking that by such measures I kept myself free.

When spring came, the horses were let out in the barnyard. Mack stood against the barn wall trying to scratch his neck and haunches, but Flora trotted up and down and reared at the fences, clattering her hooves against the rails. Snowdrifts dwindled quickly, revealing the hard gray and brown earth, the familiar rise and fall of the ground, plain and bare after the fantastic landscape of winter. There was a great feeling of opening out, of release. We just wore rubbers now, over our shoes; our feet felt ridiculously light. One Saturday we went out to the stable and found all the doors open, letting in the unaccustomed sunlight and fresh air. Henry was there, just idling around looking at his collection of calendars which were tacked up behind the stalls in a part of the stable my mother had probably never seen.

"Come to say good-bye to your old friend Mack?" Henry said. "Here, you give him a taste of oats." He poured some oats into Laird's cupped hands and Laird went to feed Mack. Mack's teeth were in bad shape. He ate very slowly, patiently shifting the oats around in his mouth, trying to find a stump of a molar to grind it on. "Poor old Mack," said Henry mournfully. "When a horse's teeth's gone, he's gone. That's about the way."

"Are you going to shoot him today?" I said. Mack and Flora had been in the stable so long I had almost forgotten they were going to be shot.

Henry didn't answer me. Instead he started to sing in a high, trembly, mocking-sorrowful voice, *Oh, there's no more work, for poor Uncle Ned, he's gone where the good darkies go.* Mack's thick, blackish tongue worked diligently at Laird's hand. I went out before the song was ended and sat down on the gangway.

I had never seen them shoot a horse, but I knew where it was done. Last summer Laird and I had come upon a horse's entrails before they were buried. We had thought it was a big black snake, coiled up in the sun. That was around in the field that ran up beside the barn. I thought that if we went inside the barn, and found a wide crack or a knothole to look through, we would be able to see them do it. It was not something I wanted to see; just the same, if a thing really happened, it was better to see it, and know.

My father came down from the house, carrying the gun.

"What are you doing here?" he said.

"Nothing."

"Go on up and play around the house."

He sent Laird out of the stable. I said to Laird, "Do you want to see them shoot Mack?" and without waiting for an answer led him around to the front door of the barn, opened it carefully, and went in. "Be quiet or they'll hear us," I said. We could hear Henry and my father talking in the stable, then the heavy, shuffling steps of Mack being backed out of his stall.

In the loft it was cold and dark. Thin, crisscrossed beams of sunlight fell through the cracks. The hay was low. It was a rolling country, hills and hollows, slipping under our feet. About four feet up was a beam going around the walls. We piled hay up in one corner and I boosted Laird up and hoisted myself. The beam was not very wide; we crept along it with our hands flat on the barn walls. There were plenty of knotholes, and I found one that gave me the view I wanted—a corner of the barnyard, the gate, part of the field. Laird did not have a knothole and began to complain.

I showed him a widened crack between two boards. "Be quiet and wait. If they hear you you'll get us in trouble."

My father came in sight carrying the gun. Henry was leading Mack by the halter. He dropped it and took out his cigarette papers and tobacco; he rolled cigarettes for my father and himself. While this was going on Mack nosed around in the old, dead grass along the fence. Then my father opened the gate and they took Mack through. Henry led Mack away from the path to a patch of ground and they talked together, not loud enough for us to hear. Mack again began searching for a mouthful of fresh grass, which was not to be found. My father walked away in a straight line, and stopped short at a distance which seemed to suit him. Henry was walking away from Mack too, but sideways, still negligently holding on to the halter. My father raised the gun and Mack looked up as if he had noticed something and my father shot him.

Mack did not collapse at once but swayed, lurched sideways and fell, first on his side; then he rolled over on his back and, amazingly, kicked his legs for a few seconds in the air. At this Henry laughed, as if Mack had done a trick for him. Laird, who had drawn a long, groaning breath of surprise when the shot was fired, said out loud, "He's not dead." And it seemed to me it might be true. But his legs stopped, he rolled on his side again, his muscles quivered and sank. The two men walked over and looked at him in a businesslike way; they bent down and examined his forehead where the bullet had gone in, and now I saw his blood on the brown grass.

"Now they just skin him and cut him up," I said. "Let's go." My legs were a little shaky and I jumped gratefully down into the hay. "Now you've seen how they shoot a horse," I said in a congratulatory way, as if I had seen it many times before. "Let's see if any barn cat's had kittens in the hay." Laird jumped. He seemed young and obedient again. Suddenly I remembered how, when he was little, I had brought him into the barn and told him to climb the ladder to the top beam. That was in the spring, too, when the hay was low. I had done it out of a need for excitement, a desire for something to happen so that I could tell about it. He was wearing a little bulky brown and white checked coat, made down from one of mine. He went all the way up just as I told him, and sat down on the top beam with the hay far below him on one side, and the barn floor and some old machinery on the other. Then I ran screaming to my father, "Laird's up on the top beam!" My father came, my mother came, my father went up the ladder talking very quietly and brought Laird down under his arm, at which my mother leaned against the ladder and began to cry. They said to me, "Why weren't you watching him?" but nobody ever knew the truth. Laird did not know enough to tell. But whenever I saw the brown and white checked coat hanging in the closet, or at the bottom of the rag bag, which was where it ended up, I felt a weight in my stomach, the sadness of unexorcised guilt.

I looked at Laird, who did not even remember this, and I did not like the look on this thin, winter-pale face. His expression was not frightened or upset, but remote, concentrating. "Listen," I said, in an unusually bright and friendly voice, "you aren't going to tell, are you?"

"No," he said absently.

"Promise."

"Promise," he said. I grabbed the hand behind his back to make sure he was not crossing his fingers. Even so, he might have a nightmare; it might come out that way. I decided I had better work hard to get all thoughts of what he had seen out of his mind—which, it seemed to me, could not hold very many things at a time. I got some money I had saved and that afternoon we went into Jubilee and saw a show, with Judy Canova, at which we both laughed a great deal. After that I thought it would be all right.

Two weeks later I knew they were going to shoot Flora. I knew from the night before, when I heard my mother ask if the hay was holding out all right, and my father said, "Well, after tomorrow there'll just be the cow, and we should be able to put her out to grass in another week." So I knew it was Flora's turn in the morning.

This time I didn't think of watching it. That was something to see just one time. I had not thought about it very often since, but sometimes when I was busy, working at school, or standing in front of the mirror combing my hair and wondering if I would be pretty when I grew up, the whole scene would flash into my mind: I would see the easy, practiced way my father raised the gun, and hear Henry laughing when Mack kicked his legs in the air. I did not have any great feeling of horror and opposition, such as a city child might have had; I was too used to seeing the death of animals as a necessity by which we lived. Yet I felt a little ashamed, and there was a new wariness, a sense of holding off, in my attitude to my father and his work.

It was a fine day, and we were going around the yard picking up tree branches that had been torn off in winter storms. This was something we had been told to do, and also we wanted to use them to make a teepee. We heard Flora whinny, and then my father's voice and Henry's shouting, and we ran down to the barnyard to see what was going on.

The stable door was open. Henry had just brought Flora out, and she had broken away from him. She was running free in the barnyard, from one end to the other. We climbed up on the fence. It was exciting to see her running, whinnying, going up on her hind legs, prancing and threatening like a horse in a Western movie, an unbroken ranch horse, though she was just an old driver, an old sorrel mare. My father and Henry ran after her and tried to grab the dangling halter. They tried to work her into a corner, and they had almost succeeded when she made a run between them, wild eyed, and disappeared around the corner of the barn. We heard the rails clatter down as she got over the fence, and Henry yelled, "She's into the field now!"

That meant she was in the long L-shaped field that ran up by the house. If she got around the center, heading toward the lane, the gate was open; the truck had been driven into the field this morning. My father shouted to me, because I was on the other side of the fence, nearest the lane, "Go shut the gate!"

I could run very fast. I ran across the garden, past the tree where our swing was hung, and jumped across a ditch into the lane. There was the open gate. She had not got out, I could not see her up on the road; she must have run to the other end of the field. The gate was heavy. I lifted it out of the gravel and carried it across the roadway. I had it halfway across when she came in sight, galloping straight toward me. There was just time to get the chain on. Laird came scrambling through the ditch to help me.

Instead of shutting the gate, I opened it as wide as I could. I did not make the decision to do this, it was just what I did. Flora never slowed down; she galloped straight past me, and Laird jumped up and down, yelling, "Shut it, shut it!" even after it was too late. My father and Henry appeared in the field a moment too late to see what I had done. They only saw Flora heading for the township road. They would think I had not got there in time.

They did not waste any time asking about it. They went back to the barn and got the gun and the knives they used, and put these in the truck; then they turned the truck around and came bouncing up the field toward us. Laird called to them, "Let me go, too, let me go, too!" and Henry stopped the truck and they took him. in. I shut the gate after they were all gone.

I supposed Laird would tell. I wondered what would happen to me. I had never disobeyed my father before, and I could not understand why I had done it. Flora would not really get away. They would catch up with her in the truck. Or if they did not catch her this morning somebody would see her and telephone us this afternoon or tomorrow. There was no wild country here for her to run to, only farms. What was more, my father had paid for her, we needed the meat to feed the foxes, we needed the foxes to make our living. All I had done was make more work for my father who worked hard enough already. And when my father found out about it he was not going to trust me any more; he would know that I was not entirely on his side. I was on Flora's side, and that made me no use to anybody, not even to her. Just the same, I did not regret it; when she came running at me and I held the gate open, that was the only thing I could do.

I went back to the house, and my mother said, "What's all the commotion?" I told her that Flora had kicked down the fence and got away. "Your poor father," she said, "now he'll have to go chasing over the countryside. Well, there isn't any use planning dinner before one." She put up the ironing board. I wanted to tell her, but thought better of it and went upstairs and sat on my bed.

Lately I had been trying to make my part of the room fancy, spreading the bed with old lace curtains, and fixing myself a dressing table with some leftovers of cretonne for a skirt. I planned to put up some kind of barricade between my bed and Laird's, to keep my section separate from his. In the sunlight, the lace curtains were just dusty rags. We did not sing at night any more. One night when I was singing Laird said, "You sound silly," and I went right on but the next night I did not start. There was not so much need to anyway, we were no longer afraid. We knew it was just old furniture over there, old jumble and confusion. We did not keep to the rules. I still stayed awake after Laird was asleep and told myself stories, but even in these stories something different was happening, mysterious alterations took place. A story might start off in the old way, with a spectacular danger, a fire or wild animals, and for a while I might rescue people; then things would change around, and instead, somebody would be rescuing me. It might be a boy from our class at school, or even Mr. Campbell, our teacher, who tickled girls under the arms. And at this point the story concerned itself at great length with what I looked like— how long my hair was, and what kind of dress I had on; by the time I had these details worked out the real excitement of the story was lost.

It was later than one o'clock when the truck came back. The tarpaulin was over the back, which meant there was meat in it. My mother had to heat dinner up all over again. Henry and my father had changed from their bloody overalls into ordinary working overalls in the barn, and they washed their arms and necks and faces at the sink, and splashed water on their hair and combed it. Laird lifted his arm to show off a streak of blood. "We shot old Flora," he said, "and cut her up in fifty pieces."

"Well I don't want to hear about it," my mother said. "And don't come to my table like that."

My father made him go and wash the blood off.

We sat down and my father said grace and Henry pasted his chewing gum on the end of his fork, the way he always did; when he took it off he would have us admire the pattern. We began to pass the bowls of steaming, overcooked vegetables. Laird looked across the table at me and said proudly, distinctly, "Anyway it was her fault Flora got away."

"What?" my father said.

"She could of shut the gate and she didn't. She just open' it up and Flora run out."

"Is that right?" my father said.

Everybody at the table was looking at me. I nodded, swallowing food with great difficulty. To my shame, tears flooded my eyes.

My father made a curt sound of disgust. "What did you do that for?"

I did not answer. I put down my fork and waited to be sent from the table, still not looking up.

But this did not happen. For some time nobody said anything, then Laird said matter-of-factly, "She's crying."

"Never mind," my father said. He spoke with resignation, even good humor, the words which absolved and dismissed me for good. "She's only a girl," he said.

I didn't protest that, even in my heart. Maybe it was true.

QUESTIONS

1. If the narrator was shy of her father and reluctant to ask him questions, why does she willingly and proudly work out-of-doors "under his eyes"? (510)

2. Why does the narrator think that work done out-of-doors, and in her father's service, "was ritualistically important"? (511) Does the narrator understand what purpose the ritual served?

3. Why did the narrator want her father to feel as she did that her mother had no business in the out-of-doors world of the farm?

4. Why does the narrator no longer feel "safe" as the word *girl* begins to change in meaning for her? (513)

5. In what sense does the narrator think she keeps herself "free" by slamming doors and sitting awkwardly in opposition to her grandmother's instructions? (513)

6. Why does the narrator think, "if a thing really happened, it was better to see it, and know." (514)

7. Why does the narrator decide to watch her father shoot Mack?

8. After seeing Mack shot, why does the narrator feel "a little ashamed" and have "a new wariness, a sense of holding off" in her attitude toward her "father and his work"? (516)

9. Why does the narrator open the gate wide for Flora?

10. Why does the narrator think that opening the gate was the only thing she could do? Why is she unable to understand why she opened the gate?

11. Why does being on "Flora's side" make the narrator, in her own mind, of "no use to anybody"? (517)

12. What does the narrator think might be true about her father's comment that "she's only a girl"? (519)

FOR FURTHER REFLECTION

1. What conclusion does the narrator reach about boys and girls?

2. Do the narrator and her father agree that she chooses certain actions because she is a girl?

3. Does this story teach us that boys and girls choose different courses of action because of their gender? Explain.

4. Do you think that letting Flora escape was the girl's last important act of childhood or her first important act as an adult?

5. In raising children to understand the workings of the world, do you agree with the narrator that "if a thing really happened, it is better to see it, and know"?

6. Do the other men in this story—the hired man Henry and the salesman—provide the narrator with reliable information on how boys and girls are different?

7. How does Laird's transformation in this story serve as a commentary on the narrator's transformation?

FREDERICK DOUGLASS

Frederick Douglass was born into slavery in rural Maryland in 1818. Sent to work in Baltimore, he was taught to read by the mistress of the house and regarded this achievement as a turning point in his life. Another such point was his violent resistance to a beating by the man to whom he had been bound as a field slave at age 17. Three years later, he escaped to the North, married, and worked menial jobs until his debut as an orator at an antislavery convention in 1841.

To expand his audience and to document the authenticity of his story, Douglass published his autobiography, *Narrative of the Life of Frederick Douglass, an American Slave,* in 1845. The book was critically acclaimed and sold well both in the United States and in Europe. Douglass left for England later the same year, where he spent two years writing and lecturing. He returned to the United States after abolitionist friends purchased his legal emancipation.

From 1847 to 1863, Douglass published his own weekly paper, the *North Star,* leading to a break with his mentor William Lloyd Garrison. Douglass also produced a number of other periodicals, as well as two extensions of his narrative—*Life and Times of Frederick Douglass* and *My Bondage and My Freedom.* In 1848, he played a prominent role at the women's rights convention in Seneca Falls, and he was a lifelong supporter of the women's suffrage movement. During the Civil War he was an adviser to President Lincoln and recruited blacks, including his own sons, for the Union army. He was appointed to several government positions, including recorder of deeds for the District of Columbia and United States minister and consul general to Haiti. Douglass died in 1895.

ABOUT
Narrative of the Life of Frederick Douglass, an American Slave

The compelling autobiography of an extraordinary man born into slavery, *Narrative of the Life of Frederick Douglass, an American Slave* is also a powerful inquiry into the question of what it means to be human. From the opening sentences of the narrative, Douglass delineates the context from which this question emerges—the fact that slave owners typically thought of slaves as animals. Douglass does not know how old he is, and he quickly asserts that this is not unusual, since most slaves "know as little of their ages as horses know of theirs" (p. 47). It is instructive that this initial comparison of slaves to animals does not serve to express something about the minds of the slave owners; instead, it expresses something about the minds of the slaves that is the consequence of being born into an environment constructed and carefully maintained by their owners. In an environment that does not permit the idea that slaves are human, the only perspective available to them is that of their owners. Their own perspective therefore becomes an additional barrier to thinking of themselves as human.

Learning to read and write is essential to the process whereby Douglass comes to see himself as human. As he describes it, the acquisition of these skills is inseparable from the dawning of self-consciousness. The world that reading gives Douglass access to opens before him, but the strongest effect of his literacy is the light it casts on the world he already knows. His anguish is so great that he "would at times feel that learning to read had been a curse rather than a blessing." It allows him to see his "wretched condition, without the remedy" (p. 84). Self-consciousness, the trait that most distinguishes humans from animals, produces such despair in Douglass that he confesses he often wished himself "a beast" (p. 84).

Douglass portrays the breadth of slavery's ability to dehumanize through his insights into the mentality of slave owners. Douglass suggests that if slaves are made rather than born, the same is sometimes true of slave owners. The mistress who began teaching him to read and write "at first lacked the depravity indispensable to shutting [him] up in mental darkness" (p. 81). Under the influence of her husband and, more generally, the institution of slavery, "the tender heart became stone, and the lamblike disposition gave way to one of tiger-like fierceness" (p. 82). The mistress not only stops teaching Douglass to read and write, but she is even more vigilant than her husband in preventing him from learning. The transformation of his mistress raises the question of how much of the behavior of slave owners toward their slaves was learned and how much was internally motivated. Douglass would have us believe that the mistress was the victim of her circumstances, yet the brutality other slave owners seemed to come by so easily makes it difficult to determine whether the behavior was learned or inherent.

Edward Covey undoubtedly counts among the slave owners who play the role as if born for it; his harsh treatment breaks Douglass "in body, soul, and spirit" (p. 105). Following his eloquent lament for the freedom he cannot have, represented by the ships sailing on Chesapeake Bay, Douglass writes, "You have seen how a man was made a slave; you shall see how a slave was made a man" (p. 107). The first part of this statement could refer to the methods employed by Covey, if not to all the owners at whose hands Douglass suffered. The second part refers to the story that follows, in which Douglass resists the whipping Covey intends to give him for disobeying. They fight for two hours, with Covey "getting entirely the worst end of the bargain" (p. 113). Douglass is never whipped again, and he describes this incident as "the turning-point in [his] career as a slave" and says that it "revived within [him] a sense of [his] own manhood" (p. 113). Douglass emphasizes the importance of literacy in developing his sense of himself as human. Is he suggesting, however, that his refusal to submit to Covey's punishment was ultimately more important in shaping his sense of self?

In a letter that prefaces the narrative, Wendell Phillips, social activist and friend of Douglass's, recalls "the old fable of 'The Man and the Lion,' where the lion complained that he should not be so misrepresented 'when the lions wrote history' " (p. 43). As Phillips observes, Douglass's narrative is history written from the perspective of those who previously had no voice. The very existence of the narrative makes it a testament to its author's humanity and, therefore, a document of revisionist history. However, what gives Douglass's narrative its universal relevance is his acute awareness of the complexities of human psychology. He observes that slaves usually spoke of themselves as content and of their masters as kind, concluding that slaves "suppress the truth rather than take the consequences of telling it, and in so doing prove themselves a part of the human family" (p. 62). Douglass is ever mindful that our humanity encompasses our failings no less than our capacity for nobility.

Note: All page references are from the Penguin Classics edition of *Narrative of the Life of Frederick Douglass, an American Slave* (1986).

DISCUSSION QUESTIONS

1. Why does Douglass believe "slavery proved as injurious to [his master's wife] as it did to [him]"? (81)

2. After his confrontation with Mr. Covey, what does Douglass mean when he writes "however long I might remain a slave in form, the day had passed forever when I could be a slave in fact"? (113)

3. Why is Douglass able to "understand the deep meaning of those rude and apparently incoherent songs" sung by slaves only when he no longer is a slave himself? (57)

4. When Douglass writes, "You have seen how a man was made a slave; you shall see how a slave was made a man," what does he understand a man to be? (107)

5. Douglass describes knowledge as "valuable bread" and the Liberator, an antislavery paper, as his "meat and drink." (83, 151) How does literacy sustain him?

6. How is Douglass able to maintain his religious faith when that of his owners is used to justify their treatment of him?

7. Why does Douglass consider holiday celebrations as part of the "inhumanity of slavery"? (115)

8. Why does Douglass describe the sails on Chesapeake Bay as "so many shrouded ghosts"? (106)

FOR FURTHER REFLECTION

1. To what extent can a piece of autobiographical writing also be read as a work of historical objectivity?

2. Can literacy be a curse as well as a blessing?

SAUL BELLOW

Saul Bellow was born to Russian immigrant parents in a suburb of Montreal in 1915. His family moved to Chicago in 1924. Before leaving for Paris on a Guggenheim Fellowship in 1943, he taught at a teacher training college and worked for the editorial department of Encyclopaedia Britannica. He served in the Merchant Marine during World War II.

Bellow's first two novels, *Dangling Man* (1944) and *The Victim* (1947), attracted a small following, but it was his next novel, *The Adventures of Augie March* (1953), that put Bellow on the literary map. The style and structure of the novel, a freewheeling picaresque comedy, signaled a dramatic shift in American fiction and won Bellow the first of three National Book Awards.

During the 1967 Arab-Israeli conflict, Bellow served as a war correspondent for *Newsday*. He spent most of his teaching career at the University of Chicago. Bellow's other works of fiction include *Henderson the Rain King* (1959), Herzog (1964), *Mr. Sammler's Planet* (1970), and *Humboldt's Gift* (1975, winner of the Pulitzer Prize). His most recent book is *Ravelstein* (2000). Bellow was awarded the Nobel Prize in Literature in 1976.

ABOUT
Seize the Day

The possibilities for self-creation, material success, and absolute freedom are the basis of a powerful American myth, one that can just as easily destroy as empower those who embrace it. A long line of literary and historical figures, going back at least to Benjamin Franklin, give us insight into this myth. Because we are a nation of immigrants whose institutions aim to make the circumstances of birth a mere starting point rather than a predictor of our fate, our capacity to invent ourselves is as limitless as our imagination. Without the practical barriers imposed by a rigid class system, vast wealth becomes not only a possibility but a measure of one's inner worth; if we can't play the game well enough to win, the fault doesn't lie in the game. Our democratic system of government promises freedom from political oppression, but this freedom can encourage us to resist societal restrictions. A democratic government is responsible to its citizens, sometimes fostering the notion that they can reap the benefits of community while being responsible to no one but themselves.

Tommy Wilhelm in *Seize the Day* is both inspired and burdened by the American myth of success. At the age of twenty, he changed his name from Wilky Adler to Tommy Wilhelm, a name signifying the person he dreams of becoming. He thereby recalls James Gatz, who by calling himself Jay Gatsby thinks he can conjure up the man Daisy Buchanan will find irresistible. Unlike Gatsby, however, Wilhelm has not fled his past; he confronts it daily through his father, who still calls him Wilky. Wilhelm has "never . . . succeeded in feeling like Tommy, and in his soul had always remained Wilky" (p. 25). But he remains optimistic, though the distance between the man he is and the man he aspires to be is an endless source of despair.

Wilhelm's financial troubles have more than practical implications. He feels that "everyone was supposed to have money" (p. 30), and his conversations with Dr. Tamkin strengthen his belief that with just a modest amount of will and talent, he could rid himself of financial worry. Tamkin assures Wilhelm that it will be "easy" for him to make much more in the market than the fifteen thousand he needs. Just as Wilhelm believes that he will one day become the person his name represents, so he clings to the hope that easy money awaits him. He assumes that his father would accept him if he had more money. Like Willy Loman, Wilhelm links his self-worth to his financial situation. If it really is easy to have more money than one needs, then financial failure must result from some character flaw.

Having quit his longtime job, left his wife and children, and taken a room in a residential hotel, Wilhelm seems intent on unburdening himself of the attachments and responsibilities that limit his freedom. He shares with Huck Finn the belief that personal autonomy somehow leads to personal fulfillment. But he is far from content when the story begins, sensing that "a huge trouble long presaged but till now formless was due" (p. 4). Wilhelm is bewildered by the fact that he has gone to such lengths to set himself free yet still feels trapped. Images of confinement proliferate. Beneath them is Wilhelm's desperate loneliness. Tamkin's assertion that we are all slaves to our "pretender souls" only further confuses the issue for Wilhelm. Is freedom a state of mind, rather than a description of external conditions? He cannot be sure, just as he can never be sure if Tamkin's pronouncements are revelation or simply a means by which Tamkin gets what he wants.

Bellow explores these themes within a tight structure that gives *Seize the Day* (1956) a formal resemblance to his first two novels, *Dangling Man* (1944) and *The Victim* (1947). *The Adventures of Augie March* (1953) heralded a new expansiveness in Bellow's fiction, against which *Seize the Day* would appear an exception. But the novella's comedy is in keeping with *Augie March* and, in fact, much of Bellow's later work. *Seize the Day*, which looks both backward and forward, occupies a unique place in Bellow's career; it is also a powerful commentary on distinctly American ideals.

Note: All page references are from the Penguin edition of *Seize the Day* (1996).

DISCUSSION QUESTIONS

1. Wilhelm wonders if "the making of mistakes expressed the very purpose of his life and the essence of his being here" and whether "he was supposed to make them and suffer from them on this earth." (56) Are we meant to think he is right?

2. When Wilhelm tells his father about the loss of his investment, he says that "one word from you, just a word, would go a long way." (109–110) What kind of word does Wilhelm want to hear?

3. Why does Dr. Adler still call his son Wilky?

4. Why does Wilhelm believe that Wilky is "his inescapable self"? (25)

5. On his way to the market with Tamkin, Wilhelm thinks that "everyone seems to know something." (78) What is it Wilhelm feels they know?

6. When Wilhelm returns to the market with Mr. Rappaport and realizes his money is gone, why is he so careful to conceal the depth of his distress?

7. Why does Wilhelm agree to accompany Mr. Rappaport to the cigar store instead of returning with Tamkin to the market?

8. As he talks with Tamkin and they track the commodities prices, Wilhelm thinks to himself, "Oh, this was a day of reckoning." (96) In what sense might this be true?

9. Wilhelm senses at the beginning of the novel "that a huge trouble long presaged but till now formless was due." (4) What does this trouble turn out to be? What form does it take?

FOR FURTHER REFLECTION

1. How much of our identity is determined by our parents?

2. Does America encourage individual freedom at the expense of communal bonds? Are these two things ultimately incompatible?

CONNECTING THEMES

The selections in this anthology are arranged chronologically (by author's date of birth) and can be read and discussed in that order. However, it is possible to consider them in the light of common themes. A few of the authors represented in *Great Conversations 1* were familiar with the works of the others—both as predecessors and contemporaries—and their writings seem to respond to one another directly. Readers will notice how many of the authors, even though greatly separated in time and place, echo one another, or respond to a similar subject in strikingly different ways.

It is likely that readers moving sequentially through this book will begin to notice these interconnections among the fifteen selections and two novels. The following list of readings and themes offers a guided alternative to a strictly chronological approach. Some of the more extensive thematic clusters could give direction to a book group for as many as seven or eight meetings. Other clusters consist of only two selections, providing material for a single meeting.

Using these clusters as examples, discussion groups will likely find other, equally interesting ways to organize their reading lists. We hope that all readers of *Great Conversations 1* will enter into the dialogue with these authors, as contemporary participants.

I. The Individual and the Community

Gilgamesh

Aeschylus

Montaigne

Emerson

Tocqueville

Douglass

Conrad

Ibsen

Freud

Veblen

II. Coming of Age and Life Passages

Gilgamesh

Whitman

Conrad

Jung

Bellow

Munro

III. Aging, Maturity, and Mortality

Gilgamesh

Whitman

Freud

Jung

Olsen

Bellow

IV. Men and Women

Gilgamesh

Veblen

Olsen

Munro

V. The Self and Its Inner Resources

Montaigne

Pascal

Emerson

VI. Friendship

Gilgamesh

Montaigne

Conrad

VII. The Claims and Boundaries of Science

Pascal

Poincaré

VIII. The Restlessness of Human Nature

Pascal

Tocqueville

IX. Humans and God

Aeschylus

Pascal

Emerson

Olsen

ACKNOWLEDGMENTS

All possible care has been taken to trace ownership and secure permission for each selection in this anthology. The Great Books Foundation wishes to thank the following authors, publishers, and representatives for permission to reprint copyrighted material:

The *Epic of Gilgamesh*, from THE EPIC OF GILGAMESH, a verse rendition by Danny P. Jackson. Copyright 1997 by Bolchazy-Carducci Publishers. Reprinted by permission of the publishers.

Prometheus Bound, from THE COMPLETE GREEK TRAGEDIES, by Aeschylus, translated by David Grene, edited by David Grene and Richmond Lattimore. Copyright 1942 by the University of Chicago. Reprinted by permission of the University of Chicago Press.

Of Friendship and *Of Solitude*, from THE COMPLETE ESSAYS OF MONTAIGNE, by Michel de Montaigne. Translated by Donald M. Frame. Copyright 1948, 1953, 1958 by the Board of Trustees of the Leland Stanford Jr. University. Renewed 1970, 1975, 1986 by Donald M. Frame. Reprinted by permission of Stanford University Press.

Pensées, from PENSÉES, by Blaise Pascal, translated by A. J. Krailsheimer. Copyright 1966 by A. J. Krailsheimer. Reprinted by permission of Penguin Books, Ltd.

Thoughts for the Times on War and Death, from THE COLLECTED PAPERS, VOLUME 4, by Sigmund Freud. Authorized translation under the supervision of Joan Riviere. Published by Basic Books, Inc. by arrangement with The Hogarth Press, Ltd. and the Institute of Psycho-Analysis, London. Reprinted by permission of Basic Books, a member of Perseus Books, L.L.C.

The Theory of the Leisure Class, from "Conspicuous Consumption," by Thorstein Veblen, and "Introduction" by C. Wright Mills, from THE THEORY OF THE LEISURE CLASS. "Introduction": Copyright 1953, renewed 1981 by C. Wright Mills. "Conspicuous Consumption": Copyright 1953, renewed 1981 by New American Library. Reprinted by permission of Dutton Signet, a division of Penguin Group (USA) Inc.

Tell Me a Riddle, from TELL ME A RIDDLE, by Tillie Olsen, introduction by John Leonard. Copyright 1956, 1957, 1960, 1961 by Tillie Olsen. Reprinted by permission of Dell Publishing, a division of Random House, Inc.

Boys and Girls, from DANCE OF THE HAPPY SHADES, by Alice Munro. Copyright 1968 by Alice Munro. Reprinted by permission of William Morris Agency, Inc. on behalf of the author.